A Modern Guide to Austrian Economics

ELGAR MODERN GUIDES

Elgar Modern Guides offer a carefully curated review of a selected topic, edited or authored by a leading scholar in the field. They survey the significant trends and issues of contemporary research for both advanced students and academic researchers.

The books provide an invaluable appraisal and stimulating guide to the current research landscape, offering state-of-the-art discussions and selective overviews covering the critical matters of interest alongside recent developments. Combining incisive insight with a rigorous and thoughtful perspective on the essential issues, the books are designed to offer an inspiring introduction and unique guide to the diversity of modern debates.

Elgar Modern Guides will become an essential go-to companion for researchers and graduate students but will also prove stimulating for a wider academic audience interested in the subject matter. They will be invaluable to anyone who wants to understand as well as simply learn.

Titles in the series include:

A Modern Guide to Sports Economics
Edited by Ruud H. Koning and Stefan Kesenne

A Modern Guide to Labour and the Platform Economy
Edited by Jan Drahokoupil and Kurt Vandaele

A Modern Guide to Financial Shocks and Crises
Edited by Giovanni Ferri and Vincenzo D'Apice

A Modern Guide to Local and Regional Politics
Edited by Colin Copus, Richard Kerley and Alistair Jones

A Modern Guide to Food Economics
Edited by Jutta Roosen and Jill E. Hobbs

A Modern Guide to Post-Keynesian Institutional Economics
Edited by Charles J. Whalen

A Modern Guide to Creative Economies
Edited by Roberta Comunian, Alessandra Faggian, Jarna Heinonen and Nick Wilson

A Modern Guide to Tourism Economics
Edited by Robertico Croes and Yang Yang

A Modern Guide to Austrian Economics
Edited by Per L. Bylund

A Modern Guide to Austrian Economics

Edited by

Per L. Bylund

Johnny D. Pope Chair and Associate Professor, School of Entrepreneurship, Spears School of Business, Oklahoma State University, USA

ELGAR MODERN GUIDES

Edward Elgar
PUBLISHING

Cheltenham, UK • Northampton, MA, USA

Published by
Edward Elgar Publishing Limited
The Lypiatts
15 Lansdown Road
Cheltenham
Glos GL50 2JA
UK

Edward Elgar Publishing, Inc.
William Pratt House
9 Dewey Court
Northampton
Massachusetts 01060
USA

Paperback edition 2024

A catalogue record for this book
is available from the British Library

Library of Congress Control Number: 2022942986

This book is available electronically in the **Elgar**online
Economics subject collection
http://dx.doi.org/10.4337/9781789904406

ISBN 978 1 78990 439 0 (cased)
ISBN 978 1 78990 440 6 (eBook)
ISBN 978 1 0353 3895 5 (paperback)

Printed and bound by CPI Group (UK) Ltd, Croydon, CR0 4YY

Contents

Contributors

Peter J. Boettke is Professor of Economics and Philosophy at George Mason University.

Per L. Bylund is Johnny D. Pope Chair and Associate Professor of Entrepreneurship in the School of Entrepreneurship at Oklahoma State University.

Nicolás Cachanosky is Associate Professor of Economics Metropolitan State University of Denver.

Ginny Seung Choi is Senior Fellow in the F. A. Hayek Program for Advanced Study in Philosophy, Politics, and Economics.

Richard G. Ellefritz is Assistant Professor of Sociology at University of The Bahamas.

Kristoffer J. M. Hansen is Research Assistant at the Institute for Economic Policy, Leipzig University.

David Howden is Professor of Economics at Saint Louis University – Madrid Campus.

Peter G. Klein is the W. W. Caruth Chair and Professor of Entrepreneurship at Baylor University's Hankamer School of Business.

Karras J. Lambert is a PhD student in the Department of Economics at George Mason University.

Peter Lewin is Clinical Professor of Management at the Naveen Jindal School of Management, University of Texas at Dallas.

Roderick T. Long is Professor of Philosophy at Auburn University.

William J. Luther is Associate Professor of Economics at Florida Atlantic University.

Mateusz Machaj is Associate Professor at the Institute of Economic Sciences of the University of Wroclaw.

Matthew McCaffrey is Associate Professor of Entrepreneurship at the University of Manchester.

Robert P. Murphy is Senior Fellow at the Mises Institute.

Jonathan R. Newman is Assistant Professor of Economics and Finance at Bryan College.

Mark D. Packard is Associate Professor at Florida Atlantic University.

Joseph T. Salerno is Academic Vice-President at the Mises Institute.

Frederic Sautet is Associate Professor in the Catholic University of America's Busch School of Business.

Arkadiusz Sieroń is Assistant Professor of Economics at Institute of Economic Sciences, University of Wroclaw.

Nikhil Sridhar is an independent researcher.

Virgil Henry Storr is Professor of Economics at George Mason University.

Krzysztof Turowski is Assistant Professor at the Theoretical Computer Science Department at the Jagiellonian University.

Acknowledgments

The editor gratefully acknowledges help with formatting from Fernando D'Andrea.

Introduction to *A Modern Guide to Austrian Economics*

Per L. Bylund

Over 150 years have passed since the publication of Carl Menger's ground-breaking *Grundsätze der Volkswirtschaftslehre* (1871) and, thereby, the founding of what is now referred to as the Austrian school of economics. The school has made many fundamentally important contributions to economic theory since then. Some of these have been adopted by other schools of thought and have been integrated into the corpus of mainstream economics, whereas many other concepts, arguments, explanations, and approaches have not.

Over the course of this century and a half, the school's influence has waxed and waned. It has also shifted and moved beyond the economics discipline and economic theory. As a respected and influential tradition in economics, the Austrian school has strongly contributed to or started several important debates in theory and methodology. The *Methodenstreit* (method dispute) in the 1880s, the socialist calculation debate in the 1920s and 1930s, and the capital controversy in the 1930s are examples of this. But today, and over the course of the recent decades, the Austrian school has little if any influence in the economics discipline within the academy. This should not be interpreted as indicative of its demise or lacking usefulness of its body of theory. Instead, the school has gained significant influence applied to business theory and practice, particularly in the fields of management and entrepreneurship where Austrian theories are core contributions (Klein & Bylund, 2014).

This shift is curious because the Austrian school, a highly theoretical approach to understanding the economy, has not changed to facilitate this shift and novel application of its theory. The theory continues to be developed, refined, and extended, as it has been since Menger's treatise, but the core of it remains the same in both structure and substance. This should be expected, since Austrian economic theory, especially as structured and formalized by Ludwig von Mises into the system of praxeology (see Long's chapter in this volume), is a purely deductive and therefore strictly theory-first approach to economic understanding.

Economic theory to the "Austrians" is, as it was traditionally in economics and the study of political economy, a logical endeavor to uncover the mechanisms and processes of the economy to thereby gain a deeper understanding of how it works. Such an approach to theorizing is today unfashionable, if not considered altogether "unscientific." It also provides little basis for running statistical regressions and exactly predicting the future, and consequently is of apparent limited use for policymakers and in statecraft. Austrian economists would beg to differ, however. In their view, economic theory cannot be used to predict exact outcomes. The future is always uncertain and will depend on exactly how individuals, relying on subjective understanding and valuations, will react to the specifics of situations. But economic theory can provide understanding for the economic processes that determine the structure and functioning of the economy, and therefore knowledge of the causal effects of specific interventions. In other words, to Austrians economic theory is impotent as a planning tool—it cannot be used to produce reliable forecasts—but is indispensable for understanding the causes of observable phenomena and the structural effects of specific influences and interventions.

The Austrian school has a different goal and makes a different claim than mainstream economics. It does not pretend that the economy is a machine that can (and perhaps should?) be operated and optimized within given parameters. There is no optimum as the economy is not a static system. Instead, Austrians view the economy as organic and ever in flux. It not only affects or is the playground for our actions—the economy *is* our actions. Therefore, the aggregate phenomena that we observe are and must be explained from the perspective of action. This bottom-up approach is core to Austrian economic theory and theorizing. But the school's core assumption of methodological individualism should not be understood as atomism, which is the straw man preferred by many critics. Austrian economics not only recognizes and attempts to understand the emergent phenomena that are core to society and have an important impact on our lives, but seeks to explain their causal nature. As Menger (2007 [1871]) begins his treatise, "All things are subject to the law of cause and effect." Indeed, it is from this perspective that Austrians approach and attempt to understand the economy: as a *process*. Austrian economic theory is both causal and realist—it does not use formalized modeling, it limits its use of mathematical analysis and is focused on understanding real phenomena in the economy and therefore has no interest in developing models of theoretically optimal states. To put it simply and somewhat bluntly, Austrian economists are interested in understanding the meaning, causes, and effects of real prices as they are in the economy—not prices as they could or should be in a theoretical model.

As Austrian economics is *causal-realist*, its economic theory provides timeless universal understanding for the workings of an economy in terms of mechanisms and processes. It should be no surprise, then, that entrepreneurship to Austrians is a core aspect to understand market economies—the "driving force" of the market, to use Mises's celebrated words. Austrians also study productive capital in terms of its heterogeneity and combinability into capital structures, not simply as a dollar value. As Lachmann (1978 [1956], p. xv) put it, "Beer barrels and blast furnaces, harbour installations and hotel-room furniture are capital not by virtue of their physical properties but by virtue of their economic functions." This economic function may be different for different types of capital even if the market value (in terms of prices) is the same.

The aim for Austrian economic theory is always to understand the real world as it is and could be. Because of its core focus on causal-realism and understanding, Austrian economics helps scholars and practitioners alike—its economic theory is a framework for making sense of what we see and experience. This is perhaps why Austrian economics was rediscovered within and has become influential in business school disciplines to a degree and in a way that mainstream economics cannot. Austrian economics does not prescribe to entrepreneurs and businessmen what they should do but offers a structured theoretical framework that allows them to understand what they see. In fact, many business practitioners have through experience developed a tacit understanding—an intuition of sorts—of the economy that is typically highly Austrian. Austrian economics provides a language and terminology as well as a structure and framework for this understanding. It connects the dots and thereby allows practitioners to leverage their business intuition.

This volume is not directed towards practitioners specifically, however. While practitioners undoubtedly will find much of value in the following pages, the aim is to provide a starting point for scholars interested in contributing to Austrian theory and/or using it in applied research. Each chapter can be read independently without the context of the remainder of the book. In other words, scholars with interest in entrepreneurship can, if they so choose, limit their reading to those chapters while a scholar in money or business cycles can focus on those chapters, respectively. But the chapters are also intended to together provide a comprehensive, as far as is possible in a single volume, overview of the current state of Austrian economics scholarship and what lies ahead. In other words, reading the book from cover to cover (or the chapters in some other order) will provide the reader a crash course in the current state of research in Austrian economics. To support this broadly interested reader, the chapters are ordered from the core and out as follows.

Chapter 1 deals with the specific Austrian method of praxeology and provides the reader with an overview and understanding of what praxeology is and the reasons Austrians rely on it. Chapter 2 provides a reinterpretation of the Austrian approach using the lens of realist phenomenology.

The following three chapters deal with aspects of entrepreneurship and its function in the market process. Chapter 3 introduces and analyzes the concept of alertness, the entrepreneurial quality originally elaborated on by Kirzner

(1973) that allows for discovering opportunities in the market. Chapter 4 introduces the judgment-based approach to entrepreneurship, which aims to understand entrepreneurial action and the forming of firms. Chapter 5 elaborates on the importance of including the disruptive entrepreneur to understand the market process and argues that market process models without this role are unfit for economic theorizing.

Chapter 6 elaborates on the role and scholarly understanding of spontaneous orders, the emergent phenomena that are common in and distinctive for the social world and which are therefore necessary for any understanding of the economy. Chapter 7 then discusses the social and moral aspects of markets understood as interactions and relationships between individuals.

Chapter 8 provides the reader with a deeper understanding for the Austrian (Misesian) argument for why a socialist economy, in which the means of production are commonly or state owned, is impossible. Chapter 9 provides an overview of the Austrian conception and theory of money, its supply and demand, and the understanding of money as not being neutral in the economy. Chapter 10 sheds light on how banking systems work, specifically the private commercial banking sector, giving special attention to fractional-reserve banking. Chapter 11 discusses the emergence of crypto currencies and contextualizes this recent development with the Austrian theory of money. Chapter 12 provides a discussion on the pure time preference theory of interest, which conceptualizes market interest rates as largely representing the social rate of time preference.

Chapter 13 provides an overview and history of Austrian capital theory and discusses how it relates to the theory of the firm. Chapter 14 introduces the Austrian business cycle theory and reviews its recent influence in macroeconomic public discourse. Chapter 15 applies Austrian theory and theorizing to sociology and outlines the nature and implications of an Austrian sociology.

Each of the chapters is written by leading scholars in that particular aspect or application of Austrian economics. Their chapters not only introduce the current state of understanding within each study, but also suggest directions for future research by pointing toward contemporary debates and their potential conclusions, underdeveloped aspects and extensions of theory, and remaining applications of interest. Together these chapters summarize where Austrian economics is currently at—and where it is (likely) heading.

REFERENCES

Kirzner, I. M. (1973). *Competition and Entrepreneurship*. University of Chicago Press.
Klein, P. G., & Bylund, P. L. (2014). The place of Austrian economics in contemporary entrepreneurship research. *Review of Austrian Economics*, 27(3), 259–279.

Lachmann, L. M. (1978 [1956]). *Capital and Its Structure*. Kansas City, MO: Sheed Andrews and McMeel.

Menger, C. (2007 [1871]). *Principles of Economics* (J. Dingwall & B. F. Hoselitz, Trans.). Ludwig von Mises Institute.

1. Praxeology

Roderick T. Long

PRAXEOLOGY AND ITS CRITICS

Praxeology, the purportedly *a priori* foundation of economic science endorsed by Ludwig von Mises and many (though not all) other Austrian economists, is often attacked for being unduly rationalistic and dogmatic; but many such criticisms are based on a misunderstanding of what is actually being claimed for praxeology. This chapter attempts to sort out what the praxeological approach entails and how it holds up to common criticisms, before sketching some future lines of needed research in the praxeological project.

What Is Praxeology?

Praxeology (from Greek *praxis*, action, and the suffix *logia*, meaning, roughly, the scientific study of something) refers to a science of, or set of principles about, human action (or perhaps simply about action per se, understood as the application of means to ends) that is thought by many (though not all) thinkers in the Austrian School tradition, and most especially by Ludwig von Mises, to have the following two characteristics. First, praxeology is *a priori* – that is, knowable without being derived from sensory experience – by contrast with *a posteriori* knowledge, which *is* so derived. (*A priori* and *a posteriori* are Latin for "on the basis of what is prior [to experience]" and "on the basis of what is posterior [to experience]," respectively.) Second, praxeology is the foundation of economics – the set of truths about human action from which the fundamental principles of economic science can be derived.

Earlier Austrian economists had based their economic reasoning on fundamental propositions about the nature of human action (e.g. Menger, 1994), but had not explicitly described them as *a priori*; this was specifically Mises's innovation,[1] elaborated in his three major methodological works (Mises, 1962, 1985, 2003), as well as in the lengthy opening methodological section of his general economic treatise *Human Action* (Mises, 1996).

As an example of the way that Mises thinks general economic principles can be derived from *a priori* truths about human action, consider the *law of dimin-*

ishing marginal utility, which states that each additional unit of a good affords the agent a lower utility than the previous unit. This law is often understood as an empirical generalization about human psychology, specifically about our tendency to become satiated as we consume more of the good in question. So understood, the law would be open to exceptions; for example, in the case of a highly addictive good, we might assign a higher utility to later increments of the good than to our initial sample.

But Mises insists that while this notion of satiation may be a largely true empirical generalization about how our preference ranking changes over time, it is not at all what the law of diminishing marginal utility is getting at. Rather, the point is that (so long as our preference rankings do *not* change) we necessarily apply the first unit of a good to our most urgent want, the second unit of a good to the second, and so on, simply because it would make no *sense* to describe something as our most urgent want unless it were the one whose satisfaction we sought first (Mises, 1996, p. 124). Hence the law of diminishing marginal utility, unlike the law (or generalization) of the satiation of wants, is not derived from observation; we can grasp it simply through considering it by means of our rational faculty, as with the propositions of mathematics and logic.

Objections and Replies

The doctrine of praxeology is frequently characterized by critics as unduly rationalistic and dogmatic, but Mises's claims about praxeology are often misunderstood. For example, even largely sympathetic critics (e.g. Caldwell, 2004, p. 195; Nozick, 1997; Steele, 1992; Vaughn, 1994, p. 77; cf. Lavoie, 1994, p. 60) have insisted that the application of praxeological categories to the real world requires auxiliary premises derived from experience, as if this were a *criticism* of Mises; but in fact it is precisely what Mises teaches. In *The Ultimate Foundation of Economic Science*, for example, Mises writes:

> Into the chain of praxeological reasoning the praxeologist introduces certain assumptions concerning the conditions of the environment in which an action takes place. Then he tries to find out how these special conditions affect the result to which his reasoning must lead. The question whether or not the real conditions of the external world correspond to these assumptions is to be answered by experience. But if the answer is in the affirmative, all the conclusions drawn by logically correct praxeological reasoning strictly describe what is going on in reality. (Mises 1962, pp. 44–45)

Even Mises's student Israel Kirzner, a prominent Austrian theorist in his own right, reports being "surprised" when, upon asking Mises "how a person can know that human beings other than himself are indeed purposeful," he was told that this is something we learn "by observation" and not *a priori*, and that it is only once we have established this fact that we can then go on to apply the *a priori* categories of praxeology to their actions (Kirzner, 2001, pp. 88–89). Perhaps, then, it would be best to characterize praxeology not simply as the *a priori* science of human action, but rather as the science of those aspects of human action that can be grasped *a priori*.

Although Mises's best-known student, Friedrich Hayek, gradually moved away from Misesian praxeology over the course of his career, in his early writings, such as *The Counter-Revolution of Science* (1952) and the essays collected in *Individualism and Economic Order*, one can see him holding what is at least a closely related position; "all propositions of economic theory," he writes, "refer to things which are defined in terms of human attitudes toward them" (Hayek, 1948a, p. 52, n. 18), which in turn implies that "we can, from the concepts of the objects, analytically conclude something about what the actions will be," since once we "define an object in terms of a person's attitude toward it, it follows, of course, that the definition of the object implies a statement about the attitude of the person toward the thing" (Hayek, 1948b, pp. 62–63; "analytic" in this context means "true by definition").

The Misesian idea that the application of *a priori* praxeological principles to real-life situations requires auxiliary premises drawn from experience is also endorsed by the early Hayek. Consider, for example, his analysis of the classical *law of rent* into two components, one *a priori* and exceptionless, and one *a posteriori* and not exceptionless:

> One is part of pure economic theory and asserts that whenever in the production of one commodity different (scarce) factors are required in proportions which can be varied, and of which one can be used only for this purpose (or only for comparatively few) while the others are of a more general usefulness, a change in the value of the product will affect the value of the former more than that of the latter. The second proposition is the empirical statement that land is as a rule in the position of the first kind of factor, that is, that people know of many more uses of their labor than they will know for a particular piece of land. The first of these propositions, like all propositions of pure economic theory, is a statement about the implications of certain human attitudes toward things and as such necessarily true irrespective of time and place. The second is an assertion that the conditions postulated in the first proposition prevail at a given time and with respect to a given piece of land. (Hayek, 1952, p. 32)

In a sense, then, the principles of praxeology are *hypothetical* in form: *if* such-and-such conditions hold, then necessarily some further such-and-such must be true. Praxeology cannot tell you whether a change in the value of some product having both land and labor as inputs will result in a greater change in the value of the land than in the value of the labor; it can only tell you that a change in the value of some product having both land and labor as inputs will result in a greater change in the value of the land than in the value of the labor *on the hypothesis* that people know of more uses for labor than for land. (Compare: geometry cannot tell me how many sides my next slice of pizza will have; it can only tell me how many sides it will have *if* my next slice of pizza is square (or triangular, or whatever). The truth of the conditional (if *p* then *q*) is *a priori*; but the truth of the antecedent (*p*) is empirical, and so the truth of the consequent (*q*) is so as well.)

Not all proponents of Misesian praxeology understand its *a priori* character in quite the same way, however. Murray Rothbard, for example – another prominent Austrian who studied under Mises – takes the principles of praxeology to be broadly empirical (Rothbard, 1957), but to be nonetheless deserving of being called aprioristic because the observations on which they are based are so fundamental to and pervasive in human experience that they are inevitably prior to ordinary empirical investigations.

Mises's and Hayek's insistence that the fundamental principles of economics are *a priori* and exceptionless is easily misunderstood as involving a claim to *infallibility* regarding them. The truths of mathematics are likewise *a priori* and exceptionless, yet that fact is perfectly compatible with the possibility of getting them wrong and making mistakes in our calculations.

Milton Friedman, one of the most prominent representatives of the rival Chicago School tradition in economics, has criticized praxeology in the following terms:

> That methodological approach, I think, has very negative influences … [It] tends to make people intolerant. If you and I are both praxeologists, and we disagree about whether some proposition or statement is correct, how do we resolve that disagreement? We can yell, we can argue, we can try to find a logical flaw in one another's thing, but in the end we have no way to resolve it except by fighting, by saying you're wrong and I'm right. (Quoted in Ebenstein, 2001, p. 273)

Friedman seems to be thinking of the contrast between empirical and praxeological evidence as a contrast between evidence that is *public*, available to all for inspection, and evidence that is *private*, some sort of subjective inner voice. But logic and mathematics, for example, are *paradigmatically* public; we do not each examine our own private number 17, for example. And that is why seeking to "find a logical flaw in one another's thing" is a perfectly appropriate way of dealing with disagreement about *a priori* matters. In Gottlob Frege's terms, Friedman seems to be confusing the *logical* realm with the *psychological* realm (Frege, 1977; c.f. Long, 2004, 2006a).

Mises has also been criticized for his claim that, from a praxeological perspective, all human action is rational. But it's important to understand the narrow character of Mises's claim. If I start humming "Happy Birthday" whenever I see a kitten, because I am in the grip of a conviction that kittens are likely to turn all of a sudden into angry rhinoceroses, but that this transformation can be prevented by singing "Happy Birthday," my action is rational simply in the sense that *given* my beliefs about what kittens are likely to do and how they can be prevented from doing such, and *given* my desire to avoid angry rhinoceroses, singing "Happy Birthday" is an appropriately chosen means to the end of avoiding the rhinoceroses. In calling my action rational, Mises is not endorsing my positive views about the causal powers and liabilities of kittens. Relatedly, David Ramsay Steele (1992) criticizes Mises for ascribing consistent preference orderings to all economic agents; but Steele's proffered counterexamples to Mises's thesis are an example of consistency *over* time, whereas all Mises is claiming is consistency *at* a time (c.f. Long, 2004; Rothbard, 1997, pp. 216–217).

Austrian economist Don Lavoie rejects what he sees as the "Euclidean" approach of Misesian praxeology in favor of an approach in which the grasping of praxeological principles is as much a matter of falsifiable, *a posteriori* "interpretive" observation as is those principles' application (Lavoie, 1986, 1994). But as I've argued elsewhere (Long, 2004), along Kantian and Wittgensteinian lines, our *ability* to grasp praxeological principles and our *ability* to apply them may be interdependent even if one is *a priori* and the other *a posteriori*. Certainly, we might never be able to grasp praxeological principles in the absence of a background of social interaction, communication, and interpretation; in the same way, we would likely be unable to grasp mathematical truths without sensory experience of and interaction with collections of material objects, yet that doesn't render mathematics a mere generalization about the behavior of such objects. Sensory experience may be required as the *occasion* for our developing *a priori* principles, without those conceptions somehow being *inferred* from such experience.

ISSUES FOR FUTURE RESEARCH

Analytic or Synthetic?

Many issues in praxeology invite further research. One is whether praxeological propositions are *analytic* – that is, true by definition, in that their truth can be ascertained simply through an *analysis* of the meanings of the relevant terms – or whether they are instead synthetic *a priori* in Immanuel Kant's sense: synthetic in that they are not true by definition, but involve *synthesizing*, putting together, one concept with a different concept that is not already contained in the first concept; *a priori* in that our knowledge of such truths is nevertheless not derived from experience. (Kant thought that mathematics, for example, was synthetic *a priori* rather than analytic, since if one tries to establish the truth of "2 + 2 = 4" as analytic by saying that "4" is *defined* as

"2 + 2," one will be left unable to account for the truth of "3 + 1 = 4," since "4" cannot be defined *both* as "2 + 2" and as "3 + 1."[2] Yet mathematics is plausibly *a priori* nonetheless.)

Hayek, as we've seen, regards praxeological principles as analytic; for Hans Hoppe, by contrast, they are synthetic *a priori* (Hoppe, 1995, pp. 17–18). In *Human Action*, Mises regards them, and indeed all *a priori* truths, as analytic: "Aprioristic reasoning is purely conceptual and deductive. It cannot produce anything else but tautologies and analytic judgments" (Mises, 1996, p. 38). Yet in his later work, *The Ultimate Foundation of Economic Science*, Mises defends the existence of synthetic *a priori* statements, before unexpectedly concluding that in the case of praxeology (though not necessarily in other areas of thought), the distinction between analytic and synthetic *a priori* is "of verbal interest only" (Mises, 1962, p. 44). This topic calls for further exploration, especially in light of the fact that many philosophers, ranging the gamut from Willard Van Orman Quine (1951) to Ayn Rand (1990), have questioned the coherence of the analytic-synthetic distinction itself.[3]

The Action Axiom

Part of the solution to the analytic-synthetic puzzle may lie in the so-called "action axiom" (as this term is used in Austrian economics, which is not always how it is used in other intellectual traditions). While statements of praxeological principles often seem to be "true by definition," the basic fact of human action is often described differently, as a fact about *reality* (not just a relationship among concepts) to which one is committed on pain of pragmatic incoherence, since any attempt to deny it will itself be an action (cf. Rothbard, 1997, pp. 68–69).[4] Even if many of the theses of praxeology (like the aforementioned law of diminishing marginal utility) seem to follow simply from the meanings of their constituent terms and so to be analytic, the action axiom seems to establish a tie, not between one concept and another, but between a concept and its real-life exemplification, in a way that seems more synthetic *a priori*. Without the action axiom, the web of concepts that constitute praxeology might be conceived of as a web of concepts without instances, like facts about unicorns or the like; but once the reality of human action has been established, all the various hypotheticals that constitute praxeology gain a toehold in reality.[5]

But what exactly does the axiom action assert? That human beings act? If that's taken as a claim about a particular biological species, it can hardly be *a priori*, and indeed we've already seen Mises denying that it is so (in his exchange with Kirzner). If instead "human" is being understood not biologically but praxeologically, as meaning something like "rational agent," then "human beings act" will be merely one more analytic tautology, and the pragmatic incoherence to which, e.g. Mises's and Rothbard's point will be question-begging. Perhaps all that the action axiom establishes, then, is that action *exists*? Would that perhaps be enough?

Which Are the Agents?

There's a related question as to how far the emphasis on *human* action is justified. Is the application of means to ends not also found among non-human animals? Or if animals are said not to act, or not to act in the same sense that humans do, then what precisely are they missing?

Turning from the subhuman to the superhuman, Mises argues that an omnipotent God would be unable to act, since "action can only be imputed to a discontented being, and repeated action only to a being who lacks the power to remove his uneasiness once and for all at one stroke" (Mises, 1996, p. 69). But is it really true that all action is prompted by dissatisfaction with the way things are? Do we not sometimes act, not to *change* a situation, but to *keep* it from changing? In that case we might be described as being dissatisfied with the way things *would* be if we didn't act; but since the counterfactual scenario we're seeking to avoid never occurs in the actual timeline (assuming our action is successful), isn't our dissatisfaction purely hypothetical?

Mises goes on to claim that for an omnipotent being "the categories of ends and means do not exist, since such a being can achieve every end without the employment of any means" (1996, p. 69). Hence once again an omnipotent God could not act, at least so long as action is understood as applying means in order to achieve ends. But aren't there many cases in which achieving an end by *these* means rather than *those* is actually part of the end? If I'm climbing Mount Everest, it's not because I simply want to be at the top (at least if I am like most climbers of Everest); rather, I want to get to the top *by climbing*. If I were simply to be carried to the summit by helicopter (or, for that matter, teleportation), I would not have achieved my goal. So, is Mises justified in ruling out the possibility that an omnipotent God might also wish, not merely to accomplish certain ends, but to accomplish them by some means and not others?

Impositionism or Reflectionism?

Mises tells us that we "see reality, not as it 'is' and may appear to a perfect being, but only as the quality of our mind and of our senses enables us to see it" (1962, p. 18). Mises here is often interpreted (whether accurately or not) as holding the view, often attributed likewise to Kant (again, whether accurately or not) that our *a priori* categories are true of the world we experience because the structure of our mind *imposes* them on experience – a position that Barry Smith (1990) calls "impositionism." Murray Rothbard, by contrast, takes *a priori* categories to be features of extramental reality that we *discover*, not something we impose – a position Smith calls "reflectionism" (Rothbard 1997, pp. 64, 105). Here there is room both for the exegetical question as to how to understand the positions of Mises and Rothbard, and more importantly the deeper philosophical question as to whether imposition or reflectionism is correct.

It is also possible to question whether the opposition between reflectionism and impositionism so much as makes sense. I've argued elsewhere (Long, 2004, cf. 2006b) that insofar as impositionism conceives of logical categories as imposed by the mind on a reality that, but for the mind's imposition, would not be subject to them, it requires the very conceivability of an illogical reality that it is at pains to deny; and likewise, insofar as reflectionism conceives of logical categories as imposed by *reality* on a *mind* that, but for reality's imposition, would lack them, it requires the very conceivability of an illogical mind that it is correspondingly at pains to deny. If that's right, then the logical character of reality and the logical character of the mind may turn out to be two sides of the same fact, without any possibility of grounding one in the priority of the other.

Praxeology and Determinism

For Mises, "[t]he logical structure of his mind enjoins upon man [a belief in] determinism" (Mises, 1985, p. 73), since action (whose reality Mises regards, as we've seen, as undeniable on pain of pragmatic incoherence) involves the application of means to ends, which implies causality, which implies necessitation. For Rothbard, by contrast, it is the thesis of causal determinism that is pragmatically incoherent, since if determinism is true, then "man's mind is ... not free to think and come to conclusions about reality," including the conclusion of determinism itself (Rothbard, 2011, p. 6).

Praxeology presumably cannot commit us *both* to the truth *and* to the falsity of causal determinism, so these two arguments can't both be correct. (Note that they *might* possibly both be incorrect.) So what is the right thing to say about the praxeological status of determinism? Is Mises perhaps too quick to assume either that the *existence* of causation implies the *universality* of causation, or that causation inherently implies *necessitation* (or both)? Is Rothbard perhaps too quick to assume that having one's beliefs necessitated by antecedent circumstances must involve having one's beliefs necessitated by factors that *bypass* one's reasoning process rather than operating *through* it?

The Boundaries of Praxeology

The final area for future research that I shall point to is perhaps the most funda-mental of all. Praxeologists (I've claimed) are committed to the view that *some* economic principles are *a priori*, while *others*, those needed for the application of the former, are auxiliary premises knowable only *a posteriori*. But where does the *a priori* portion of economics stop and the *a posteriori* portion begin?

As an example: Hayek claimed that his 1927 article "Economics and Knowledge" was "an attempt to persuade Mises" that "what was *a priori* was only the logic of individual action," and that as soon as economic analysis is extended to "the interaction of many people," it enters "the empirical field," since "the empirical element enters in people learning about what the other people do." To Hayek's surprise, Mises "approved the article as if he had not been aware that it was a criticism of his own views" (Caldwell, 2004, pp. 221, 421).

Austrians have reacted in a variety of ways to the question of Mises's agree-ment or disagreement with Hayek on this point. Lawrence White, for example, argues that while Hayek was correct in regarding the capacity of economic agents to learn from market feedback as empirical rather than *a priori*, he was mistaken in regarding this as a disagreement with Mises, since (as we've seen) for Mises the application of praxeological principles to actual situations is an empirical matter (White, 1984, p. 25, n. 90). Israel Kirzner, by contrast, regards the ability to learn from market feedback as *part* of the Misesian concept of action rather than merely auxiliary to it, thus lending this ability something closer to an *a priori* praxeological status (Kirzner, 1973, p. 32); on this reading, perhaps Mises's appearance of agreement with Hayek was either misunderstanding or mere politeness. Here we are presented with both an exegetical question (what was Mises's view?) and a deeper philosophical question (what *should* it have been?); the latter, in particular, is not confined to this dispute over market feedback but ramifies throughout the entire range of economic phenomena.

NOTES

1. The term "praxeology" originates not with Mises but rather with Louis Bourdeau (1882) and Alfred Espinas (1890), but this early usage has no strong connection with Mises's approach. With the variant spelling "praxiology," the term is also used by a variety of different schools of thought in a variety of different senses (Auspitz, Gasparski, Milicki, & Szaniawski, 1992); with both spellings, it is often used in connection with Polish philosopher Tadeusz Kotarbiński, on whom see Hiz (1954).

2.   Many rather more complicated efforts have been made to derive the truths of mathematics from analytic definitions of basic mathematical operations, but this project has not met with success.

3.   For some of my own suggestions in this area, see Long, 2004, 2005a, 2005b.

4.   Compare Aristotle and Descartes on the axiomatic status of the law of non-contradiction and the fact of one's own existence, respectively.

5.   In the words of Henry Hazlitt: "The deductive side of economics is no less important than the factual. One can say of it what Santayana says of logic (and what could equally well be said of mathematics), that it 'traces the radiation of truth,' so that 'when one term of a logical system is known to describe a fact, the whole system attaching to that term becomes, as it were, incandescent'" (Hazlitt, 1996, pp. 176–177).

REFERENCES

Auspitz, J. L., Gasparski, W. W., Milicki, M. K., & Szaniawski, K. (Eds). (1992). *Praxiologies and the Philosophy of Economics*. New Brunswick: Transaction Publishers.

Bourdeau, L. (1882). *Théorie des Sciences*, vol. 2. Paris: Librairie Germer Baillière.

Caldwell, B. J. (2004). *Hayek's Challenge: An Intellectual Biography of F. A. Hayek*. Chicago: University of Chicago Press.

Ebenstein, A. (2001). *Friedrich Hayek: A Biography*. New York: Palgrave.

Espinas, A. (1890). Les Origines de la Technologie. *Revue Philosophique de La France et de l'Étranger, 30*, 113–135.

Frege, G. (1977). *The Frege Reader* (M. Beaney, Ed.). Oxford: Blackwell.

Hayek, F. A. von. (1948a). Economics and Knowledge. In *Individualism and Economic Order* (pp. 33–56). Chicago: University of Chicago Press.

Hayek, F. A. von. (1948b). Fact of the Social Sciences. In *Individualism and Economic Order* (pp. 57–76). Chicago: University of Chicago Press.

Hayek, F. A. von. (1952). *The Counter-Revolution of Science*. Glencoe: The Free Press.

Hazlitt, H. (1996). *Economics in One Lesson*, 50th Anniversary Edition. San Francisco: Laissez Faire Books.

Hiz, H. (1954). Kotarbinski's Praxeology. *Philosophy and Phenomenological Research, 15*(2), 238.

Hoppe, H.-H. (1995). *Economic Science and the Austrian Method*. Auburn: Ludwig von Mises Institute.

Kirzner, I. M. (1973). *Competition and Entrepreneurship*. University of Chicago Press.

Kirzner, I. M. (2001). *Ludwig von Mises: The Man and His Economics*. Wilmington: ISI Books.

Lavoie, D. (1986). Euclideanism versus Hermeneutics: A Reinterpretation of Misesian Apriorism. In I. M. Kirzner (Ed.), *Subjectivism, Intelligibility, and Economic Understanding: Essays in Honor of Ludwig M. Lachmann on his Eightieth Birthday* (pp. 192–210). London: Macmillan.

Lavoie, D. (1994). The Interpretive Turn. In P. J. Boettke (Ed.), *The Elgar Companion to Austrian Economics* (pp. 54–62). Cheltenham, UK and Northampton, MA, USA: Edward Elgar Publishing.

Long, R. T. (2004). Anti-Psychologism in Economics: Wittgenstein and Mises. *Review of Austrian Economics, 17*(4), 345–369.

Long, R. T. (2005a). Praxeology: Who Needs It. *Journal of Ayn Rand Studies*, 6(2, Centenary Symposium, Part II: Ayn Rand among the Austrians), 299–316.

Long, R. T. (2005b). Reference and Necessity: A Rand-Kripke Synthesis? *Journal of Ayn Rand Studies*, 7(1), 209–228.

Long, R. T. (2006a). Realism and Abstraction in Economics: Aristotle and Mises versus Friedman. *Quarterly Journal of Austrian Economics*, 9(3), 3–23.

Long, R. T. (2006b). Rule-Following, Praxeology, and Anarchy. *New Perspectives on Political Economy*, 2(1), 36–46.

Menger, C. (1994). *Principles of Economics*. Grove City: Libertarian Press.

Mises, L. von. (1962). *The Ultimate Foundation of Economic Science: An Essay on Method*. Princeton: D. van Nostrand Company.

Mises, L. von. (1985). *Theory and History: An Interpretation of Social and Economic Evolution*. Auburn: Ludwig von Mises Institute.

Mises, L. von. (1996). *Human Action: A Treatise on Economics*, 4th Edition. San Francisco: Fox & Wilkes.

Mises, L. von. (2003). *Epistemological Problems of Economics*, 3rd Edition. Auburn: Ludwig von Mises Institute.

Nozick, R. (1997). On Austrian Methodology. In *Socratic Puzzles* (pp. 110–141). Cambridge MA: Harvard University Press.

Quine, W. V. O. (1951). Two Dogmas of Empiricism. *Philosophical Review*, 60(1), 20–43.

Rand, A. (1990). *Introduction to Objectivist Epistemology*, 2nd Edition (H. Binswanger & L. Peikoff, Eds). New York: Penguin.

Rothbard, M. N. (1957). In Defense of "Extreme Apriorism." *Southern Economic Journal*, 23(3), 314–320.

Rothbard, M. N. (1997). *The Logic of Action I: Method, Money, and the Austrian School*. Cheltenham, UK and Northampton, MA, USA: Edward Elgar Publishing.

Rothbard, M. N. (2011). *Economic Controversies*. Auburn: Ludwig von Mises Institute.

Smith, B. (1990). Aristotle, Menger, Mises: An Essay in the Metaphysics of Economics. In B. J. Caldwell (Ed.), *Carl Menger and His Legacy in Economics, Annual Supplement to Volume 22: History of Political Economy* (pp. 263–288). Durham: Duke University Press.

Steele, D. R. (1992). *From Marx to Mises: Post-capitalist Society and the Challenge of Economic Calculation*. La Salle, IL: Open Court Publishing.

Vaughn, K. I. (1994). *Austrian Economics in America*. Cambridge: Cambridge University Press.

White, L. H. (1984). *The Methodology of the Austrian School Economists*. Auburn: Ludwig von Mises Institute.

2.   Austrian phenomenology

Mark D. Packard

INTRODUCTION

While, broadly speaking, Austrians are a rather homogenous bunch of quirky and heterodox thinkers, outsiders to the Austrian school are often unaware of the deep and sometimes bitter disagreements that Austrians have waged within its own camp of scholars. While virtually all Austrians embrace the label 'subjectivist,' there are profound divides over what that term means (or ought to mean) and what philosophical assumptions it shoulders. As a result, Austrian scholars have generated distinct approaches to economic theory and methodology, and have generated similar but distinctive theories of, e.g., the business cycle, the fatal flaws of socialist economy planning, the process of entrepreneurship, and so forth.

At the center of these debates is the philosophical legacy of Ludwig von Mises, who developed a distinctive rationalist philosophy of science that has generated immense dialogue, commentary, elaboration, contention, and confusion. Various scholars have read deeply into Mises's words to justify the adoption of distinctive and conflicting philosophical positions as the foundational basis for the Austrian school. Others have rejected Mises's efforts within the philosophy of science altogether as a mistaken and absurd leap into 'neo-Kantianism.'

In this chapter I will proffer a new historical interpretation—that none of the prior arguments are correct, and that Mises has been altogether misunderstood at one level or another. Specifically, I develop a novel historical analysis that will place Mises within a camp of philosophers of science that once and briefly held significant prominence in the early twentieth century, but have been lost to history for various reasons—the camp of *realist phenomenology*. Mises's membership within this camp is not explicit—while it is clear that Mises knew the work of some of its members, he also leaves the clear impression that his work is derived originally and to a large extent independently of other thinkers. However, I will endeavor to show that it is possible, even likely, that Mises was familiar with the realist phenomenologists of the time and that their independent efforts are highly similar and reconcilable—far more so than the hermeneuticists and, later, the critical realists. In essence, Mises's position is a middle-ground position between these Austrian camps, a position that embraces both causal realism *and* phenomenology—the position of realist phenomenology. Thus, I will conclude that the counterhistorical (Bylund & Packard, 2022a) study of the realist phenomenologists, including Reinach, Scheler, Ingarden, Stein, and others, proffers a robust and powerful foundation for Austrian subjectivism—one that may, if I might be permitted to voice a fanciful hope, finally serve to reconcile the camps and put an end to the longstanding philosophy wars within the Austrian school.

THE PHILOSOPHY WARS

There has been much debate over the merits of a hermeneutic versus a causal or, specifically, a critical realist interpretation of praxeology (e.g. Lachmann, 1990; Lavoie, 1990, 2011; Martin, 2009; Rothbard, 1989; Runde, 2001; Storr, 2011) to the extent that, for many, it has become a tired argument. A particularly key aspect of the debate involves questions regarding Mises's own intellectual heritage and the origination of his rather unique epistemology. The phenomenology movement of the early twentieth century garnered a rather significant intellectual following, which included Mises Circle member Alfred Schütz and, later, many of the Austrian revival, including Ludwig Lachmann and Don Lavoie among others. Other Austrians, however, including Murray Rothbard (1989) and Hans-Hermann Hoppe (1989), were hostile toward this movement, resulting in a rift within the Austrian revival that remains today.

Concerns within the Austrian school over phenomenology pertain primarily to its supposed radical idealism. However, the phenomenological movement and the interpretive dimension more broadly contain a multiplicity of perspectives. The 'transcendental' idealist version(s) that Rothbard and Hoppe attacked is certainly a popular one within modern sociology, but it is not the only one. Even hermeneutics, which is more a methodology than a meta-theory,[1] hosts diverse opinions. This diversity of thought was lost within the meta-theoretical debates of the Austrian school on either side, where scholars would often refer to the diverse field of phenomenology only as "the hermeneutical or interpretive dimension of science" (Lavoie, 2011, p. 102). This oversight obscured important nuance, caused the Austrian camps to talk past each other (Storr, 2010, 2011), and led to an overall unproductive debate (Horwitz, 2004).

My thesis herein is that the Austrian school—the Misesean branch at least (I will steer clear of the methodological disputes between Mises and Hayek that are, to my reading, far less pronounced than some have made them out to be)—is in fact phenomenological, despite whatever angst is felt over that term. The contemporary Austrian school's general ignorance of the phenomenology movement and its history is regretful, as it has caused misunderstandings that have impeded progress and caused rifts among its ranks. I thus aim to remediate this ignorance by reviewing the historical origination of phenomenology and its ties to the Austrian school. In particular, I recount the historical rift in the phenomenology movement, which led to the division of 'realist' and 'transcendental' branches of phenomenology. I then place Mises's praxeology firmly within the branch of realist phenomenology, as a more moderate and 'causal realist' branch of phenomenology that offers the foundational subjectivism of phenomenology (that realism does not) without the baggage of idealism.

WAS MISES A PHENOMENOLOGIST?

Mises was to a significant extent before his time in economic philosophy and, as such, was largely unable to couch his own philosophical position neatly within an existing meta-theoretical framework. His 'causal realism,' as it has come to be known, built on and extended Dilthey's (1976, 1989), Weber's (1978, 2011), and, of course, Menger's (2009) pioneering work on social scientific method by developing a dualist meta-theory and method oriented to the study of social phenomena while the rest of his field plowed forward (mis)using positivist methods designed only for the study of natural and non-conscious objects and phenomena.

With more recent philosophical developments, however, scholars of the Austrian revival sought to fit Austrian theory, and Misesean praxeology especially, into the developing meta-theoretical frameworks that had since arisen. Two distinct frameworks have been offered in particular: hermeneutics and critical realism.

Hermeneutics

Philosophical hermeneutics is an interpretive philosophy of social science originally pioneered by Wilhelm Dilthey toward the end of the nineteenth century. Dilthey adamantly rejected a single philosophy of science, as he perceived the natural and social sciences to be innately distinctive. Under Dilthey's influence, Edmund Husserl developed *phenomenology* as a philosophy of *social* science, which emphasizes the centrality of human consciousness and intentionality to the social sciences as well as the boundedness of human awareness and knowledge. Elaborating Husserl's phenomenology, Martin Heidegger and, later, Hans-Georg Gadamer and Paul Ricœur (among others) further elaborated Dilthey's hermeneutic method into a formal social scientific meta-theory. The essential insight of philosophical hermeneutics, and its interpretive methodology, is that we cannot interpret human action (e.g. text and speech acts) correctly unless we grasp the meanings that the actors themselves ascribe to those particular actions. Thus, as social science deals with conscious and intentional behaviors, the hermeneutical method pursues a better and fuller understanding of those subjective intentions and, thus, facilitates a more correct interpretation of the purposes ascribed to behaviors. In short, positivistic empirical science is doomed to mislead because one cannot 'observe' intentions; but a hermeneutical method gets us, at least, closer to social 'truth.'

The introduction of philosophical hermeneutics into the Austrian school came by way of Ludwig Lachmann,[2] who found particular interest in the importance of interpretation early in his career (Lachmann, 1943, 1971) which led to his later discovering and advocating philosophical hermeneutics (Lachmann, 1990). It was Lavoie, Lachmann's student, however, that provided the Austrian school the most complete arguments for philosophical hermeneutics as a meta-theoretical foundation for praxeology (Lavoie, 1986, 1990, 1991, 1994, 2011).

Lachmann's and Lavoie's interpretations of Mises through the lens of hermeneutics is hardly without merit. Mises employs many of the same themes and, sometimes, the very same concepts that philosophical hermeneutics also develops. For example, both Mises and hermeneutics build from and upon Dilthey's (and Weber's) methodological dualism and concept of *Verstehen*. They are both explicitly subjectivist and share a "deprecation of quantitative approaches to the study of history" (Storr, 2010, p. 149). They are also both strictly post-modern (in the broader sense of the term):

> Modernism can be defined as the rationalist and/or empiricist view that knowledge is the result of the knowing subject achieving a detached objectivity in relation to the objects of study. The 'truth' is thought to follow from the strict application of 'scientific methods' in theorizing (where mathematics and logical deduction is privileged as a superior form of reasoning), and in empirical work (where the verification or falsification of hypotheses through statistical testing is privileged) ... It has been the dominant philosophical orientation of the social and natural sciences since the Enlightenment. (Lavoie, 2005: 3)

Intentionality, interpretation, and the subjectivity of meaning are key post-modern themes imbued throughout Mises's writings. Echoing very precisely the main tenets of philosophical hermeneutics, Mises (1998, p. 26) rejected the idea that:

> it is possible to grasp human action intellectually if one refuses to comprehend it as meaningful and purposeful behavior aiming at the attainment of definite ends. Behaviorism and positivism want to apply the methods of the empirical natural sciences to the reality of human action. They interpret it as a response to stimuli. But these stimuli themselves are not open to description by the methods of the natural

sciences. Every attempt to describe them must refer to the meaning which acting men attach to them.

A fair reading of both philosophical hermeneutics and Mises can hardly deny that, in very many respects, "Mises look[s] remarkably similar to the contributors to the growth of knowledge and hermeneutics traditions" (Lavoie, 2011, p. 117).

The primary criticisms of a hermeneutical approach to praxeology have been, summarily, "nihilism, relativism, and solipsism" (Rothbard, 1989, p. 46). That is, philosophical hermeneutics at least since Heidegger (2010) adopts a 'transcendental idealism' in which conscious experience is the only given, from which all knowledge is derived as an intersubjectively reconstructed interpretation. This view suggests that there is no reality without a conscious being to perceive it,[3] and that 'truth' itself is culturally relative. While this 'post-truth' philosophical movement has gained recent steam due, it seems, to its usefulness as a political cudgel, most scientists, including the subjectivist Austrians, reject it outright. Mises is clearly unwilling to step into such a neo-Kantian idealism, claiming for his apriorism the status of real and objective truth:

> It is consequently incorrect to assert that aprioristic insight and pure reasoning do not convey any information about reality and the structure of the universe. The fundamental logical relations and the categories of thought and action are the ultimate source of all human knowledge. They are adequate to the structure of reality, they reveal this structure to the human mind and, in this sense, they are for man basic ontological facts. (Mises, 1998, p. 86)

Critical Realism

Although the Austrian school was a strong critic of the *positivism* of classical and neo-classical economics, its departure from positivism into subjectivism was not a full leap into radical idealism. Austrians would readily admit the existence of 'reality' *per se* and, thus, at least some objective truths. Thus, for many, the departure from positivism landed the Austrian school in a form of causal *realism*. As David Gordon put it in a 1996 speech, "Austrian economics and a realistic philosophy seem made for each other," and most contemporary Austrians have readily adopted *critical realism* as its foundation (Beaulier & Boettke, 2004; Lewis, 2005; Martin, 2009; Runde, 2001).

A moderate departure from positivism, but also antagonistic toward the more idealistic modern phenomenologies, Roy Bhaskar (1978, 1998, 2009) offered critical realism as a 'post-positivist' middle ground. Critical realism takes a more nuanced stance than positivism on questions of ontology, epistemology, human agency, and method, in essence taking a middling or straddled position between functionalist objectivism and interpretivist subjectivism (Packard, 2017). Critical realism posits an essentially compatibilist notion of human agency, and puts the freedom of will at a secondary position, capable of altering social structures yet strongly beholden to them. The agent's ability to alter social structure rather than remaining slave to them, as per positivism, arises, for critical realism, from experiential variance. That is, because individual agents are heterogeneous along multiple dimensions, we tend to experience and perceive reality differently. This permits a heterogeneity in causal interpretation, which can lead to differences in derived reactions and learning. Those differences play out to distinct outcomes, the more successful generating conformity through observation and discourse and, thereby, producing new social structures different from the old. In essence, critical realism's volition amounts to little more than deciding between existing structure and new experience—it is freedom of interpretation, and little more, allowing interpretation to thereby set forth a new structural routine by which one's actions will subsequently become determined.

Certainly, critical realism also holds some merit for Austrian scholarship. For example, it aligns in many ways with Hayek's (1952) foray into cognitive psychology in *The Sensory Order*. Hayek's own philosophy, and that of his friends Karl Popper and Donald Campbell (Campbell, 1974; Popper, 1974, 1978, 1987), is sometimes described as an *evolutionary* realism, very much like, but in subtle ways different from, Bhaskar's critical realism.[4] Another variant of realism would be Anthony Giddens's (1984) structuration theory. Each of these realist meta-theories, while differing on the interactive mechanisms between epistemology, human agency, and the ontological realm, share an understanding of the essential *nature* of these, including the ontological reality and causal determinism of social phenomena.

However, critical realism's straddling of objectivism and subjectivism is philosophically tenuous. While it attempts to offer a semi-voluntarist (i.e. compatibilist) approach that reconciles social determinism with human agency and self-determinism, foundationally it collapses into a determinist position (King, 1999; Packard, 2017). In this foundational sense, then, critical realism fundamentally misaligns with Mises's voluntarist self-determinism.

> What the term 'freedom of the will' refers to is the fact that the ideas that induce a man to make a decision (a choice) are, like all other ideas, not 'produced' by external 'facts,' do not 'mirror' the conditions of reality, and are not 'uniquely determined' by any ascertainable external factor to which we could impute them in the way in which we impute in all other occurrences an effect to a definite cause. There is nothing else that could be said about a definite instance of a man's acting and choosing than to ascribe it to this man's individuality. (Mises, 1962, pp. 57–58)

For Mises, as with Menger (2009), the essential condition of human agency and free will separated the natural sciences from the social sciences, a conclusion shared by interpretivists such as the phenomenologists, but not by the (social) realists.

Critical realism's determinist–self-determinist (i.e. methodological holist–individualist) stratification results, according to King (1999, pp. 283–284), in two key antinomies: (1) that "although society is dependent on individuals, it is at the same time irreducible to individuals" and thus independent of them, and that, (2) "although social action is always meaningful, there are objective material factors which cannot be reduced to individual interpretation." These contradictions are especially concerning for Misesean praxeology, which holds methodological individualism, intentionality, and subjective interpretation to be foundational tenets. If praxeology recognizes that social collectives are wholly dependent on the individuals that comprise them and that social meaning can always be reduced to individual interpretations (collectively), as Mises understood, then praxeology finds itself fully within the domain of *interpretivism*, and not *realism*. Critical realism, while in many respects aligned with Mises's praxeology (and even more aligned with Hayek's non-praxeological approach), is in other fundamental ways misaligned and, even, philosophically incommensurable, making it a rather shaky foundation.

The Austrian proponents of hermeneutics are (were) absolutely correct in their recognition of the ties between Mises and interpretive phenomenology and of a foundational misalignment between Mises and modern-day realism. Post-positivist realism is fundamentally misaligned with Misesean anti-positivism and subjectivism (cf. Burrell & Morgan, 1979), as it is foundationally objectivist, with subjectivist components built incommensurably within (Packard, 2017). Mises's strict and coherent subjectivism falls squarely within the realm of interpretivism, alignable, in principle, with phenomenology. Yet, as Austrian realists argue, it is also realist in the sense that is incommensurable with the transcendental idealism of prevailing phenomenologies. Thus, it seems, we find Mises without a philosophical home.

ALFRED SCHÜTZ

Storr (2010) argues that, perhaps, a Schützian interpretation of Mises is apropos given their shared academic heritage and the fact that Alfred Schütz explicitly intended his work to be an extension of Mises's (Hülsmann, 2007). While I find this argument compelling and believe that Schütz offers important additions to Misesean meta-theory, Mises's own rationalistic epistemology goes well beyond Schütz's application of the phenomenological method to the social sciences. Perhaps most glaringly, a Schützian reading of Mises is too narrow, encapsulating only a small part of Mises's contribution to method. For example, Schütz cannot account for Mises's methodological apriorism, which is typically attributed to the influence of Kant. This is not meant as a criticism of Schütz, but it does suggest that Schütz's work alone is an insufficient foundation for praxeology.

To my own reading, Mises's work on social scientific epistemology seems to align far better with phenomenological philosophy than with critical realism. His arguments mirror quite precisely the same criticisms of positivism and the emphases on conscious intentionality and subjectivism of phenomenology. Said more unambiguously (and, perhaps, controversially), *Mises was a phenomenologist*, though not a hermeneuticist, as I will argue next. A thorough layout of the evidence for this conclusion would require a full volume. Fortunately, such a case should not be necessary, as will be implied in the following outline of realist phenomenology.

PHENOMENOLOGY'S HISTORY

Let us first turn briefly to some background history, i.e. to the origins of different variants within the larger phenomenological movement, and how phenomenology (and especially hermeneutics) came to be so vehemently discarded within the modern praxeology movement. Phenomenology is a large camp, comprising multiple threads or offshoots spawning from Edmund Husserl's seminal work, *Logical Investigations*, published in two volumes in 1900 and 1901. In it, Husserl follows and builds from the pioneering work of Brentano and Dilthey, both of whom also greatly influenced Menger and the Austrian school (Smith, 1992a, 1994), to harshly attack the positivist paradigm, arguing that the social sciences are inherently distinct from the natural sciences. Husserl sought to reconcile logical realism with philosophical psychology. Amid the so-called *Psychologismus-Streit* (i.e. the 'psychologism dispute'), Husserl's thought landed into a subjectivist, anti-psychologistic perspective, offering in this work a *realist* phenomenological account in which mental acts (i.e. *intentionality*) are directed *at* objects, but that such objects are real and not subject to the consciousness itself. Placing intentionality at the heart of social science, he argued that social phenomena must be understood from the first-person point of view—intentions and meaning could not be observed—suggesting a very different scientific method for the social sciences. *Logical Investigations* attracted a great deal of attention and interest among young thinkers, who began to flood to Göttingen, where Husserl held an associate professorship (*Extraordinariat*).

Husserl would, in the subsequent decade, take a 'transcendental turn' into Kantian[5] transcendentalist idealism. This shift in thought came about through or as a result of his development and elaboration of the *eidetic* or *phenomenological method*, by which conscious experience would be 'bracketed,' meaning that the phenomenologist would dispel any assumptions about the true reality of one's conscious experience (for one could be hallucinating, for example, and yet such hallucination would have real effects on behavior). There are, even, purely mental or transcendent objects that 'constitute themselves' in consciousness, having no basis in 'real' or physical experience. This line of reasoning ultimately led Husserl to conclude that all objects, both mental and physical, are constituted *intersubjectively*. "An object existing in itself is never one with which consciousness or the Ego pertaining to consciousness has nothing to do" (Husserl, 1982, p. 106). This led, ultimately, to Husserl's bracketing of phenomenology to conscious phenomena *en toto*, dropping concerns about objective reality into the bucket of agnosticism.

Husserl's turn into transcendental idealism threw the young field of phenomenology into disarray, dubbed the "the realism-idealism controversy" (Ingarden, 1929, 1975). Some—Adolf Reinach and Max Scheler of particular note—would not follow Husserl into transcendentalism. These advocated and developed what is now known as *realist* or *realistic* phenomenology, which embraced the central tenets of phenomenology (consciousness, subjectivism, intentionality, interpretation, etc.), but held fast to the vital role that objective reality plays in what is perceived. But most phenomenologists followed Husserl into transcendentalism, including Martin Heidegger, Jean-Paul Sartre, and Maurice Merleau-Ponty. Husserl's transcendental or constitutive phenomenology would spawn variations of it, such as existentialism (e.g. Sartre, Merleau-Ponty, de Beauvoir) and philosophical hermeneutics (e.g. Heidegger, Gadamer, Ricœur), from which additional branches would further segment, such as Rorty's *neopragmatism*, Foucault's *poststructuralism*, Derrida's *deconstructionism*, and Butler's *performativism*. These later branches begin to push what most historians believe was a soft transcendentalism (not dismissive of reality but merely agnostic about its relevance to sociology) even further into radical relativism.

Of note, it is these more recent radical offshoots from transcendental phenomenology that drew the ire and antagonism of Hoppe (1989), Rothbard (1989), and other Austrian critics, confounding the more recent and radical relativist approaches with the earlier and less radical branches. This should not be taken as a criticism of these formative Austrians—their confusion is certainly understandable, as these radical offshoots explicitly build on and from the work of earlier transcendental phenomenologists.[6] However, as a result of this misunderstanding and ignorance of the complex history of phenomenological thought, it is extremely difficult to tease out what criticisms hold any merit whatsoever. Lavoie (1990: 9) thus lamented that, "although there are some interesting issues in the criticisms that have been raised so far of the hermeneutical Austrians, the critics, by and large, have not shown a very sophisticated appreciation of economics." While this retort is unfair, it is true that the critics of a hermeneutical approach have unfairly reproached the phenomenological tradition for the sins of its offspring. Indeed, there were many early phenomenologists—of the Munich and Göttingen circles—who also critiqued the transitioning phenomenological movement in much the same way that Hoppe and Rothbard did and, so, did not follow Husserl into his transcendental turn, maintaining and building from, instead, the realism of his earlier work.

REALIST PHENOMENOLOGY

Two early phenomenologists of note who stayed behind at the transcendental turn were Adolf Reinach and Max Scheler. These, along with others (e.g. Celms, Daubert, Ingarden, Pfänder, Stein, von Hildebrand, etc.) criticized Husserl's turn into idealism and built instead on his earlier foundations of a *realist* or *realistic* phenomenology. This now obscure branch of phenomenology is, I think, most apposite to Misesean praxeology. Because hermeneutics is methodologically focused and represents many different strands of phenomenology,[7] it offers a somewhat confused and uncompelling foundation for social science. Arguably, realist phenomenology is a more comprehensible and unconfounded phenomenological foundation, which maintains a metaphysical realism that Austrian scholars crucially maintain (whereas hermeneutical philosophers are uncommitted to it), while maintaining the quintessentially Austrian *subjectivist* social ontology that critical realism (at least partially) abandons.

While there is no clear evidence that Mises knew of Reinach's work,[8] there are strong tendrils of Reinach's contribution to philosophy throughout Mises's thought (Smith, 1990). For example, Mises adopted Reinach's conception of *states of affairs*,[9] a foundational meta-theoretical concept that he employs heavily throughout *Human Action*. Also, years before Mises developed his *aprioristic* method, apparently from Kant's influence, Reinach developed an elaborate theoretical elaboration of *apriorism*, applying it much further than Kant's limited scope into real-world contexts, just as Mises did with the science of human action.

Mises *was* aware of and had read Scheler, however, and cites him favorably in *Epistemological Problems of Economics*. Mises was likely brought into further contact with Scheler's ideas through Alfred Schütz, who had engaged deeply with Scheler's work throughout his career and even translated some of his work. While most historians place Schütz in the transcendental camp, he was widely influenced by the realist camp, which influence undoubtedly had some proximal impact on Mises.

Adolf Reinach

Reinach has been described as "among the ablest of the remarkable set of students whom Husserl had attracted" (MacIntyre, 2006, p. 9). Husserl himself marveled at Reinach's ability to distil and explain complex ideas to him—even his own: "It was really Reinach who introduced me to my *Logical investigations*, and in an excellent way" (Husserl, quoted in Oesterreicher, 1952, p. 100). Thus, "the Göttingen students of phenomenology ... refer to Reinach, not to Husserl, as their real teacher in phenomenology" (Spiegelberg, 1982, pp. 191–192).

German-born, Reinach enlisted in the German army for the First World War in 1914 and was killed in action in 1917 at the young age of 33, cutting much too short an extremely promising career. If not for his untimely death, Reinach's popularity among students, his intellect, and an ability to present clear arguments may have altered the trajectory of the phenomenological movement. Instead, his early demise led to his life's work receiving "pathetically little attention, particularly within the English language" (DuBois, 1995, p. 2).

Before the war, Reinach had already made something of a lasting impact on the field, having published several works, including a critique of Kant's (mis)interpretation of Hume and a revisionary elaboration of his *apriorism*, a theory of negative judgment, and an influential *a priori* theory of civil law. In fact, this last work has already been successfully integrated into modern Austrian legal theory and private property, apparently brought to the attention of the Austrian school by Barry Smith.[10] Yet it is his larger body of work, and especially his work on judgment, logic, and the *a priori*, which has so far been overlooked by not just the Austrians but virtually the whole field of philosophy and social science, that is, or may be, especially important to Austrian theory generally, and Misesean praxeology specifically.

Judgment and states of affairs

One of the most foundational contributions of Husserl and, especially, Reinach was a critical advancement of our understanding of an ontology–epistemology dualism. Whereas Brentano and Frege pushed philosophers toward a theory of mental representations (representationalism), which allowed a deeper understanding of heterogeneity in judgments (i.e. empirical perception does not impose the same mental understanding across actors), Husserl and Reinach further recognized "a heterogeneous category of judgment-*correlates*, a category of entities in the world which would make judgments or sentences true or false" (Smith, 1982, p. 293).

Reinach's notion of a 'state of affairs' (*Sachverhalte*) is uniquely robust and central to realist phenomenology and has become widely (but not universally;

see Armstrong, 1997) accepted in philosophy. Reinach conceives of a 'state of affairs' differently than did Husserl (Seron, 2015). For Reinach (1982, pp. 334, 338), these states of affairs are not "objects in the strict sense" but are "objectual correlates" of judgments. In other words, a state of affairs is a *thought* or *assessment* regarding the relational and characteristic nature of 'things.' The referent of the concept that I know as 'that ball' is an object, but a state of affairs includes the nature of its existence (from a phenomenological standpoint)—its roundness, softness, color, position, etc., as well as its concept and purpose are all part of the *state of affairs* with respect to that ball, as I might perceive or experience it. The thought 'an orange ball is on my desk' is a state of affairs.

A state of affairs *occurs* or *obtains*, it does not *exist*, which has implications for ontological coherence. It *need not* obtain in order to be a 'state of affairs,' it need only be imagined. If a state of affairs 'existed' in an ontological sense, then we would arrive at a logical complication where *not A* (for some state of affairs A) can only mean the absence of and not the negation of A, as is logically proper. If A were my earlier example of a state of affairs, then *not A* would be some real (ontological) object 'not-orange-ball-on-my-desk.' This is, clearly, not what we mean by *not A*. However, if A as a state of affairs *occurs* or *obtains* rather than *exists*, then *not A* implies that A *does not occur* (i.e. there is no orange ball on my desk), which is logically coherent.

There are five facts or criteria for Reinach's states of affairs (Seron, 2015):

1. states of affairs are believed or asserted;
2. states of affairs sit relationally within what we today call a causal mental model;
3. only states of affairs can present modalities (i.e. *is*, *may be*, *will not*, etc.);
4. states of affairs can be positive or negative (there are, of course, no negative *things*); and
5. while objects can be 'seen,' only states of affairs can be *known* or *understood.*

The veracity or obtaining of a particular imagined state of affairs is *given* by reality itself and its empirical effects on one's subjective experience. My observation of an orange ball on my desk *gives* that state of affairs—it has obtained.

In short, while an *object* is, or refers to, an ontological reality *per se*, a *state of affairs* is an epistemological representation only, typically meant to represent reality as it is, i.e. to represent real objects as they were, are, or will be. But a state of affairs is a proposition *about* how the world was, is, or will be, and may or may not be true. Ontology, then, corresponds to *obtained* states of affairs only. Epistemology's realm is far broader, comprising *all* states of affairs, obtained or not. The laws of *logic*, then, are "nothing other than general principles expressing relations between states of affairs" (Reinach, 1982, p. 339). This is a foundational assertion that becomes critical in his elaboration of the *a priori*, as we shall soon see.

For Mises, as with Reinach, human action is based in and on *states of affairs*, and not on reality *per se*. Mises adopts a Reinachian interpretation of states of affairs, and its *givenness*, throughout his presentation of praxeology. For example:

> Acting man is eager to substitute a more satisfactory *state of affairs* for a less satisfactory. His mind imagines conditions which suit him better, and his action aims at bringing about this desired state. (Mises, 1998, p. 13, emphasis added)

> We cannot approach our subject if we disregard the meaning which action man attaches to the situation, i.e., the *given state of affairs*, and to his own behavior with regard to this situation. (Mises, 1998, p. 26, emphasis added)

Judgment, then, is for Reinach outwardly intentional or 'projected,' an epistemic claim of some state of affairs. Such claims are made true or false by the 'obtaining' of their ontological *correlate*, i.e. by the claimed state of affairs' referent. Thus, "a judgment is true precisely when its intentional state of affairs stands in perfect coincidence with the corresponding 'disposition of the things' on the side of the object" (Smith, 1997, p. 588). That is, a judgment is true if the state of affairs it refers to obtains (or obtained). This state of affairs can be positive (is/was/will be) or negative (is not/was not/will not be). The 'obtaining' of a state of affairs is an ontological matter—"'states of affairs' obtain (*bestehen*) indifferently of what consciousness apprehends them, and of whether they are apprehended by any consciousness at all" (Reinach, 1969, p. 213)—providing the foundational ontological independence of a realist phenomenology that Husserl had abandoned.

Reinach's judgment concept stood in strong contrast with the prevailing orthodoxy, which "had rested on a conception of the judgment as a compound of concepts or presentations. Judgments thus conceived have no direct ontological correlates of their own: they are true or false in virtue of the existence or non-existence of a corresponding combination amongst the ontological correlates of their constituent concepts" (Smith, 1982, p. 293). Mises refers regularly to judgments (and especially value judgments) as a characteristic process of human life. But his concept of judgment is essentially Reinachian, as I think a careful reading reveals.

The *a priori*
The goal of logic, and of scientific exploration, for Reinach is in ascertaining the *essences* of things, their situatedness, and their 'necessary relations' with

other things. These are *ontologically objective* (interrelational) properties, independent of mental acts. The primary aim of phenomenology is then, for Reinach, the intuition of essences, i.e. the true and objective nature of things and their relations (DuBois, 1995). "There is no accidentally-being-so in essences; rather, there is a necessarily-having-to-be-so, and an essentially -cannot-be-otherwise" (Reinach, 1969, p. 210). Through the phenomenological method, states of affairs, and their properties, are 'given' and intuited, although, Scheler (2017) argues, never in their entirety.

For Reinach (1976), then, a knowledge of essences produces for us a logical capacity to deduce *a priori* necessarily true states of affairs, or judgments of states of affairs, that necessarily *must* obtain to the extent that our knowledge of essences is accurate and complete. Said differently, there are states of affairs that, given the extent of (true) knowledge that we so far possess, will necessarily obtain as there is no logically coherent alternative state of affairs that otherwise *could* obtain. This allows both positive and negative *a priori* judgments. For example, within a controlled environment, a physicist can predict with apodictic certainty the physical reaction of two billiard balls colliding *given* also a sufficiently complete knowledge of the nature of the balls (their composition and shape), their situatedness (e.g. on what surface, air resistance, etc.), and their relations (e.g. Newton's laws of motion). And because we grasp the genetic essence of an acorn, we may be *a priori* certain that a planted acorn *will not* germinate into a new pumpkin plant. These are, for Reinach, knowable *a priori* out of a knowledge of the essences of the objects, of their situatedness within reality, and of their necessary causal relations with other objects.

In this way, Reinach pushes apriorism much further than did Kant or, for that matter, even Mises. There came to be a dark antagonism toward aprioristic rationalism among philosophers—in large part due to the forays into idealism of its primary advocates, Descartes and Kant. But, Reinach maintains, the *a priori* "does not mean anything dark or mystical" (Reinach, 2012, p. 5). The only barriers to such apriorism, for Reinach, is not in its impossibility, as empiricists claim, but only in our present failure to have sufficiently uncovered the essences of things. Once we understand natural essences, we can derive logically necessary predictions from them *given* the particular situatedness of those essences. Connecting these insights to Misesean praxeology is, then, a simple matter. Hülsmann (2007, p. 673) explains:

> Some of the empirical conditions under which human action can take place are universally given. For example, all human actions occur during the passage of time and all acting persons age in the course of time. Other empirical conditions such as the use of money are of a more contingent nature. But however universal or contingent these conditions are, it remains true that *once* they are given, they cause certain objective effects, which are the subject matter of the a priori theory of human action.

Mises's praxeological argument is, in Reinach's language, that the *essence* of human action is its *intentionality*. But this essence of humanity could not be abductively intuited through the same scientific methods as other essences can, because of its innate unobservability, which would have proved a devastating barrier to social science.[11] Mises's groundbreaking insight was in deriving it through argumentation. But the result is the same: an essence is grasped and established as true and certain, from which other states of affairs can be deductively theorized.

Max Scheler

The most influential realist phenomenologist of the time was Max Scheler, a German whose large (and, at the time, well-known) intellectual legacy was squelched after his death in 1928 by the Nazi regime, against which he had been outspoken. Scheler contributed to many areas of philosophy, including metaphysics, politics, ethics, religion, and history. His work in all of these areas, I think, will prove helpful to the development of Austrian thought. But I will introduce to readers only one foundational development that Austrian scholars will find particularly interesting—his subjective axiology.

Scheler's value theory

Experience, Scheler (1973) explains, is value-laden, and objects of experience are only bearers or purveyors of values. Value does not *inhere* in objects, just as the color orange does not inhere in the ball on my desk, but is only given as phenomenal experience. Thus, he explicitly rejects what is, in economics, the notion of value as 'utility.'

> One inquires in vain as to what in all the world such 'powers,' 'capabilities,' and 'dispositions' should consist of. Are we to admit special 'axiological powers,' or are these powers none other than those which natural science ascribes to things, such as adhesion, cohesion, gravity, etc.? ... Values *are not* such powers; they are rather the effects, the desires and feelings *themselves*. However, this leads to a value theory of quite a different type. (Scheler, 1973, p. 16)

This "value theory of quite a different type" is a subjective value theory that Austrian readers will find both very familiar and highly insightful.

For Scheler, the value of a painting is not in its objective nature or properties, but in the experience of it, which is given as a *value-phenomenon*. 'Value-phenomena' are, in Scheler's conception, dualistic in nature—they entail an objective change on the one hand and a subjective experience of the change on the other. The consumption of food entails objective aliment and the biological changes that such entails *as well as* a subjective experience of taste and relief from hunger pangs. The latter is *intuitively given* and then *brought to givenness* with the object(s) of experience through *value-ception*. By 'value-ception' he does not mean 'the noticing of feelings' but rather, in the language of his phenomenology, an 'inner intuition' of the subjective value experience.

Value-phenomena are different from the intentional act of *valuing*, which is an act of creation and meaning-making. Like Mises, Scheler argues that we are inherently drawn toward greater positive values and away from lesser or negative values. The good life, for Scheler, is as Davis and Steinbock (2021) summarize, "a movement and openness to the higher or deeper values," the escaping of negative values for positive ones and, particularly, love. "There is no experience of the good in itself in general, but only the good in itself for me, and this constitutes in part the experience of vocation peculiar to each unique person as creatively becoming."

One can clearly see the similarities between Scheler's presentation of subjective value and the Austrian school's conception (Menger, 2007; Mises, 1998), and particularly more recent elaborations of Austrian subjective value theory (e.g. Bylund & Packard, 2022b). But Scheler's theory of value is built upon philosophical ethics and axiology and is thus highly complementary to the economics-centered value theorizing of the Austrian school. Thus, while the Austrian school still has the strongest and most theoretically sound of the economic value theories, there is still very much it could gain from Scheler's value theory.

MOVING FORWARD

Mises was a pioneer in developing a unique and remarkably advanced meta-theoretical foundation for this own market process theory. But philosophy was not his primary interest nor his focus. Although his framework is sufficiently sound to bolster an advanced and superior theory of economics, generally, a lack of further advancement at the meta-theoretical level in contemporary theorizing has resulted in rather paltry advancement of Mises's extensive work since then. In a very real sense, nearly all of the contemporary advancements of Austrian theorizing have merely been incremental elaborations and applications of theory that Mises already set forth. Austrian economics, to push forward to new heights, will I think require advancements in meta-theory.

To do so, I perceive that the most successful path forward will be a *counter-historical* one (Bylund & Packard, 2022a). Counterhistory is, essentially, the revisiting of historical scientific and philosophical debates. By reconsidering theories that at one time lost their day, we might find advanced arguments that proffer new insights and advancement in the modern era, where we face problems derived from those paths taken long ago.

A Counterhistory of Realist Phenomenology

My aim in this chapter has been to introduce readers, both within the Austrian school and without, to the broader tradition of phenomenology and its prospects as a foundational meta-theory. Of course, phenomenology, generally, has already been the center of a somewhat heated debate that has rent the Austrian school into factions. But philosophical hermeneutics—the center of contention—is hardly the only branch of phenomenology. In fact, while there are significant merits to the hermeneutical tradition that should certainly be a part of Austrian discourse, its development and presentation has been tangled as a result of its development by phenomenologists of similar but different meta-theoretical positions. Dilthey, the original modern hermeneuticist, was in fact a causal realist who developed hermeneutics as an interpretive methodology. Heidegger and his followers then advanced hermeneutics atop different forms of existentialism, with varying degrees of (un)realism. As a result, the criticisms and defense of hermeneutics are simultaneously both valid and invalid.

A better versing in the history of phenomenology and its many branches offers us a clearer view into the promise of phenomenology for Austrian economics. I have specifically advocated the *realist* branch of phenomenology, which seems to offer precisely the causal realist foundations that the Austrian school requires, embracing a *meta-physical* realism without scientistic *social* reification. Attempts to reify social phenomena into the same categorical ontology as wind, electricity, and gravity and study them as such is a mistake that both Mises and Hayek clearly refuted. *Causal realism* (i.e. that social phenomena have real effects) simply does not imply ontological objectivity, as social realists suppose.

Austrian (ontological) subjectivism is categorically misfit with social realisms such as critical realism. But it is highly aligned with realist phenomenology's social ontological subjectivism, without the transcendental idealism.

Even a brief review of the realist phenomenologists reveals a vast array of insights that are clearly 'Austrian' in nature. I have mentioned a few already, such as Reinach's dualism and conception of judgment and Scheler's subjective value theory. Both of these forgotten thinkers have done much more work that ought to be of profound interest to Austrian scholars. Other realist phenomenologists have made other interesting contributions. For example, I recently discovered and built upon Edith Stein's theory of empathy. Roman Ingarden has done significant work on aesthetics and the value of art, which may be of interest to Austrian scholars. There is a trove of insights within this obscure branch of philosophy that I have argued is the most closely aligned with Misesean praxeology.

CONCLUSION

Much tends to get lost in the path dependencies of historical evolution. For example, the prevailing positivism of modern economics is, to a large extent, the result of the Second World War, which shifted the center of economic thought from anti-positivist Europe to positivist America. In a similar way, the First World War and the rise of the Nazi regime effectively squelched the promise of realist phenomenology as a sound and nuanced alternative to the radical positions of both the neo-Kantian transcendentalists as well as the positivists. Modern efforts to move on from these two unsatisfactory extremes has produced only tenuous platforms that have been rightly criticized for their problematic assumptions.

I see two ways forward from here. We can either continue the current Austrian program of reinventing a realist subjectivism as a foundation for our theorizing, or else we can employ a counterhistorical method to rediscover the groundwork already laid by truly brilliant thinkers of the past. Menger's and Mises's work on meta-theory is sound and important, but remains underdeveloped. It has been a challenge, for example, to explain and justify our methodological dualism within a philosophical zeitgeist that is extremely dismissive of any dualist foundation. Some of the best arguments that I have seen for this have been made by the realist phenomenologists. Let us look back as we try to move forward. There is far too much value in that history to leave it there.

NOTES

1. Both Gadamer and Ricœur attempted to develop the hermeneutical method into its own meta-theory, which is what is meant by 'philosophical hermeneutics.' But using the term 'hermeneutics' in this way has been problematic, as a hermeneutic method was adopted by many different phenomenological positions. Even Gadamer and Ricœur each developed somewhat distinct philosophies for hermeneutics. It is much more apropos, I think, to describe hermeneutics as the interpretive methodology that Dilthey rescued, and not as a *specific* interpretive meta-theory.
2. While some have noted connections between Schütz and the hermeneutic tradition (e.g. Staudigl & Berguno, 2014), Schütz was not, himself, part of the early hermeneutics camp.
3. Historians of, at least, Heidegger and Gadamer (and perhaps others of the phenomenology movement, such as Rorty) have argued that an interpretation of radical relativism may be an over-reading, that although these thinkers strongly emphasized the cultural relativism of what is considered to be 'truth' in response to the rise of logical positivism in social science, they may not have meant to suggest that there is no independent reality whatsoever.
4. See Alvarez and Barney (2007, 2010) for a partial delineation of these types of realism.

5.	Kant was rather unclear on the meaning of 'transcendental idealism,' of which there remains wide debate. It seems to be, in most respects, simply representationalism, which should be hardly controversial, given that representationalism is the predominant understanding of perception today. Some, however, contend that Kant's position, following Berkeley, is more radically idealistic. I take no position on this debate. Here are Kant's (1998, p. 426) own words: "I understand by the *transcendental idealism* of all appearances the doctrine that they are all together to be regarded as mere representations and not as things in themselves, and accordingly that space and time are only sensible forms of our intuition, but not determinations given for themselves or conditions of objects as things in themselves. To this idealism is opposed *transcendental realism*, which regards space and time as something given in themselves (independent of our sensibility). The transcendental realist therefore represents outer appearances (if their reality is conceded) as things in themselves, which would exist independently of us and our sensibility and thus would also be outside us according to pure concepts of the understanding."

6.	For example, Rorty, in his seminal *Philosophy and the Mirror of Nature*, positions his own philosophy as a branch of hermeneutics, although he moves much further into idealism than did Heidegger or Gadamer.

7.	While Dilthey advocates hermeneutics from what appears to be a realist position, Heidegger's and Ricœur's hermeneutical philosophies were existentialist, and Gadamer's dialogical hermeneutics was also influenced by his neo-Kantian training.

8.	Smith (1990, pp. 279–280) notes that Mises's unawareness of Reinach's work "is hardly surprising, given that ... the special nature of Austrian Aristotelian apriorism was appreciated by very few at the time when Mises was working out the philosophical foundations of his praxeology."

9.	There is significant ambiguity regarding the historical origins of the modern philosophical concept of a 'state of affairs.' While Smith (1992b) traces the idea all the way back to Aristotle, the modern concept has been credited informally to Brentano and Husserl. However, the formalization of the modern concept, and the one that Mises adopts, was developed, formalized, and elaborated by Reinach (1982).

10.	In 2001, the Mises Institute hosted a symposium to integrate Reinach's legal philosophy with Rothbard's, later published as a special issue of the *Quarterly Journal of Austrian Economics* in 2004.

11.	To see how such a failure to capture the essence of humanity undermines the human and social sciences, we need only look to the reproducibility project's devastating failures.

REFERENCES

Alvarez, S. A., & Barney, J. B. 2007. Discovery and creation: Alternative theories of entrepreneurial action. *Strategic Entrepreneurship Journal*, 1(1–2): 11–26.

Alvarez, S. A., & Barney, J. B. 2010. Entrepreneurship and epistemology: The philosophical underpinnings of the study of entrepreneurial opportunities. *Academy of Management Annals*, 4(1): 557–583.

Armstrong, D. 1997. *A world of states of affairs*. Cambridge: Cambridge University Press.

Beaulier, S. A., & Boettke, P. J. 2004. The really real in economics. In P. Lewis (Ed.), *Transforming economics: Perspectives on the critical realist project*: 187–201. New York: Routledge.

Bhaskar, R. 1978. *A realist theory of science*. Brighton: Harvester.

Bhaskar, R. 1998. *The possibility of naturalism: A philosophical critique of the contemporary human sciences*. London: Routledge.

Bhaskar, R. 2009. *Scientific realism and human emancipation*. New York: Routledge.

Burrell, G., & Morgan, G. 1979. *Sociological paradigms and organisational analysis: Elements of the sociology of corporate life*. London: Heinemann.

Bylund, P. L., & Packard, M. D. 2022a. Back to the future: Can counterhistory accelerate theoretical advancement in management? *Academy of Management Perspectives*, 36(2): 801–819.

Bylund, P. L., & Packard, M. D. 2022b. Subjective value in entrepreneurship. *Small Business Economics*, 58: 1243–1360.

Campbell, D. T. 1974. Evolutionary epistemology. In P. A. Schlipp (Ed.), *The philosophy of Karl Popper*: 413–463. LaSalle, IL: Open Court.

Davis, Z., & Steinbock, A. 2021. Max Scheler. In E. N. Zalta (Ed.), *The Stanford encyclopedia of philosophy*, Fall: Metaphysics Research Lab, Stanford University.

Dilthey, W. 1976. The development of hermeneutics. In H. Rickman (Ed.), *Selected writings*: 246–263. New York: Cambridge University Press.

Dilthey, W. 1989. *Introduction to the human sciences*. Princeton, NJ: Princeton University Press.

DuBois, J. M. 1995. *Judgment and sachverhalt: An introduction to Adolf Reinach's phenomenological realism*. Dordrecht: Kluwer Academic.

Giddens, A. 1984. *The constitution of society*. Los Angeles, CA: University of California Press.

Hayek, F. A. v. 1952. *The sensory order*. Chicago, IL: University of Chicago Press.

Heidegger, M. 2010. *Being and time* (J. Stambaugh, Trans.). Albany, NY: SUNY Press.

Hoppe, H.-H. 1989. In defense of extreme rationalism: Thoughts on Donald McCloskey's *The rhetoric of economics*. *Review of Austrian Economics*, 3(1): 179–214.

Horwitz, S. 2004. Money and the interpretive turn: Some considerations. *Symposium*, 8(2): 249–266.

Hülsmann, J. G. 2007. *Mises: The last knight of liberalism*. Auburn, AL: Ludwig von Mises Institute.

Husserl, E. 1982. *Ideas pertaining to a pure phenomenology and to a phenomenological philosophy, First book: General introduction to a pure phenomenology* (F. Kersten, Trans.). The Hague: Martinus Nijhoff.

Ingarden, R. S. 1929. Bemerkungen zum Problem Idealismus-Realismus. *Jahrbuch für Philosophie und Phänomenologische Forschung, Ergänzungsband: Festschrift, Edmund Husserl zum 70. Geburtstag gewidmet*. Halle: Niemeyer.

Ingarden, R. S. 1975. *On the motives which led Husserl to transcendental idealism*. The Hague: Martinus Nijhoff.

Kant, I. 1998. *Critique of pure reason* (P. Guyer, Trans.). Cambridge: Cmbridge University Press.

King, A. 1999. The impossibility of naturalism: The antinomies of Bhaskar's realism. *Journal for the Theory of Social Behaviour*, 29(3): 267–288.

Lachmann, L. M. 1943. The role of expectations in economics as a social science. *Economica*, 10(37): 12–23.

Lachmann, L. M. 1971. *The legacy of Max Weber*. Berkeley, CA: Glendessary Press.

Lachmann, L. M. 1990. Austrian economics: A hermeneutic approach. In D. Lavoie (Ed.), *Economics and hermeneutics*: 132. London: Routledge.

Lavoie, D. 1986. Euclideanism versus hermeneutics: A reinterpretation of Misesian apriorism. In I. M. Kirzner (Ed.), *Subjectivism, intelligibility, and economic understanding*. New York: New York University Press.

Lavoie, D. 1990. *Economics and hermeneutics*. London: Routledge.

Lavoie, D. 1991. The discovery and interpretation of profit opportunities: Culture and the Kirznerian entrepreneur. In B. Berger (Ed.), *The culture of the entrepreneur*: 48. San Francisco, CA: Institute for Contemporary Studies.

Lavoie, D. 1994. Cultural studies and the conditions for entrepreneurship. In T. W. Boxx & G. M. Quinlivan (Eds), *The cultural context of economics and politics*. Lanham, MD: University Press of America.

Lavoie, D. 2005. Introduction: Expectations and the meaning of institutions. In D. Lavoie (Ed.), *Expectations and the meaning of institutions*. New York: Routledge.

Lavoie, D. 2011. The interpretive dimension of economics: Science, hermeneutics, and praxeology. *Review of Austrian Economics*, 24(2): 91–128.

Lewis, P. 2005. Boettke, the Austrian school and the reclamation of reality in modern economics. *Review of Austrian Economics*, 18(1): 83–108.

MacIntyre, A. 2006. *Edith Stein: A philosophical prologue, 1913–1922*. Lanham, MD: Rowman and Littlefield.

Martin, A. 2009. Critical realism and the Austrian paradox. *Cambridge Journal of Economics*, 33(3): 517–530.

Menger, C. 2007. *Principles of economics*. Auburn, AL: Ludwig von Mises Institute.

Menger, C. 2009. *Investigations into the method of the social sciences* (F. J. Nock, Trans.). Auburn, AL: Ludwig von Mises Institute.

Mises, L. v. 1962. *The ultimate foundation of economic science*. Princeton, NJ: D. Van Nostrand.

Mises, L. v. 1998. *Human action: A treatise on economics*. Auburn, AL: Ludwig von Mises Institute.

Oesterreicher, J. M. 1952. *Walls are crumbling: 7 Jewish philosophers discover Christ*. New York: Devin-Adair.

Packard, M. D. 2017. Where did interpretivism go in the theory of entrepreneurship? *Journal of Business Venturing*, 32(5): 536–549.

Popper, K. R. 1974. *The philosophy of Karl Popper*. La Salle, IL: Open Court.

Popper, K. R. 1978. Natural selection and the emergence of mind. *Dialectica*, 32(3–4): 339–355.

Popper, K. R. 1987. Campbell on the evolutionary theory of knowledge. In G. Radnitzky, & W. W. I. Bartley (Eds), *Evolutionary epistemology, rationality, and the sociology of knowledge*: 113–120. La Salle, IL: Open Court.

Reinach, A. 1969. Concerning phenomenology. *The Personalist*, 50: 210–211.

Reinach, A. 1976. Kant's interpretation of Hume's problem. *Southwestern Journal of Philosophy*, 7(2): 161–188.

Reinach, A. 1982. On the theory of the negative judgment. In B. Smith (Ed.), *Parts and moments: Studies in logic and formal ontology*: 315–378. Munich: Philosophia Verlag.

Reinach, A. 2012. *The apriori foundations of the civil law: Along with the lecture "Concerning Phenomenology."* Berlin: Ontos Verlag.

Rothbard, M. N. 1989. The hermeneutical invasion of philosophy and economics. *Review of Austrian Economics*, 3(1): 45–59.

Runde, J. 2001. Bringing social structure back into economics: On critical realism and Hayek's scientism essay. *Review of Austrian Economics*, 14(1): 5–24.

Scheler, M. 1973. *Formalism in ethics and non-formal ethics of values: A new attempt toward the foundation of an ethical personalism.* Evanston, IL: Northwestern University Press.

Scheler, M. 2017. *On the eternal in man.* New York: Routledge.

Seron, D. 2015. Adolf Reinach's philosophy of logic. In B. Leclercq, S. Richard, & D. Seron (Eds), *Objects and pseudo-objects: Ontological deserts and jungles from Bretano to Carnap*: 167–182. Berlin: De Gruyter.

Smith, B. 1982. Introduction to Adolf Reinach, "On the theory of the negative judgment." In B. Smith (Ed.), *Parts and moments: Studies in logic and formal ontology*: 289–313. Berlin: Philosophia Verlag.

Smith, B. 1990. Aristotle, Menger, Mises: An essay in the metaphysics of economics. *History of Political Economy*, 22(5): 263–288.

Smith, B. 1992a. Austrian philosophy and Austrian economics. In J. L. Auspitz, W. W. Gasparski, M. K. Mklicki, & K. Szaniawski (Eds), *Praxiologies and the philosophy of economics*: 245–272. New Brunswick, NJ: Transaction Publishers.

Smith, B. 1992b. Sachverhalt, *Historisches Wörterbuch der Philosophie*, Vol. 8: 1102–1113. Basel: Scheidegger and Spiess.

Smith, B. 1994. *Austrian philosophy: The legacy of Franz Brentano*. Chicago, IL: Open Court.

Smith, B. 1997. Realistic phenomenology. In L. E. Embree, E. A. Behnke, D. Carr, J. C. Evans, J. Huertas-Jourda, J. J. Kockelmans, W. R. McKenna, A. Mickunas, J. N. Mohanty, & T. M. Seebohm (Eds), *Encyclopedia of phenomenology*. The Hague: Kluwer.

Spiegelberg, H. 1982. *The phenomenological movement*, 3rd ed. The Hague: Martinus Nijhoff.

Staudigl, M., & Berguno, G. 2014. *Schutzian phenomenology and hermeneutic traditions*. Dordrecht: Springer.

Storr, V. H. 2010. Schütz on meaning and culture. *Review of Austrian Economics*, 23(2): 147–163.

Storr, V. H. 2011. On the hermeneutics debate: An introduction to a symposium on Don Lavoie's "The interpretive dimension of economics: Science, hermeneutics, and praxeology." *Review of Austrian Economics*, 24(2): 85–89.

Weber, M. 1978. *Economy and society: An outline of interpretive sociology*. Berkeley, CA: University of California Press.

Weber, M. 2011. *Methodology of social sciences* (E. A. Shils & H. A. Finch, Trans.). New York: Routledge.

3. Alertness: an Aristotelian approach

Frederic Sautet

INTRODUCTION

Alertness is the cornerstone of Israel Kirzner's theory of human action.[1] It is at the heart of the "entrepreneurial element," which Kirzner sees as missing from the Robbinsian view of the human person. The notion of alertness as it relates to market process theory and entrepreneurship first appeared in an article that Israel Kirzner published in 1967 entitled, "Methodological Individualism, Market Equilibrium, and Market Process" (2015b). But it was in *Competition and Entrepreneurship* (C&E), published in 1973, that Kirzner more fully developed and used the notion. Alertness has had a most important impact in the field of entrepreneurship studies.[2]

Alertness has been the subject of controversies over the years, and in some ways the idea has remained somewhat elusive. It is the aim of this chapter to shed as much light as possible on the concept. First we look at the way Kirzner attempted to define alertness in C&E in 1973. We focus on several aspects of alertness: identification of means and ends, concatenation of events in the market process, knowledge, pure profit, uncertainty, creativity, judgment, and ownership. With each, we endeavor to stick as closely as possible to Kirzner's original intent, and we assess—and defend as the case may be—his view against that of other scholars who have often been critical of the notion. From Kirzner's work, three functions of alertness can be established, which lead to the following definition of alertness: a propensity to transcend the current framework of means and ends.

In the last two sections of the chapter we attempt to give more substance to the notion of alertness as a propensity. To that effect, we use the Aristotelian theory of the immateriality of the intellect, as found in his work on the nature of the human soul. We contend that Aristotle's theory offers the best framework to explain the essence of alertness as the human propensity to discover hitherto unknown gains from trade, as Kirzner saw it in 1973.[3]

THE FUNDAMENTALS OF ALERTNESS IN KIRZNER'S *COMPETITION AND ENTREPRENEURSHIP*

The first mention of "alertness" in Israel Kirzner's C&E is in chapter 1, on page 12. Therein Kirzner defines the entrepreneurial element in the behavior of economic agents as "their alertness to previously unnoticed changes in circumstances which may make it possible to get far more in exchange for whatever they have to offer than was hitherto possible." Note that in this first use of the term, Kirzner links alertness to exchange and to the realization (by the agent) that more gains from trade are possible than was previously thought.

Chapter 2 of C&E more formally introduces the concept of alertness into the economics literature. In this chapter, two theories about human behavior are important to understand what Kirzner means by alertness. First, Lionel Robbins's famed presentation of the nature of economic behavior, as it developed in the later part of the nineteenth century in price theory (Robbins, 1935). Lord Robbins sees the determination of market data (prices, quantity, product qualities, production methods, etc.) as the result of the interactions of the economizing activities of individual agents. Agents engage in economizing behavior because means are scarce and must be allocated in order to achieve competing ends. It is the scarcity (a) of resources/means, and (b) of goals/ends that are achievable by the agent that bring about economizing behavior. In that sense, individuals seek to secure efficiency or to maximize goal satisfaction by fulfilling the most meaningful (to the agent) goals possible with the least number of resources available. Hence in the economic view of the human person, agents are maximizers or optimizers.

The problem, as Kirzner states, is that Robbins's "analytical vision of economizing, maximizing, or efficiency-intent individual market participants is ... misleadingly incomplete" (Kirzner, 2013). The reason is that the view of economizing individuals cannot explain the existence of a market process without introducing further exogenous elements. Economizing behavior cannot explain the changes in the data of the market that anyone can witness through casual observation. Robbinsian theory can explain the existence of (partial) equilibrium, but cannot explain changes in the market, unless we assume every possible change to be exogenous to market participants, which is not theoretically satisfying.

This brings us to the second theory of human behavior that Kirzner uses in C&E, chapter 2. Kirzner contrasts Robbins's purely economizing approach with the broader Misesian concept of *homo agens*. Mises's *homo agens* encompasses Robbinsian maximizing behavior, but also goes beyond. *Homo agens* does not confine economic analysis to a world of already given means and ends, it opens up the analysis to the possibility that agents can engage in new courses of action that improve their situation. In other words, individual agents do not simply improve their situation through solving an allocation (of resources) problem (what Kirzner calls a "mechanical computation"). They can also improve their situation through "*the very perception of the ends-means framework* within which allocation and economizing are to take place" (Kirzner, 2013, p. 26; emphasis in original).

Kirzner defines alertness in order to explain this very point. The key (and only) difference between Robbinsian economizing behavior and Misesian *homo agens* is the idea that agents can define the goals they want to achieve and the means to achieve them, as opposed to having those goals and means given exogenously (i.e., as an underlying assumption explaining economizing behavior). *Homo agens* includes economizing behavior, as well as the identification of what will be economized upon (namely goals and resources to achieve them). The crucial concept that enables this identification is alertness. Hence, alertness is the *bridge* between a mechanistic theory of economic behavior and an open-ended view of human action. Without alertness, Kirzner affirms, one cannot understand economic behavior other than within the strict confines of the closed world of Robbinsian economizing in which what needs to be economized is given from the start.

In this vein, Kirzner states: "Mises's *homo agens* ... is endowed not only with the propensity to pursue goals efficiently, once ends and means are clearly identified, but also with the drive and alertness needed to identify which ends to strive for and which means are available" (Kirzner, 2013, p. 27). Here Kirzner links alertness to the *identification* of the end the agent may want to pursue and to the means available to do so. "Identification" is the first, and most fundamental, function of alertness.[4]

ALERTNESS, ENDOGENIZATION AND THE CONCATENATION OF MARKET PHENOMENA

It is because of the function of identification of new goals and means that changes in market data become endogenous. In this view, market evolution can be explained through its internal dynamic of change, rather than by assuming external shocks to situations of equilibrium. Kirznerian alertness in that sense is key to any theory of the "market process," as developed in the modern Austrian tradition. Hence the second function of alertness is "endogenization" of the market process.

Another way of looking at the issue of endogenization is to think in terms of market *process* and *concatenation* of market events. If the entrepreneurial function is capable of generating genuine change, some economists have argued that events in the market cannot be related to one another. In this view, entrepreneurs introduce new information in a way that is unrelated to earlier market events. There is no systematic process at work: entrepreneurial action is akin to random changes. For George Shackle, for example, a choice made by an entrepreneur can in no way be determined by the past, as every choice is "originative" (Shackle, 1983). There is entrepreneurship but market phenomena are "floating" independently of each other. (This is in opposition to the neoclassical view in which there is no entrepreneurship to speak of and all market phenomena are deterministic.)

By contrast, Kirzner contends that alertness is precisely the attribute that makes possible non-determined entrepreneurial discoveries that are, at the same time, dependent (to some extent at least) on earlier market conditions. In Kirzner's words:

> My "alertness" view of the entrepreneurial role rejects the thesis that if we attribute genuine novelty to the entrepreneur, we must necessarily treat entrepreneurially generated market events as not related to earlier market events in any systematic way. The genuine novelty I attribute to the entrepreneur consists in his spontaneous *discovery* of the opportunities marked out by earlier market conditions (or by future market conditions as they would be in the absence of his own actions). It is the opportunity for pure profit that those market conditions made possible that switches on the alertness of potential entrepreneurs, generating entrepreneurial discovery. (Kirzner, 2015a, p. 147; italics in original)

In that sense, Kirzner's theory is part of a "middle ground." Therein, the second function of alertness enables the market process to be explained in terms of genuine novelty, while relating entrepreneurial decisions to past events in a systematic way.

ALERTNESS AND KNOWLEDGE

In a section of chapter 2 of C&E entitled "The Entrepreneur in the Market," Kirzner discusses alertness in regard to knowledge. In a world of perfect knowledge (even knowledge defined in a stochastic way), the computation of the solution to the maximizing problem leading to the optimum course of action is always possible in one way or another. In this world, Kirzner explains, there is no need for alertness since the knowledge necessary to pursue the best course of action is always available to the decision maker: "his plans can be shown to be in principle implicit in the data which constitutes his knowledge of all the present and future circumstances relevant to his situation" (Kirzner, 2013, p. 30).

If we drop the assumption of perfect knowledge, and adopt the Hayekian view that the knowledge available to each decision maker is highly imperfect (in the sense of genuine ignorance being pervasive), and that knowledge is dispersed throughout society and not available to anyone in its totality, then the Robbinsian approach can only generate a very imperfect and incomplete solution to the problem of choosing among competing goals and scarce means. We can surmise that in such a world of truly imperfect knowledge, there almost always exist better goals to pursue and better means to obtain those goals than those that the decision maker already knows (but these better goals and means are truly unknown to the decision maker). Hence in the world of truly imperfect knowledge, alertness plays a vital function: it enables the social observer to explain "how the market process supplies new information to the participants—how the decision-makers revise their view of the ends-means framework relevant to their situations" (Kirzner, 2013, p. 31). In other words, without alertness, there is no explanation of the way individuals may overcome (to some extent at least) the genuine ignorance in which they find themselves. (We discuss below the issue of uncertainty, which is an extension of the analysis of imperfect knowledge.)

In this approach, Kirzner explains, "participants do not merely react to given market data, but rather display entrepreneurial alertness to possible changes in these data—an alertness which can be used to explain how such changes can occur in general" (Kirzner, 2013, p. 31). In other words, Kirzner opens up the door (a) to market participants being more than mere recipients of the information given to them by market data (i.e., Robbinsian maximizers), and instead invites the social observer to see market participants as (b) providers of information through the realization that some market data (prices, quality, products, etc.) do not reflect what these very same participants think is the true state of the market. It is only through alertness that market participants can become *active* participants in the marketplace as opposed to being mere passive ones.

In order to clearly establish the role of alertness in decision making, Kirzner introduces into the analysis the device of the pure entrepreneur, i.e., "a decision-maker whose entire role arises out of his alertness to hitherto unnoticed opportunities" (Kirzner, 2013, p. 31). This participant is an imaginary figure whose role is purely meant to show the function of alertness. A market only populated with pure Robbinsian maximizers cannot explain changes in terms of new products or new prices except through external shocks. It can only explain allocative efficiency in a closed world. By contrast, a market populated with pure entrepreneurs (as well as Robbinsian maximizers) who display "alertness to the existence of price differences between inputs and outputs" (Kirzner, 2013, p. 37) can discover the information necessary for new production to take place. A third function of alertness, therefore, is to enable new information necessary to individuals' plans to be carried out. Without alertness, there would be no new information at the disposal of participants.

The discussion of the role of knowledge in C&E doesn't stop here. In the section entitled "Entrepreneurship and Knowledge" in chapter 2, Kirzner explores the issue of conceiving entrepreneurship as having superior knowledge. It is tempting indeed to understand the entrepreneurial function as one that derives from knowledge and information asymmetries. The entrepreneur in this view possesses superior knowledge in an area that can be exploited, and in that sense entrepreneurship is a scarce resource. This is the way entrepreneurship is often conceived in the neoclassical literature (e.g., Leibenstein, 1968, p. 75; Schultz, 1975). The issue with this approach is that it treats entrepreneurship as a factor of production, albeit a special one, among other factors in the marketplace. In other words, if entrepreneurship is a factor, it could conceivably be hired, the way any scarce resource can be hired in the market. This is not the way Kirzner conceives the function of the entrepreneurial element. Entrepreneurship, in Kirzner's view, cannot be a scarce resource to be allocated, since it is the very function that allocates resources in the first place. Hence, entrepreneurship, and therefore alertness, cannot be understood as the *possession* of superior (and asymmetrical) knowledge of market data.

Instead Kirzner proposes to define alertness itself as "the 'knowledge' of where to find market data." As Kirzner puts it: "I speak of the essentially entrepreneurial element in human action in terms of alertness to information, rather than of its possession." In other words, "the kind of 'knowledge' required for entrepreneurship is 'knowing where to look for knowledge' rather than [having] knowledge of substantive market information." And Kirzner states further that "the word which captures most closely this kind of 'knowledge' seems to be alertness."[5] Therefore, alertness does not involve the *possession* of superior knowledge as entrepreneurship is traditionally conceived in neoclassical economics (when it is conceived at all). Alertness is itself, according to Kirzner, a form of knowledge, one that cannot be bought and sold as a factor of production, but a knowledge that enables the discovery of other forms of knowledge. In that sense, alertness is the "highest order of knowledge" (Kirzner, 2013, p. 54), one that is necessary to obtain other forms of knowledge.

ALERTNESS AND PURE PROFIT

Among the debates that stemmed from the publication of C&E, those on the roles of pure profit and uncertainty in Kirzner's theory have been extremely disputed. Kirzner argues that alertness (the entrepreneurial element in human action), pure profit, and sheer uncertainty are inseparable: if one is present, the other two are as well.

As indicated above, entrepreneurship can only exist in the context of truly imperfect knowledge and information. This means that knowledge is not only dispersed, but also that participants truly ignore the possibility that their ignorance could be reduced. Participants don't know what their ignorance is made of.[6] Because of the nature of truly imperfect knowledge, opportunities for gains from trade may not be perceived, and therefore situations of pure profit may be found. Since asset prices reflect only the knowledge that is already known to participants, the participants' ignorance of available knowledge may lead to situations of mispriced assets. In such situations, there is scope for entrepreneurial activity. Pure profit may be available to those who correctly identify the mispricing of assets. Pure profit exists because of radical ignorance. It is not a return, but an income linked to the correct identification of mispriced assets and to the correction of those very prices. Pure profit is always to be understood as containing no element of compensation for the services of the entrepreneur or of any factor of production.

Pure profit has another important role in Kirzner's theory. Not only is it an income that is obtained when an opportunity (i.e., mispriced assets) is discovered and price differences are successfully exploited, it is also an incentive that "switches on" entrepreneurial alertness. The potential of "pure gain (or avoidance of loss) to be derived from replacing action based on less accurate prescience by action based on the more realistically envisaged future" (Kirzner, 1982, p. 151) is a powerful incentive to orient the entrepreneurial gaze towards the existence of pure profit, that is, errors in the price system. Alertness therefore, in the social context of the market, can be influenced ("switched on") by the potential discovery of pure profit.

Kirzner also sees the exploitation of pure profit opportunities as participating in the process of market equilibration. Hence, for Kirzner, the notion of alertness is key to the equilibration properties of the market system. Kirzner seems to refer to the notion of equilibration in the Hayekian sense of coordination of plans. As we saw above, it is an important aspect of the "middle ground" view that Kirzner holds. The market process consists of entrepreneurial discoveries that are marked out by earlier market conditions. There is a systematic process at work: "entrepreneurial discoveries are the steps through which any possible tendency toward market equilibrium must proceed." Indeed, "entrepreneurial activities make up ... the process of mutual discovery by which alone we can imagine equilibrium ever to be approached" (Kirzner, 2015a, p. 147). There is no doubt that in Kirzner's theory one cannot dissociate alertness and some idea of equilibration in the market process.

This view has been the subject of numerous debates and many have criticized it. As Mises (1949, p. 288, 1962) argued, what matters is not whether there exists a tendency towards full plan coordination, but whether unsuccessful entrepreneurs are eliminated from the market.[7] George Selgin hammers the idea that tendencies to equilibrium are fundamentally unimportant to the understanding of the market process. What matters for Selgin is that entrepreneurial action, and therefore alertness, "leads to the systematic elimination of entrepreneurial profit and loss" (this is also the position of Foss & Klein, 2012; Selgin, 1987, p. 39).

ALERTNESS AND UNCERTAINTY

Jack High (1982) contends that there is no uncertainty in Kirzner's theory of entrepreneurship in C&E. For uncertainty to be present, one not only needs to have genuine ignorance on the part of decision makers, but also production in time. C&E only presents, High contends, a theory of instantaneous arbitrage.

A close reading of Kirzner's C&E, however, permits a different interpretation than High's. As the following quotation shows, Kirzner is perfectly aware in C&E of the importance of production in time, and the sheer uncertainty it may bring in the context of radical ignorance: "even the alert entrepreneur, discovering what *seems* to be an attractive opportunity, may have considerable misgivings concerning the venture. And the longer the time before the venture's required outlay can be expected to bring the hoped-for revenues, the less sure of himself the entrepreneur is likely to be" (Kirzner, 2013, p. 62; italics in original).[8]

Although the book seems to focus mostly on the notion of instantaneous arbitrage, entrepreneurial activity in C&E also takes place in time, and unquestionably involves sheer uncertainty. The point Kirzner makes is that the scope for entrepreneurship does not depend on any particular attitude towards uncertainty on the part of market participants. It depends on the existence of *alert* market participants. Alertness (to situations of gains that were hitherto unknown) is the defining feature of the entrepreneurial element, whether entrepreneurial activity involves complex production in time (with all the uncertainty associated with it) or not. Hence the Kirznerian alert entrepreneur shoulders uncertainty aside when he or she identifies the existence of *potential* gains from trade.[9] What is meant by "shouldering aside uncertainty" is that in spite of the unavoidably speculative character of an entrepreneurial realization, the entrepreneur considers that an "opportunity for profit *does* exist" (Kirzner, 2013, p. 69; italics in original). Alertness is a human propensity to "sniff out" potential gains from trade in spite of the unknowability of the future.[10]

ALERTNESS TO WHAT? UNCERTAINTY, CREATIVITY, AND JUDGMENT

Some critics see Kirznerian alertness as a passive reaction to what exists and not an active anticipation of what is to come (Foss & Klein, 2012, p. 39). Part of that view comes from Kirzner's own description of entrepreneurship as a responding agency in C&E. At first it may seem that Kirzner's critics have a point. It is necessary to look at what precisely Kirzner said. As Kirzner puts it: "I feel it necessary to draw attention to entrepreneurship as a *responding agency*. I view the entrepreneur not as a source of innovative ideas ex nihilo, but as being *alert* to the opportunities that exist *already* and are waiting to be noticed" (Kirzner, 2013, p. 59). That famous and often quoted reference to entrepreneurship as a responding agency is part of a discussion of Schumpeter's view of the entrepreneurial role. Because of the entrepreneur's innovative activity, Schumpeter sees the entrepreneur as a disequilibrating force, whereas Kirzner theorizes it primarily as an equilibrating tendency.

It was Kirzner's goal in C&E to present a theory of the market process which takes seriously Hayek's knowledge problem, and thus provides the underlying disequilibrium theory for the standard neoclassical theory of the allocation of scarce resources (i.e., prices tend towards costs and least-cost technologies are deployed). Kirzner's goal was to show how such a process comes about in a way that doesn't assume what it is that we are to prove. In such a context, entrepreneurship is seen as the driving force that discovers and marshals knowledge and sets the market process in motion. Kirzner's primary, but certainly not sole, concern in his 1973 book is to explain the allocative properties of the market system in order to establish its self-correcting characteristic in the context of true ignorance (see Sautet, 2018 for more on the topic). Yet, as we have seen, even in C&E Kirzner turns to the possibility of production in time, and therefore to entrepreneurial decision making taking place in the sheer uncertainty of the future.

Following the publication of C&E, Kirzner refined his analysis of uncertainty and entrepreneurship. In "Uncertainty, Discovery, and Human Action," Kirzner argues that alertness can also be understood as man's motivated propensity to formulate an image of the future.[11] Kirzner more explicitly acknowledges the importance of production in time through the idea that "alertness must ... embrace the awareness of the ways in which the human agent can, by imaginative, bold leaps of faith, and determination, in fact *create* the future for which his present acts are designed" (Kirzner, 1982, p. 150). Alertness is here explicitly linked to uncertainty. When production in time takes place, uncertainty exists, and the future is therefore open to creation and error (as opposed to the case of instantaneous arbitrages, which are certain once discovered). In such a context, alertness embraces creation because the future is not mechanically unfolding. It is to be created, to some extent at least, through the decisions to be made and the actions to be taken.[12]

Kirzner walks a fine line. Some critics reject the idea of the usefulness of alertness in the context of an uncertain future. How can one be alert to an opportunity that is not in existence now since it will come into existence in the future? Future opportunities cannot be theorized as already in existence in the present, that is, waiting to be grasped. Surely, opportunities are just conjectures about the future. In *Organizing Entrepreneurial Judgment: A New Approach to the Firm*, Foss and Klein specifically define opportunities as imagined and subjective, rather than discovered.[13] Yet, what Kirzner emphasizes repeatedly with his notion of alertness in the context of uncertainty is the idea that human beings have formidable powers of creativity, of imagination, of being able to see "around the corner," in spite of the uncertainty of the future. Participants in a market are capable of having a "vision" of the future, one that can help them act and realize gains from trade that only come to exist over time.

This is where alertness leads to judgment. To be alert in the context of an uncertain future means not only to come to realize that an opportunity for pure profit may exist—an opportunity to seize gains from trade that were hitherto unknown—but also to formulate the best possible image of the future as it will unfold under the influence of our actions. In the context of the uncertainty of the future, any opportunity discovered may not be realized; discovery is always speculative. Judgment is needed to assess relevance to future possible states of the world and to assess one's own influence on the future.

This is High's position when he states: "A person who has alertly conceived a number of ways in which the future might unfold also chooses which of those images will guide his action." High continues: "we must form an opinion of how we should act," and this can be done by exercising judgment (High, 1982, p. 165). Alertness does not involve judgment precisely because it precedes it.[14] Kirzner considers that the object of judgment must first be noticed before any judgment can take place (judgment is judgment of something). He links the notions of alertness and judgment together, although the latter is secondary to the former.[15] As High states it, "judgment is the mental process of assigning relevance to those things we already know" (High, 1982, p. 167).

Nicolai Foss and Peter Klein have been most critical of Kirzner's position (e.g., Foss & Klein, 2010, p. 104, 2012, pp. 28, 39). In their view, alertness "does not itself involve judgment, and does not, in this understanding, have a direct effect on the allocation of resources" (Foss & Klein, 2012, p. 54). Instead they propose an account of opportunity exploitation that does not rest on alertness, but combines the Knightian concept of judgment and the notion of capital heterogeneity. They rest their approach on the theory of Frank Knight, who saw the essence of entrepreneurship in judgment.

JUDGMENT IMPLIES OWNERSHIP: WHAT ABOUT ALERTNESS?

According to Foss and Klein, "judgment implies asset ownership" (2012, p. 20; see also pp. 21, 40) because judgment is decision making about the employment of resources. This position is the opposite of Kirzner's, which contends that alertness (and the entrepreneurial element) is unrelated to asset ownership. The two views have been the subject of many commentaries since the publication of C&E.

As we saw above, Kirzner distinguishes the purely entrepreneurial role from other roles in the marketplace, including that of the capitalist, who is traditionally seen as owning assets. Isolating alertness as the essence of entrepreneurship leads Kirzner to see the entrepreneurial function as separated from that of owning assets. The pure entrepreneur does not own assets, his function is distinct from other functions in the marketplace. Kirzner's approach is similar to that of John Bates Clark or of Mises for that matter. Mises considers the construct of the pure entrepreneur as distinct from the capitalist in his analysis of uncertainty and functional distribution (Mises, 1998, pp. 253–254). Separating the entrepreneurial function from asset ownership is "extremely important in the precise definition of pure entrepreneurial profits and their analytical separation from other receipts" (Kirzner, 2013, p. 38).

In a famous passage in C&E, Kirzner states: "the discovery of a profit opportunity means the discovery of something obtainable for nothing at all. No investment at all is required; the free ten-dollar bill is discovered to be already within one's grasp" (Kirzner, 2013, p. 39). There is clearly no relationship between the discovery of a profit opportunity and the ownership of assets or other resources. Entrepreneurial discovery costs nothing, and requires no asset to be given up in the process. All this means that there is no opportunity cost to being alert, which is fundamentally conceivable only if the source of alertness is immaterial (see last section below).

The difference between the judgment view and the alertness approach revolves around the essence of the entrepreneur in the marketplace. Foss and Klein contend that the entrepreneurial function must include the capitalist function because entrepreneurial judgment is about asset allocation. But Kirzner insists that, "analytically the purely entrepreneurial role does not overlap that of the capitalist, even though, in a world in which almost all production processes are more or less time-consuming, entrepreneurial profit opportunities typically require capital" (Kirzner, 2013, p. 40). The difficulty is realizing that even though one may argue that no real-world entrepreneur exists without asset ownership, the entrepreneurial *function* can be analytically distinguished from that of the capitalist. It would be impossible otherwise to separate analytically pure entrepreneurial profits from pure interest and from other types of rents (see Sautet, 2018, pp. 133–136 for an extensive discussion). Ultimately, alertness is not related to asset ownership because "alertness is not an action, but a praxeologically necessary aspect of all action" (Koppl, 2002, p. 8).

ALERTNESS AS A PROPENSITY

As a way to conclude the first part of the chapter, we ask the question whether alertness is a propensity. In C&E on page 27, Kirzner explains that there exists in human action broadly conceived (as Mises would have it), a "propensity for alertness toward fresh goals and the discovery of hitherto unknown resources with which *homo agens* is endowed." Herein, Kirzner does not directly state that alertness is a propensity, but simply that there exists a propensity for alertness within each human being. In other words, alertness is a category of action that is always present to varying degrees in human decision making. That propensity for alertness is also what Kirzner calls the "entrepreneurial element" in human action. There is equivalency, in Kirzner's theory, between alertness on the one hand and what it means to be entrepreneurial on the other. Entrepreneurs are alert decision makers, and any decision maker who is alert (which is potentially any human being) is also an entrepreneur.[16]

We saw above that Kirzner sees alertness as a type of knowledge. In addition to the notion of a "higher order of knowledge" that Kirzner uses in C&E, we should also use the term "propensity," which describes well the idea that alertness is not a capability, and is not a resource that can be deployed at will. Kirzner actually says just this in "Uncertainty, Discovery, and Human Action," in which he defines alertness as a "motivated propensity" to formulate an image of the future (1982, p. 149). In other words, alertness can be simply defined as a *human propensity to transcend the current framework of means and ends*. This is not just a question of semantics. The term "propensity" sits well in the middle ground between a deterministic view of human action on the one hand (relating for instance to the notion of "capability"), and a more Shacklean understanding of choice on the other. (See below for an analysis of the term "propensity" using Aristotle's theory.)

ALERTNESS AND THE REJECTION OF PURPOSE AND TELEOLOGY IN MODERN ECONOMICS

In the last two sections of the chapter, we will attempt to engage in some "philosophical speculations" in order to deepen our understanding of the essence of alertness.

The influence of the Enlightenment on the physical sciences and their impersonal method of inquiry also affected the early development of political economy. With the establishment of wealth as the subject matter of political economy in the early nineteenth century came also a strong reaction against all sorts of "metaphysical speculations" in science, and especially the rejection of forms of anthropomorphism and animism: natural-world phenomena are not the result of spirits animating them, but of forces determining them. The nineteenth century was characterized as "cosmological and objectivist" in contrast to the "anthropological and subjectivist" views of the eighteenth century (Röpke, 1950, p. 68). As part of that long movement, philosophers and scientists rejected the old Aristotelian framework, which had governed science since the Middle Ages. Aristotle had famously established four causes for any event: material, formal, efficient, and final. Modern economics essentially retained the notion of material and efficient causes, and lost interest in the other two.[17]

As the nineteenth century wore out, it became more and more accepted that economics should follow the model of the physical sciences and analogies were made between the force of self-interest and the force of gravity. For instance, Senior described the pursuit of wealth as similar to gravitation in physics. The attraction of physics can be found in the works of the best economists of the time. Jevons talks of the "mechanics of utility and self-interest" and Edgeworth of the "economic calculus," which is akin to analyzing the forces in physics. Maffeo Pantaleoni, dubbed the Alfred Marshall of Italy, also stressed the maximization principle as resting on hedonistic and egotistic considerations (Kirzner, 2009, pp. 72–73). The recurrent idea was that self-interest is the key to turning economics into a science like mechanics. If, in Aristotelian terms, self-interest represents the efficient and material causes, perhaps it becomes clearer why modern economics has been more interested in incentives (related to material and efficient causality), than in entrepreneurship (which proceeds from telos and formal causality).

All this culminates, perhaps surprisingly, in the early works of Joseph Schumpeter. Determined to establish a scientific approach to economics devoid of all the "metaphysical speculations" that one can find when theorizing about human action, Schumpeter focuses on what he sees as the objective, impersonal, and measurable aspect of economics: the quantities of goods that are exchanged. In the Walrasian mindset, Schumpeter stipulates that it is the existence of interdependencies between various goods that should constitute the study of economics. The goal was to remove the unpredictable human element from the picture so as to avoid investigating the nature of human behavior. In so doing, economics could replace the concept of human purpose by functional relationships as found in utility functions, for instance.[18] With Schumpeter's work—but also with that of Walras, Edgeworth, Pantaleoni, and others—many economists came to reject explicitly any teleological notion (i.e., the Aristotelian final cause) from their discipline. Purpose and other "metaphysical considerations," to use Schumpeter's expression, have no place in a science that focuses on functional relationships.[19]

What economists perhaps did not realize fully at the time is that once man's ability to formulate a purpose is removed from the explanation of action, human beings are, ipso facto, reduced to their physical (and biological) constituents. Man is considered purely as a physical being—i.e., the Newtonian vision of the human individual. In the late nineteenth and even more so in the early twentieth century, the human element came to be eliminated and replaced with a utility machine based on a utility function. We may then speak of "mechanomorphism" when economists ascribe "mechanical properties to what is otherwise recognized as an aspect of human affairs or when [they treat] an economic system as though it were a mechanical system" (Mittermaier, 1986, p. 237). Attributing mechanical behavior to creative agents is one of the gravest errors of modern economics. Hence man *qua* man was replaced by *homo economicus*, the cyborg optimizer (Mirowski, 1998).

In this context, it is not by chance that Robbins talks of "ends" and "means" in his definition of economics (Robbins, 1935, p. 16), and not of "purpose." It is true that the two terms are often used interchangeably. But if man is seen as a cyborg, he cannot truly establish purposes, he can only execute a plan according to his given preferences (and other constraints). Strictly speaking, the Robbinsian maximizer is not a purpose-oriented being when he or she acts.[20] By contrast, Kirzner insists on the importance of purpose in human action. In fact, purpose cannot be thought of without alertness. Indeed, what enables human beings to formulate new purposes is their alertness.

THE IMMATERIALITY OF THE INTELLECT: AN ARISTOTELIAN VIEW OF THE ESSENCE OF ALERTNESS

The problem for modern economics is that upholding purpose (and therefore alertness) as the final cause of human action would amount to rejecting what is called "psychophysical reductionism," i.e., the position in the philosophy of the mind which argues that everything that exists can be reduced to its physical components. The "truth" of reductionism has been dominating science for a long time, even if some scholars have been skeptical of it. Those, such as philosopher Thomas Nagel, who openly question it (not only in philosophy but also in biology) expose themselves to strong criticism and contempt. In *Mind and Cosmos* (2012), Nagel presents a skeptical view of reductionism and offers an alternative theory, which he calls "natural teleology," that is, the hypothesis that the universe has an internal logic that drives its evolution from the basic components of matter found in the early stages to the complex molecules that make life possible. Orthodox science, especially in the domain of biology, does not ascribe goals or direction to matter. It recognizes no such thing as a telos of the universe, let alone of matter or of biological compounds. Nagel has been labeled a "teleologist" by some of his critics, which for them is just one step removed from being a creationist. In philosophy and the physical sciences in general, especially biology, anything remotely teleological is considered non-scientific.

Modern economics is in a peculiar place, in comparison. Standard neoclassical economics assumes that (a) agents are non-purposeful (preferences and the environment determine their actions) and (b) the construct of equilibrium is somehow preordained by the interactions of men's actions on the one hand and the patterns of available resources and technology on the other. Hence the whole edifice of neoclassical economics is deterministic (even when it is laid out in stochastic terms) and not teleological.[21] Austrian economics upholds a different view: human beings can formulate purposes. While economics cannot speculate (and refrains from speculating) as to why human beings can formulate purposes,[22] it presupposes that human beings differ radically in their essence from other objects in the world: they can choose means to attain purposes.

If alertness is the propensity to transcend the current framework of means and ends/goals, or if it is the propensity to recognize something that the decision maker (let alone others in the marketplace) has hitherto not realized, it must imply the idea that the human person is somehow not bound by the determinants of the past. Hence, a strict reductionist view could not explain the essence of alertness. In "What Is Alertness?", Roger Koppl states: "Alertness is the uncaused cause whose effect is change" (2002, p. 3). In his paper, Koppl recasts the notion of alertness in the language of Alfred Schutz's phenomenological approach to social science, and argues that alertness is the propensity to problematize open possibilities. Presenting alertness as an "uncaused cause" is not language that can be found in Kirzner. This approach, however, opens up a very important dimension that could help explain what is meant by "propensity." But the idea of uncaused cause also raises an issue: it brings "metaphysical speculations" into the field of science, something that modern economics has avoided at all costs, particularly through the removal of the idea of purpose in human action, as we saw above. We believe, however, that alertness can be best explained through Aristotelian lenses.[23]

Hylomorphism—Aristotle's theory that understands the soul of the human person both as its causal form and as a substance—can help us understand the essence of alertness. In this view, the soul includes the intellect. The intellect—an aspect of the soul—is immaterial. In that sense, it has no place in modern science, as it cannot be reduced to physical phenomena.[24] A key idea in Aristotle's theory is that the soul has two functions: it causes motion and it discriminates (or distinguishes). With regard to the latter, discriminating is the work of reasoning and sense perception. When the senses perceive external objects, they distinguish one object from another. Similarly when the intellect thinks, it discriminates by establishing the different forms of different intelligible things. Each of these processes are relevant to alertness.

Following Aristotle, one can assert that alertness is a function of the human intellect, and it is therefore also an aspect of the immaterial human soul. In *On the Soul* (Aristotle, 2002),[25] Aristotle uses the ideas of actuality and potentiality (or potency) in the cases of the senses and of the intellect.[26] Human beings possess the sense of sight, for instance, because our eyes are capable of seeing many shapes and colors outside of themselves. They are not limited to the actuality of one color and shape. In potency, eyes can distinguish many colors and shapes. In that sense, it is the potentiality rather than the actuality of sight that matters.[27] But sight is at the same time limited by the physical characteristics of the organs that enable it: the human eye can only see some light waves that can be perceived as colors and not others.

When it comes to the intellect, Aristotle explains that our intellect has the potential of determining the causal form of anything that can be perceived or thought because "the intellect, in its being-at-work, *is* the things it thinks."[28] Because the intellect becomes the things it thinks, the intellect, in Aristotle's view, is capable of thinking and understanding potentially everything about the concrete and abstract world. For Aristotle, the sheer size and complexity of reality does not put a limit on the human intellect. Hence the intellect is not actually any thing, but *potentially* every thing.[29] According to Aristotle, if our thinking was located only in a bodily organ (such as the brain), then we could only process, in principle, some objects of reality, as our intellect (being finite) could only be moved from potentiality to actuality in those cases.[30] Aristotle rejects that idea for the reason that no bodily organ directly corresponds to the activity of the intellect.[31] Hence the intellect is immaterial and not limited by material characteristics.[32]

If we think of alertness the way Aristotle thinks of the intellect, we can establish that alertness is the *potentiality* to see and recognize gains from trade that were hitherto unknown. Hence alertness is a limitless potentiality because the (immaterial) intellect is capable of receiving, imagining, and understanding the causal forms of countless (concrete and abstract) objects.[33] The action of recognizing new gains from trade is not purely sensorial. Clearly it involves the senses, but it mostly involves the intellect, as it implies an *understanding* of reality. In Aristotle's view, the understanding or the thinking of what is perceived by the senses is the result of the intellect moving from potency to actuality.[34] It is also the intellect that is capable of bringing together all the data of the various senses (plus those stored in various parts of the brain). Alertness therefore is not mere perception, as it involves primarily the intellect "being-at-work" in order to generate the causal forms of whatever object it is focusing on.[35] Moreover, Aristotle argues that one type of intellect is contemplative and another is practical. The first reasons for the sake of reason itself. The second reasons for the sake of something and is concerned with action (Aristotle: 433a10). Alertness is more likely to be an aspect of the practical intellect than of the contemplative.

The activity of the intellect that involves alertness may focus on concrete (external) objects, in which case each of them is "potentially something intelligible." This means that alertness will enable the intellect to think the object and to become actively the object. Aristotle also remarks that in the case of immaterial or abstract objects, "what thinks and what is thought are the same thing" (429b30). This, presumably, has some importance in the context of the discovery of opportunities for entrepreneurial action that involve time and uncertainty. In such a case, what is intelligible is not only an external object, but it is also what is directly conceived by the intellect: it's an *idea* about the future. In other words, in the case of abstract objects, the intellect can *create* the intelligible form, which sounds very much like what entrepreneurs do. Another way of understanding alertness in the Aristotelian context is therefore to see alertness as the function of the intellect that discovers something intelligible (i.e., gains from trade) but that is still in potency. The discovered gains from trade are themselves in potency and will be actualized through the entrepreneur's actions.

All this doubtlessly relates to imagination. Aristotle states that "one sort of thinking is imagination, and another sort of thinking is conceiving that something is the case" (Book III, chapter 3: 427b30). Further, he states: "sometimes, by means of the imaginings and thoughts in the soul, just as if one were seeing, one reasons out and plans what is going to happen in response to what is present" (Book III, chapter 7: 431b). It cannot be clearer. Aristotle sees a role for the intellect in *imagining as if one were seeing*. This leads to planning the future, using current available resources. This is very similar in many ways to Kirznerian alertness, which may involve imagination, since gains from trade are most of the time only in potency and in the future.[36]

Aristotle also affirms that "sense perception when directed to its proper object is always truthful ... but it is possible to think things through falsely" (Book III, chapter 3: 427b10). This may shed a new light on Kirzner's view of "entrepreneurial errors." Kirzner sees error in at least two ways. First, agents may not perceive that new gains from trade could have been discovered. In Aristotelian terms, the intellect failed to conceive (or imagine) that something was the case, that is, it failed to ascribe forms to objects that could have received them (errors of overpessimism in Kirzner's typology). Second, agents may believe that new gains from trade were available when they weren't. This is a case of the intellect thinking things through falsely or imagining things in a faulty way, that is, it attempted to ascribe forms to objects that never materialized (errors of overoptimism in Kirzner's typology). Intellectual error is especially likely, Aristotle explains, when the object of the intellect is a compound of intelligible things, instead of being unique and indivisible (Book III, chapter 6). By analogy, the more complex and uncertain an entrepreneurial opportunity for profit will be (in terms of inputs, outputs, and time), the more errors may potentially occur because the intellect may fail at integrating the elements together. All the errors mentioned here are often labeled as resulting from a "lack of alertness." We see that the Aristotelian framework helps us put content behind that idea.[37]

Aristotle is aware that sense perception can also be faulty at times.[38] Most interestingly, he states: "it is possible even for there to be a false appearance of things about which, at the same time, there is a true conception; for example, the sun appears to be a foot wide, but one believes it to be bigger than the inhabited world" (Book III, chapter 3: 428b). This may have considerable implications for alertness, as one can argue that the entrepreneurial function is also about conceiving correctly of the existence of gains from trade when no one else could "see" them. The "false appearance of things" (i.e., the true ignorance on the part of other agents of the existence of potential gains from trade) corrected by the right conception of the entrepreneur is another way of thinking of alertness in the context of Aristotle's theory.

Alertness is a human propensity to transcend the current framework of means/ends, which in the context of Aristotelian thought amounts to establishing new material, formal, efficient, and final causes. Alertness is therefore linked to the four causes in the Aristotelian causal theory: material (the new means discovered by the entrepreneur, but which are only meaningful in the light of formal causation), formal (determining the contour, so to speak, of new gains from trade), efficient (the "alert" agent doing the acting is the entrepreneur), and final (determining the purpose of the entrepreneurial discovery). Of the four causes, the formal and final causes matter most in the context of Kirznerian entrepreneurship because establishing forms is the primary role of the intellect (and therefore of alertness).[39]

The Aristotelian framework enables us to argue that opportunities for profit are (potentially) discoverable because they are the result of the human intellect coming to know that which it was in potentiality. It doesn't mean the opportunity "exists out there." It means that the human intellect is potentially capable of conforming (or creating) to the form of a concrete (or abstract) object that was hitherto unknown.[40] Understanding alertness as a propensity, as we discussed above, has now a very specific meaning. That propensity is a potentiality (or potency) of the human intellect to recognize or define new causal forms and a new telos of objects (present or future gains from trade) that didn't possess them in the first place because they were truly unknown (at least in the mind of the entrepreneur). This potentiality emanates from the human intellect, which, through its immateriality, is capable of introducing novelty in the (subjectively perceived) world (by the agent doing the acting). Moreover, as we mentioned above, if alertness emanates from an immaterial intellect, then it implies that the propensity to be alert is effected without any opportunity cost: no resources are used up, so to speak, by the immaterial intellect in the process of being alert.

CONCLUSION

Alertness is the central concept of Kirzner's theory of the entrepreneurial function in human action. Yet, as central as it is to Kirzner's theory, alertness has
not always been well understood. Our interpretation of Kirzner's theory leads
us to adopt the position that it is best to understand alertness as a propensity.
Hence we offer the following definition of the concept: alertness is a human
propensity to transcend the current framework of means and ends. We also
establish three functions of alertness: (a) *identification* of new ends and means;
(b) *endogenization* of the market process and the concatenation of market
events; and (c) *the enabling of new information* necessary for individuals'
plans to be carried out.

We use Aristotle's theory of the soul and the intellect in order to establish
the nature and source of alertness. The human propensity to identify new
means and ends is, in the Aristotelian theory of the intellect, a potentiality
through which the intellect is capable of conforming to (or creating) the
form of an object that was hitherto unknown. In other words, alertness, in the
context of the means/ends framework as understood in the economic theory of
human action, is what permits the human intellect to know that which it was
in potentiality.

Misesian methodology forbids economics to venture into philosophy, and
probably for good reasons.[41] Yet Austrian economics assumes, most of the
time implicitly, an open-ended world and a human mind capable of sheer
creation. Clearly, the materialist view of the human person cannot explain the
validity of this approach. Even if we surmise that the open-endedness of the
world is a sort of illusion that can be explained through the complexity of the
social system and some cognitive limits of the human mind (which can only
be real and numerous in a physical view of the mind), we are still left with the
problem of the entrepreneurial element being able to "see," to "recognize," and
to "realize" knowledge that was hitherto truly not known.

Instead, it has to be the case that the human intellect (and therefore alertness)
is itself open-ended, and therefore immaterial, as in the hylomorphic tradition
of the human soul known to Aristotelian scholars. The Aristotelian approach
permits us to see alertness as the true source of change (i.e., the identification
of a new means and ends framework), as it solves the Parmenidean problem
in which modern economics finds itself.[42] Without an acknowledgment of
Aristotelian formal and final causality, there are phenomena which could
appear as "uncaused causes." But when we consider Aristotelian formal and
final causality, we are enabled to "see" the causes as they actually are. It is
our contention that only then can Kirznerian alertness be understood as the
"uncaused cause" whose effect is genuine change.

NOTES

1. The author would like to thank Israel Kirzner, Michael Pakaluk, Paul Radich, and Dennis Teti for their comments on previous drafts of the chapter. The usual caveat applies.

2. While the notion was almost unused in the decade that followed the publication of C&E, in the 1990s things started to change. For instance, from 2004 to 2008 the notion of alertness appeared in 57 articles in top academic journals on entrepreneurship, most of them in direct relation to Kirzner's work. See Boettke and Sautet (2013).

3. We use the terms "gains from trade" throughout the chapter. We use them interchangeably with, and as synonyms of, "entrepreneurial opportunity for pure profit." Indeed, we are only concerned with gains from trade that remain positive once all costs have been accounted for.

4. The notion of "ends" here encompasses goals that are personal and contingent. This is different from the notion of "end" in moral philosophy wherein ends are objective and inherent to the nature of the thing.

5. Kirzner (2013, p. 54). Kirzner (1979, p. 8) defines alertness as "the knowledge of where to obtain information (or other resources) and how to deploy it."

6. It is important here to insist on the idea of "truly" imperfect knowledge. The notion of imperfect knowledge is commonly admitted in neoclassical equilibrium models. In such cases, knowledge or information is imperfect because it is too costly to obtain. The notion of "truly" imperfect knowledge refers to the idea that participants don't know what it is that they don't know.

7. As Kirzner himself states in C&E (2013, p. 68): "The market, Mises emphasizes again and again, tends to eliminate from the entrepreneurial role all except those able 'to anticipate better than other people the future demand of the consumers.'"

8. Kirzner mentions the uncertainty associated with entrepreneurship and production in time in several passages in C&E (2013). On page 14: "The time duration of a production process does not, except by introducing the uncertainties involved in an unknown future, alter its entrepreneurial aspect." On page 41 (italics in original): "all the revenue received by this final sale has resulted from the final decision to sell (and this final decision, although *planned* at the time of the original decision to buy, was not at all *assured* until actually made)." On page 69: "In a world of uncertainty every entrepreneurial decision, no matter how much alertness it reflects, must to some extent constitute a gamble."

9. Production in time implies that any gains discovered are potential rather than certain. Until output has been produced and sold at a price that covers all costs (including capital costs), the opportunity for profit that was discovered remains potential rather than certain. While the exploitation of an opportunity is part of the telos of any entrepreneur, it is not part of the theory Kirzner developed. Exploiting something discovered may (and most of the time will) involve the entrepreneurial element, but insofar as it is only about fulfilling a plan, it is not part, according to Kirzner, of alert entrepreneurial activity.

10. As Kirzner (2018, p. 149) puts it, "We have no assurance that a man walking down the street will, after his walk, have absorbed knowledge of all the facts to which he has been exposed; we do, in talking of human action, assume at least a tendency for man to notice those that constitute possible opportunities for gainful action on his part."

11. See Kirzner (1982, p. 149). Note that here Kirzner explicitly defines alertness as a propensity.

12. Kirzner frames also alertness in terms of "the endeavor to secure greater correspondence between the individual's future as he envisages it and his future as it will in fact unfold" (1982, p. 151).

13. See Sautet (2018, pp. 127–30), for a response to Foss and Klein's position.

14. Although broadly conceived, alertness involves imagination and creativity. See Kirzner (1982, p. 151).

15. As Kirzner himself puts it in C&E: "my emphasis on the element of alertness in action has been intended to point out that, far from being numbed by the inescapable uncertainty of our world, men *act upon their judgments* of what opportunities have been left unexploited by others" (Kirzner, 2013, p. 69; italics in original).

16. As Mises stated: "In any real and living economy every actor is always an entrepreneur" (1998, p. 253).

17. Francis Bacon, René Descartes, and Isaac Newton are probably most responsible for the death of Aristotelian formal and final causality. Consciously or not, economists in the nineteenth century followed Newton in simplifying the analysis to one or two sources of causality. For a development of this theme, see for instance Richard Hassing (1997) and Alasdair MacIntyre (2007).

18. As Kirzner (2009, pp. 73–74) explains it, Schumpeter is of the view, in *The Nature and Essence of Economic Theory* published in 1906, that "economists must consider the changes in 'economic quantities' as if they were caused automatically without paying attention to the human beings who may have been involved in the appearance of such changes."

19. Some economists and philosophers opposed that approach. Max Weber, for instance, saw purpose as the most salient aspect of human action, as it establishes the cause of an action through the *Verstehen* (understanding) of its motive (Kirzner, 2009, p. 161). Weber saw motivation and purpose as essential elements distinguishing human action from other phenomena.

20. Some philosophers (mostly in the natural law tradition) have insisted on this very point. According to Francis Slade (1997), for instance, "end" does not mean "purpose." Human beings have purposes and motives, whereas ends are qualities of all kinds of things. Slade uses the example of medicine, the end of which is in the restoration and maintenance of the condition of health, irrespective of what the physician does with his or her knowledge. Human beings have purposes (or intentions) by which "they determine themselves to certain actions" (1997, p. 83). Ends exist independently of our willing them and irrespective of our actions and decisions. Hence, as Slade explains, "man has an end (telos); individual human beings have 'intentions' or 'purposes' in executing their acts. Purpose (*proairesis*) … is what we propose to ourselves to do" (1997, p. 84). For Aristotle there exist natural ends of the human person, such as happiness (*eudaimonia*). This is not what Robbins refers to in his definition of economics.

21. Buchanan and Vanberg (1991) agree that the market system is non-teleological, but, by contrast, they also see it as non-deterministic. Social orders result from evolutionary processes that can also be described as non-linear, complex adaptive systems. Their most virulent critique, however, is aimed at the idea of equilibrium. They see a "teleological thrust" and some "residual teleology" with regard to neoclassical equilibrium (1991, pp. 172–174). It is most important, in

Buchanan's and Vanberg's view, to reject strongly any teleological view of the social order.

22. This is the notion of "methodological dualism," which stands in opposition to "methodological monism" which argues the truth of reductionism.

23. As David Gordon (2006) and others have explained, Austrian economics finds its roots in Aristotelian philosophy. Our attempt, however, to use Aristotelian concepts as found in Aristotle's *On the Soul* to explain alertness is, to the best of our knowledge, new.

24. The idea that the human intellect is immaterial (or has an immaterial aspect) is generally linked in philosophy to a defense of the ontological freedom of the will. See Boethius (2009), for instance. For a modern defense of the Aristotelian view of the soul and the intellect, see for instance Dodds (2009) and George (2020).

25. Henceforth, all the references to Aristotle come from this same book.

26. Aristotle's view of potentiality and actuality of a substance ultimately derives from his theory of change in response to the Parmenidean challenge (i.e., there is no such thing as genuine change). Aristotle responded to Parmenides stating that a substance can undergo a change, and especially can go from privation of a form to having a form without losing its identity, because it possessed the change in potentiality.

27. This said, the actuality is "that-for-the-sake-of-which" the potentiality exists.

28. Quote is in Book III, chapter 7: 431b 10 (sic), italics in original. "The soul," Aristotle says, "is in a certain way all beings, for beings are either perceptible or intelligible, while knowledge in a certain way is the things it knows, and perception is the things it perceives" (431b 20). Joe Sachs (the translator of the Green Lion Press edition of *On the Soul*) uses the term "being-at-work," which translates the Greek *energein* to mean that the intellect (or the senses as the case may be) is moving from potency to actuality.

29. More generally, see Aristotle, Book III. The intellect is a power of the immaterial soul. In coming to know, it receives that which it was in potentiality, without being deprived of anything. The intellect receives the form of the known object—a tree for example—such that the intellect conforms to the form of the tree, and in that sense "becomes" the tree, intellectually. In the words of Aristotle: "The soul is a place of forms, except that this is not the whole soul, but the thinking soul, and it is not the form in its being-at-work-staying-itself, but in potency" (429a 20).

30. The same way our natural sight is limited to certain light frequencies. Other parts of the soul have corresponding functions in the body, such as those of the senses (smell, touch, etc.). In Aristotle's view (Book III, chapter 2), separate senses provide different information, but they cannot, of themselves, tell that sweet is different from white. If we know that sweet is different from white, it is because both are apparent to some one thing that is capable of integrating them and knows that they are different and distinguished. This one thing is the intellect.

31. This activity, in Aristotle's words, refers to "thinking things through" and "conceiving that something is the case."

32. Aristotle didn't see the brain as an organ linked to the activities of the intellect. We now know that the brain has a very important role in human thinking. But even if some of the functions associated with the mind (such as memory and language) can be located in the brain, Aristotle's view that pure thinking (i.e., the establishing of causal forms) doesn't have a corresponding organ still remains logically valid. See Dodds (2009) and George (2020).

33. While alertness emanates from the immateriality of the intellect, there is a material component to the intellect (and therefore to alertness) in Aristotle's theory in the relationship between the intellect and some organs of the body, especially with regards to the senses, as well as to memory, language, etc. In that sense, experience and prior learning could influence memory and therefore alertness. See for instance Arentz et al. (2013).

34. See Aristotle, Book III, chapter 3.

35. According to Joe Sachs's introductory notes to Book III, Aristotle uses two dozen words to describe various kinds of thinking the intellect can engage in. Among them, some may describe or relate to the function of alertness. For instance to recognize (*gnōrizein*), to judge or to distinguish (*krinein*), and to discern (*gignōskein*).

36. "Imagination" in Greek is *phantasia*, which derives from *phaos* (light). Aristotle explains (Book III, chapter 3: 429a) that we cannot see without light, hence to imagine is to shed some new light onto something. In a footnote Joe Sachs explains that "imagination allows practical thinking to go beyond present perceptions and consider distant possibilities and novel combinations of things" (p. 146, footnote 17).

37. Another source of error could be the lack of appetite. Indeed, Aristotle affirms (Book III, chapter 10) that the intellect doesn't cause motion, but that desire (appetite) does. Hence the practical intellect may identify the right thing to pursue, but without enough desire, one may remain undecided. Since this goes beyond alertness, we only mention it *in passim*.

38. See Aristotle, 428a ff.

39. As Aristotle explains, the intellect is most necessary to the soul "by becoming all things [and] by forming all things" (Book III, chapter 5).

40. That "object" is, most of the time, potential gains from trade to be realized in the future.

41. Even Kirzner does not see the need to engage in "philosophical speculations" when it comes to explaining the essence of the entrepreneurial element, as he told the present author.

42. An example is the Austrian idea that value scales do not pre-exist action and are emergent during the agent's action. In our view, it cannot, at a most fundamental level, be explained by reductionism.

REFERENCES

Arentz, J., Sautet, F. E., & Storr, V. H. (2013). Prior-Knowledge and Opportunity Identification. *Small Business Economics*, *41*(2), 461–478.

Aristotle. (2002). *On the Soul and on Memory and Recollection*. Santa Fe, NM: Green Lion Press.

Boethius, A. M. S. (2009). *The Consolation of Philosophy*. Cambridge MA: Harvard University Press.

Boettke, P. J., & Sautet, F. E. (2013). Introduction to the Liberty Fund Edition. In *Competition and Entrepreneurship*. Indianapolis, IN: Liberty Fund.

Buchanan, J. M., & Vanberg, V. J. (1991). The Market as a Creative Process. *Economics and Philosophy*, *7*(2), 167–186.

Dodds, M. J. (2009). Hylomorphism and Human Wholeness: Perspectives on the Mind-Brain Problem. *Theology and Science*, *7*(2), 141–162.

Foss, N. J., & Klein, P. G. (2010). Entrepreneurial Alertness and Opportunity Discovery: Origins, Aattributes, Critique. In H. Landström & F. Lohrke (Eds), *Historical Foundations of Entrepreneurship Research* (pp. 98–120). Cheltenham, UK and Northampton, MA, USA: Edward Elgar Publishing.

Foss, N. J., & Klein, P. G. (2012). *Organizing Entrepreneurial Judgment: A New Approach to the Firm.* Cambridge: Cambridge University Press.

George, M. (2020). Neuroscience and the Human Soul. *The Aquinas Review 2019–2020, 23*, 123–152.

Gordon, D. (2006). *The Philosophical Origins of Austrian Economics.* Auburn AL: Ludwig von Mises Institute.

Hassing, R. (1997). Introduction: Final Causality in Nature and Human Affairs. In R. Hassing (Ed.), *Studies in Philosophy and the History of Philosophy* (pp. 1–51). Washington, DC: Catholic University of America Press.

High, J. (1982). Alertness and Judgment: Comment on Kirzner. In I. Kirzner (Ed.), *Alertness and Judgment: Comment on Kirzner. Method, Process and Austrian Economics: Essays in Honor of Ludwig von Mises.* Washington, DC: Lexington Books.

Kirzner, I. M. (1973). *Competition and Entrepreneurship.* Chicago, IL: University of Chicago Press.

Kirzner, I. M. (1979). Producer, Entrepreneur, and the Right to Property. In I. M. Kirzner (Ed.), *Perception, Opportunity, and Profit: Studies in the Theory of Entrepreneurship.* Chicago, IL: University of Chicago Press.

Kirzner, I. M. (1982). Uncertainty, Discovery, and Human Action: A Study of Entrepreneurial Profile in the Misesian System. In I. M. Kirzner (Ed.), *Method, Process, and Austrian Economics: Essays in Honor of Ludwig von Mises* (pp. 139–159). Lexington, MA: Lexington Books.

Kirzner, I. M. (2009). *The Economic Point of View: The Collected Works of Israel M. Kirzner* (P. J. Boettke & F. E. Sautet, Eds). Indianapolis, IN: Liberty Fund.

Kirzner, I. M. (2013). *Competition and Entrepreneurship, The Collected Works of Israel Kirzner* (P. J. Williamson & F. E. Sautet, Eds). Indianapolis, IN: Liberty Fund.

Kirzner, I. M. (2015a). Entrepreneurship, Economics, and Economists. In P. J. Boettke & F. E. Sautet (Eds), *Austrian Subjectivism and the Emergence of Entrepreneurship Theory: The Collected Works of Israel M. Kirzner* (pp. 139–150). Indianapolis, IN: Liberty Fund.

Kirzner, I. M. (2015b). Methodological Individualism, Market Equilibrium, and Market Process. In P. J. Boettke & F. E. Sautet (Eds), *Austrian Subjectivism and the Emergence of Entrepreneurship Theory: The Collected Works of Israel M. Kirzner* (pp. 175–189). Indianapolis, IN: Liberty Fund.

Kirzner, I. M. (2018). Hayek, Knowledge and Market Processes: The Essence of Entrepreneurship and the Nature and Significance of Market Process. In P. J. Boettke & F. E. Sautet (Eds), *The Collected Works of Israel M. Kirzner* (pp. 134–155). Indianapolis, IN: Liberty Fund.

Koppl, R. (2002). What Is Alertness? *Journal Des Economistes et Des Etudes Humaines, 12*(1). https://doi.org/10.2202/1145-6396.1044

Leibenstein, H. (1968). Entrepreneurship and Development. *American Economic Review, 58*(2), 72–83.

MacIntyre, A. (2007). *After Virtue: A Study in Moral Theory* (3rd Ed.). Notre Dame, IN: University of Notre Dame Press.

Mirowski, P. (1998). Machine Dreams: Economic Agents as Cyborgs. In J. B. Davis (Ed.), *New Economics and Its History* (pp. 13–40). Durham, NC: Duke University Press.

Mises, L. von. (1949). *Human Action*. New Haven, CT: Fox & Wilkes and Foundation for Economic Education.

Mises, L. von. (1962). Profit and Loss. In *Planning for Freedom*. South Holland, IL: Libertarian Press.

Mises, L. von. (1998). *Human Action: The Scholar's Edition*. Auburn, AL: Mises Institute.

Mittermaier, K. (1986). Mechanomorphism. Subjectivism Intelligibility and Economic Understanding. In I. M. Kirzner (Ed.), *Essays in Honor of Ludwig M. Lachmann on His Eightieth Birthday* (pp. 236–251.). London: Macmillan.

Nagel, T. (2012). *Mind and Cosmos*. Oxford: Oxford University Press.

Robbins, L. (1935). *An Essay on the Nature and Significance of Economic Science* (2nd Ed.). London: Macmillan.

Röpke, W. (1950). *The Social Crisis of Our Time*. Chicago, IL: University of Chicago Press.

Sautet, F. E. (2018). The Battle for the Essence of Entrepreneurship. *Review of Austrian Economics*, *31*(1), 123–139.

Schultz, T. W. (1975). The Value of the Ability to Deal with Disequilibria. *Journal of Economic Literature*, *13*(3), 827–846.

Selgin, G. A. (1987). Praxeology and Understanding: An Analysis of the Controversy. *Review of Austrian Economics*, *2*, 19–58.

Shackle, G. L. S. (1983). Review Article: Decisions, Process and the Market. *Journal of Economic Studies*, *10*(3), 56–66.

Slade, F. (1997). Ends and Purposes. Final Causality in Nature and Human Affairs. In R. Hassing (Ed.), *Studies in Philosophy and the History of Philosophy* (pp. 83–85). Washington, DC: Catholic University of America Press.

4. Entrepreneurial judgment

Peter G. Klein and Matthew McCaffrey

INTRODUCTION

It is well known that entrepreneurship plays a crucial role in Austrian economics, a sentiment captured in Ludwig von Mises's remark that entrepreneurs are "the driving force of the market economy." Yet while the Austrian tradition has already proved a rich source of insight about entrepreneurship, the firm, innovation, economic growth, and related topics, there remains wide scope for expanding and applying Austrian theory. In fact, the long history of Austrian economics, combined with its recent rapid growth, means that the number of its theoretical, empirical, and policy studies is now large enough that it is useful to summarize their past achievements and future prospects.

With that in mind, this chapter explores a series of central themes in contemporary Austrian entrepreneurship research that we group under the heading of *entrepreneurial judgment*. These themes are crucial elements in what is now known as the judgment-based approach to entrepreneurship (JBA). The JBA has a distinguished pedigree in Austrian work and has been growing substantially in recent years both there and in other areas of social science and management research (c.f. Foss & Klein, 2012, 2015; Foss, Klein, & McCaffrey, 2019 for surveys). In what follows, we first outline the history and major themes of the JBA, including decision-making under uncertainty, the ownership and use of heterogeneous capital assets, the delegation of authority within the firm and its implications for organization, and the social function of the profit and loss test. We then discuss trends in the judgment literature and explore some open questions and debates that continue to animate this body of research.[1]

THE HISTORICAL BACKGROUND OF THE JUDGMENT-BASED APPROACH

We begin by briefly sketching the history of the JBA, especially within the Austrian tradition. The foundations of what would become the JBA were first laid by the early French economists. In the eighteenth century, Richard

Cantillon placed the entrepreneur front and center in his economic analysis and particularly emphasized the problem of decision-making under uncertainty (Cantillon, 2001 [1755]). In the following century, Jean-Baptiste Say similarly argued that entrepreneurs earn a special income from their ability to correctly estimate future prices in uncertain markets (Say, 1971 [1821]). Say's French liberal followers likewise stressed the importance of entrepreneurs in creating and coordinating market activity (Salerno, 1988).

Beginning with the "marginalist revolution," many scholars in and around the Austrian tradition contributed to developing the JBA, including Carl Menger, Victor Mataja, Eugen von Böhm-Bawerk, John Bates Clark, Frank Fetter, Frank Knight, and Ludwig von Mises.[2] Naturally, not all of these writers produced extensive theories of entrepreneurship: some are fragmented or nascent. Likewise, while some Austrians have consciously worked to integrate and build upon the ideas of earlier writers, others developed their own theories. Nevertheless, Austrian works share several themes, especially in answering questions about the unique economic function of entrepreneurship and explaining the real-world entrepreneurial decisions that produce profit and loss.

For example, Carl Menger, the founder of the Austrian school, did not write extensively on entrepreneurship, but he did sketch a series of economic functions that entrepreneurs perform:

> entrepreneurial activity includes: (a) obtaining *information* about the economic situation; (b) economic *calculation*—all the various computations that must be made if a production process is to be efficient (provided that it is economic in other respects); (c) the *act of will* by which goods of higher order (or goods in general— under conditions of developed commerce, where any economic good can be exchanged for any other) are assigned to a particular production process; and finally (d) *supervision* of the execution of the production plan so that it may be carried through as economically as possible. (Menger, 1871, p. 68; emphasis in original)

Each of these activities can be linked to the theories of later economists. For example, Menger's student Viktor Mataja expanded Menger's analysis of the stages of production and made a variety of suggestions about the complexities of entrepreneurial decision-making in managing production (Möller & McCaffrey, 2021a). These hints were also developed by Eugen von Böhm-Bawerk, who talked about the need for entrepreneurs to coordinate production (McCaffrey & Salerno, 2014). Böhm-Bawerk stressed in particular the heterogeneous nature of production goods and the need to organize them. Further steps were then taken by American economists working in the Mengerian tradition. John Bates Clark emphasized the way entrepreneurs make the "supreme decisions" that ultimately guide a business in dynamic markets (Clark, 1918, p. 122). Frank A. Fetter explicitly described entrepreneurship as a problem of decision-making and of bearing uncertainty and explored the roles of judgment and luck in generating profit and loss (McCaffrey, 2016).

Despite the fact that all of these writers at least hinted at the idea of uncertainty as distinct from probabilistic risk, this notion was not discussed extensively until the works of Frank Knight and Ludwig von Mises. Knight is best known today for his distinction between risk and uncertainty, while Mises spoke of "class probability" and "case probability" (Knight, 1921; Mises, 1949). Although there are differences in the details of their accounts, Knight and Mises worked in the same direction, namely, toward identifying a unique type of decision problem that entrepreneurs must solve that cannot be insured or otherwise accounted for in the costs of the business enterprise. Uncertainty (no matter exactly how we conceptualize it) implies the need for a specialized kind of decision-making that cannot be defined according to strict rules or expressed as a maximizing behavior. Following Knight and numerous other economists, we call this type of decision-making *judgment*.

The exercise of judgment is the defining characteristic of entrepreneurship and the entrepreneurial function, and also the fundamental explanation of profits and losses in the market economy. A key theme in Mises's writings is the importance of the profit and loss test in sorting successful entrepreneurs from unsuccessful ones. Profit and loss constantly rearrange the pattern of ownership in society according to entrepreneurs' degrees of success in satisfying consumer wants. Herein lies the crucial welfare implication of the market economy: the constant push toward the greater satisfaction of the masses through the most effective use of scarce factors of production.

To summarize the key claims of the JBA: factors of production are scarce and heterogeneous and must be combined and recombined continuously in order to serve the most urgent needs of consumers. This does not happen spontaneously: some kind of decision-making authority is required to guide the process. Such authority falls to those who own the factors of production and bear ultimate power to decide how they are used. These owner-decision-makers are entrepreneurs. Entrepreneurs govern the production process directly and indirectly. Directly they can make decisions about what, where, and how to produce; indirectly, they delegate authority over these decisions within business firms. However, production takes time, and the future is uncertain, meaning that error and failure are ever-present possibilities. Because entrepreneurs are the ultimate owners and decision-makers, the success or failure of business ventures falls on them. Only by successfully anticipating the future state of the market can entrepreneurs arrange production now in such a way as to earn a profit later. The "rewards" and "punishments" of the profit and loss system constantly rearrange the pattern of ownership and ultimate decision-making authority in society, and ceaselessly work to align entrepreneurs' decisions with consumers' wants.

THE JBA AND CONTEMPORARY ENTREPRENEURSHIP RESEARCH

The roots of the JBA can be traced to the beginning of the Austrian tradition. Yet with the exception of some passing remarks in Ludwig Lachmann's (1956) book on capital and Murray Rothbard's updated statement of the entrepreneur's role in production (1962), the approach lay mostly dormant for the first few decades of the Austrian revival, beginning in the 1950s and 1960s. Partly this was due to the influence of Israel Kirzner, whose *Competition and Entrepreneurship* (1973) took a different approach, conceptualizing entrepreneurship as alertness to or the discovery of profit opportunities. While Kirzner's work was positioned as an explanation for the competitive market process, not as a theory of entrepreneurship per se, it soon became regarded as the dominant "Austrian" take on the subject. Moreover, although the Kirznerian approach did not have much influence on mainstream microeconomics, it was cited frequently by mainstream entrepreneurship scholars (Klein & Bylund, 2014) who had been looking for more rigorous theoretical foundations than were widely available at the time. Thanks to Shane and Venkataraman (2000), Shane (2003), and similar works, entrepreneurship as studied and taught in business schools became defined as the discovery, evaluation, and exploitation of profit opportunities.

More recently, the opportunity-discovery approach has been criticized from a variety of perspectives. Alvarez and Barney (2007) and Wood and McKinley (2010) argue that opportunities do not exist prior to action, but must be created, subjectively, by entrepreneurial imagination and effort. The literature on entrepreneurial "effectuation" views entrepreneurs not as formulating a goal and then assembling the resources necessary to obtain it, but as acting cautiously, incrementally, and experimentally. Effectual reasoning involves starting with resources at hand, imagining potential actions and outcomes, and choosing outcomes with the smallest affordable loss (Sarasvathy, 2009).

Foss and Klein (2012, 2020), building on the JBA, offer a more pragmatic critique, urging entrepreneurship to drop the opportunity construct altogether and focus on the entrepreneur's beliefs, actions, and results under conditions of uncertainty. Opportunities are manifest ex post, when entrepreneurial outcomes are successful. What entrepreneurship scholars mean by "opportunity" is simply a business idea, plan, or belief, which may or may not turn out as the entrepreneur imagines. Instead of focusing on metaphorical opportunities, entrepreneurship researchers and teachers should focus on action in the Misesian sense.

Specifically, entrepreneurship begins with the entrepreneur's beliefs about the present (resource characteristics and availability, scientific and technical conditions, consumer preferences), possible futures (production outcomes, consumer demands, legal and regulatory issues), and her ability to bring about various possible futures (beliefs about causality, self-efficacy, confidence). As with all human action, the entrepreneur desires to bring about a particular future that, from her subjective perspective, is preferred to the present. Entrepreneurship proper begins once investments are made—i.e., when resources are acquired, combined, and committed to various production plans. This could involve the creation of a new firm but could also manifest in a new product or new organizational practice, or even in a decision to maintain existing plans or resource deployments.

After actions have been taken (i.e., after investments have been made), the entrepreneur learns whether those actions did in fact bring about the anticipated desirable future. These results are in some sense objective (profits and losses, the market value of the entrepreneur's assets, the survival of the venture), though obviously there are elements of subjective interpretation at play in terms of non-financial goals or the meaning the entrepreneur attaches to financial or other objective metrics. Finally, there is an adjustment stage in which the entrepreneur either learns and plans to take different actions in the future or runs out of capital and is forced to exit. The implication of this action-based approach to entrepreneurship is that opportunity is at best a metaphorical construct, at worst ambiguous and misleading. It makes far more sense, from the perspective of JBA theorists, to treat concrete judgments such as investment decisions or choices about how to combine capital assets rather than metaphorical opportunities (whether "discovered" or "created") as units of analysis or core constructs (Foss, Foss, Klein, & Klein, 2007; Klein & Foss, 2008).

To this end, it is also important to clarify the nature of judgment and explore its economic, cognitive, and other relevant characteristics. For example, some work suggests that intuition or "gut feeling" are at the heart of judgmental decision-making (Foss & Klein, 2015; Klein, 2016). Others prefer to think in terms of empathic accuracy (McMullen, 2015), customer need diagnosis (Godley & Casson, 2015), or identifying emergent demand routines (Giménez Roche & Calcei, 2021) as the bases of judgment. An important caveat is that, while it is useful not only for our theorizing but also for teaching that we articulate, as much as possible, what judgment is and how it works, the very nature of judgment is that it is not susceptible to a complete, formal articulation or analysis. Judgment is decision-making about the uncertain future, typically without a formal model or decision rule; to the extent that we can parameterize and systematize these decisions, they are not judgments!

Because judgment is manifest in ownership—ultimate decision authority (or residual rights of control) over productive resources—the quality of an entrepreneur's judgments will be reflected in the skill with which she can create and capture value by deploying these resources under conditions of uncertainty. Note that judgment as an abstract economic function (the act of judging the uncertain future) is different from "judgment" as that term is sometimes used in everyday discourse as a synonym for wisdom or prudence. Judgments can be good or bad, accurate or inaccurate, generating profits or leading to losses. Foss et al. (2021) capture the skill with which judgment is exercised with the construct of "ownership competence" (Foss, Klein, Lien, Zellweger, & Zenger, 2021). This is different from the standard approach to ownership in economics and management—mainly derived from agency and incomplete contracting theories—which focuses on the incentive effects of ownership. These concepts and theories neglect ownership's role as an instrument to match judgment about resource use and governance with the firm's evolving environment under uncertainty. Business owners own with different levels of competence, and differences in ownership competence matter for value creation. Ownership competence—the skill with which ownership is used as an instrument to create value—can be decomposed into matching competence (*what to own*), governance competence (*how to own*), and timing competence (*when to own*). Property rights of use, appropriation, and transfer relate to these three ownership competences.

Note that this broader conceptualization of entrepreneurial action moves us away from an exclusive focus on the creation of new firms, which many scholars take to be the complete domain of entrepreneurship. The JBA sees entrepreneurship as more like stewardship or responsibility for productive assets, decisions about which must always be made in conditions of uncertainty. A decision not to devote resources to a new venture or product (in particular, when competitors are pursuing similar ventures or products) reflects the decision-maker's idiosyncratic judgment about the uncertain future, and this is an entrepreneurial act in the sense used by the Austrians and other leading theorists like Frank Knight (1921).

Similarly, the JBA diverges from Joseph Schumpeter's view of entrepreneurship as the creation of "new combinations," i.e., from the idea of entrepreneurship as a species of innovation. Entrepreneurship and innovation are often intertwined, but the exercise of judgment does not necessarily involve the creation of innovative products, processes, or business models. This division between Schumpeter and the Austrians is worth clarifying, as Schumpeter was partly influenced by his teachers Böhm-Bawerk and Friedrich von Wieser. Yet he also was a fiercely independent thinker with strong affinities to the general equilibrium theory of Léon Walras (McCaffrey, 2009). His close ties to the Austrians have, however, sometimes resulted in his views being conflated with theirs, leading to some confusion that could be avoided through greater attention to the JBA. For example, beginning with Schumpeter, an excessive focus on entrepreneurship in relation to equilibrium constructs has inspired a fruitless and seemingly endless debate within the Austrian school about whether entrepreneurship is equilibrating or disequilibrating. This debate is mostly irrelevant and misleading from the perspective of the JBA, which focuses instead on profit and loss as a method of selecting successful entrepreneurial activities (see, e.g., Klein, 2008; McCaffrey, Foss, Klein, & Salerno, 2021).

The importance of the JBA extends beyond debating the foundations of entrepreneurship research, however: it also provides original answers to a variety of research questions. A series of examples relate to unconventional or non-market forms of entrepreneurial activity.

The first case involves non-traditional forms of business organization. How should decision-making authority be distributed and how does this affect the size and shape of firms? While the conventionally structured business firm with a managerial hierarchy dominates the commercial world, there is tremendous variation in how businesses are organized. In the last few decades especially there has been an ongoing experimentation with various forms of business with little or no hierarchy or central management and consequently with a great deal of dispersed or "democratic" decision-making by employees. These experiments make for fascinating case studies, but the JBA provides a useful way to untangle fact from fiction and look more closely at the costs and benefits of these alternatives to the traditional firm. For example, it is common to find that while a company may reject formal hierarchy, it is often replaced by informal hierarchy and other subtle means of retaining the functions of management (Foss & Klein, 2014). In practice, the "original judgment" of owner-entrepreneurs always exists in some form or another, even if on paper a company has no formal top-down decision structure (Möller & McCaffrey, 2021b).

Austrian economists have, understandably, focused their research on conventional for-profit entrepreneurship. However, judgmental decision-making under conditions of uncertainty is not limited to the marketplace and, in a sense, is a feature of all human action. As a result, there is a sense in which we can speak of entrepreneurial action in many areas of the economy and society beyond those captured in traditional theories of profit-seeking market entrepreneurship. For example, social entrepreneurship sits on the boundary of the marketplace. Social enterprises combine standard business methods with broader "social" missions. The latter typically involve the alleviation of economic problems such as poverty and homelessness or finding solutions to broader social issues such as providing care or support for marginalized groups (e.g., Abu-Saifan, 2012; Alvord, Brown, & Letts, 2004; Martin & Osberg, 2007; Seelos & Mair, 2005). Despite receiving tremendous attention in the literature, however, there is still widespread disagreement about how to define and study social entrepreneurship, and how to capture exactly what social entrepreneurs do (Saebi, Foss, & Linder, 2019). This is especially true of the economic function of social entrepreneurship, which remains somewhat vague and elusive (McCaffrey, 2017a).

The JBA offers a fresh take on social entrepreneurship by looking at entrepreneurs' decisions about how to balance the "economic" and "social" sides of business. Supported by Austrian economic theory, the JBA helps explain that there is less tension between the dual purposes of social enterprises than is often thought: in a sense, *all* market entrepreneurship is already social in that it creates value for many people in society, beginning with its customers but also including a wide range of other stakeholders. Beyond this, however, we can think of social entrepreneurship as a way for entrepreneurs to navigate the trade-off between profit-seeking and charity. By deciding how to produce for a social purpose (and how to price products and remunerate factors of production), entrepreneurs decide where to set the boundaries of the use of economic calculation. In other words, they decide the scope of the profit and loss test (McCaffrey, 2017a). Rather than a unique and clearly differentiated type of business organization, then, social entrepreneurship simply represents points on the more extreme end of a spectrum of profit-seeking and charity.

Another example of an alternative to market entrepreneurship is political entrepreneurship. This concept has been defined in various ways and is usually associated with rent-seeking and related concepts drawn from the public choice literature. However, the JBA offers a different way to conceptualize entrepreneurial behavior in the political sphere. That is, political entrepreneurs can be thought of as the owners and ultimate decision-makers with government (McCaffrey & Salerno, 2011). Political entrepreneurs make judgments about how to use scarce resources, and they also confront an uncertain future. Crucially, however, they finance their activities through taxation, borrowing, and inflation rather than through successfully using scarce resources to satisfy consumers. They also act without the guidance of a system of market prices and the profit and loss test. As a result, the welfare implications of political entrepreneurship run in the opposite direction to those of market entrepreneurship.

A fourth, more specific case is military organization. This field often struggles with classic questions from economics and management relating to problems like the size and shape of military organizations, their internal incentive compatibility and efficient use of scarce resources, the uncertainty and incomplete information facing their leaders, and so on (McCaffrey, 2014, 2015b). These and other topics can be analyzed from the perspective of the JBA. The most crucial of these is the idea that the profit and loss test of the market, along with the use of money prices to allocate scarce resources, provides an indispensable framework for decision-making that does not exist in the military sphere. Military organizers therefore confront similar limitations as bureaucrats attempting to centrally plan a national economy.

ENTREPRENEURIAL JUDGMENT IN OTHER FIELDS OF MANAGEMENT

Entrepreneurship is by now a distinct discipline with its own research questions and trends. Nevertheless, the JBA has applications to many other fields of management research in addition to economics and entrepreneurship research as such.

For example, in finance, ideas from Austrian theories of money, banking, and financial markets have been influential in investment theory, particularly the notion of "value investing" (Calandro, 2004, 2009; Grimm, 2012; Spitznagel, 2013). And while business cycle theory is usually considered outside the domain of entrepreneurship, there are important parallels between Austrian capital theory and concepts of resource heterogeneity from transaction cost economics and the resource-based view of the firm (Agarwal, Barney, Foss, & Klein, 2009). The Austrian theory of the business cycle, which assigns special importance to entrepreneurial behavior, has enjoyed a renaissance since the global financial crisis of 2008, which mainstream macroeconomics was ill equipped to anticipate or remedy. In the wake of the crisis it became particularly clear that many economists had failed to look realistically at the way entrepreneurs behaved in the boom period, and how their decisions affected the severity of the bust. In response, a new literature has emerged that focuses on using Austrian ideas to explain entrepreneurs' decision processes during the businesses cycle (Engelhardt, 2012).

The JBA also sheds light on how entrepreneurs respond to external shocks, the Covid-19 disruptions of 2020–2021 being an obvious example (Klein, 2020). First, increased uncertainty—not only about markets and customers, but also about unprecedented policy responses—places an increased premium on superior judgment (or high levels of ownership competence). The Covid-19 shocks also illustrate the limits to quantitative forecasting tools! Second, the policy response to Covid, including lockdowns, business closures and capacity restrictions, travel restrictions, and the like, limit the ability of entrepreneurs to deploy and redeploy resource combinations, directing their attention instead to finding alternative business models, sources of supply, and product characteristics, as well as decisions about how to use the excess capacity created by demand slowdowns such as retraining or restructuring (Klein, Knudsen, Lien, & Timmermans, 2020). Most important, restrictions on economic activity, both voluntary and involuntary, impede the market process of matching actual ownership to individuals and groups with high levels of ownership competence.

A straightforward application of Austrian entrepreneurship theory is the problem of entrepreneurial finance. If entrepreneurial judgment under uncertainty is sufficiently tacit and idiosyncratic that entrepreneurs cannot convince outside parties to invest—the central idea behind Knight's (1921) theory of the firm—then we would expect to see new ventures financed exclusively through bootstrapping or debt. However, investments from business angels and venture capitalists are increasingly important in modern economies. Foss, Klein, and Murtinu (2022) address this seeming paradox by pointing out that new-venture funding represents investment both in projects (resources with salvage values) and in entrepreneurs (tacit, subjective judgments and capabilities). Angels and venture capitalists, as well as individuals who start new companies, are exercising a measure of entrepreneurial judgment in judging potential founders. These founders face a trade-off between choosing resources that are more closely complementary to their own idiosyncratic judgments—so that outside equity investors are betting purely on the entrepreneur—and choosing resources that are less specific, so the investor has more protection against failure of the venture.

Contemporary marketing research also has much in common with the JBA, given their joint focus on identifying and satisfying customers. Strategic marketing, in particular the resource-advantage theory, closely resembles Austrian thinking in several ways, such as its emphasis on action, time, and knowledge (D'Andrea, 2020). Several of the core elements of the JBA have also been used to develop new theoretical frameworks in marketing that stress entrepreneurs' role in "facilitating value" for consumers by understanding their valuations and preferences (Hastings, D'Andrea, & Bylund, 2019).

The JBA, like Austrian economic theory in general, strives for realism and practicality. It should not come as a surprise then that it has a role to play in business history as well as theory. Austrians can and should contribute to the "historical turn" in management studies, and in some sense they already are. For example, leading historians of entrepreneurship like Mark Casson often draw on Austrian ideas to interpret historical cases (e.g., Casson & Casson, 2013). To take another example, research has explored how institutions historically influenced entrepreneurial decision-making and steered economies away from productive market entrepreneurship in settings as diverse as ancient China and the United States during the Great Depression (Bylund & McCaffrey, 2017; McCaffrey, 2017b).

THE INSTITUTIONAL CONTEXT OF ENTREPRENEURSHIP

While judgment per se is abstract and universal, specific acts of entrepreneurial judgment must be understood in a particular context. Mainstream economics typically models context as a straightforward effect such that changes in the constraints actors face lead to predictable and uniform behavioral responses.

This is the approach taken by much of the economics-based literature on entrepreneurship that looks at how changes in contextual variables such as rates of taxation, social insurance, regulation, etc. affect self-employment and business formation. The consensus in this literature is that targeted policies designed to promote particular types of firms (startups, high-growth firms, tech firms) tend to channel resources to politically favored, but economically inefficient projects and companies, mainly because bureaucrats without "skin in the game" lack the information, incentives, and ownership abilities to allocate resources to their most highly valued uses. Rather, a policy environment featuring the rule of law, competition, sound money, and low levels of corruption allows entrepreneurs and market forces to determine outcomes.

With its roots in the Austrian tradition, the JBA emphasizes not only formal policies, but also the role of subjective interpretation of individuals, events, and resources (Packard, 2017). As noted above, the entrepreneur's beliefs about cause and effect are also subjective and may be tacit (though in some sense testable against reality). Hence the JBA allows the context to shape not only the objective constraints that surround the formation and exercise of entrepreneurial judgments and interpretations but also those judgments and interpretations themselves (McCaffrey, 2018). When institutions and policies change, entrepreneurs respond, not just because these changes translate into objective changes in the context surrounding them, but also because these changes prompt different interpretations of, for example, their longer-run implications.

One way to understand the role of institutions in this context is that, by providing structure to the social world, institutions make it easier for decision-makers to anticipate the future, mitigating the effects of uncertainty (Foss & Garzarelli, 2007; Lachmann, 1971). Lachmann (1971, p. 75) describes an institution as a "recurrent pattern of conduct" that helps individuals plan by making the behavior of other individuals more predictable. "An institution provides a means of orientation to a large number of actors. It enables them to co-ordinate their actions by means of orientation to a common signpost" (Lachmann 1971, p. 49). This squares with North's (1991) well-known definition of institutions as "humanly devised constraints that structure political, economic and social interaction," including both informal constraints and formal legal rules. "Together with the standard constraints of economics they define the choice set and therefore determine transaction and production costs and hence the profitability and feasibility of engaging in economic activity" (North, 1991, p. 97).

There is substantial work on how the institutional environment—including the legal system, the political and regulatory environment, social norms and culture, and the like—affects startups and self-employment (Bjørnskov & Foss, 2016; Bradley, Kim, Klein, McMullen, & Wennberg, 2021; Bradley &

Klein, 2016). This literature includes institutionalist perspectives in sociology (Nee, 1998; Scott, 1995) as well as empirical studies in the New Institutional Economics (North, 1990; Williamson, 2000). It usually emphasizes that stable rules enable complex exchange across time and space. More stable institutions mean more predictability, more secure property rights, more complete contracts, and so on. In turn, more entrepreneurial projects will be undertaken. Bjørnskov and Foss (2008, 2013) argue that incentives to engage in entrepreneurial behaviors are particularly influenced by the extent to which private property rights are protected and enforced. This includes dimensions such as generality (i.e., equals are treated equally), transparency, and accountability in public decision-making. Depending on how well public institutions, the constitution, and so on guard against rent-seeking, resources will be devoted to productive entrepreneurship (Baumol, 1990).

This literature usually does not explicitly address how entrepreneurs steer the combination and recombination of heterogeneous resources under uncertainty, the focus of the JBA. Still, its arguments are highly relevant to entrepreneurial judgment. Thus, Bjørnskov and Foss (2013) link economic production theory and institutional arguments in the context of the JBA. They focus on the flexibility with which resources can be combined and recombined, corresponding to the production theory notion of the "elasticity of factor substitution" (Klump & de La Grandville, 2000). If this elasticity is high, then resources are more easily allocated to highly valued uses. Foss and Bjørnskov argue also that the elasticity of substitution is endogenous to institutional variables. Thus, "good" institutions—which present entrepreneurs with low transaction costs when they search for resources, bargain over the terms at which they can acquire or contract for these, monitor resources, etc.—positively influence the flexibility with which resources can be identified, allocated, combined, etc. by these entrepreneurs.

As hinted above, the JBA provides a framework for thinking about some of the more complex relationships between institutions and entrepreneurial behavior. Baumol (1990) argued that entrepreneurs channel their efforts into activities that carry the greatest rewards; as a result, if rent-seeking or organized crime are remunerated more than servicing customers in the marketplace, entrepreneurial talent will flow to the former activities. Yet Baumol's insight, while important, overlooks several important aspects of entrepreneurial decision-making. First, Baumol conceived of entrepreneurship in Schumpeterian terms as innovation, whereas we argue that it is much broader and subtler than this. Any study of institutions must therefore consider their effects on entrepreneurs' perceptions, expectations, and judgment in addition to their capacity for innovation. Second, Baumol's argument—again like Schumpeter's—overlooks the importance of uncertainty and error in entrepreneurial decision-making. He more or less assumes that institutions channel entrepreneurship in one direction or another in a straightforward way, and that entrepreneurs are successful in their efforts to seek out the greatest rewards, as determined by the "rules of the game" established by prevailing institutions. Once more though, the JBA offers a more nuanced picture in which entrepreneurs can err in deciding which activities will provide the greatest rewards; they can furthermore fail in the tasks they choose (e.g., they can fail to successfully lobby government for favorable treatment); and they are not restricted to only one type of activity but will likely choose a combination of productive and unproductive behaviors. Third, entrepreneurs are not passive victims of the institutional environment: to varying degrees they can also act to change that environment. This process too is fraught with uncertainty (Bylund & McCaffrey, 2017). It also raises another crucial point found in the JBA, namely, the question of how the nature of entrepreneurial behavior changes outside the institutional context of a system of market prices. This hints at the ideas of social and political entrepreneurship discussed above, but also at more specific challenges entrepreneurs face when trying to directly alter fundamental ideas, beliefs, and norms in society.

ECONOMIC POLICY

The practical and realist nature of Austrian economics means that many of its core concepts and theories are ideally suited for application to economic policy, and the theory of entrepreneurship is no exception. In fact, this is an important advantage of the JBA, as some researchers have expressed skepticism about the ability of other Austrian approaches to contribute more than general principles of policy analysis. For example, some work suggests that Hayekian spontaneous order theories have little to offer in terms of concrete policy advice (Elert & Henrekson, 2019). Likewise, the Kirznerian approach to policy, which focuses on the way the institutional environment switches off or blocks entrepreneurial alertness, has also been criticized (McCaffrey, 2015a). There is therefore a golden "opportunity" to apply the JBA research agenda in the direction of policy.

A JBA account of public policy will draw on a combination of the ideas discussed in previous sections. Here we focus on only one of these: the crucial concept of ownership. Understanding how ownership occurs in specific situations can in turn tell us much about how policy decisions are made, resources are allocated, welfare is improved or destroyed, and so on. For example, we have already suggested that we can think of political action to allocate resources as a problem of ownership and entrepreneurial decision-making, albeit with very different welfare implications than market entrepreneurship. Political entrepreneurship in this sense can also be understood more clearly using the notion of "ownership competence" mentioned above. For instance, we should expect that, given that political owners do not acquire their decision rights through the profit and loss test, they will not demonstrate the same ownership competences as market entrepreneurs. As a result, the decision processes of political decision-makers and market entrepreneurs will vary drastically, as will their welfare implications.

A similar example is found in cases where government systematically intervenes in the entrepreneurial process through taxation, regulation, and other controls that forcibly alter the pattern of ownership in society. Such a system of interventionism amounts to "*institutionalized* uninvited co-ownership" (Hülsmann, 2006, emphasis in original). Moreover, it involves a systematic redistribution of decision-making authority from entrepreneurs to political decision-makers. For instance, if government bails out an auto manufacturer, that company surrenders at least a part of its decision-making power, and the entrepreneurs who nominally control it become its managers. The judgment of entrepreneurs competing in the market and bearing uncertainty is replaced with the judgment of policymakers without skin in the game and who lack the guidance of the profit and loss test.

These general examples help to show that the JBA is capable of developing concrete policy advice: specifically, it can be used to analyze subtle or informal changes in decision authority that nevertheless have a great impact on human welfare. By examining the way that policy affects the distribution of ownership and decision-making, the JBA thus offers a novel account of the relationship between public policy and entrepreneurship.

CONCLUSION

What is today called the judgment-based approach to entrepreneurship has been a key feature of Austrian economics research since the works of Carl Menger. It continues to grow and thrive as a research agenda in that tradition, while also attracting increasing attention in the social sciences and management disciplines. We have summarized the key concepts of the JBA and explained a variety of ongoing debates and research strands within the literature. We conclude with some remarks about the place of the JBA within the entrepreneurship field and some suggestions for further work.

The recent revival of the JBA in the context of contemporary entrepreneurship theory coincides with a flourishing of alternative theoretical perspective and approaches, all of which challenge the opportunity-discovery approach building on Kirzner and developed by scholars such as Shane and Venkataraman (2000) and Shane (2003). These include the "opportunity creation" or "opportunity construction" approach (Alvarez & Barney, 2007; Wood & McKinley, 2010), the effectuation model (Sarasvathy, 2009), theories of entrepreneurial bricolage (Baker & Nelson, 2005), and models of "external enablers" (Davidsson, 2015; Kimjeon & Davidsson, 2021). Some of these critiques are ontological (i.e., dealing with the nature of entrepreneurial opportunities) and others cognitive (focusing on how entrepreneurs think). The JBA can be considered a methodological critique of the opportunity-discovery approach in that it argues that beliefs, actions, and results are sufficient for understanding the core phenomena of entrepreneurship and that, therefore, the opportunity construct is unnecessary (Foss & Klein, 2020) and that the emphasis on "discovery" misleads scholars and practitioners to ignore the fundamental uncertainty associated with human action.

At one level, the JBA can be considered a reframing or reinterpretation of familiar issues and practices associated with the entrepreneurial process such as market analysis, scenario planning and other forecasting tools, business model design, resource assembly, prototyping, market testing, performance measurement, and the like. In this sense, the JBA does not tell entrepreneurs to do something different from what they already do; rather, it helps researchers, teachers, policymakers, journalists, and others understand and conceptualize entrepreneurship and its vital role in society.

We have already touched on a number of outstanding issues and problems. One promising area is the dimensionalization and further analysis of uncertainty (or case probability); for example, Packard, Clark, and Klein (2017) distinguish between uncertainty about means (resources, team members, technical plans) and uncertainty about ends (products, services, market conditions), suggesting that entrepreneurs typically focus on exercising judgment, and attempting to reduce uncertainty, about these dimensions sequentially rather than simultaneously. Foss et al. (2022), following Langlois and Cosgel (1993), interpret Knightian uncertainty in terms of the entrepreneur's ability to articulate and communicate her judgments to other parties (rather than her ability to formalize her beliefs to herself). Existing work in cognitive psychology on shared cognition or shared mental models can be helpful here. There is also more to be done on the market process by which entrepreneurs compete under conditions of uncertainty and the effectiveness of alternative institutions for sorting high- and low-ability entrepreneurs and matching ownership with ownership competence.

The JBA also has implications for the theory of delegation, in which entrepreneur-owners delegate proximate decision authority to subordinates who exercise what might be called "derived judgment" on behalf of owners (Foss et al., 2007). The contractual and other means by which this delegation takes place under different conditions deserve further study. Note that, unlike agency models in which the roles of principal and agent are given ex ante, the JBA suggests that agents with superior judgment or higher levels of ownership competence will tend to become principals via bargaining or market sorting. Moreover, the JBA suggests that non-market actors such as politicians, judges, bureaucrats, and the like can exercise a form of delegated judgment (on behalf of citizens or taxpayers) but cannot exercise residual control rights as they are not owners of the resources they control. The means by which citizens or taxpayers delegate authority to these political actors, while monitoring and constraining that authority, is analogous to the techniques used by owners exercising original judgment to engage employees exercising derived judgment. Bringing the JBA into the analysis of non-market decision-making should yield new insight on a variety of social, political, and institutional topics.

NOTES

1. This chapter draws heavily on several of our published works, including Foss and Klein, 2012; Foss, Klein, and McCaffrey, 2019; Foss, Klein, Lien, Zellweger, and Zenger, 2021; McCaffrey, 2015a, 2017a.
2. See, respectively, Foss and Klein, 2010, 2012; Martin, 1979; McCaffrey, 2016; McCaffrey & Salerno, 2014; Möller & McCaffrey, 2021a; Salerno, 2008. Other notable scholars have contributed to Austrian entrepreneurship theory along different lines than those studied in this chapter. These writers include Friedrich von Wieser, Joseph Schumpeter, and, most important, Israel Kirzner. On Kirzner's work, see the chapter by Sautet in this volume, as well as McCaffrey, Foss, Klein, and Salerno, 2021.

REFERENCES

Abu-Saifan, S. (2012). Social Entrepreneurship: Definition and Boundaries. *Technology Innovation Management Review*, *2*(2), 22–27.

Agarwal, R., Barney, J. B., Foss, N. J., & Klein, P. G. (2009). Heterogeneous Resources and the Financial Crisis: Implications of Strategic Management Theory. *Strategic Organization*, *7*(4), 467–484.

Alvarez, S. A., & Barney, J. B. (2007). Discovery and Creation: Alternative Theories of Entrepreneurial Action. *Strategic Entrepreneurship Journal*, *1*(1–2), 11–26.

Alvord, S. H., Brown, L. D., & Letts, C. W. (2004). Social Entrepreneurship and Societal Transformation. *Journal of Applied Behavioral Science*, *40*(3), 260–282.

Baker, T., & Nelson, R. E. (2005). Creating Something from Nothing: Resource Construction through Entrepreneurial Bricolage. *Administrative Science Quarterly*, *50*(3), 329–366.

Baumol, W. J. (1990). Entrepreneurship: Productive, Unproductive, and Destructive. *Journal of Political Economy*, *98*(5, Part 1, October), 893–921.

Bjørnskov, C., & Foss, N. J. (2008). Economic Freedom and Entrepreneurial Activity: Some Cross-Country Evidence. *Public Choice*, *134*(3–4), 307–328.

Bjørnskov, C., & Foss, N. J. (2013). How Strategic Entrepreneurship and the Institutional Context Drive Economic Growth. *Strategic Entrepreneurship Journal*, *7*(1), 50–69.

Bjørnskov, C., & Foss, N. J. (2016). Institutions, Entrepreneurship, and Economic Growth: What Do We Know and What Do We Still Need to Know? *Academy of Management Perspectives*, *30*(3), 292–315.

Bradley, S. W., Kim, P. H., Klein, P. G., McMullen, J. S., & Wennberg, K. (2021). Policy for Innovative Entrepreneurship: Institutions, Interventions, and Societal Challenges. *Strategic Entrepreneurship Journal*, *15*(2), 167–184.

Bradley, S. W., & Klein, P. G. (2016). Institutions, Economic Freedom, and Entrepreneurship: The Contribution of Management Scholarship. *Academy of Management Perspectives*, *30*(3), 211–221.

Bylund, P. L., & McCaffrey, M. (2017). A Theory of Entrepreneurship and Institutional Uncertainty. *Journal of Business Venturing*, *32*(5), 461–475.

Calandro, J. (2004). Reflexivity, Business Cycles, and the New Economy. *Quarterly Journal of Austrian Economics*, *7*(3), 45–69.

Calandro, J. (2009). *Applied Value Investing*. New York: McGraw-Hill.

Cantillon, R. (2001 [1755]). *Essay on the Nature of Commerce in General*. New Brunswick, NJ: Transaction.

Casson, M. C., & Casson, C. (2013). *The Entrepreneur in History: From Medieval Merchant to Modern Business Leader*. New York: Macmillan.

Clark, J. B. (1918). *Essentials of Economic Theory as Applied to Modern Problems of Industry and Public Policy*. New York: Macmillan.

D'Andrea, F. A. M. C. (2020). Strategic Marketing and Austrian Economics: The Foundations of Resource-Advantage Theory. *Review of Austrian Economics*, *33*(4), 481–501.

Davidsson, P. (2015). Entrepreneurial Opportunities and the Entrepreneurship Nexus: A Re-Conceptualization. *Journal of Business Venturing*, *30*(5), 674–695.

Elert, N., & Henrekson, M. (2019). The Collaborative Innovation Bloc: A New Mission for Austrian Economics. *Review of Austrian Economics*, *32*(4), 295–320.

Engelhardt, L. (2012). Expansionary Monetary Policy and Decreasing Entrepreneurial Quality. *Quarterly Journal of Austrian Economics*, *15*(2), 172–194.

Foss, K., Foss, N. J., Klein, P. G., & Klein, S. K. (2007). The Entrepreneurial Organization of Heterogeneous Capital. *Journal of Management Studies*, *44*(7), 1165–1186.

Foss, N. J., & Garzarelli, G. (2007). Institutions as Knowledge Capital: Ludwig M. Lachmann's Interpretative Institutionalism. *Cambridge Journal of Economics*, *31*(5), 789–804.

Foss, N. J., & Klein, P. G. (2010). Alertness, Action, and the Antecedents of Entrepreneurship. *Journal of Private Enterprise*, *25*(2), 145–164.

Foss, N. J., & Klein, P. G. (2012). *Organizing Entrepreneurial Judgment: A New Approach to the Firm*. Cambridge: Cambridge University Press.

Foss, N. J., & Klein, P. G. (2014). Why Managers Still Matter. *MIT Sloan Management Review*, *56*(1), 73–80.

Foss, N. J., & Klein, P. G. (2015). Introduction to a Forum on the Judgment-Based Approach to Entrepreneurship: Accomplishments, Challenges, New Directions. *Journal of Institutional Economics*, *11*(3), 585–599.

Foss, N. J., & Klein, P. G. (2020). Entrepreneurial Opportunities: Who Needs Them? *Academy of Management Perspectives*, *34*(3), 366–377.

Foss, N. J., Klein, P. G., Lien, L. B., Zellweger, T., & Zenger, T. (2021). Ownership Competence. *Strategic Management Journal*, *42*(2), 302–328.

Foss, N. J., Klein, P. G., & McCaffrey, M. (2019). *Austrian Perspectives on Entrepreneurship, Strategy, and Organization*. Cambridge: Cambridge University Press.

Foss, N. J., Klein, P. G., & Murtinu, S. (2022). *Entrepreneurial Finance under Knightian Uncertainty*. Milan: IT.

Giménez Roche, G. A., & Calcei, D. (2021). The Role of Demand Routines in Entrepreneurial Judgment. *Small Business Economics*, *56*(1), 209–235.

Godley, A. C., & Casson, M. C. (2015). "Doctor, Doctor …": Entrepreneurial Diagnosis and Market Making. *Journal of Institutional Economics*, *11*(3), 601–621.

Grimm, R. C. (2012). Fundamental Analysis as a Traditional Austrian Approach to Common Stock Selection. *Quarterly Journal of Austrian Economics*, *15*(2), 221–236.

Hastings, H., D'Andrea, F. A. M. C., & Bylund, P. L. (2019). Towards a Value-Dominant Logic of Marketing. *MISES: Interdisciplinary Journal of Philosophy, Law and Economics*, *7*(3). https://doi.org/10.30800/mises.2019.v7.1240

Hülsmann, J. G. (2006). The Political Economy of Moral Hazard. *Politická Ekonomie*, *54*(1), 35–47.

Kimjeon, J., & Davidsson, P. (2021). External Enablers of Entrepreneurship: A Review and Agenda for Accumulation of Strategically Actionable Knowledge. *Entrepreneurship Theory and Practice*, 104225872110106.

Kirzner, I. M. (1973). *Competition and Entrepreneurship*. Chicago, IL: University of Chicago Press.

Klein, P. G. (2008). The Mundane Economics of the Austrian School. *Quarterly Journal of Austrian Economics*, *11*(3–4), 165–187.

Klein, P. G. (2016). Why Entrepreneurs Need Firms, and the Theory of the Firm Needs Entrepreneurship Theory. *Revista de Administração*, *51*(3), 323–326.

Klein, P. G. (2020). Uncertainty and Entrepreneurial Judgment during a Health Crisis. *Strategic Entrepreneurship Journal*, *14*(4), 563–565.

Klein, P. G., & Bylund, P. L. (2014). The Place of Austrian Economics in Contemporary Entrepreneurship Research. *Review of Austrian Economics*, *27*(3), 259–279.

Klein, P. G., & Foss, N. J. (2008). The Unit of Analysis in Entrepreneurship Research: Opportunities or Investments? *International Journal of Entrepreneurship Education*, *6*(3), 145–170.

Klein, P. G., Knudsen, S., Lien, L. B., & Timmermans, B. (2020). Recessions Give Businesses Time to Improve—if Governments Let Them. https://blogs.lse.ac.uk/businessreview/2020/06/25/recessions-give-businesses-time-to-improve-if-governments-let-them/

Klump, R., & de La Grandville, O. (2000). Economic Growth and the Elasticity of Substitution: Two Theorems and Some Suggestions. *American Economic Review*, *90*(1), 282–291.

Knight, F. H. (1921). *Risk, Uncertainty, and Profit*. Boston, MA: Houghton Mifflin.

Lachmann, L. M. (1956). *Capital and Its Structure*. Kansas City, MO: Sheed Andrews and McMeel.

Lachmann, L. M. (1971). *The Legacy of Max Weber*. Berkeley, CA: Glendessary.

Langlois, R. N., & Cosgel, M. M. (1993). Frank Knight on Risk, Uncertainty, and the Firm: A New Interpretation. *Economic Inquiry*, *31*(3), 456–465.

Martin, D. T. (1979). Alternative Views of Mengerian Entrepreneurship. *History of Political Economy*, *11*(2), 271–285.

Martin, R. L., & Osberg, S. (2007). Social Enterprise: The Case for Definition. *Stanford Social Innovation Review*, *5*(2), 28–39.

McCaffrey, M. (2009). Entrepreneurship, Economic Evolution, and the End of Capitalism: Reconsidering Schumpeter's Thesis. *Quarterly Journal of Austrian Economics*, *12*(4), 3–21.

McCaffrey, M. (2014). The Political Economy of *The Art of War*. *Comparative Strategy*, *33*(4), 354–371.

McCaffrey, M. (2015a). Economic Policy and Entrepreneurship: Alertness or Judgment? In D. Howden & P. L. Bylund (Eds), *The Next Generation of Austrian Economics: Essays in Honor of Joseph T. Salerno*. Auburn, AL: Ludwig von Mises Institute.

McCaffrey, M. (2015b). The Economics of Peace and War in the Chinese Military Classics. *Economics of Peace and Security Journal*, *10*(1). https://doi.org/10.15355/epsj.10.1.23

McCaffrey, M. (2016). Good Judgment, Good Luck: Frank Fetter's Neglected Theory of Entrepreneurship. *Review of Political Economy*, *28*(4), 504–522.

McCaffrey, M. (2017a). Economic Calculation and the Limits of Social Entrepreneurship. In M. McCaffrey (Ed.), *The Economic Theory of Costs* (pp. 243–263). New York: Routledge.

McCaffrey, M. (2017b). Military Strategy and Unproductive Entrepreneurship in Warring States China. *Management and Organizational History*, *12*(2), 99–118.

McCaffrey, M. (2018). William Baumol's "Entrepreneurship: Productive, Unproductive, and Destructive." In G. Javadian, V. K. Gupta, D. K. Dutta, Grace Chun Guo, A. E. Osorio, & B. Ozkazanc-pan (Eds), *Foundational Research in Entrepreneurship Studies* (pp. 179–201). Cham: Springer International.

McCaffrey, M., Foss, N. J., Klein, P. G., & Salerno, J. T. (2021). Breaking out of the Kirznerian box: A Reply to Sautet. *Review of Austrian Economics*. https://doi.org/10.1007/s11138-021-00552-x

McCaffrey, M., & Salerno, J. T. (2011). A Theory of Political Entrepreneurship. *Modern Economy*, *2*(4), 552–560.

McCaffrey, M., & Salerno, J. T. (2014). Böhm-Bawerk's Approach to Entrepreneurship. *Journal of the History of Economic Thought*, *36*(4), 435–454.

McMullen, J. S. (2015). Entrepreneurial Judgment as Empathic Accuracy: A Sequential Decision-Making Approach to Entrepreneurial Action. *Journal of Institutional Economics*, *11*(3), 651–681.

Menger, C. (1871). *Principles of Economics*. New York: New York University Press.

Mises, L. von. (1949). *Human Action*. New Haven, CT: Fox & Wilkes and Foundation for Economic Education.

Möller, U., & McCaffrey, M. (2021a). Entrepreneurship and Firm Strategy: Integrating Resources, Capabilities, and Judgment through an Austrian Framework. *Entrepreneurship Research Journal*. https://doi.org/10.1515/erj-2020-0519

Möller, U., & McCaffrey, M. (2021b). Levels without Bosses? Entrepreneurship and Valve's Organizational Design. In M. McCaffrey (Ed.), *The Invisible Hand in Virtual Worlds* (pp. 211–240). Cambridge: Cambridge University Press.

Nee, V. (1998). Sources of the New Institutionalism. In M. C. Brinton & V. Nee (Eds), *In the New Institutionalism in Sociology* (pp. 1–16). New York: Russell Sage Foundation.

North, D. C. (1990). *Institutions, Institutional Change, and Economic Performance*. Cambridge, MA: Harvard University Press.

North, D. C. (1991). Institutions. *Journal of Economic Perspectives*, *5*(1), 97–112.

Packard, M. D. (2017). Where Did Interpretivism Go in the Theory of Entrepreneurship? *Journal of Business Venturing*, *32*(5), 536–549.

Packard, M. D., Clark, B. B., & Klein, P. G. (2017). Uncertainty Types and Transitions in the Entrepreneurial Process. *Organization Science*, *28*(5), 840–856.

Rothbard, M. N. (1962). *Man, Economy, and State*. Princeton, NJ: Van Nostrand Company.

Saebi, T., Foss, N. J., & Linder, S. (2019). Social Entrepreneurship Research: Past Achievements and Future Promises. *Journal of Management*, *45*(1), 70–95.

Salerno, J. T. (1988). The Neglect of the French Liberal School in Anglo-American Economics: A Critique of Received Explanations. *Review of Austrian Economics*, *2*(1), 113–156.

Salerno, J. T. (2008). The Entrepreneur: Real and Imagined. *Quarterly Journal of Austrian Economics*, *11*(3–4), 188–207.

Sarasvathy, S. D. (2009). *Effectuation: Elements of Entrepreneurial Expertise.* Cheltenham, UK and Northampton, MA, USA: Edward Elgar Publishing.

Say, J.-B. (1971 [1821]). *A Treatise on Political Economy, or the Production, Distribution, and Consumption of Wealth.* New York: Augustus M. Kelley.

Scott, W. R. (1995). *Institutions and Organizations.* Thousand Oaks, CA: Sage.

Seelos, C., & Mair, J. (2005). Social Entrepreneurship: Creating New Business Models to Serve the Poor. *Business Horizons*, *48*(3), 241–246.

Shane, S. A. (2003). *A General Theory of Entrepreneurship: The Individual-Opportunity Nexus.* Cheltenham, UK and Northampton, MA, USA: Edward Elgar Publishing.

Shane, S. A., & Venkataraman, S. (2000). The Promise of Entrepreneurship as a Field of Research. *Academy of Management Review*, *25*(1), 217–226.

Spitznagel, M. (2013). *The Dao of Capital: Austrian Investing in a Distorted World.* Chichester: John Wiley & Sons.

Williamson, O. E. (2000). The New Institutional Economics: Taking Stock, Looking Ahead. *Journal of Economic Literature*, *38*(3), 595–613.

Wood, M. S., & McKinley, W. (2010). The Production of Entrepreneurial Opportunity: A Constructivist Perspective. *Strategic Entrepreneurship Journal*, *4*(1), 66–84.

5. Entrepreneurship and the market process

Per L. Bylund

Ludwig von Mises famously observed that entrepreneurship is the "driving force" of the market process. He was not the first Austrian economist to discuss entrepreneurship—the school's founder Carl Menger had discussed what characterizes entrepreneurial activity already in his *magnum opus* (see Menger, 2007 [1871], p. 160). But Mises unambiguously placed the entrepreneur at the center of his theory as both the source of value creation and the solution to the economic calculation problem (see Mises, 1951 [1922], 1935 [1920]).

With entrepreneurship being core to its economic theory, Austrian economics has gained significant influence in business school disciplines such as entrepreneurship and management over the past decades (Klein & Bylund, 2014). But not in economics proper, where Austrian economics was once an influential school of thought. In modern economics, curiously, entrepreneurship is all but forgotten (Baumol, 1968). Even the timing of economics turning its back on entrepreneurship is curious as it coincides with economics not only striving to become a physics of the social sciences but also increasingly distancing itself from its legacy—and the economic reasoning of Austrian economics.

Although Austrians can and should pride themselves with having a theory of entrepreneurship, or in any case an economic theory that *includes* entrepreneurship, it is typically limited to being an aspect of the market process. For example, Hayek (1945) notes how entrepreneurs adapt to events they neither have nor need to have knowledge about by responding to price changes. Similarly, Kirzner (1973) argues that entrepreneurship as alertness to opportunity contributes to equilibrating the economy (see also Sautet, 2022). In more recent theory development, Foss and Klein (2012) argue, alongside Knight (1921), that entrepreneurship is about exercising judgment (see also Klein & McCaffrey, 2022) by establishing business firms within which they can conduct controlled experiments.

While far from a comprehensive list of Austrian conceptions of entrepreneurship, these three entrepreneurship theories have something important in common: they treat entrepreneurship as an important component in but not the *driving force* of the market process.

The first two conceptualize the entrepreneur as primarily a responsive agent. For Hayek, entrepreneurs respond directly to price movements by adjusting their purchasing and production efforts accordingly. For Kirzner, entrepreneurs earn profits by correcting previous mistakes, thereby contributing "toward the systematic elimination of error" (Kirzner, 1978b, p. 74). Both explain entrepreneurship as a force that equilibrates and improves on the overall market, but neither conception of entrepreneurship explains the driving force of the process.

The judgment-based approach, in contrast, focuses on the entrepreneur as an active owner-decision-maker, a capital owner who bears the uncertainty of production. But the aim here is to explain why entrepreneurs need firms (Foss & Klein, 2012), not if and when those firms aim to or in fact cause changes to the market process.

These theories exemplify how modern Austrian theorizing on entrepreneurship largely misses the mark (at least from a Misesian perspective). This is also how I will use them in this chapter: as illustrations of how Austrian theorizing over the past decades fail to recognize the Misesian conception of entrepreneurship and, therefore, also Mises's understanding for the market process.

While these theories indeed address, albeit indirectly or even only implicitly, the *workings* of the market process, they do not explain (or attempt to explain) its *driving force*. This is much more than a difference in emphasis or leaving out an aspect for simplification. The market process without its driving force is an altogether different phenomenon.

Mises, in fact, was very clear about the importance of entrepreneurship as the driving force of the market process. He wrote: "In eliminating the entrepreneur one eliminates the driving force of the whole market system" (Mises, 1949, p. 249). The function of the entrepreneur, then, is not simply *a* driving force out of potentially many but is *the* driving force. And it is the driving force of *the whole market system* which leaves no room for other possible "forces." To Mises, entrepreneurship is the driving force of the market process. Period.

But this raises the question of how Mises's conception of entrepreneurship relates to other Austrian entrepreneurship theories, including the ones that were just mentioned, that conceive of the entrepreneur as primarily a *responsive* agent. Put differently, and to make the contrast to the aforementioned theories clear, how can the entrepreneur be the market's driving force yet merely respond to changes?

This seeming tension arises out of Mises's uncharacteristically ambiguous discussion on entrepreneurs and promoters.

MISES'S ENTREPRENEUR AND THE PROMOTER

Mises (1949, p. 254) relied on a broad praxeological definition of entrepreneurship as "acting man exclusively seen from the aspect of the uncertainty inherent in every action." Defined this way, economic theory finds a specific explanation for the function of uncertainty-bearing alongside the functions of capital ownership, land ownership, and labor. This broad conception of entrepreneurship is compatible with the aforementioned aspects of entrepreneurial action (adjusting, error-correcting, and judgmental decision-making), but is also too broad to provide specific explanations. Mises consequently distinguished between this general definition and a specific type of entrepreneurship—a subset of the general function—that is of particular importance to economic theory: the promoter-entrepreneur or, simply, promoter.

Mises's promoter in several ways resembles Schumpeter's (1934 [1911]) heroic conception of the entrepreneur. To Schumpeter, the entrepreneur is a disequilibrating innovator, the cause of equilibrium-busting "creative destruction" that is the core characteristic of the industrial evolution of economic capitalism (Schumpeter, 1947). As Mises (1949, p. 256) stated: "The driving force of the market, the element tending toward unceasing innovation and improvement, is provided by the restlessness of the promoter and his eagerness to make profits as large as possible."

Giving the promoter this type of fundamental importance in the market process, one would expect Mises to do much more than note its role and importance for economics. Why did he not develop a theory of the promoter? The simple answer is that Mises believed that he could not pursue the promoter praxeologically, i.e. deductively inferred from the action axiom, and therefore the distinction was beyond reach for economic theory:

> It is to be admitted that the notion of the entrepreneur-promoter cannot be defined with praxeological rigor. (In this it is like the notion of money which also defies—different from the notion of a medium of exchange—a rigid praxeological definition.) However, economics cannot do without the promoter concept. (Mises, 1949, p. 256)

This conclusion, that a concept that "economics cannot do without" also "cannot be defined" through economic reasoning, must have been difficult to accept for Mises. After all, it suggests a clear and important limit to economic theory (e.g. Bylund, 2021b). Mises may have been too quick to admit defeat, however. Bylund (2020) suggests the promoter can in fact be defined with praxeological rigor using a different theoretical model than the "evenly rotating economy" that Mises relied on. In Bylund's model, which he refers to as the "specialization deadlock" (Bylund, 2016, pp. 60–65), actions are distinguished based on their positioning relative to the economic boundaries of the existing market. Actions are here either within-boundary adjustments, which do not challenge the structure or extent of the market but are primarily (but not exclusively) responsive, or pioneering, meaning they take place beyond the market's extent. It is in the former category—the non-promoter-entrepreneurs—that we typically find Austrian entrepreneurship theories such as the ones mentioned above, which we will elaborate on in the next section.

Bylund's distinction is not novel but is in fact Mises's. What is new is that Bylund (2020) provides the means for a praxeological definition and therefore a basis for theoretically analyzing the promoter specifically. We can therefore use it to produce an argument for what entrepreneurship means, from a Misesian perspective, for and within the market process, respectively. In other words, the Bylund-Mises distinction between general/non-promoter-entrepreneurship and promoter-entrepreneurship allows us to elaborate on the meaning of the "driving force" for the market process and its implications for economic action in general.

As a result, this also affects our understanding for the economic calculation problem, which to Mises was fundamentally a "problem of ... economic dynamics" (1951 [1922], p. 139) that could be solved only through the "division of intellectual labor" of property-owning entrepreneurs. Mises's conclusion, as we will see, follows from the proper understanding of the promoter's role in driving the market process through revolutionizing production.

THE BOUNDARIES OF THE MARKET PROCESS

It was claimed above that the listed entrepreneurship theories, and especially those by Hayek and Kirzner, focus on within-system adjustments. From a mainstream economics perspective, this should appear both true and inconsequential. After all, seeing the economy as an equilibrium system, as non-Austrians typically do, allows for no economic action beyond the system's boundaries. But this conclusion, while formally accurate, depends on using the wrong analytical frame. Austrian economics, in contrast to modern mainstream economics, is not a theory of the economy as an equilibrium system, but of the market as a *process*.

As the market process progresses, society experiences economic growth from expanding productive capability through capital accumulation and a deepening of the division of labor. When it retrogresses, society consumes rather than accumulates productive capital and, as a result, experiences decreasing productivity and, therefore, becomes poorer. The third and only remaining logical alternative, a stationary economy, is to Austrians a theoretical impossibility. Here, wealth and incomes remain unchanged and total profits therefore equal total losses (cf. Mises, 1949, pp. 251–252). In such a state of affairs, which resembles the general equilibrium model, actions are precluded as they are undertaken in order to effect change. Thus, the market process must either progress or retrogress (Bylund, 2018).

The question is then what causes this progression or retrogression, i.e. how the boundaries of the market process get shifted. Bylund (2016) distinguishes between two types of causes, which we might summarize as exogenous and endogenous to the market's production. Exogenous changes such as population growth, which facilitates incremental deepening of the division of labor (Smith, 1976 [1776]), or the discovery of new resources (cf. Schumpeter, 1934 [1911]), shift economic circumstances by increasing the economy's output potential. Economic actors are thereby induced to respond with adjustments to their production undertakings.

A similar argument can be made for when consumer preferences change, which causes the capital structures already put in place to become maladapted. Entrepreneurs respond by adjusting their investments and production undertakings to better serve consumers and, as a result, earn profits (cf. Mises, 2008). However, unlike increased population or resource availability, this would not typically increase total output.

In both of these cases, as Bylund (2016) notes, actors within the economic system are primarily responsive. From their point of view, the boundaries to the economic landscape in which they make investments and undertake production are exogenously given and provide immutable limits to what actions are possible. They also indicate the nature and extent of the adjustments that are possible to make. In other words, economic action takes place within the boundaries of the present state of the market.

WITHIN-SYSTEM ADJUSTMENTS

While Hayek and Kirzner conceive of the entrepreneur as acting within a market process, they both subscribe to the view of entrepreneurship as responsive to given circumstances. They take the boundaries of the market process as given and attempt maximizing, or at any rate improving, adjustments of production for profit.

In Hayek's case, entrepreneurs have production plans, which may be implemented to varying degrees, that they adjust as circumstances change. In his well-known example in "The Use of Knowledge in Society," the relative scarcity of tin increases and its market price thus increases significantly. The reason for this price increase, whether due to a disaster in a large tin mine (lower actual supply) or the discovery of new valuable uses for tin (increased actual demand), does not matter for their response. As Hayek puts it:

> It does not matter for our purpose—and it is very significant that it does not matter—which of these two causes has made tin more scarce. All that the users of tin need to know is that some of the tin they used to consume is now more profitably employed elsewhere, and that in consequence they must economize tin. There is no need for the great majority of them even to know where the more urgent need has arisen, or in favor of what other needs they ought to husband the supply. (Hayek, 1945, p. 526)

The task of Hayek's entrepreneur is here the same regardless of what causes the higher price (and whether the entrepreneur is aware of this cause): to adjust production by contributing to a better (more cost-effective) allocation of tin. Indeed, the "marvel" of the market system is to Hayek that the price system accumulates and communicates the relevant information—the relative scarcities—so that actors do not need to gather and comprehend "the knowledge of the particular circumstances of time and place" (1945, p. 521).

Kirzner's (1973) theory is in many ways similar to Hayek's (see e.g. Salerno, 1993) but focuses on another aspect of entrepreneurial action: its equilibrative effects. By discovering opportunities for profit, which are already existent in the market, the entrepreneur can correct those "errors" (imperfect solutions) made by previous actors and, as a result, push the market's resource allocation closer to general equilibrium. Like Hayek, Kirzner produces a knowledge argument in which entrepreneurs' alertness to opportunity allows them to alleviate some of the previous errors made due to ignorance and which are, therefore, incorporated in the market's production structure (cf. Kirzner, 2019).

Hayek and Kirzner focus on different but complementary aspects of the same process: Hayek's argument is primarily on how the system automatically adjusts its allocation to changing circumstances whereas Kirzner focuses on how entrepreneurs refine production. It should be noted that, to Kirzner, the equilibrium toward which entrepreneurial corrections push the market is a moving target that is ultimately unreachable because market data (especially consumer wants) change. In the end, therefore, the corrections that Kirzner's entrepreneurs bring about are in fact adjustments to changes in the data, much as is the case for Hayek's entrepreneurs.

The judgment-based approach is complementary to Hayek's and Kirzner's arguments by focusing on what affords the entrepreneur the decision-making power and ability to make adjustments and act on opportunities. Entrepreneurial judgment is manifest in ownership and is exercised through decision-making over owned resources. The business firm is then the means by which the entrepreneur can delegate and distribute decision rights to take advantage of employees' specific knowledge and uncertainty-bearing abilities (Foss, Foss,

& Klein, 2007; see also Knight, 1921). The entrepreneur maintains ownership and their original judgment continuously determines the scope of the firm through investing and divesting (Foss, Klein, & Bjørnskov, 2019). Klein and McCaffrey (2022, p. 66) note: "Entrepreneurs govern the production process directly and indirectly. Directly they can make decisions about what, where, and how to produce; indirectly, they delegate authority over these decisions within business firms."

The judgment-based approach does not necessarily preclude boundary-shifting actions such as novel innovations. It is therefore conceivable that judgmental entrepreneurs can use their ownership prerogative to make production decisions that challenge and potentially shift the boundaries of the market process. However, proponents of the judgment-based approach are critical of how innovation scholars disregard or diminish that "entrepreneurship is very often something much more mundane" (Foss & Klein, 2012, p. 17). Especially Schumpeter, they say, has "disassociated the firm and the entrepreneur" (Foss & Klein, 2012, p. 17).[1] The judgment-based approach thus

> diverges from Joseph Schumpeter's view of entrepreneurship as the creation of "new combinations," i.e., from the idea of entrepreneurship as a species of innovation. Entrepreneurship and innovation are often intertwined, but the exercise of judgment does not necessarily involve the creation of innovative products, processes, or business models. (Klein and McCaffrey, 2022, p. 69)

The judgment-based approach's explicit emphasis on regular, mundane entrepreneurship (firm-building) offers interesting insights into the workings of the market. However, by making this choice these scholars also all but exclude the driving force of the market process. The theory consequently ends up focusing primarily, if not exclusively, on within-system adjustments, which it aims to explain using firm organizing.

In sum, then, these three theories consider economic action, and particularly entrepreneurship, as taking place *within* the existing boundaries of the market process. While those boundaries may shift over time, such changes are assumed to have primarily exogenous causes. Entrepreneurs do not drive this type of change; they respond to it. Consequently, these theories leave little if any room for the promoter—the "driving force" of the market process (Bylund, 2020).

THE DRIVING FORCE OF THE MARKET PROCESS

The promoter, writes Mises, is responsible for making the "great adjustments" to the production structure that make the economy able to best serve consumers. Rather than making the "many small adjustments [that] are necessary too," the economic function and impact of promoters "does *not* merely consist in determining the general plan for the utilization of resources" (Mises, 1949, p. 300; emphasis added). In other words, as Bylund (2020) argues, the role of the promoter is not to deal with allocation of resources within the system, whether or not such new allocations lead to improvements, but, rather, to *revolutionize* production (cf. Schumpeter, 1934 [1911]).

The question then becomes, how does one revolutionize the market process such that its production better serves consumers? The theories of Hayek and Kirzner, discussed above, make clear that the market process already includes mechanisms that bring about adjustments to changes (the price mechanism) as well as refinements to the production structure (entrepreneurial alertness). Similarly, the judgment-based approach provides a framework for understanding how entrepreneurs, dealing primarily with mundane production, exercise judgment through owner decision-making in firms. Thus, the answer to how production can be revolutionized rather than improved must provide an explanation as to how production can be taken *beyond* within-system adjustments, refinements, and reallocations. In other words, the promoter cannot be limited by the boundaries within which other entrepreneurs act; the "great adjustments" the promoter brings about are not mere refinements of the existing production structure or reallocations of resources and do not emerge from responsive behavior. Instead, promoters undertake productions that seek to or in effect do undermine the present order by challenging the boundaries and, as a result, the structure of production within the market process.

One way of conceptualizing this type of entrepreneurship is to think of the promoter as an innovator. Schumpeter (1934 [1911], p. 66) suggests that the entrepreneur-innovator can be "defined by the carrying out of new combinations." Specifically, he notes five cases of such innovative development: (1) the introduction of a new good or (2) method of production, (3) opening a new market, (4) increasing the supply of factors, or (5) changing the organization of any industry. While these cases would indeed have a significant effect on what can be produced in the market, they do not accurately capture Mises's promoter. For example, increasing the supply of factors does not revolutionize the structure of the market process but should merely cause adjustments in the Hayekian sense.

Bylund (2016) conceptualizes the promoter as an innovator in the realm of production in general by imagining and producing a novel division of labor and capital. Such innovation can be in the form of producing a new good, as with Schumpeter's (1), but only if it entails building a new production structure. Specifically, the promoter's undertaking goes beyond present market conditions by implementing a novel, imagined yet to be tried out division of labor. Within an advanced specialized market economy, this would typically take place in the form of task-splitting and the replacement of existing market production with a new (type of) process (Bylund, 2015a, 2015b). As this new process depends on expertise and specializations that do not yet exist in the market, such production is largely incompatible with the existing production structure and thus takes place beyond the boundaries of the market process. When implemented, these new processes not only are distinct from the existing market but were pursued because they are such—the entrepreneur *chose* to deviate from existing market production.

When such novel undertakings are successful, Bylund (2016, 2020) argues, other entrepreneurs will attempt to emulate the original promoter's production to capture some of their above-normal profits. This, in turn, creates new markets between the competitors and their rivalrous bidding for the new capital and labor services thus determines market prices for those specializations. This process eventually leads to the innovation being subsumed into the market process as it replaces previous productions. As a result, the boundaries of the market process shift outward, its overall division of labor deepens, and productivity increases.

A TALE OF TWO MARKET PROCESSES

From our discussion above we can infer two distinct views of the market process. First, the market process of Hayek, Kirzner, and the "mundane" entrepreneurship of the judgment-based approach. Far from a stationary economy, this market process progresses albeit slowly. Within its boundaries, the actions of Kirznerian entrepreneurs take production ever closer to equilibrium by exploiting opportunities and, thereby, correct errors (Kirzner, 1978a). Equilibrium is a moving target, however, as consumers want change, causing entrepreneurs to make adjustments to their now-maladjusted production plans. Similarly, exogenous shocks cause factor prices to change, which require Hayekian adjustments to realign production with new relative valuations.

These changes occur within the boundaries of the market process and therefore primarily affect the market system's efficiency. This is a matter of (re)allocating resources toward more valuable uses, but through exchange and using the price mechanism. Entrepreneurs busy themselves making adjustments for profit, which continuously shift the market toward efficient production.

Rather than having static boundaries, exogenous influences can bring about changes to the extent of the market. This happens primarily through changes in population size, which affect what productions are possible in the market. As Adam Smith (1976 [1776]) noted, a population increase facilitates more intensive division of labor (cf. Durkheim, 1933 [1892]), and consequently an increased extent of the market. The market process thus progresses, but the progression is *incremental* and in response to changing conditions. This should rarely overwhelm the adjustment efforts by responsive entrepreneurs, whose actions therefore are equilibrating and improve the economy's value-productive efficiency within the present boundaries.

The promoter-driven market process takes a very different shape. Here, the promoter's implementation of revolutionizing innovations leads to spasmodic shifts of the market boundaries outward as new divisions of labor are subsumed by the market. Rather than incremental progression, this market process progresses through leaps forward with the successes of promoter-entrepreneurs' novel productions and efforts by emulating entrepreneurs. Note that these progressions are due to *endogenous* changes: the actions of promoters revolutionize what productions are (and become) possible. The market process generates its growth from within as promoters pursue novel production means that cannot be reached through adjustments or market exchange (Bylund, 2016).

These two market processes are clearly different in structure and behavior. While they can provide insights separately as analytical models, the real world does not offer the luxury of observing them independently or choosing one over the other. The empirical market includes elements from both. As Mises (1949, p. 256) noted, "[t]here are in the market pacemakers and others who only imitate the procedures of their more agile fellow citizens," which is why "economics cannot do without the promoter concept." The former—the pacemakers—are the promoters, the driving force of the market process that shifts the market boundaries *from within*. The latter—the imitators—are responsive to the changes effected by the promoters, and deal with Hayekian adjustments, Kirznerian error-correcting, and "mundane" business. We need both to understand the real market process.

EXCLUDING THE DRIVING FORCE

Let us now produce a combined model of the market process to examine the interaction between promoters and non-promoters. This will help illustrate not only the difference between the models but will also illuminate the issues involved with excluding the promoter from theories of the market process. We can do this either by introducing the promoter to the world of only within-system adjustments or the other way around, but *the result would be the same*. The promoter's actions trump those of entrepreneurs making adjustments to new or newly revealed market data because the promoter determines (when successful) the economic conditions in the market by shifting its boundaries and therefore the parameters within which other actors make economic decisions. Promoters, in other words, effect changes to which non-promoters must adjust.

In the first market process model above, all entrepreneurs were responsive agents busying themselves with within-system adjustments. They adjust their production undertakings when conditions change, or perhaps in anticipation of change, such as rising or falling factor prices. As Hayek argued, it does not matter to these actors what the actual cause of those changes is, because all they need to know is communicated through the market prices—and especially their change (rise or fall) relative to other prices. In other words, non-promoters respond to changes whether they are of exogenous origin or caused by promoters—the cause is inconsequential. Hayekian entrepreneurs have the means to deal with the price changes that promoters bring about. The difference between a promoterless world and one that includes promoters lies only in the frequency (and extent of the impact) of such changes and, therefore, the need to make necessary adjustments. If such changes happen very frequently, adjustments to production plans may need to be carried out continuously for non-promoters' undertakings to remain somewhat aligned with expected consumer wants.

The situation is similar for Kirznerian entrepreneurs, who are in the business of finding and correcting errors remaining or arising in previous entrepreneurial decisions: "they perceive price discrepancies" (Kirzner, 1973, p. 122). Strictly interpreted, then, Kirznerian pure entrepreneurs, who do not own capital of their own, will be presented with new opportunities as promoters cause changes to the market process. To the extent that the former are alert to those new opportunities, they may profit greatly from the disruptions promoters bring about. While Kirznerian entrepreneurs act to equilibrate the market process within its present boundaries, the focus on error corrections suggests the resultant equilibration process continues even as promoters challenge and disrupt those very boundaries. The distance to equilibrium, the amount of error presently existent in the system, changes over time: it increases with each promoter-caused disruption and then decreases through Kirznerian error correction, then increases again with the next disruption, and so on. The alert entrepreneur, who deals with adjustments within the market boundaries through spotting and correcting errors, is still a purely equilibrating force. As Kirzner notes, the pure entrepreneur neither owns capital nor deals with production that extends over time and therefore cannot be harmed or set back by the promoter's disruption. "Entrepreneurship does not consist of grasping a free ten-dollar bill which one has already discovered to be resting in one's hand; it consists in realizing that it is in one's hand and that it is available for the grasping" (Kirzner, 1973, p. 47).

In contrast, for the judgmental mundane entrepreneur, who owns capital and exercises judgment by making decisions about resource usage, the entry of the promoter can cause substantial practical problems. The added uncertainty from potential disruptions to the market process imposes costs that go far beyond what the Kirznerian entrepreneur faces because the production plan may need to be revised and thus the firm's internal capital structure reformed or even dismantled (cf. Lachmann, 1978 [1956]). This can be a very costly and time-consuming process, which adds to the entrepreneur's burden.

The point here is that these three conceptions of entrepreneurship (and others, which we have excluded) take place within a market process that may be and often is disrupted, with varying frequency, by promoter-entrepreneurs. Thus, we must conclude that the models offered by, for example, Hayek and Kirzner, are important *aspects* of the market process, but that they only consider a highly simplified model—a *mechanism*—in which the boundaries and parameters are largely unchanging. Yet the real market process is continuously affected by boundary-shifting, parameter-upsetting actions by promoters.

To again use Hayek's example of the tin market, the argument that entrepreneurs respond to higher prices of tin without knowing (or needing to know) the cause of those higher prices is accurate but severely lacking because it is incomplete. Hayek properly notes that if "somewhere in the world a new opportunity for the use of some raw material, say tin, has arisen," then the higher price will cause entrepreneurs using tin in their productions to economize on their usage. This is of course an accurate observation. However, Hayek's argument begins with the higher price, which is in fact determined through exchange within the market process. But if the price rises due to a new opportunity to use tin, as quoted above, then we are missing two important steps preceding the higher price: the discovery and implementation of the new use of tin and the consequent bidding up of tin prices.

Hayek's argument excludes what precedes and determines the higher price. Granted, it is of little importance for the responsive adjustment argument that Hayek makes, but it is a necessary component of Mises's conception of the market process. In fact, Hayek here excludes what Mises would likely consider the important components of the market process: the actions of the promoter and the implications thereof on price. What follows is, in comparison, rather uninteresting.

MISES'S MARKET PROCESS AND ECONOMIC CALCULATION

Restating Hayek's tin example in Misesian market process terms, a promoter imagines a new use for tin that implies a new type of production process and perhaps the production of a new type of good. The promoter must finance the undertaking and find factors, including labor, that have the skills/uses necessary to establish the imagined production process. In other words, the promoter uses capital that has been redirected from other uses, which means the relative scarcity and therefore prices for those factors increase. This is not part of Hayek's tin example but will cause the same adjustment processes as the rise in tin price. But, so far, there is no effect on tin prices.

As the promoter establishes their process and commences production, demand for tin rises accordingly. But how much? The promoter imagines that the new process will produce more value than existing processes, which of course is necessary for undertaking this line of production. Based on this appraisement of future value, the promoter is willing *and able* to offer higher prices and thus outbid other entrepreneurs who wish to use tin in production. Not only has market demand for tin increased, but the promoter, due to the new and expected higher-valued use, is the higher bidder and manages to secure sufficient supply while other producers, who already used tin, will not. Thus, the promoter causes the tin price to rise.

It is at this point that Hayek's argument begins. But note that the prices of tin (and other resources) rise as part of the bidding process as the promoter attempts to secure sufficient supply in their new production process. If the promoter buys the supply of tin from seller X, then other sellers may increase the price in anticipation of demand increasing also for their tin offered for sale. But it may also be that the in-flow of new customers, who were previously served by seller X, causes them to increase their selling price as a result. We cannot determine how or when the price increases among other sellers of tin. In other words, other entrepreneurs who rely on tin in their productions will adjust their production *as prices rise*, not necessarily as prices have already been established at a higher level. It is not a higher final price that causes the economizing of tin but increased relative scarcity and the therefore rising prices as the promoter bids for tin. Mises's market process thus includes also the dynamism of production actions as prices are *in flux*—as they are being adjusted due to production decisions and market actions.

Note that Mises's conception of the market process, which *includes* the promoter as its very driving force, dovetails with his economic calculation argument (Mises, 1935 [1920]; 1951 [1922]). In it, Mises (1949, p. 332) argues that factor prices are determined by entrepreneurs who "appear as bidders at an auction, as it were, in which the owners of the factors of production put up for sale land, capital goods, and labor." This auction is ever ongoing in the market, but it is not merely about responsive entrepreneurs making adjustments due to changing prices. Adjustments to price changes is only one side of the story. The auction also includes bidders who are promoters and who therefore bid on factors using different value expectations: their undertakings are expected, by them, to produce more value than existing productions and, therefore, they are willing and consider themselves able to bid much higher than the prices determined through previous price determinations. It is the expected (or, rather, imagined) value of their contribution to consumers that limits the price they're willing to pay (Bylund, 2021a), whether or not it is correct. This is why they are able to outbid existing producers competing to purchase the same resources.

In other words, Mises's (1935 [1920]; cf. Turowski & Machaj, 2022) economic calculation argument is incomplete without a proper understanding for the role of the promoter, who is the first to secure supply of certain factors, by virtue of higher willingness to pay, and thereby indirectly determines the final market price (e.g. Böhm-Bawerk 1959 [1889], pp. 215–235). Many critics of (and respondents to) Mises's original argument (e.g. Lange, 1936, 1937) have mistaken Mises's market process for Hayek's or Kirzner's per the discussion above (e.g. Camarinha Lopes, 2021). But, as we have seen, the market process without the promoter is a very different place than the real market process. In fact, the economic calculation problem is greatly diminished within the rather stable market process consisting of only within-system adjustments *because the boundaries are largely stable.* Here, the price system reduces to a mechanism for aggregating dispersed information and communicating relative valuations in a common denominator, as with Hayek (1945). This is naturally a problem that requires a solution in planned economies, but it is not Mises's problem. It is not the reason Mises concluded that socialism is impossible (Bylund, Lingle, & Packard, 2022).

THE IMPACT OF THE PROMOTER

In Mises's market process, the boundaries are shifted outward by the specific actions of (successful) promoters, which in turn disrupt the resource allocations between and among other production processes throughout the market. In terms of prices, a single promoter changes relative prices for the inputs used in their novel production but also, thereby, causes other producers to pursue using alternative inputs, which further shifts prices. Factor prices are therefore constantly in flux with entrepreneurs continuously seeking their most valuable uses.

The existence or mere potential of promoter-entrepreneurship in the market contributes to making all economic action uncertain because the past and present can no longer reliably predict the future. Not only do relative prices change, but existing producers cannot trust that their market niche will remain or that they will be able to continue to earn profits selling their outputs. The decision to continue producing must therefore rest on the assumption that one's particular business will not soon be disrupted directly or indirectly by a promoter.

In market production, therefore, adjustments cannot profitably be made to already realized price changes in the sense discussed above in the cases of Hayek and Kirzner. The only adjustments that can turn out profitable are adjustments to imagined consumer value. Hence, the direction for price determination from the imagined consumer value of future goods to present factor supply through entrepreneurs' competitive bids. Entrepreneurship is consequently future oriented and never actually responsive. For this reason, Mises emphasizes, similar to Knight (1921), that the entrepreneur necessarily relies on their judgment and understanding of what the future market will be, which is the only way of earning profits: "A prospective entrepreneur does not consult the calculus of probability which is of no avail in the field of understanding. He trusts his own ability to understand future market conditions better than his less gifted fellow men" (Mises, 1949, pp. 296–297).

This is why, writes Mises, the economic uncertainty borne by the entrepreneur is not a matter of lacking knowledge, technological or otherwise. It is a matter of bearing the uncertainty of *value*, which ultimately is determined through the experience of the consumer (Bylund & Packard, 2021): "The technologist may determine the optimum for a production aggregate's utilization. But this technological optimum may differ from that which *the entrepreneur on the ground of his judgment concerning future market conditions enters into his economic calculation*" (Mises, 1949, p. 345; emphasis added).

The market process, then, is determined by the actions taken by promoters, which ultimately determine both the direction of progression and the extent of the market. Because the promoter's actions challenge and bring about a shift in the boundaries of the market process, the only possible guidance for entrepreneurs, both promoters and non-promoters, is their expected value contribution as recognized by (future) consumers. While promoters seek to create new value, their doing so—and the mere potential of someone acting like a promoter—significantly limits the scope, effect, and value of within-system adjustments. In fact, such adjustments made *in response to* price changes are only feasible under the assumption that the pursued business opportunity will largely remain intact despite the changing prices. But that assumption appears rather tenuous in the presence of promoters.

While the importance of non-promoters in the market process cannot be denied, their impact on the economy is significantly circumscribed and undermined by promoter-entrepreneurship. What adjustments they make in response to price changes are unlikely to maintain profitability in a Misesian market process unless they are adjustments made *to anticipated changes in consumer value*, which is an imaginative and proactive action, not responsive as such. The scope for responsive entrepreneurial adjustments is severely circumscribed in a promoter-driven market process.

DIRECTIONS FOR FUTURE RESEARCH

The argument put forth in this chapter is that the promoter is not only an important concept that "economics cannot do without," but that the inclusion of promoter-entrepreneurship fundamentally changes the nature of economic theorizing and also our conception of the market process. Specifically, the promoter as the driving force (Bylund, 2020) determines the nature of the process and the direction, scope, and velocity of its progression. The promoter as a disruptor or architect of "great adjustments" is the cause of fundamental market dynamics and thereby makes present economic conditions merely a starting point for the pursuit of creating future value. The market's future value potential is determined and limited only by the imagination of entrepreneurs.

In contrast, the market process without the promoter is a matter of making continuous adjustments to production in response to changing market data. Change is here predominantly incremental rather than spasmodic and the unfolding of the process is therefore comparatively slow and predictably equilibrating. As a result, the promoterless market process reduces to an equilibrium system of sorts, with the ability to respond to exogenous shocks through within-system adjustments.

As it is the latter that has typically been assumed by those attempting to respond to Mises's calculation problem, the offered solutions are wide of the mark. As Mises notes in *Socialism* (1951 [1922], p. 139), the "problem of economic calculation is of economic dynamics: it is no problem of economic statics." Yet we find that the promoterless market process is, especially compared to the promoter-driven market process, largely static.

Most Austrian theorizing, as well as debates, both within the Austrian tradition and with non-Austrians, have taken place within or using the limited dynamics of the promoterless market process. While this work is undoubtedly important, it is based on overly simplified assumptions and grants too much ground to the equilibrium models of mainstream economic theory. It also risks confusing scholars about the nature of Misesian economics.

As has been presented here, a proper understanding of the promoter, as the driving force of the market process, suggests there remain a number of unanswered questions within Austrian economic theory. On the one hand, the promoter opens new areas for research, which were previously beyond theoretical reach. One example of this is the specifics of the promoter's role and impact on the economy and how it differs from those of the non-promoter. Another is the role of the promoter in economic growth, which adds a micro perspective to the systemic creation of universal prosperity.

On the other hand, proper understanding of the promoter-entrepreneur provides a sounder foundation for existent theories in Austrian economics. For example, while Austrians have uncovered the mechanics of economic growth as resultant from the increased rates of saving and the accumulation of capital, the role of the promoter in this process has not been sufficiently studied (for an exception, see Bylund, 2016). Similarly, Austrian capital theory (e.g. Hayek, 1941; Lachmann, 1978 [1956]; Cachanosky & Lewin, 2022) presents how the capital structure adjusts to changes in the interest rate, but the mechanics of such changes, especially the extension and contraction of the roundaboutness of production, are severely undertheorized (Bylund, 2015b). This argument also ties into the Austrian theory of the business cycle (Newman & Sieroń, 2022), which lacks a detailed theory of the micro-level processes and mechanisms behind the unsustainable boom and the inevitable bust. The promoter should play an important role here, as everywhere, and could contribute greatly to the sophistication of the Misesian theory.

NOTE

1.   This is a curious rejection of Schumpeter's work. In *The Theory of Economic Development*, Schumpeter's early and main work on entrepreneurship, he notes that "new combinations are, as a rule, embodied, as it were, in new firms which generally do not arise out of the old ones but start producing beside them" (Schumpeter, 1934 [1911], p. 66).

REFERENCES

Baumol, W. J. (1968). Entrepreneurship in Economic Theory. *American Economic Review, 58* (2: Papers and Proceedings of the Eightieth Annual Meeting of the American Economic Association), 64–71.

Böhm-Bawerk, E. von. (1959 [1889]). *Positive Theory of Capital*, Vol. 2. Grove City, PA: Libertarian Press.

Bylund, P. L. (2015a). Explaining Firm Emergence: Specialization, Transaction Costs, and the Integration Process. *Managerial and Decision Economics, 36*(4), 221–238.

Bylund, P. L. (2015b). The Realm of Entrepreneurship in the Market: Capital Theory, Production, and Change. In P. L. Bylund & D. Howden (Eds), *The Next Generation of Austrian Economics: Essays in Honor of Joseph T. Salerno*. Auburn, AL: Mises Institute.

Bylund, P. L. (2016). *The Problem of Production: A New Theory of the Firm*. New York: Routledge.

Bylund, P. L. (2018). The Management Problem of Socialism: Cost at the Expense of Value. In M. McCaffrey (Ed.), *The Economic Theory of Costs Foundations and New Directions*. New York: Routledge.

Bylund, P. L. (2020). Finding the Entrepreneur-Promoter: A Praxeological Inquiry. *Quarterly Journal of Austrian Economics, 23*(3–4), 355–389.

Bylund, P. L. (2021a). The Austrian Free Enterprise Ethic: A Mengerian Comment on Kirzner (2019). *Review of Austrian Economics, 34*(4), 495–501.

Bylund, P. L. (2021b). Understanding the Limits of Pure Theory in Economics: Knight and Mises. In *Research in the History of Economic Thought and Methodology* (pp. 3–18). Bingley: Emerald Publishing.

Bylund, P. L., Lingle, C., & Packard, M. D. (2022). Politicized Revisionism: Comment on Lopes. *Cambridge Journal of Economics, 46*(3), 609–612.

Bylund, P. L., & Packard, M. D. (2021). Subjective Value in Entrepreneurship. *Small Business Economics*. https://doi.org/10.1007/s11187-021-00451-2

Cachanosky, N., & Lewin, P. (2022). Capital Theory and the Theory of the Firm. In P. L. Bylund (Ed.), *A Modern Guide to Austrian Economics*. Cheltenham, UK and Northampton, MA, USA: Edward Elgar Publishing.

Camarinha Lopes, T. (2021). Technical or Political? The Socialist Economic Calculation Debate. *Cambridge Journal of Economics*, *45*(4), 787–810.

Durkheim, E. (1933 [1892]). *The Division of Labor in Society* (Trans. G. Simpson). New York: Free Press.

Foss, K., Foss, N. J., & Klein, P. G. (2007). Original and Derived Judgment: An Entrepreneurial Theory of Economic Organization. *Organization Studies*, *28*(12), 1893–1912.

Foss, N. J., & Klein, P. G. (2012). *Organizing Entrepreneurial Judgment: A New Approach to the Firm*. Cambridge: Cambridge University Press.

Foss, N. J., Klein, P. G., & Bjørnskov, C. (2019). The Context of Entrepreneurial Judgment: Organizations, Markets, and Institutions. *Journal of Management Studies*. https://doi.org/10.1111/joms.12428

Hayek, F. A. von. (1941). *The Pure Theory of Capital*. Chicago, IL: Chicago University Press.

Hayek, F. A. von. (1945). The Use of Knowledge in Society. *American Economic Review*. https://doi.org/10.2307/1809376

Kirzner, I. M. (1973). *Competition and Entrepreneurship*. Chicago, IL: University of Chicago Press.

Kirzner, I. M. (1978a). Economics and Error. In L. M. Spadaro (Ed.), *New Directions in Austrian Economics* (pp. 57–76). Kansas City, MO: Sheed Andrews and McMeel.

Kirzner, I. M. (1978b). Entrepreneurship, Entitlement, and Economic Justice. *Eastern Economic Journal*, *4*(1), 9–25.

Kirzner, I. M. (2019). The Ethics of Pure Entrepreneurship: An Austrian Economics Perspective. *Review of Austrian Economics*, *32*(2), 89–99.

Klein, P. G., & Bylund, P. L. (2014). The Place of Austrian Economics in Contemporary Entrepreneurship Research. *Review of Austrian Economics*, *27*(3), 259–279.

Klein, P. G., & McCaffrey, M. (2022). Entrepreneurial Judgment. In P. L. Bylund (Ed.), *A Modern Guide to Austrian Economics*. Cheltenham, UK and Northampton, MA, USA: Edward Elgar Publishing.

Knight, F. H. (1921). *Risk, Uncertainty, and Profit*. Boston, MA: Houghton Mifflin.

Lachmann, L. M. (1978 [1956]). *Capital and Its Structure* (2nd Edn). San Francisco, CA: Institute for Humane Studies.

Lange, O. (1936). On the Economic Theory of Socialism: Part 1. *Review of Economic Studies*, *4*(1), 53–71.

Lange, O. (1937). On the Economic Theory of Socialism: Part 2. *Review of Economic Studies*, *4*(2), 123.

Menger, C. (2007 [1871]). *Principles of Economics* (Trans. J. Dingwall & B. F. Hoselitz). Auburn, AL: Ludwig von Mises Institute.

Mises, L. von. (1935 [1920]). Economic Calculation in the Socialist Commonwealth. In F. A. von Hayek (Ed.), *Collectivist Economic Planning* (pp. 87–130). London: Routledge and Keegan Paul.

Mises, L. von. (1949). *Human Action*. New Haven, CT: Fox & Wilkes and Foundation for Economic Education.

Mises, L. von. (1951 [1922]). *Socialism: An Economic and Sociological Analysis* (Trans. J Kahane). New Haven, CT: Yale University Press.

Mises, L. von. (2008). Profit and Loss. In *Planning for Freedom: Let the Market System Work* (pp. 143–172). Indianapolis, IN: Liberty Fund.

Newman, J.R., & Sieroń, A. (2022). Austrian Business Cycle Theory: Current Research Trends and Future Directions. In P. L. Bylund (Ed.), *A Modern Guide to*

Austrian Economics. Cheltenham, UK and Northampton, MA, USA: Edward Elgar Publishing.

Salerno, J. T. (1993). Mises and Hayek Dehomogenized. *Review of Austrian Economics*, *6*(2), 113–146.

Sautet, F. E. (2022). Alertness: An Aristotelian Approach. In P. L. Bylund (Ed.), *A Modern Guide to Austrian Economics*. Cheltenham, UK and Northampton, MA, USA: Edward Elgar Publishing.

Schumpeter, J. A. (1934 [1911]). *The Theory of Economic Development: An Inquiry into Profits, Capital, Credit, Interest, and the Business Cycle*. Cambridge, MA: Harvard University Press.

Schumpeter, J. A. (1947). *Capitalism, Socialism, and Democracy* (2nd Edn). New York: Harper & Bros.

Smith, A. (1976 [1776]). *An Inquiry into the Nature and Causes of the Wealth of Nations*. Oxford: Oxford University Press.

Turowski, K., & Machaj, M. (2022). Economic Calculation and Socialism. In P. L. Bylund (Ed.), *A Modern Guide to Austrian Economics*. Cheltenham, UK and Northampton, MA, USA: Edward Elgar Publishing.

6. Spontaneous order

Karras J. Lambert and Peter J. Boettke

INTRODUCTION: RECENT LITERATURE ON SPONTANEOUS ORDER

The concept of spontaneous order has a rich intellectual pedigree that extends well beyond the ideas of the Austrian School and the discipline of economics narrowly conceived. Usually traced to the political economy writings of major figures of the Scottish Enlightenment such as Adam Ferguson and Adam Smith, spontaneous orders are considered to be social institutions "which are indeed the result of human action, but not the execution of any human design" (Ferguson, 1995 [1776], p. 119). Among members of the Austrian School of economics, the term is most commonly associated with the work of F. A. Hayek, who devoted considerable attention in his later writings to the spontaneous origins of a variety of social institutions including markets, law, language, and culture.[1]

While contemporary works in the broader Austrian tradition continue to make use of and reference the notion of spontaneous order, there has arguably been little meaningful theoretical development since the work of Hayek. A good number of the publications on the topic have simply been restatements of the same theme, providing commentary on the works of the Scottish classical liberals and, among the Austrians, Menger and Hayek. Barry (1982) offers a chronological intellectual history of the idea from the Spanish Scholastics through Scottish Enlightenment thinkers to Carl Menger. Hamowy (1987) focuses more narrowly on the contributions of Scottish Enlightenment thinkers. More recently, Horwitz (2001) examines commonalities in the writings of Adam Smith, Menger, and Hayek with respect to spontaneous order while Sieroń (2019) connects Menger's theory of social institutions with Hayek's writing on spontaneous order, Mises' contributions to monetary theory, and Bruno Leoni's work in legal theory. Boettke (1990) and Vaughn (1999) focus specifically on Hayek's work concerning spontaneous order while Sugden (1989) picks up on a Hayekian theme in arguing that social conventions can emerge as self-perpetuating spontaneous orders.

Austrian-influenced historical work has also demonstrated that social cooperation and a functioning legal framework can emerge and be sustained through the voluntary actions of individuals without creation or enforcement by a centralized state apparatus. While the legal positivist view maintains that law is the product of deliberate design, Benson (1989, p. 647) argues that the body of modern mercantile law, which enabled the proliferation of commercial transactions throughout Europe after the eleventh century, was initially and for some time "voluntarily produced, voluntarily adjudicated and voluntarily enforced." Leeson (2008), meanwhile, looks to precolonial Africa for two historical examples that suggest the effectiveness of spontaneous social orders in enabling coordination without command in the face of threats of violent theft and social heterogeneity.

Scholars working in disciplines outside economics have also incorporated the concept of spontaneous order into their work. Nozick (1974, pp. 18–19) acknowledges the Mengerian analysis of the origin of money and notes how "there is a certain lovely quality to explanations of this sort" on account of the fact that such explanations "minimize the use of notions constituting the phenomena to be explained." Nozick then lists a number of examples of what he terms "invisible-hand explanations" in scientific literature. These examples include Mises' work on economic calculation, the Austrian theory of the trade cycle, and Hayek's writing on knowledge.

Ullmann-Margalit (1978, p. 270) follows Nozick with respect to exploring "invisible-hand explanations" and defines "the invisible-hand process" as "the aggregate mechanism which takes as 'input' the dispersed actions of the participating individuals and produces as 'output' the overall social pattern." She also joins Hayek (1979, p. 155) in arguing that the traditional classification of phenomena as either natural or artificial is deficient in the realm of human action, as such a polarity ignores those phenomena which are the result of human action but not of human design. Ullmann-Margalit (1978, p. 289, emphasis in original) also argues "the case can be made that an invisible-hand explanation may be offered to account not just for the *generation* but also for the *degeneration*, or disintegration, of a well-structured social pattern." The potential for social disintegration that Ullmann-Margalit identifies was also acknowledged by Mises, which we touch upon later in this chapter.

Application of the concept of spontaneous order has even extended into the realm of art and media studies. Essays in Cantor and Cox (2009) bring economic reasoning to bear in analysis of classic literature, placing particular emphasis on spontaneous orders in language and culture. Cantor (2012) contrasts "top-down" and "bottom-up" models of order as depicted in pop culture, specifically films and television shows. Miller (2018) and Mildenberger (2018) offer case studies of spontaneous order and disorder respectively within the medium of video games.

There is also a strand in the "experimental economics" literature which investigates the self-generating properties of spontaneous orders within laboratory settings. Referencing Hayek's theoretical work on the economics of knowledge, Smith (1982) utilizes a double oral auction to test whether decentralized markets function well while considerably economizing on informational requirements. Smith (1982, p. 167) dubs as the "Hayek Hypothesis" the proposition that "strict privacy together with the trading rules of a market institution are sufficient to produce competitive market outcomes at or near 100% efficiency." Georgalos and Hey (2020, p. 912) "investigate whether Spontaneous Order can emerge, without it being imposed by the government" and "find strong evidence in favour of the emergence of Spontaneous Order, with communication being an important factor."

Some economists working in the tradition of the Austrian School tend to avoid using the term "spontaneous order" altogether. For instance, Rothbard (1995, p. 48) separates the "paradigm of Misesian praxeology" from "the fundamentally irrational 'evolved rules,' 'knowledge,' 'plans,' and 'spontaneous order' paradigm of Hayek." Salerno (1990, p. 26) similarly distinguishes the "social rationalism" of Ludwig von Mises from the "'spontaneous order' and social evolutionist positions staked out by F. A. Hayek." Salerno argues that Mises understood a market-based society characterized by private property and exchange to be a "rational" and not a "spontaneous" order on account of the fact that "all social interactions and relationships are thought out in advance and that, therefore, society originates and evolves as a product of reason and teleological striving."

Given the limited theoretical development of the concept of spontaneous order since Hayek's work and the just-mentioned analytical schism that has developed within the modern Austrian School, we believe an attempt toward clarification at the theoretical level might prove especially useful in establishing a foundation from which future work in the Austrian tradition may proceed. To that end, we highlight the common theoretical threads that connect the ideas of Menger to both Mises and Hayek in relation to viewing market institutions as products of purposive human action but not objects of design. Since this volume is concerned with the Austrian School of economics, we focus our attention on the study of markets and the institutions that promote market exchange and avoid commenting on the application of the idea of spontaneous order within scientific domains such as psychology and biology. After discussing the extent to which each of Menger, Mises, and Hayek can be said to work with the concept of spontaneous order, we conclude by suggesting where scholarly efforts might be productively directed in the near future for those interested in working on topics related to spontaneous orders and the market process.

CARL MENGER: THE EXACT UNDERSTANDING OF THE ORGANIC ORIGINS OF SOCIAL INSTITUTIONS

Menger on the Organic Origin of Money

From his first pathbreaking volume on economic theory, *Principles of Economics*, Carl Menger established that the explanations of all economic phenomena, particularly money prices, ultimately require reference to the subjective valuations of individuals with respect to concrete quantities of goods. When his first work was met with a lukewarm reception by his intended audience in the German academy, Menger turned the brunt of his attention to methodological issues and produced a second major volume a decade later, *Investigations into the Method of the Social Sciences*, which considers fundamental theoretical problems in economics and the social sciences more broadly. Most of Menger's explicit discussion concerning what we now refer to as "spontaneous order" appears in Book Three of this later work. There, Menger distinguishes between "organic" and "pragmatic" origins of social institutions.

Menger considers a social institution to have an "organic" origin when the institution results not from a singular or "common will" but from the actions undertaken according to private interests by myriad individuals in society. Since the theoretical explanation of institutions with "pragmatic" origin requires little intellectual difficulty, Menger considers it a principal task of social scientific investigation to theoretically explain those institutions that do not owe their origins to the design of a single intelligence. For Menger (1981, p. 146), "a noteworthy, perhaps the most noteworthy, problem of the social sciences" concerns "How can it be that institutions which serve the common welfare and are extremely significant for its development come into being without a common will directed toward establishing them?" To answer this question, it is not enough to merely state that some social phenomena arose absent a single directing will. Instead, the mechanism and causal sequence must be worked out in "exact" fashion by building up from the purposive actions of individuals.

Although Menger lists a number of institutions which can be said to have emerged in "organic" fashion, his explanation of the origin of money is prominently featured in each of his major works, including both of the aforementioned volumes as well as his 1892 journal article "On the Origins of Money." Logically working backwards from the existence of the institution of money to the purposive actions of individuals seeking to satisfy their wants, Menger explains the transition from direct exchange to indirect exchange by noting the differing marketability across goods. Those who first grasp the benefits of indirect exchange will trade for goods which do not provide satisfaction in consumption directly but can be more readily exchanged for what they actually wish to acquire. Each person who recognizes this and exchanges for goods believed to be especially marketable drives demand for these media of exchange further until eventually one or a very small number of commodities remain and become generally accepted mediums of exchange, at which point they serve as "money" within the area. According to Menger (2007 [1976], p. 260, emphasis in original), "as each economizing individual becomes increasingly more aware of his economic interest, he is led by this *interest, without any agreement, without legislative compulsion, and even without regard to the public interest,* to give his commodities in exchange for other, more saleable, commodities."

Despite such a strong affirmation in favor of the "organic" origin of money, Menger does not deny that "pragmatic" modification is possible once the institution of money emerges. For instance, standardized metallic coinage can serve to facilitate exchanges even better than when commodity money is left in the form of bullion. Nevertheless, Menger demonstrates that money traces its "organic" origin to the voluntary actions of all individuals in society and cannot first be imposed by the command of some king or director. As Menger (1981, p. 155, emphasis in original) recognizes, "the origin of money can truly be brought to our full understanding only by our learning to understand the *social* institution discussed here as the unintended result, as the unplanned outcome of specifically *individual* efforts of members of a society."

This is not to say, of course, that intentionality is not present at each step in the cumulative process by which a common medium of exchange emerges from the self-interested actions of individuals. Nevertheless, it can be said that no individual's intention corresponds exactly with the eventual function of the institution that forms. In the case of money, no particular individual needs to imagine nor intend that engaging in acts of indirect exchange will result in the widespread use of a standardized commodity on one side of every exchange which in turn makes economic calculation possible. At the beginning of the process by which a common medium of exchange emerges, an individual needs to merely strive to acquire a more marketable good for one believed to be less marketable in order to more closely attain one's personal ends. To drive the adoption of a common medium of exchange or to facilitate economic calculation need not be the intention of any particular individual but results nevertheless from the composite of the voluntary actions of all. In this sense, Menger (1981, p. 133, emphasis in original) identifies money as a social phenomenon which is "the unintended result of individual human efforts (pursuing *individual interests*) without a *common will* directed toward their establishment."

One of Menger's (2007 [1976], p. 49) stated aims in his first work was that of "establishing a price theory based upon reality and placing all price phenomena (including interest, wages, ground rent, etc.) together under one unified point of view." It is noteworthy, then, that he later conceived "the prices of goods, interest rates, ground rents, wages, and a thousand other phenomena of social life in general and of economy in particular" to be "to no small extent the unintended result of social development" (Menger, 1981, p. 147). Price formation does not occur according to a "common will" but falls within ranges according to the respective valuations of the individuals engaging in market exchange. No central administration needs to determine and enforce prices at which goods must be exchanged. In fact, such comprehensive intervention into the price structure of the market would prove disastrous, as the abolition of a price structure that emerges from voluntary exchanges in goods of all orders would render impossible meaningful economic calculation through profit and loss accounting. Menger (1981, p. 177) foreshadowed the work of his followers when declaring the "partially superficial pragmatism" of those seeking to "create something new in the realm of political institutions" to be "a pragmatism that contrary to the intention of its representatives inexorably leads to socialism."

Menger on the Organic Origins of Law

Law is another notable social institution that Menger traces back to "organic" origins through "exact" theoretical understanding. Menger identifies common law as preceding the formation of communities and states, though also open to "pragmatic" modification once civilization has progressed to a certain stage. Menger (1981, p. 225) writes, "There is scarcely need to remark that law usually comes into being and develops in an advanced community by way of legislation, or by way of an express agreement of the members of society directed toward establishing it, that is, predominantly in a pragmatic manner." However, "It was otherwise at the first beginnings of civilization, in epochs when the intercourse of people inhabiting a definite territory was slight, when their integration was not strong, when the awareness of integration was, furthermore, imperfect." In these early times, "we cannot yet properly speak of law as the expression of the organized *total will* of a nation" and therefore "the genesis of law is not pragmatic."

Since in primitive conditions "each individual, even if not directly harmed, feels threatened most seriously in *his* interests by acts of violence," individuals gradually come to imagine the benefits that would result from "the limitation of individual despotism." This realization, like the realization that indirect exchange provides an effective solution to the limitations of direct exchange, was not "thought of as an organized unit." Instead, it arose "*in the minds of individual members of the population* with the increasing awareness of *their interest, the individuals' interest*." After law is established first in thought and then serves as a binding force for a national community, it is passed down according to tradition and custom.

Despite this "organic" origin of law, Menger also recognizes that strong men who assume positions of power in a society may impose "laws" of their own. Menger distinguishes these top-down legislative impositions from the laws that previously arose from the natural interplay of self-interested individuals, referring to the former instead as "statutes." Since rulers naturally wish for their own imposed statutes to be recognized and obeyed as territorial laws, Menger recognizes that over time there tends to be a blurring between those laws of human society that arose organically and permitted societal development from those that were imposed by particularly powerful individuals.

It is important to note that Menger does not consider "exact research" into the "organic" origins of social institutions to be the sole interest of economists or sociologists. "For the understanding of social phenomena in their entirety," Menger (1981, p. 135) writes, "the *pragmatic* interpretation is, in any case, just as indispensable as the 'organic.'" As mentioned above in regard to the coining of commodity money, Menger does not regard social institutions that arose without full intentional design to necessarily be immune to improvement through intentional modification. With respect to law, Menger considers the "assertion" that "common law ... benefits the [common good] nonetheless to a higher degree than a corresponding positive legislation could" to be "erroneous in every conceivable respect," noting that "common law has also proved harmful to the common good often enough, and on the contrary, legislation has just as often changed common law in a way benefiting the common good." Thus, Menger took a more practical view of the function of law and acknowledged that human intentionality could create or modify laws otherwise inherited from ancestors for the purpose of furthering social cooperation.

Carl Menger utilized and elaborated the theoretical analysis of those social institutions which are not the intended result of any singular will but arise from the self-interested actions of all those living within a society. In doing so, he set a clear course for future economists of the Austrian School to follow in examining the "organic" origins of many social institutions such as money and law, which are vital for human social cooperation. By rooting his analysis on the actions of individuals and tracing out the consequences to society at large, he pioneered the compositive method and provided, in the words of Mises (1998 [1949], p. 402), both "an irrefutable praxeological theory of the origin of money" and "the elucidation of fundamental principles of praxeology and its methods of research."

LUDWIG VON MISES: RATIONALIZING SPONTANEOUS ORDERS

Mises on Economic Calculation and Will

While never a direct student of Menger, Mises met the Austrian School founder privately on a number of occasions and participated in the seminar of Eugen von Böhm-Bawerk, who was one of Menger's principal followers. Furthermore, Mises (2009, p. 25) writes that it was only upon reading Menger's *Principles of Economics* that he became an economist. Building from Menger's theoretical investigations concerning the origin of money and the transition from direct to indirect exchange, Mises' articulation and emphasis of the fundamental importance of economic calculation is arguably the connecting thread throughout his work and central to his development of catallactic theory.

For his part, Mises endorses Menger's account of the origin of money and approach to the explanation of social phenomena more generally. In opposition to explanations that assume the imposition of a singular design and favorably quoting Menger's description of social institutions with organic origin, Mises (1998 [1949], p. 404) writes:

> It is necessary to comprehend that one does not contribute anything to the scientific conception of human action and social phenomena if one declares that the state or a charismatic leader or an inspiration which descended upon all the people have created them. Neither do such statements refute the teachings of a theory showing how such phenomena can be acknowledged as "the unintentional outcome, the resultant not deliberately designed and aimed at by specifically individual endeavors of the members of a society."

Mises moved beyond Menger's theory of price formation in the sense that he exhaustively described the differences between an economy characterized by private ownership and exchange in goods of all orders and one wherein private ownership and exchange in higher-order goods is abolished.[2] It is sufficient for the purposes of this chapter to summarize Mises' argument concerning the impossibility of economic calculation under socialism in the following way.

The attempted direction of economic activity according to that of a single plan would preclude the possibility of economizing altogether. Without access to the exhaustive web of prices generated from the exchange of goods of all orders for money, a central planner cannot compare the costs and proceeds of utilizing various means for the achievement of certain ends. Profit and loss calculation is rendered impossible, as the planner would lack a common extensive magnitude by which to compare physically heterogeneous inputs and outputs. It is impossible for a single mind to generate a price structure, which must be formed out of the estimations and actions of all who voluntarily take part in the division of labor in order to capture true resource costs.

Here Menger's repeated references to a "common will" in contrasting the "pragmatic" interpretations of social phenomena with the "organic" becomes significant. After all, Mises (1998 [1949], p. 691, emphasis in original) states "the essential mark of socialism is that *one will* alone acts." If we understand the market as "a process, actuated by the interplay of the actions of the various individuals cooperating under the division of labor," we might conceive the social order generated as a consequence as one produced by *many wills acting* (Mises, 1998 [1949], p. 259).

The profits and loss system undergirds the selective process of the market, according to which the individuals partaking in the division of labor are naturally sorted into lines of production where they are deemed best able to transform available means into the most desired ends demanded by consumers. The substitution of a singular will for the myriad individual wills underlying the voluntary actions of the market process thereby also substitutes the ends of the planner for all of the individual ends that are pursued concurrently in market exchange. While the institutions of the market order may result from the actions of individuals without relying on any central design, it is also true that the continued adherence to these same institutions safeguard social cooperation and all of the benefits that result. Menger recognized that the zeal of pragmatic-minded institutional reformers leads inexorably to socialism. Mises, in turn, recognized that the realization of socialism must eliminate the very institutions that have made possible the advanced degree of civilization we enjoy.

Mises on Reason and the Law of Association

Mises makes no apologies for his support of rationalism. According to Mises (2003 [1960], p. 143), "science belongs completely to the domain of rationality. There can no more be a science of the irrational than there can be irrational science. The irrational lies outside the domain of human reasoning and science." In the struggle for the attainment of a higher standard of living, "man has only one tool to fight error: reason" (Mises 1998 [1949], p. 187).

A major theme Mises returns to throughout *Human Action* is the importance for individuals who enjoy the benefits derived from social cooperation to intellectually grasp the increased productivity possible under the division of labor. Unlike a number of classical liberals before him, Mises recognizes that the social and intellectual progress of mankind is by no means guaranteed. The adoption of ideologies antagonistic to the market order produce actions inimical to the realization of the benefits of association through the nexus of the division of labor and indirect exchange. "Man is free in the sense that he must daily choose anew between policies that lead to success and those that lead to disaster, social disintegration, and barbarism" (Mises 1998 [1949], p. 193). Mises recognizes reason to be the only means by which fallacies may be refuted and the inevitable results of the abolition or impairment of market institutions may be revealed and diverted. "The main objective of praxeology and economics is to substitute consistent correct ideologies for the contradictory tenets of popular eclecticism," Mises (1998 [1949], p. 185) writes. "There is no other means of preventing social disintegration and of safeguarding the steady improvement of human conditions than those provided by reason."

Mises does not use the phrase "spontaneous order" in his writings and he even seems to take a stand directly opposed to the idea that human society might be understood as a spontaneous order when he writes "any given social order was thought out and designed before it could be realized" (Mises 1998 [1949], p. 188). He soon after clarifies, however, that by "social order" he is referring to "the actions of individuals with regard to their fellow men and of already formed groups of individuals with regard to other groups," not "the connecting of individual actions into an integrated system of social organization." Just as Menger's theoretical explanation of the origin of money relies upon individuals grasping the benefits of indirect exchange before an exchange takes place, Mises argues that individuals must likewise grasp the benefits of peaceful cooperation before it can be practiced.

While Mises (1998 [1949], p. 143) views society as "the outcome of conscious and purposeful behavior," he also recognizes "this does not mean that individuals have concluded contracts by virtue of which they have founded human society." Just as money was voluntarily adopted step by step rather than imposed by a king, Mises considers society, "the total complex of the mutual relations created by such concerted actions," to be the result of the voluntary actions of individuals who cooperate with each other in order to better attain their own ends. "It is not necessary that the individuals concerned become aware of the fact that such mutuality results in the establishment of social bonds and in the emergence of a social system" since "the individual does not plan and execute actions intended to construct society. His conduct and the corresponding conduct of others generate social bodies" (Mises, 1998 [1949], p. 188). It is in this sense that we may understand "the order that emerges under a system of division of labor and private property was not the result of anyone's design or intention, but was the composite of all the separate striving of individuals to realize their purposes and plans" (Boettke, 1990, p. 71).

A key concept that underscores Mises' conception of the social order is the law of association, which teaches that "the division of labor brings advantage to all who take part in it" (Mises, 1998 [1949], p. 159). Mises recognizes that the greater productive powers of the division of labor permits the development of human social bonds in the first place. "If and as far as labor under the division of labor is more productive than isolated labor, and if and as far as man is able to realize this fact, human action itself tends toward cooperation and association" (Mises, 1998 [1949], p. 160). Inversely, "in a hypothetical world in which the division of labor would not increase productivity, there would not be any society. There would not be any sentiments of benevolence and good will" (Mises, 1998 [1949], p. 144).

For Mises, it is no virtue to be ignorant of the benefits from cooperation. Even if he admits that "it is permissible to contend that the immense majority of our contemporaries are mentally and intellectually not adjusted to life in the market society although they themselves and their fathers have unwittingly created this society by their actions," Mises (1998 [1949], p. 316) considers "this maladjustment [to consist] in nothing else than in the failure to recognize erroneous doctrines as such." Only reason can expose the fallacies in doctrines that deny the mutual advantages to be derived from participation in the division of labor. For Mises, this is the task of the economist and the cause to which he dedicated his life's work.

F. A. HAYEK: THE SPONTANEOUS ORDER APPROACH TO UNDERSTANDING HUMAN SOCIETY

Hayek on Spontaneous Orders

F. A. Hayek is undoubtedly the Austrian School economist most commonly associated with the idea of spontaneous order. According to Smith (2015, p. 224), "So pervasive is the idea of spontaneous order in Hayek's work, and so profitably did he explore its implications, that it is no exaggeration to say that it forms the spine of his life's work." While this common thread can arguably be identified throughout nearly all of Hayek's work,[3] it is most pronounced in Hayek's later writings, especially from *The Constitution of Liberty* onwards.

Hayek (1967, p. 92) defines a spontaneous order as "a sort of order over the particular manifestation of which we have little control, because the rules which determine it determine only its abstract character, while the detail depends the particular circumstances known only to its individual members." Spontaneous orders, despite having a recognizable *function*, have no singular *purpose*, but instead "can be used for, and will assist in the pursuit of, a great many different, divergent, and even conflicting individual purposes. Thus the order of the market, in particular, rests not on common purposes but on reciprocity" (Hayek, 1967, p. 163).

Hayek favors using the term "catallaxy" to describe the market economy since there is not a single hierarchy of ends being served by the rules of the order. In this respect, the connection is evident between Hayek's conception of spontaneous order and his interest in the socialist calculation debate:

> The chief point about the catallaxy is that, as a spontaneous order, its orderliness does *not* rest on its orientation on a single hierarchy of ends, and that, therefore, it will *not* secure that for it as a whole the more important comes before the less important. This is the chief cause of its condemnation by its opponents, and it could be said that most of the socialist demands amount to nothing less than that the catallaxy should be turned into an economy proper (i.e., the purposeless spontaneous order into a purpose-oriented organization) in order to assure that the more important be never sacrificed to the less important. (Hayek, 1967, p. 164)

Hayek adopted a distinction that Mises (1951, pp. 295–297) previously touched upon between an "organism" and an "organization." Where an "organization" is operated by a single will according to a single hierarchy of ends, an "organism" is the result of multiple wills interacting in pursuit of their own individual ends. Mises identifies coercion, or more specifically the absence thereof, as a key aspect in the operation of the division of labor. Mises (1951, p. 297) writes:

> Organizations are possible only as long as they are not directed against the organic or do it any injury. All attempts to coerce the living will of human beings into the service of something they do not want must fail. An organization cannot flourish unless it is founded on the will of those organized and serves their purposes.

Since the choice is not between a plan and no plan but the single plan devised by one will versus the plans of many individuals, Hayek (1948, p. 79) raises the question of "who is to do the planning." Hayek answers in support of the multitude of individuals comprising a society, as they, unlike central planners, are able to utilize knowledge of time and place to solve "the economic problem of society," which Hayek sees as "a problem of how to secure the best use of resources known to any of the members of society, for ends whose relative importance only these individuals know" (Hayek, 1948, p. 78).

Preoccupation with this problem led Hayek (1948, pp. 10–11) to contrast the social contract or "design" theories of social institutions with the "true" form of individualism which appreciates spontaneous processes and institutions not under the design of a single mind. "While design theories necessarily lead to the conclusion that social processes can be made to serve human ends only if they are subjected to the control of individual human reason, and thus lead directly to socialism," Hayek writes, "true individualism believes on the contrary that, if left free, men will often achieve more than individual human reason could design or foresee." We might say then that a spontaneous order is truly a *voluntary* order. On this theme, Collins (2021, p. 3) remarks that for Hayek, "rather than being the result of deliberate design, social order reflected the organic and voluntary associations of many people over time seeking to satisfy their private preferences."

Like Menger, Hayek is careful not to impugn hierarchical organization as such, but cautions against the heedless extension of organizational logic across all social relations. Mises' argument concerning the impossibility of economic calculation under socialism makes clear that an organization not embedded within a market order cannot *economize* in the proper sense of the word and therefore a world-encompassing socialist state would bring forth the disintegration of the social division of labor. Organizations based upon coercion will not permit the same degree of utilization of comparative costs and adjustments to changing conditions as would be possible in a strictly voluntary order. As Hayek (1960, p. 37) writes:

> The argument for liberty is not an argument against organization, which is one of the most powerful means that human reason can employ, but an argument against all exclusive, privileged, monopolistic organization, against the use of coercion to prevent others from trying to do better ... Organization is therefore likely to be beneficial and effective so long as it is voluntary and is imbedded in a free sphere and will either have to adjust itself to circumstances not taken into account in its conception or fail. To turn the whole of society into a single organization built and directed according to a single plan would be to extinguish the very forces that shaped the individual human minds that planned it.

Here, Hayek echoes Mises' characterization of a socialist system as an organization under which one will alone act. Where an entrepreneur can create a firm on the basis of voluntary employment and purchase contracts on the market according to the conditions of specialization under the division of labor, the substitution of a single plan for the plans of all individuals in their private roles as entrepreneurs eradicates the very mechanism by which the costs of resources can be ascertained and meaningfully compared. Absent the market process, which involves the free exchange of goods according to voluntarily decided money prices, the mental operation of cost accounting made possible by the formation of the price structure is rendered impossible.

Hayek, like Mises and Menger before him, appreciates the self-ordering nature of individual actions within the frame of the market order and recognizes that a single mind cannot replicate the function of a social process which was never designed in the first place but which emerged from the private actions of individuals pursuing their own plans.

Hayek on Rationality and Rules

In his later works, Hayek often pits the British empiricism of David Hume against the French rationalism of René Descartes. Hayek identifies in the former an appreciation for spontaneity and the absence of coercion in human affairs while he ascribes to the latter the belief that all social institutions which should be allowed to persist must be deliberately designed according to specific purposes in advance of their emergence. Often describing this French tradition as "constructivist" or "Cartesian" rationalism, Hayek (1967, p. 85) considers, "rationalism in this sense [to be] the doctrine which assumes that all institutions which benefit humanity have in the past and ought in the future to be invented in clear awareness of the desirable effects that they produce." Later, Hayek (1978, p. 3) expresses "the basic conception of this [rationalistic] constructivism" as the idea that "since man himself created the institutions of society and civilization, he must be able to alter them at will so as to satisfy his desires or wishes."

Hayek thus positions Cartesian rationalism to be the distaste of social orders which can be said to have emerged spontaneously from the purposive actions of individuals but not according to any central design. Against this "rationalistic pseudo-individualism which also leads to practical collectivism," Hayek (1948, pp. 6–7) reaffirms the Mengerian approach to studying social phenomena, namely "by tracing the combined effects of individual actions, we discover that many of the institutions on which human achievements rest have arisen and are functioning without a designing and directing mind."

Much of Hayek's later work can be read as an effort to identify the institutional arrangement necessary to safeguard the operation of the market process by which individuals pursue peaceful social cooperation. Like Menger, Hayek does not consider prevailing legal institutions to be perfect and unable to be improved upon. According to Hayek (1948, pp. 134–135), "there is not reason to assume that the historically given legal institutions are necessarily the most 'natural' in any sense." He notes, for example, how "the recognition of the principle of private property does not by any means imply that the particular delimitation of the contents of this right as determined by the existing laws are the most appropriate." He elsewhere offers the example of the extension of property rights into the realm of intellectual property, which to Hayek demonstrates a wrong turn in the "slavish application of the concept of property as it has been developed for material things" (Hayek, 1948, p. 114).

Although Hayek does not oppose any modification to prevailing social institutions on principle, he does oppose piecemeal intervention into the particular outcomes of a spontaneous order. Any changes must instead come at the level of rules, which in turn must be general and abstract so as to permit each person to peacefully pursue their own plans. Hayek (1973) draws a distinction between *nomos*, or ends-independent rules, and *thesis*, or ends-oriented rules. As the terms suggest, ends-independent rules do not aim for the realization of particular ends but seek to create a framework in which the actions of individuals may achieve better coordination. Ends-oriented rules, meanwhile, seek to intervene in such ways to achieve particular results. For Hayek (1948, p. 115), "the precise content of the permanent legal framework, the rules of civil law, are of the greatest importance for the way in which a competitive market will operate." If the goal is to achieve a state of social harmony and human flourishing, the institutions of the market order that Mises identified as necessary for economic calculation, namely sound money and private ownership in goods of both lower and higher orders, must be secured from arbitrary interference. Hayek (1948, p. 87) recognizes the price system to be such a "marvel" that he believes "if it were the result of deliberate human design ... this mechanism would have been acclaimed as one of the greatest triumphs of the human mind." Hayek, in the tradition of Menger, sought to draw appreciation for the important social phenomena underpinning civil society which nevertheless, in their totality, did not rely on any deliberate human design. Along with Mises, Hayek also feared that the proliferation of ideologies opposed to the market system would not find it difficult "to destroy the spontaneous formations which are the indispensable bases of a free civilization" (Hayek, 1948, p. 107).

SPONTANEOUS ORDER RESEARCH: LOOKING AHEAD

Carl Menger established the foundations of methodological individualism and the compositive method from which successive generations of followers in the Austrian tradition of economics have continued to develop economic and social theory, particularly Ludwig von Mises and F. A. Hayek. Each of these men committed their considerable productive energies to battling interventionist ideologies which if followed consistently would spell doom for the institutions required to support social cooperation under the division of labor. They strove not only to unmask the fallacies of detractors of the market system but each of them also put forward a positive vision of a free and prosperous social order characterized by peace and social bonds.

Since the concept of spontaneous order is simple and well established, future theoretical breakthroughs seem unlikely. More historical investigations into the emergence of market institutions outside top-down control would be welcome and history of thought treatments can be useful for keeping the ideas of past scholars alive in modern literature, but we believe that the most productive use of scholarly energy might be in taking up the mantle of the Austrian forefathers whose works we describe in this chapter and applying their ideas to modern arguments against market institutions. It is vital to continually attempt to communicate the teachings of economics such that others may realize the marvel of the pricing process, which no single individual designed yet nevertheless benefits all who take part in specialization and exchange under the division of labor. At the same time, the spread of incorrect and illogical ideologies must be refuted anew by returning to and reinvigorating the ideas of Menger, Mises, and Hayek based on the conditions and challenges of our time.

The stakes are high, as the failure to appreciate the workings of the market system and the benefits all enjoy by virtue of its operation may result in the disintegration of social cooperation and the escalation of both domestic and international discord. To repeat the words Mises (1998 [1949], p. 881) found suitable to close his *magnum opus*:

> The body of economic knowledge is an essential element in the structure of human civilization; it is the foundation upon which modern industrialism and all the moral, intellectual, technological, and therapeutical achievements of the last centuries have been built. It rests with men whether they will make the proper use of the rich treasure with which this knowledge provides them or whether they will leave it unused. But if they fail to take the best advantage of it and disregard its teachings and warnings, they will not annul economics; they will stamp out society and the human race.

NOTES

1.   While Michael Polanyi is sometimes credited for coining the term "spontaneous order," Wilhelm Röpke (1963 [1937], p. 4) had earlier used the exact phrase to describe the market economy. See D'Amico (2015, p. 117) and the references therein.
2.   See Mises (1935, 1951, pp. 111–150, 1998 [1949], pp. 201–232, 694–711) for his major contributions on the topic of the impossibility of economic calculation under socialism.
3.   See Boettke (1990) for a defense of this position.

REFERENCES

Barry, N. (1982) "The Tradition of Spontaneous Order," *Literature of Liberty*, 5(2), pp. 7–58.

Benson, B. L. (1989) "The Spontaneous Evolution of Commercial Law," *Southern Economic Journal*, 55(3), pp. 644–661.

Boettke, P. J. (1990) "The Theory of Spontaneous Order and Cultural Evolution in the Social Theory of F.A. Hayek," *Cultural Dynamics*, 3(1), pp. 61–83.

Cantor, P. A. (2012) *The Invisible Hand in Popular Culture: Liberty vs. Authority in American Film and TV*. Lexington, KY: University Press of Kentucky.

Cantor, P. A. & Cox, S. (eds.) (2009) *Literature and the Economics of Liberty: Spontaneous Order in Culture*. Auburn, AL: Ludwig von Mises Institute.

Collins, G. M. (2021) "Spontaneous Order and Civilization: Burke and Hayek on Markets, Contracts and Social Order," *Philosophy and Social Criticism*, 20(10), pp. 1–30.

D'Amico, D. (2015) "Spontaneous Order," in Coyne, C. J. & Boettke, P. (eds.) *The Oxford Handbook of Austrian Economics*. Oxford: Oxford University Press, pp. 114–142.

Ferguson, A. (1995 [1776]) *An Essay on the History of Civil Society*. Cambridge: Cambridge University Press.

Georgalos, K. & Hey, J. (2020) "Testing for the Emergence of Spontaneous Order," *Experimental Economics*, 23(3), pp. 912–932.

Hamowy, R. (1987) *The Scottish Enlightenment and the Theory of Spontaneous Orders*. Carbondale, IL: Southern Illinois University Press.

Hayek, F. A. von (1948) *Individualism and Economic Order*. Chicago, IL: University of Chicago Press.

Hayek, F. A. von (1960) *The Constitution of Liberty*. Chicago, IL: University of Chicago Press.

Hayek, F. A. von (1967) *Studies in Philosophy, Politics, and Economics*. Chicago, IL: University of Chicago Press.

Hayek, F. A. von (1973) *Law, Legislation and Liberty, Volume 1: Rules and Order*. Chicago, IL: University of Chicago Press.

Hayek, F. A. von (1978) *New Studies in Philosophy, Politics, Economics and the History of Ideas*. Chicago, IL: University of Chicago Press.

Hayek, F. A. von (1979) *Law, Legislation and Liberty, Volume 3: The Political Order of a Free People*. Chicago, IL: University of Chicago Press.

Horwitz, S. G. (2001) "From Smith to Menger to Hayek: Liberalism in the Spontaneous-Order Tradition," *Independent Review*, 6(1), pp. 81–97.

Leeson, P. T. (2008) "Coordination without Command: Stretching the Scope of Spontaneous Order," *Public Choice*, 135(1–2), pp. 67–78.

Menger, C. (1981) *Investigations into the Method of the Social Sciences with Special Reference to Economics*. New York: New York University Press.

Menger, C. (2007 [1976]) *Principles of Economics*. Ed. and trans. Dingwall, J. & Hoselitz, B. F. Auburn, AL: Ludwig von Mises Institute.

Menger, C. (2009) *On the Origins of Money*. Auburn, AL: Ludwig von Mises Institute.

Mildenberger, C. D. (2018) "Spontaneous Disorder: Conflict-Kindling Institutions in Virtual Worlds," *Journal of Institutional Economics*, 14(5), pp. 787–809.

Miller, W. G. (2018) "The Role of Spontaneous Order in Video Games: A Case Study of Destiny," *Cosmos + Taxis*, 5(3–4), pp. 63–72.

Mises, L. von (1935) "Economic Calculation in the Socialist Commonwealth," in Hayek, F. A. von (ed.) *Collectivist Economic Planning*. London: Routledge and Keegan Paul, pp. 87–130.

Mises, L. von (1951) *Socialism: An Economic and Sociological Analysis*. New Haven, CT: Yale University Press.

Mises, L. von (1998 [1949]) *Human Action: The Scholar's Edition*. Auburn, AL: Ludwig von Mises Institute.

Mises, L. von (2003 [1960]) *Epistemological Problems of Economics*. 3rd Ed. Auburn, AL: Ludwig von Mises Institute.

Mises, L. von (2009) *Memoirs*. Auburn, AL: Ludwig von Mises Institute.

Nozick, R. (1974) *Anarchy, State, and Utopia*. Oxford: Blackwell.

Röpke, W. (1963 [1937]) *Economics of the Free Society*. Chicago, IL: Henry Regnery Company.

Rothbard, M. N. (1995) "The Present State of Austrian Economics," *Journal des Economists et des Etudes Humaines*, 6(1), pp. 43–89.

Salerno, J. T. (1990) "Ludwig von Mises as Social Rationalist," *Review of Austrian Economics*, 4, pp. 26–54.

Sieroń, A. (2019) "Legacy of Menger's Theory of Social Institutions," *Studies in Logic, Grammar and Rhetoric*, 57(1), pp. 145–160.

Smith, C. (2015) "Hayek and spontaneous order," in Garrison, R. W. & Barry, N. (eds.) *Elgar Companion to Hayekian Economics*. Cheltenham, UK and Northampton, MA, USA: Edward Elgar Publishing, pp. 224–245.

Smith, V. L. (1982) "Markets as Economizers of Information: Experimental Examination of the 'Hayek Hypothesis,'" *Economic Inquiry*, 20(2), pp. 165–179.

Sugden, R. (1989) "Spontaneous Order," *Journal of Economic Perspectives*, 3(4), pp. 85–97.

Ullmann-Margalit, E. (1978) "Invisible-Hand Explanations," *Synthese*, 39(2), pp. 263–291.

Vaughn, K. I. (1999) "Hayek's Implicit Economics: Rules and the Problem of Order," *Review of Austrian Economics*, 11, pp. 129–144.

7. The social and moral aspects of markets

Ginny Seung Choi and Virgil Henry Storr

INTRODUCTION

Neoclassical economics appears to operate on curious notions of people and markets. The quintessential economic agent within neoclassical economics, *homo economicus*, is an individual who possesses perfect information and knowledge of all the environments in which she occupies and functions. She always makes decisions that provide her with the greatest benefit or satisfaction among the array of choices available to her. Because she weighs her choices purely in terms of profit or utility, she never hesitates to abandon her trading partners, suppliers, service providers, consumers, goods and services whenever a more profitable or desirable alternative appears, even if they benefit her only by a trivial amount. Furthermore, she has no attachments to anyone, anything or any place, and does not get persuaded nor hurt by other agents' actions and betrayals. In effect, *homo economicus* is an emotionless, compassionless, uncompromising, friendless and calculating being, and the market is a space populated with agents who are identical to her.

Furthermore, according to scholars of the neoclassical economic tradition, the market functions merely as a piece of machinery, a mechanism, or a computer program that automatically executes logged commands based on the initial conditions and endowments of its input elements. In addition, they tend to gloss over the process through which market exchanges that constitute the market equilibrium or steady state transpire (perhaps given their strong focus on outcomes and results). In fact, every proper market has a game theoretic or mathematical representation in neoclassical economics and *homo economicus* has a fully formulated strategy for each market.

Contrary to our neoclassical counterparts, we in the Austrian economic tradition view people as human beings. We do not perceive people as automatons; the agent in Austrian economics is not an isolated individual without any socially meaningful relationship, roaming about in institution-less deserts. Nor, for that matter, do Austrians perceive people as powerless against their own circumstances, unavoidably plagued by their biases, whose decisions and fates are instantaneously and fully determined by their environments. Instead, we understand people as complex, fallible, emotive, social beings whose actions and motivations we cannot hope to comprehend without appreciating the political, economic, social and historical contexts in which they are embedded. We also recognize the importance of subjectivity, i.e. the interpretations and meanings people attach to their worlds. Whether or not a person's interpretation of a situation is objectively the accurate one, she formulates her plan of action and the tone of her approach based on what she believes has transpired. Hence, we believe that individual economic action is driven by the knowledge and information (which is likely imperfect and incomplete, and can be mistaken) each person possesses in the moment and her judgments about her own circumstances, her expectations about the future and her perceived consequences of their intended actions (which, again, is likely imperfect and incomplete, and can be mistaken). We believe that every human action, even misguided ones, is purposeful and not reflexive nor impulsive. We view and study economic phenomena as social ramifications of individual choice, while our counterparts in neoclassical economics and other schools of thought often view them to be an aggregate or societal phenomena and analyze them as equilibria.

In this chapter, we argue that the Austrian theory of the market as a process and as the order that results from that process provides a useful framework to explore the moral and social aspects of markets. We argue that studying social interactions and relationships, and the rules of engagement that govern these interactions and relationships in the market setting, is difficult, if not impossible, within a framework that perceives the market as a series of coded commands and views human beings as atoms which mechanically and automatically execute their own sequence of encrypted instructions. In order to explore the sociality and morality of markets, we must rely on a framework that models human beings as human beings and also permits (in its theories) the possibility of meaningful and thriving social relationships developing in various institutional settings. Given our appreciation for meaning, process and human action, the Austrian framework for understanding human behavior in economic settings uniquely equips us with the tools to rigorously examine the sociality and morality of markets.

The remainder of the chapter is structured as follows. We begin with an overview of Austrian economic literature on the market order, with a particular focus on Mises and Hayek. We then examine how a richer conception of human beings in Austrian economics informs people's social interactions in market spaces. Building on the previous section, we explain that market interactions are not anonymous and people can and do make genuine personal connections in the market. The following sections argue that well-functioning markets depend on market participants following rules of just conduct and that it is through this mechanism that markets promote morality. We then offer concluding remarks.

THE MARKET PROCESS, THE MARKET ORDER

For Austrian economists, "[t]he market is not a place, a thing, or a collective entity" (Mises, 2007 [1949], p. 257). Rather, it is a process, animated by the interplay of actions of the individuals in the market who compete and cooperate under the division of labor. It is ever changing, as these individuals continuously adjust their plans in their attempts to coordinate their activities with one another (i.e. successfully trade). Coercion plays no role here; every purchase and sale are freely made by the market participants, guided by their own interpretations and evaluations of the terrain of the market. The forces that drive the market are the judgments, tastes, preferences and expectations of the individuals occupying the market space and their actions which are directed by these judgments, tastes, preferences and expectations (Ibid., pp. 257–258).

Thus, the market is also very much a product of human actions; every market phenomenon such as prices and profits can always be traced back to the deliberate choices of the individuals occupying the market. It is a result of a long evolutionary process and, as such, there is nothing inhuman, mystical, accidental or artificial about the market as our neoclassical counterparts might suggest (Ibid., pp. 258, 265). In this way, markets serve a society by bringing about a high degree of correspondence between expectations of different members while increasing their individual wealth (Hayek, 1976, p. 107).

Within the Austrian conception of the market, consumers are paramount. "The consumers," Mises (2007 [1949], p. 270) wrote,

> patronize those shops in which they can buy what they want at the cheapest price. Their buying and their abstention from buying decides who should own and run the plants and the farms. They make poor people rich and rich people poor. They determine precisely what should be produced, in what quality, and in what quantities ... If something is offered to them that they like better or that is cheaper, they desert their old purveyors.

Consumers determine who wins and who loses in markets. While "[o]nly the sellers of goods and services of the first order are in direct contact with the consumers and directly depend on their orders," Mises continued,

> they transmit the orders received from the public to all those producing goods and services of the higher orders. For the manufacturers of consumers' goods, the retailers, the service trades, and the professions are forced to acquire what they need for the conduct of their own business from those purveyors who offer them at the

cheapest price. If they were not intent upon [obeying the consumers' orders], they would be forced to go out of business ... The slightest deviation [from the consumers' orders], whether willfully brought about or caused by error, bad judgement, or inefficiency, restricts their profits or make them disappear. A more serious deviation results in losses and thus impairs or entirely absorbs their wealth.

Thus, producers are bound unconditionally to consumers' needs and wants, as well as their whims and fancies. But the directives of consumers cannot be abundantly clear and obvious to everyone. In fact, their directives tend to be communicated through their purchases, their abstentions and the urgency at which they make their purchases. In a sense, their directives seem rather intangible, not readily perceived by the blunt senses. So, consumers reward those entrepreneurs who quickly picked up on their directives with profits and punish those who misconstrued or failed to obey their directives with losses. Stated another way, consumers' orders must be interpreted, and consumers reward those entrepreneurs who do a better job of interpreting consumers' orders.

Ultimately, entrepreneurs compete with one another for the rewards awarded by the consumers. In this manner,

> [t]he consumers determine ultimately not only the prices of the consumers' goods, but no less the prices of all factors of production. They determine the income of every member of the market economy. The consumers, not the entrepreneurs, pay ultimately the wages earned by every worker, the glamorous movie star as well as the charwoman. With every penny spent the consumers determine the direction of all production processes and the details of the organization of all business activities. (Ibid., p. 271)

However, this does not imply that the power of consumers is unlimited. In every society, there exists a scarcity of resources and, therefore, conflicts over how to utilize the available resources. In essence, each consumer has to not only persuade entrepreneurs to produce the goods and services that she desires, but also be more persuasive than other consumers. Furthermore, she needs to vie with other consumers to secure the goods and services she desires which are available in limited quantities. For instance, Ann might signal to her favorite bakers that they need to bake more scones not only by buying the scones, but also by buying more scones than the combined number of cookies Patricia and Jeannette are willing to buy. In addition, not only does Ann need to compete with Patricia and Jeannette, she needs to compete against Susie for the available scones. Thus, consumers are not always buying goods and services at the cheapest prices imaginable, but often have to discover the lowest price at which they could purchase a good or service whilst keeping producers from manufacturing another good or service. Coupled with the fact that, "in reality, [producers and consumers] are the same people" (Ibid., p. 316), what at first glance seemed like an account of one side of the market dominating the other, comes into sharper focus as an account of people trying their best to juggle their own wants and the wants of others. And, as the account clearly demonstrates, catallactic competition is a social phenomenon (Ibid., p. 275). It involves the interaction of multiple people.

In addition to understanding the market as a competitive process, Austrians also understand the market as a discovery process. Hayek (2014b [1945], pp. 93–94) argued that the fundamental economic problem of a society was one "of how to secure the best use of the resources known to any of the members of society, for ends whose relative importance only these individuals know," or, rather, "a problem of the utilization of knowledge which is not given to anyone in its totality." One challenge with trying to utilize such knowledge is that it is often specific to a time and place, tacit and inarticulate. Indeed, the possessors of this knowledge may sometimes be unaware of the knowledge that they possess and the relevance of the knowledge that they possess may not become apparent until a particular set of circumstances has transpired (Arentz, Sautet & Storr, 2013). Because of the nature of this knowledge, a centrally planned economic system is simply incapable of efficiently and effectively utilizing this diffuse local knowledge (Lavoie, 2015 [1985]). Hayek believed that the only economic system that can do so is the market precisely because it can guarantee, first, the discovery of relevant knowledge by well-positioned market actors and, then, its effective use by the society.

Every act of buying or selling, Hayek explained, reveals previously unknown or unnoticed information about the market and about market conditions. For instance, through market exchange, buyers and sellers can learn about which resources that were once abundantly available are no longer so readily available and which resources that were once limited in supply are no longer as scarce. Through the market, people also learn about improvements in technological capabilities and sophistication of consumer tastes and thus discover new information. The market can also teach individuals about who can most cheaply provide a particular good whilst maintaining a particular level of quality.

The market functions because individuals then take this newly revealed or acquired information into account as they build and adjust their future plans. Through the reiteration of this competitive market process, (a) the market steers resources to those individuals who value them the most; (b) the producers providing a particular good have a comparative advantage in producing the particular good and no one among those who are not producing this good can do it better; (c) every good and service that is sold in society is sold at a price lower than at which anyone else could supply it; and (d) the collection of goods and services that a society desires and prioritizes are in fact available and sold to its members (Hayek, 2014a [1948], p. 309). And, the more open to competition the market is, the better and more likely the market is able to serve the needs of the society.

Arguably, this richer understanding of the market as an emergent social order (as opposed to a sterile mechanism that is always in equilibrium) serves as the ideal canvas on which economists could begin to examine the sociality and morality of the market. Indeed, the Austrian conception of the market pivots around the human being qua human being, and human beings are arguably socially connected moral creatures.

HUMAN BEINGS ARE CONNECTED TO ONE ANOTHER

Unlike *homo economicus*, the notion of an economic agent in Austrian economics is not a god-like figure who has perfect knowledge and information about her economic environment, and is a perfectly rational and socially isolated figure who is largely satisfied in her situation. Nor do Austrians view economic agents as socially isolated figures. As Mises (2005 [1957], pp. 159–169) described, we model our economic agent as a socially situated human being;

> [e]very individual [in Austrian economic theory] is born into a definite social and natural milieu. An individual is not simply man in general, whom history can regard in the abstract. An individual is at any instant of his life the product of all the experiences to which his ancestors were exposed plus those to which he himself has so far been exposed. An actual man lives as a member of his family, his race, his people, and his age; as a citizen of his country; as a member of a definite social group; as a practitioner of a certain vocation. He is imbued with definite religious, philosophical, metaphysical, and political ideas, which he sometimes enlarges or modifies by his own thinking.

Hence, we perceive every individual to be a product of her own situation and the economic, political, social and historical contexts into which she was born. Every action she commits is guided by her social network, and the meanings (or culture) and the various sympathies that she shares with the other members of her family, her social groups and her country (Storr, 2013).

It is hard to miss the sense of community and belonging, and the feelings of sympathy in Mises's description of the typical economic agent in Austrian theory. Indeed, we have long accepted that this sense of community, sympathy and belonging is a key motivation for human action. Austrians have also operated with the assumption that feelings of social solidarity do not make sense outside a framework of social cooperation and that they are not prerequisites to social cooperation or relationships.[1] For instance, Mises (2005 [1957],

p. 144) wrote that the "feelings of sympathy and friendship and the sense of belonging" that can emerge between members of society are not "the agents that have brought about social relationships," but rather "the fruits of social cooperation" which thrive only in the framing of social cooperation; "they did not precede the establishment of social relations and are not the seed from which they spring." Rothbard (1993 [1962], p. 85) echoed Mises, saying, "[i]n explaining the origins of society, there is no need to conjure up any mystic communion or 'sense of belonging' among individuals … In fact, it is far more likely that feelings of friendship and communion are the effects of a regime of (contractual) social cooperation rather than the cause."

Similarly, Hayek (1976) lamented how the popular interpretation of the word "economy" failed to capture key features of the market. An economy, Hayek (Ibid., p. 107) believed, evokes the image of "a complex of activities by which a given set of means is allocated in accordance with a unitary plan among the competing ends according to their relative importance." He believed that the term more aptly portrayed a (centralized) organization (e.g. a household or a firm) that directs its available resources towards the satisfaction of a single hierarchy of priorities and aims than a (decentralized) order that has emerged from the patterns begot by the repeated interactions of dissimilar individuals. Instead, Hayek recommended the use of the word "catallaxy" which was derived from a Greek word that means "to exchange," "to admit into the community" and "to change an enemy into a friend" (Ibid., p. 109). Undoubtedly, compared to economy, catallaxy better conveys a sense of patterns of mutually beneficial interactions, friendships that do not require involved parties to share the same ends, the transformation of strangers into friends and reconciliation between conflicting parties (i.e. the connectedness between human beings in the market).[2] Furthermore, using the term catallaxy reminds us that the market is an "order brought about by the mutual adjustment of many individual economies [i.e. organizations] in a market" (Ibid., pp. 108–109) in the pursuit of many different purposes.

Given how Hayek comprehended the market, it is not surprising that he was able to recognize that the Great Society is held together primarily by catallatic relations. "It is of course true," Hayek (Ibid., p. 112) admitted, "that within the overall framework of the Great Society there exists numerous networks of other relations that are in no sense economic." "But," he (Ibid., pp. 112–113) continued,

this does not alter the fact that it is the market order which makes peaceful reconciliation of the divergent purposes possible – and possible by a process which redounds to the benefit of all. That interdependence of all men … not only is the effect of the market order but could not have been brought about by any other means. What today connects the life of any European or American with what happens in Australia, Japan or Zaire are repercussions transmitted by the network of market relations.

> This is clearly seen when we reflect how little, for instance, all the technological possibilities of transportation and communication would matter if the conditions of productions were the same in all the different parts of the world.

In short, for Hayek (Ibid., p. 112), it is "the relations between the parts of being governed by the striving for the better satisfaction of their material needs" – the "cash-nexus" – that hold the Great Society together.

Granovetter (1985, p. 484, emphasis added) correctly observed that neoclassical economics, at best, has outright dismissed the notion that people form connections with one another and, at worst, viewed it as "a *frictional drag that impedes competitive markets*," if not outright dismissed. To those who view *homo economicus* as someone who would switch trading partners in an instant and without hesitation whenever she may profit or benefit more (even by a negligible amount) as an accurate representation of the typical individual in the economy, establishing and maintaining relationships with peers would of course not only seem cumbersome and stifling, but also illogical. Hence, in the neoclassical economic interpretation of the world, it makes sense that the quintessential economic agent would be a socially isolated figure and that the quintessential economic space would be devoid of any relations (e.g. Weber, 1978, pp. 635–640). In the real world, however, people tend to be social beings who not only want to be liked but to also be worthy of the care that others have for them.[3] For these sorts of people, it is probably unsurprising that they would form (and want to form) some type of relationship in the social spaces they roam. Understanding economic agents in our theories as actual human beings, the notion that people and groups/organizations (which are formed by these people) would be connected to one another is a fundamental feature of the Austrian version of the market.

Again, we perceive the market as a product of human action; more specifically, we view it as an unintended consequence of human action, an order that emerged from the patterns generated by the *repeated interactions* (i.e. relations) between dispersed individuals.[4] Recognizing that human beings are connected to one another in the market is a necessary condition for scholars to begin discussing how people's interactions and relationships in the market can become overlain with social content.

MARKET INTERACTIONS ARE NOT ANONYMOUS AND HUMAN BEINGS MAKE CONNECTIONS IN MARKETS

In the perfectly competitive market, which is arguably neoclassical economics' most idealized model of the market, buyers and sellers never seem to genuinely interact with one another. Here, a successful trade occurs whenever a buyer's willingness to pay for a good exceeds the price at which the seller is willing to sell. To the buyer, it does not matter precisely from whom she is purchasing the good; all that matters is that she is purchasing the good at the lowest possible price and that there is no other seller selling the good in the market from whom she can purchase it at a lower price. Likewise, the seller does not care to whom she is selling the good so long as she is selling it at the highest possible price and there is no other buyer in the market to whom she can sell it at a higher price. In some sense, the only personal information (if one could call it that) that matters about market participants in this market are their reservation prices for the maximization of market efficiency. Among those market participants who can successfully trade, the buyer with the highest willingness to pay must be paired with the seller with the lowest willingness to sell, the buyer with the second highest willingness to pay must be paired with the seller with the second to lowest willingness to sell, so on and so forth. And, these paired buyers and sellers *must* exchange their cash and goods at the market price. Indeed, if all that mattered was one's reservation price or some other attribute that could be easily cardinally or ordinally ordered in the real world, no one will ever need get genuinely acquainted with anyone else in the market and everyone could remain anonymous.[5, 6]

In the real world, however, much of our market interactions arguably do not tend to be with true strangers. For instance, people do not tend to say that they are going to the grocery store when they shop for groceries; they often say that they are going to Giant, Safeway, Wegmans, Whole Foods or Trader Joe's. And, because of their frequent interactions with the employees at Wegmans and Whole Foods, they regard them as more than strangers, even when interacting with a new employee at these establishments. Ultimately, many, if not most of our interactions in the market become imbued with social content (Granovetter, 1985).

Recall that the market process allows people to discover information and knowledge about the market that is local, time-dependent and hitherto unknown to the active party. Of course, a person can discover new information on her own; her own experiences and interactions in the market can teach her about the market conditions, the goods and services she desires and the people who also occupy the marketspace without having to learn this information from another person. However, as she navigates the market in pursuit of her goals, it is more likely the case that she speaks to others. These conversations may strictly be economic. To be sure, the bulk of her conversations may revolve around her asking a sales representative about the quality and various features of the goods they have on sale (e.g. "What features does this car have? How did this car perform in its safety tests?"), discussing available options and haggling with them. But she can also learn something about the sales representative through these narrowly economic conversations. For instance, she could glean whether he is polite or rude by the way he spoke to her. Additionally, she could gauge whether he respects others by the way he was condescending and dismissive of her queries. Her non-verbal interactions with him may reveal other information about him. She could discern whether or not he is organized by the cleanliness of his desk and his attire. In fact, while she may not be able to explicitly articulate her reasons, she may even be able to sense whether he is trying to defraud her by his behavior. Even if she did not know this sales representative in any meaningful sense before stepping into his dealership, she would walk out with some opinion of him based on what she had observed and learnt. The more they interact, the more repeated their dealings, the more they will learn about each other.

In real-world markets, Storr (2008) explained, meaningful conversations beyond those that narrowly pertain to the transactions and exchanges that are taking place often occur. For instance, market participants often inquire about each other's families, discuss current news, brunch together on weekends, unwind after work with drinks and exercise or play sports together outside work. Some colleagues and competitors form strong bonds over their shared and common work experiences and some market associates develop sibling-like and even romantic relationships. Consequently, for Storr (Ibid.), the market is a site where meaningful economic and extraeconomic conversations can occur and, therefore, where meaningful social relations (beyond simple economic or commercial relationships) form. For Storr (Ibid.), the market is not *merely* a social body, a social phenomenon, nor a process; the market is also a social space.

Chamlee-Wright (1997), using the case of female entrepreneurship in Ghana, also illustrated that economic relationships matter for the social lives of market participants. Her study showcased that many (if not most) female entrepreneurs shared a strong camaraderie with the other female entrepreneurs who operate in their immediate area and form tight friendships. In addition to serving a vital economic function (by, say, providing the female entrepreneurs with credit and critical business information), her study documented how these relationships also serve a vital social function. For instance, immediate market neighbors chat, gossip, share personal worries and advise one another. Market friends also help in raising each other's children, share food with one another during financial difficulties and even sell each other's wares when something unexpected or an emergency arises. At a time when tribal connections and kin networks were declining in influence and importance in urban Ghana, these sororal relationships between female entrepreneurs filled the vacuum left behind by the depreciating blood ties and provided the social and economic support these female entrepreneurs needed.

A key point made by Storr (2008) that deserves greater emphasis is that there are some relationships, like the sororal relationships shared by the Ghanaian female entrepreneurs, that were initiated in markets that might not have developed without the market and would not have developed along the precisely same course had it not been for the market. For example, active members of the labor force nowadays seem to expect their jobs to be more than a paycheck; the pay clearly still matters, but employees seem to seek out jobs that are fulfilling and meaningful. This, of course, is understandable since the demarcation between work and home is becoming increasingly blurred as people spend more and more time at work. It only seems natural in this situation that they would increasingly want to build connections with colleagues. The evidence suggests that people do form meaningful connections with their colleagues, e.g. they often go to their friends at work to share significant developments in their personal and professional lives, and celebrate and commiserate with one another; they go to happy hours together; and they socialize and play sports with each other on weekends. Frequently, their work friendships are not confined to just one another; spouses and children of colleagues regularly know one another, and people are acquainted with (or at least know of) colleagues' college friends and siblings. Moreover, having friendships at work matters for employee engagement, firm performance and lower turnover rates. Using data collected by Gallup about the workplace, Mann (2018) reported that "women who strongly agree they have a best friend at work are more than twice as likely to be engaged (63%) compared with the women who say otherwise (29%)." In addition, as a part of their recommendations, Gallup (2021, p. 17) wrote that "[t]o be competitive and maximize business performance in today's workplace, employers are responsible for fostering wellbeing" and one of the ways in which they could do so is by "encouraging friendships at work." If these friendships between colleagues did not come to exist or were not allowed to flourish, there would be immediate economic consequences to individual and firm performances. And, perhaps more crucially, these employees would have been denied the substantial improvement in their overall well-being that they might have gained had work friendships been permissible.

Of course, there are literatures (e.g. social capital in social science and network theory in economics) that highlight the economic significance of social relationships (i.e. relationships that were initially formed in society/ outside a commercial or market space). However, these literatures tended to minimize or ignore the social significance of economic relationships. Unlike neoclassical economists, Austrians do not view social relations as shackles that impede people from succeeding in markets, but rather as boosters that facilitate (if not accelerate) people's success in markets. In fact, the thread of literature that discusses the market as a social space (e.g Choi & Storr, 2018, 2019, 2020, 2021; John & Storr, 2011; Storr, 2008, 2009, 2010) suggests how these meaningful market relationships also add value to our social lives.

MARKETS DEPEND ON INDIVIDUALS FOLLOWING RULES OF JUST CONDUCT

There are some peculiarities with the model of the perfectly competitive market in which neoclassical economists take pride. In a perfectly competitive market, for instance, a buyer and a seller somehow wordlessly and instantaneously locate one another, and magically know, without any conversation or negotiation, the price at which both are willing to trade. Moreover, this price is miraculously the market's equilibrium price. Additionally, even though every market participant is a *homo economicus* whose actions are driven by self-interest (narrowly defined), no manipulations, cheating or fights happen in this space. The neoclassical marketspace is not a chaotic, hostile place as one might imagine fictional lawless pirate havens to be. Instead, it more resembles a serene, idyllic paradise where there are no rules, but its inhabitants do not behave in problematic or unexpected ways. While the perfectly competitive market does not explicitly rely on any recognized rules of engagement or conduct, for the assumed results to obtain, its economic agents do implicitly rely on unspoken, but shared expectations of acceptable behavior (i.e. norms), responsibilities and common market practices, i.e. rules of just conduct.

Despite not incorporating institutions into their models (at least not explicitly), even the perfectly competitive market and certainly all well-functioning real-world markets rely on economic agents to follow rules of just conduct.[7] To explore this, it is useful to turn to Hayek's thoughts on rules and orders. Hayek (1973) viewed orders as, basically speaking, social structures and institutions. He (Ibid., p. 36) described an order as,

> a state of affairs in which a multiplicity of elements of various kinds are so related to each other that we may learn from our acquaintance with some spatial or temporal part of the whole to form correct expectations concerning the rest, or at least expectations which have a good chance of proving correct.

Hayek identified two distinct types of orders.[8] First among these was orders of human design, "deliberate human arrangements" (Ibid., p. 38), which he called organizations, made orders and *taxis*. Because these orders were designed by human beings who are not omniscient and possessed limited knowledge, insights and intellectual capabilities, they were also "relatively simple or at least necessarily confined to such moderate degrees of complexity as the maker can still survey" and were "usually concrete in the sense ... that their existence can be intuitively perceived by inspection" (Ibid.). Made orders, due to their relative simplicity and the relative ease at which the maker could shape the order, tend to be hierarchical and united by a single goal or purpose.

For Hayek, made orders can be contrasted with grown orders – also called spontaneous orders, emergent orders and *kosmos*. Grown orders (a) can have any degree of complexity that the society requires of them; (b) have structures that, compared to made orders, are not so tangible and obvious, but could still be vaguely grasped; and (c) generally serve no single or specific purpose. In fact, spontaneous orders are "orderly structures which are the product of the action of many men but are not the result of human design" (Ibid., p. 37) and, "not having been made[,] it *cannot* legitimately be said to *have a particular purpose*, although our awareness of its existence may be extremely important for our successful pursuit of a great variety of different purposes" (Ibid., p. 38; emphasis in original).

A key difference between made and grown orders is that the former operates on commands while the latter operates on rules. Specifically, the relative simplicity of made orders and their unity under a single purpose enable the maker to structure made orders hierarchically, thereby organizing activity through commands. Those at the top of the hierarchy, given their vantage point, can broadly assess the links between the means and the ends, and make changes (i.e. command changes) to the order. Those who are not at the top of the hierarchy are compliant to the commands and are agreeable to the hierarchical arrangement because they, at least to some degree, understand their positions and roles within the order and how they contribute towards the achievement of the organization's goals.

The distinctive feature of made orders (at least for our purposes in this chapter) is how individual actions within made orders are directed by commands aimed to serve the unified purpose (i.e. ends-oriented rules). Grown orders, in contrast, operate on the basis of rules that emerge from the behavior of people and groups within the order and that, in turn, shape their conduct.

In particular, Hayek (Ibid., p. 75) thought of a rule as "a propensity or disposition to act or not to act in a certain manner, which will manifest itself in what we [call] practice or custom." Essentially, for Hayek, rules are borne out of regular, consistent and predictable actions of people – behavioral patterns – when they are faced with the same situation. These patterns of behavior, over time, increasingly correlate with people's expectations of one another, which in time morph into social rules. And not all rules will be conducive towards or be capable of supporting the prosperity of those within the grown order (or conducive towards orderliness, for that matter).[9] However, all socially accepted rules must be "ends-independent" (Ibid., p. 121) or "purpose-independent" (Ibid., p. 81). Moreover, some of these rules will not be so easily articulable or explicitly known by the people who follow them (just as how some knowledge in society is not). As Hayek (Ibid., p. 50) wrote,

> the rules governing a spontaneous order must be independent of purpose and be the same, if not necessarily for all members, at least for whole classes of members not individually designated by name. They must, as we shall see, be rules applicable to an unknown and indeterminable number of persons and instances. They will have to be applied by individuals in the light of their respective knowledge and purposes; and their application will be independent of any common purpose, which the individual need not even know.

In addition, Hayek (Ibid., p. 40) mused that there are at least two circumstances under which regular patterns would emerge and manifest into rules;

> a regular pattern will thus form itself not only if the elements all obey the same rules and their different actions are determined only by the different positions of the several individuals relatively to each other, but also ... if there are different kinds of element which act in part according to different rules.[10]

Therefore, habitual behavior at the individual level or repeated and predictable actions and reactions to the same or similar situations by members of an order generates behavioral patterns at the aggregate level that members of a grown order can come to expect from their peers. And this "solidification" of habits and expectations, in time, becomes viewed as a social rule, on which the order is eventually reliant for its proper function.

As explained earlier, for Austrians, markets can be understood as grown orders brought about by the interactions of individuals, some of whom develop made orders (e.g. firms, co-operatives, unions, industry associations and other organizations) to achieve their goals. A cursory read of Hayek's work on rules and orders may erroneously lead one to comprehend him as insinuating that the identical rules of conduct would manifest no matter the people who populate the marketspace and no matter the type of market institution at play. Hayek, however, believed that distinct sets of rules could and were likely to emerge when different people populate the marketspace and different institutions and meta-institutions are at work.[11] For instance, Hayek (Ibid., p. 40; emphasis added) wrote,

> [t]he important point is that the regularity of the conduct of the elements will determine the general character of the resulting order but not all the detail of its particular manifestation. The particular manner in which the resulting abstract order will manifest itself will depend, in addition to the rules which govern the actions of the elements, on *their initial position* and on all the particular circumstances of the immediate environment to which each of them will react in the course of the formation of that order. The order, in other words, will always be an adaptation to a large number of particular facts which will not be known in their totality to anyone. *The*

important point is that the regularity of the conduct of the elements will determine the general character of the resulting order but not all the detail of its particular manifestation.

More specifically on the market order,

[i]n a modern society based on exchange, one of the chief regularities in individual behaviour will result from the similarity of situations in which most individuals find themselves in working to earn an income; which means that they will normally prefer a larger return from their efforts to a smaller one, and often that they will increase their efforts in a particular direction if the prospects of return improve. This is a rule that will be followed at least with sufficient frequency to impress upon such a society an order of a certain kind. But the fact that most people will follow this rule will still leave the character of the resulting order very indeterminate, and by itself certainly would not be sufficient to give it a beneficial character. For the resulting order to be beneficial people must also observe some conventional rules, that is, rules which do not simply follow from their desires and their insight into relations of cause and effect, but which are normative and tell them what they ought to or ought not to do. (Ibid., p. 45)

In short, Hayek seemed to have believed that it was possible for different societies to manifest different flavors or cultures of market where people follow the same overarching rules of conduct (e.g. basic respect for private property) but are guided by different componential rules (e.g. different norms about what constitutes respecting private property).[12]

MARKETS PROMOTE MORALITY

Often the rules of conduct that emerge in market settings encourage morality. As Hayek, Rothbard and other Austrians have explained, the market is a moral teacher.

Recall that Austrian economists have long understood the market as a discovery process for a great deal of market-relevant information such as profit opportunities and prices, and that the market teaches people about who can provide a good or service, who can produce them most cheaply and who can best satisfy our economic needs.[13] It is through this same process that market participants also discover whether the people with whom they are interacting are good or bad people.

Arguably, every market transaction presents an opportunity for opportunism. In a market exchange, a buyer typically agrees to pay a seller a certain amount for a specific good or service and the seller likewise agrees to transfer ownership of the good or service to the buyer. However, the buyer and seller could engage in opportunistic behavior and refuse to pay for or deliver the good or service after the other party has fulfilled their end of the agreement.

The choice to engage in opportunism is a deliberate decision; thus, the honest and opportunistic behavior of trading partners can reveal to market participants what type of person their trading partners are with every market exchange. In a world of complete strangers or one-time interactions, it may make sense to engage in opportunism, just as neoclassical theory predicts for any situations of demanding mutual cooperation (e.g. prisoner's dilemma). However, in a world where people are not engaging complete strangers for every potential market exchange, and where repeated interactions are permitted and do take place, it no longer is the optimal strategy to always behave opportunistically at every opportunity.[14]

The market also functions as a conversation about right and wrong. Indeed, the market permits people to communicate to others that they approve or disapprove of their behaviors through the profit-and-loss mechanism. Suppose a seller decided to follow through on her agreement instead of fleeing with both the cash and the good. The buyer is likely to reward the seller for her good decision (her moral decision) with profits and can convey the intensity of her approval through repeated business with the seller and referring the seller to other buyers. Accordingly, how a market participant conducts herself in the market could affect her future business opportunities. Because people can pick up on and learn things about others' characters and personalities by observing and judging their negotiating strategies, their communication, their demeanor and their behavior within and outside the negotiations and other business-related processes, the market is fairly good at inspiring virtuous behavior.

Similarly, people can punish vices in the market. Consider a case of discrimination in the labor market. As we (Storr & Choi, 2019, pp. 223–224, emphasis added) wrote,

> [t]hrough this mechanism of rewards and punishments [i.e. the profit-and-loss mechanism], the market discourages a racist employee from discriminating against a black employer, a sexist consumer from refusing to purchase a good from a female producer, and a homophobic producer from refusing to sell to homosexual consumers. The business that refuses to hire the most productive workers or serve potential customers who are most willing and able to pay because of race, ethnicity, sexual identity, or sexual orientation will lose out to its competitors. This is, obviously, not to say that we should never expect to observe intolerance in a market setting. It is instead to suggest that indulging in this behavior in a market setting comes at a cost and that the more competitors there are in a market the less likely it is to occur.
>
> *This market mechanism can also curb other vices. Vices, no matter what they are, simply cannot flourish in the long run in a market society.*

Suppose, for instance, that an employer would like to never hire a woman. This employer would pay to express his tastes for discrimination by losing out on the chance to hire equally or better qualified female candidates for a lower wage and by losing access to half of the overall talent pool. Moreover, over time, potential employees would become aware of his tastes and some qualified male candidates may choose to not apply for a job with the employer because they disapprove of his behavior and wish to disassociate themselves from him and his actions. Hence, market pressures will compel the discriminating employer to reassess his position and hire women for his company lest he experience losses or even goes bankrupt. Here, the question would not be *whether* the market would pressure him to reassess his disposition and practices, but *when*.

Admittedly, as we argue elsewhere, the market process is capable of promoting any system of morality so long as the society considers something a virtue or a vice. The market can teach people to better on those margins and thus promote morality in that manner. Indeed, the same market forces that allow us to prosper economically can also enrich us socially and morally.

CONCLUSION

Much of the literature in market process theory (including our own work) has tended to focus on the market itself, the market actors and their interactions and social relationships. In this chapter, we argued that the Austrian theory of the market as a process and as the order that results from that process provides a useful framework to explore the social and moral aspects of markets.[15] Indeed, it is extremely challenging (if not impossible) to discuss and examine the social relationships that emerge from market settings and the ways in which people socially conduct themselves if human beings are modeled as homogenous, perfectly rational agents. Because we Austrian economists stress meaning, process and human action in our economic analysis, the Austrian framework for understanding human behavior in economic settings truly and uniquely equips us with the tools to rigorously examine the sociality and morality of markets.

There are several possible extensions and applications of this Austrian approach to exploring the social and moral aspects of markets. For instance, there is room to undertake ethnographic studies and social histories of the emergence of social relations and the moral aspects of various specific markets.

Moreover, applying insights from the Austrian approach to studying social interactions and relationships, and the rules of engagement that govern these interactions and relationships in the market setting to the context of firms, can advance our understanding of the role of social relationships in promoting entrepreneurial activity within firms. Economic sociologist Ronald Burt (2004) argued that those individuals who stand in close proximity to structural holes are more likely to have good ideas than others in a firm because there is a larger degree of homogeneity in opinions and behavior within groups than between groups. Those workers who serve as bridges or brokers across groups tend to benefit from their interactions with more heterogeneous peers and thus are more likely to form good ideas that their peers find valuable and deserving of praise. Burt's theory about structural holes, brokerage and good ideas, we believe, might benefit from applying the insights of the Austrian framework described in this chapter to the firm and its employees. In particular, mere proximity to structural holes will not necessarily "infect" individuals with good ideas. They will need to communicate with people who are dissimilar to themselves, foster rapport with one another and gain each other's confidence and trust (at least to some degree) in order to collaborate and share their own exclusive knowledge, information and opinions. Stated another way, broker-age is fruitfully understood as (a form of) entrepreneurship within the firm.

Furthermore, the social and moral insights about the market that we discuss in this chapter might also improve our understanding of rent seeking and cronyism. If our argument is correct (or at least has some potential to explain some of the moral and social behaviors we observe in market settings), it implies that having and maintaining relationships is crucial to being successful in business and in being successful and effective cronies and rent seekers. Additionally, there is potential room to apply this framework to the study of politics. It is a commonly known observation that politicians, bureaucrats and policymakers leverage their relationships to exert some influence on particular actions and decisions. Yet, to the best of our knowledge, the Austrian lens has not been applied to the role of social relationships in driving political, bureau-cratic and policy decisions, actions and changes, and how past actions in those spaces shape the development of political friendships.

A research program in the Austrian approach to social and moral implica-tions of the market process seem to be a very fertile ground.

NOTES

1.   It is probably worthwhile to note here that Mises, along with Hayek and other Austrian economists, did not seem to believe that the terms "competition" and "cooperation" were antonyms of one another as others seemed to believe. Mises (2007 [1949], p. 273) described social competition as "the striving of individuals to attain the most favorable position in the system of social cooperation."

2.   Mises (2007 [1949], p. 273) also believed in the market's ability to transform conflicts of interest and feelings of hostility into partnerships, mutuality and a sense of unity: "[s]ocial cooperation under the division of labor [i.e. the market] removes such antagonisms [i.e. irreconcilable conflicts of interest]. It substitutes partnership and mutuality for hostility. The members of society are united in a common venture."

3.   In *The Theory of Moral Sentiments*, Adam Smith (1982 [1759], pp. 113–114) also made a similar observation: "Man naturally desires, not only to be loved, but to be lovely; or to be that thing which is the natural and proper object of love. He

naturally dreads, not only to be hated, but to be hateful; or to be that thing which is the natural and proper object of hatred. He desires, not only praise, but praise-worthiness; or to be that thing which, though it should be praised by nobody, is, however, the natural and proper object of praise. He dreads, not only blame, but blame-worthiness; or to be that thing which, though it should be blamed by nobody, is, however, the natural and proper object of blame."

4. By an order that emerged from the patterns generated by the repeated interactions between dispersed individuals, we mean "the regularity of the conduct of the elements [that] determine the general character of the resulting [spontaneous] order but not all of the detail of its particular manifestation" (Hayek, 1973, p. 40).

5. Our concerns about the assumption of absolute anonymity in neoclassical theory does not imply that we do not recognize the value of some degree of anonymity (or impersonality) for markets. As trade expanded beyond towns, regions and countries, wealth exploded precisely (or at least in part) due to the impersonal nature of markets; so long as a person has the required money or resources, neither her popularity, her likability nor her appearance could severely impact her ability to acquire her wants and pursue her plans in the market. Our conten-tion here (and throughout the chapter) is with the celebration of anonymity by our neoclassical counterparts and their conviction that (a) relationships between market actors (whether they are beneficial or harmful) do not endogenously develop in market settings and (b) in the case that relationships do form, they are likely to be hindrances to individual success.

6. For the purposes of this chapter, we narrow our focus to the studies within the Austrian tradition that explicitly explore the possibility of social relationships to form in the market. Naturally, there are other studies and literatures outside Austrian economics that speak to this topic. See Choi and Storr (2020) for a more comprehensive overview.

7. Of course, it is possible to argue that the perfectly competitive market is no longer the dominant paradigm within mainstream economics. And, that new institutional economics and behavioral economics incorporate formal and infor-mal institutions (including laws, norms and biases) into their analysis of market activity. Arguably, even these approaches treat agents as (almost) automatically responding to the incentives they face within their institutional settings. The Austrian notion advanced by Lachmann (1977, p. 62) that institutions are points of orientation is very different than the new institutional economics notion that institutions are constraints.

8. In *Law, Legislation, and Liberty: Rules and Order*, Hayek (1973) discussed the two orders as if they were dichotomous and we mimic his tone here. However, as his discussions on the Great Society hinted, he saw the two orders as being two extremes of a spectrum or continuum. This is crucial, as we hopefully argue persuasively, as both made and grown orders require individuals to follow rules (whether they are in the form of commands from above or endogenously mani-fested rules of conduct) in order to function well.

9. For instance, Hayek (1973, p. 44) gave an example about how a rule stipulating that every individual must kill or flee from anyone that she encounters is not con-ducive towards a social order/orderliness and may even lead to perfect disorder. As another example, Choi and Storr (2019) discussed how the traditional practice of gift-giving in Korean culture (an endogenously manifested social rule) was not conducive towards an efficient allocation of resources (at least in more contem-porary times).

10. With regards to the example with which we began this section, the fact that the perfectly competitive market could manifest some rules of conduct and form an order, said Hayek, should not be so surprising.

11. In fact, Hayek also likely thought that, even with the same group of people and the same underlying conditions, the specific rules of conduct that manifest would vary between different iterations of the market order.

12. On the capacity of different market institutions to manifest their own distinct cultures and of different groups of people populating the same market to breed their own unique flavors/tones, see Storr (2013) and Choi and Storr (2018).

13. For instance, Hayek (2014a [1948], p. 109) believed that market participants can not only learn about their environment, but also about the people with whom they trade; "[t]he function of competition is here precisely to teach us *who* will serve us well." Similarly, Kirzner believed entrepreneurs to be agents of discovery who not only learnt about ever evolving market conditions but also learnt something about other people by merely observing their behavior and decisions as they navigated the market (Kirzner, 2013 [1973], p. 8).

14. The discussion of anonymous exchange above is relevant here.

15. Our argument in this chapter is not merely conjecture or anecdotal. For instance, our own studies (Choi & Storr, 2018, 2020; Storr & Choi, 2019, chapter 6) collectively demonstrate that the market allows people to discover hitherto unknown information about one another, form meaningful social relationships/friendships and promote virtues whilst discouraging vices.

REFERENCES

Arentz, J., Sautet, F. E., & Storr, V. H. (2013). Prior-knowledge and opportunity identification. *Small Business Economics*, *41*(2), 461–478.

Burt, R. S. (2004). Structural holes and good ideas. *American Journal of Sociology*, *110*(2), 349–399.

Chamlee-Wright, E. (1997). *The Cultural Foundations of Economic Development: Urban Female Entrepreneurship in Ghana*. London: Routledge.

Choi, G. S., & Storr, V. H. (2018). Market institutions and the evolution of culture. *Evolutionary and Institutional Economics Review*, *15*(2), 243–265.

Choi, G. S., & Storr, V. H. (2019). A culture of rent seeking. *Public Choice*, *181*(1–2), 101–126.

Choi, G. S., & Storr, V. H. (2020). Market interactions, trust and reciprocity. *PLOS ONE*, *15*(5), e0232704.

Choi, G. S., & Storr, V. H. (2021). The market as a process for the discovery of whom not to trust. *Journal of Institutional Economics*, 1–16.

Gallup. (2021). *State of the Global Workplace: 2021 Report*. Washington, DC: Gallup.

Granovetter, M. S. (1985). Economic action and social structure: A theory of embeddedness. *American Journal of Sociology*, *91*(3), 481–510.

Hayek, F. A. von. (1973). *Law, Legislation, and Liberty, Volume 1: Rules and Order*. Chicago, IL: University of Chicago Press.

Hayek, F. A. von. (1976). *Law, Legislation, and Liberty, Volume 2: The Mirage of Social Justice*. Chicago, IL: University of Chicago Press.

Hayek, F. A. von. (2014a [1948]). The meaning of competition. In B. J. Caldwell (Ed.), *The Collected Works of F.A. Hayek, Volume XV: The Market and Other Orders* (pp. 105–116). Chicago, IL: University of Chicago Press.

Hayek, F. A. von. (2014b [1945]). The use of knowledge in society. In B. J. Caldwell (Ed.), *The Collected Works of F. A. Hayek, Volume XV: The Market and Other Orders* (pp. 93–104). Chicago, IL: University of Chicago Press.

John, A., & Storr, V. H. (2011). The sociability and morality of market settlements. In D. E. Andersson, Å. E. Andersson, & C. Mellander (Eds), *Handbook of Creative Cities* (pp. 405–421). Cheltenham, UK and Northampton, MA, USA: Edward Elgar Publishing.

Kirzner, I. M. (2013 [1973]). *Competition and Entrepreneurship: The Collected Works of Israel Kirzner* (P. J. Williamson & F. E. Sautet, Eds). Indianapolis, IN: Liberty Fund.

Lachmann, L. M. (1977). Ludwig von Mises and the market process. In *Capital, Expectations and the Market Process* (pp. 181–193). Kansas City, MO: Sheed, Andrews and McMeel.

Lavoie, D. (2015 [1985]). *Rivalry and Central Planning: The Socialist Calculation Debate Reconsidered*. Arlington, VA: Mercatus Center at George Mason University.

Mann, A. (2018). Why we need best friends at work. www.gallup.com/workplace/236213/why-need-best-friends-work.aspx

Mises, L. von. (2005 [1957]). *Theory and History: An Interpretation of Social and Economic Evolution*. Indianapolis, IN: Liberty Fund.

Mises, L. von. (2007 [1949]). *Human Action: A Treatise on Economics*. Indianapolis, IN: Liberty Fund.

Rothbard, M. N. (1993 [1962]). *Man, Economy, and State: A Treatise on Economic Principles*. Auburn, AL: Ludwig von Mises Institute.

Smith, A. (1982 [1759]). *The Theory of Moral Sentiments*. Indianapolis, IN: Liberty Fund.

Storr, V. H. (2008). The market as a social space: On the meaningful extraeconomic conversations that can occur in markets. *Review of Austrian Economics, 21*(2–3), 135–150.

Storr, V. H. (2009). Why the market? Markets as social and moral spaces. *Journal of Markets and Morality, 12*(2), 272–296.

Storr, V. H. (2010). The social construction of the market. *Society, 47*(3), 200–206.

Storr, V. H. (2013). *Understanding the Culture of Markets*. London: Routledge.

Storr, V. H., & Choi, G. S. (2019). *Do Markets Corrupt Our Morals?* London: Palgrave Macmillan.

Weber, M. (1978). *Economy and Society*. Berkeley, CA: University of California Press.

8. Economic calculation and socialism
Krzysztof Turowski and Mateusz Machaj

INTRODUCTION

The rise of socialist movements in the nineteenth century undoubtedly influenced economics in one certain way: it put to prominence a question of the comparative efficiency of socialism versus capitalism. It was said for example that the socialist central planning would remove production wastes and mismanagements occurring under capitalism. Moreover, it was claimed that the profligacies such as advertisement would become useless and disappear, allowing for more resources to be used productively. On the other hand, critics of socialism asked questions about the existence of the proper incentives under an economic regime that dampens or breaks completely the dependence between efforts and income. The answers amounted to proposing various alternative schemes of recognition of efforts within a socialist community. On top of all that, there was a long strand of never-ending discussions of the alleged moral superiority of socialism, e.g. its possibility to turn men into creatures with higher morals, less envious, and more productive for the benefit of the whole of society.

The question of the efficiency of socialism became larger than academia especially after the October Revolution of 1917 in Russia, which led to the establishment of the first state under the dictatorship of the Communist Party driven by a Marxian ideology. The inquiries into the advantages and disadvantages of different property regimes gained obvious practical significance – especially since Marx's writings were a critique of an existing order rather than a guidebook for a new one.

It is within this context that Ludwig von Mises published his famous essay *Economic Calculation in the Socialist Commonwealth* in 1919. On the one hand, he was familiar with the various political discussions, especially in the German-speaking world, about problems of incentives and productivity in socialist systems (Mises, 1951, p. 159; 1998a, pp. 672–676). However, his aim was much more modest and at the same time much more fundamental: he wanted to clarify whether it was possible, given all the knowledge about resources and the already established collective rank of consumption goods to produce, to allocate these resources by a central planner at least as effectively as it is done via the price system in markets.[1] Or, to put it differently, he was asking whether there exists a rational calculation procedure in socialism.

THE DEBATE OVER CALCULATION IN SOCIALISM(S)

Mises for his task accepted the definition of socialism as an economic system in which "all the means of production are in the exclusive control of the organized community" (Mises 1951, p. 211).[2] Although it is by far not the unanimous definition, it was often assumed in his time (e.g. Ebeling, 1993), as it captures the common element of both Marxist and many non-Marxist varieties of socialism (Hülsmann, 2007, p. 376). Note that Mises, in all his caution, refrained from a definite statement about the ownership of consumption goods. For the purposes of his analysis, it was perfectly valid to have even a private property of such goods combined with any scheme of distribution.

Probably the most famous yet very straightforward vision of an allocation process under socialism was put forward by Otto Neurath. He advocated the abandonment of money and a transition to in-kind calculation by a central board. A central planner would know the input-output coefficients in all production processes and using this knowledge he could find an optimal allocation of production goods (Neurath, 1973, pp. 140–141).

Mises's argument ran counter to such schemes and consisted of five simple steps:[3]

1. There exists collective ownership of factors of production – this is the premise shared unanimously by Marx, Neurath, and other socialist writers.
2. There are no exchanges of factors of production – an obvious corollary, since there is no second party to exchange them with.
3. There are no market prices of factors of production – since there are no exchanges, no exchange ratios can arise.
4. There is no way to appraise different production processes – there is no common unit, all inputs and outputs are expressed only in heterogeneous natural units.
5. Finally, there is no guide for a rational allocation of factors of production – there is no way to compare two different methods to produce the same good or two production processes with different outputs.

The argument made by Mises applies as well to any allocation algorithm in which we assume the collective ownership of factors of production, i.e. for any socialist economy. It is not sufficient that socialists would allow citizens to possess some personal property or even grant full ownership of the consumption goods. Still, in any developed economy without market prices of factors of production "all production involving processes stretching well back in time and all the longer roundabout processes of capitalist production would be gropings in the dark" (Mises, 1990, p. 14; see also Mises, 1951, pp. 119, 122).

This article and the subsequent book titled *Socialism*, in which Mises extended his main argument by distinguishing several different types of economic systems (e.g. syndicalism and interventionism) and adding some cultural considerations caused a hot debate within economic circles. Oskar Lange, young and rising Walrasian general equilibrium theorist with Marxist political views, even commented sarcastically:

> the merit of having caused the socialists to approach this problem systematically belongs entirely to Professor Mises. Both as an expression of recognition for the great service rendered by him and as a memento of the prime importance of sound economic accounting, a statue of Professor Mises ought to occupy an honourable place in the great hall of the Ministry of Socialisation or of the Central Planning Board of the socialist state. (Lange, 1936, p. 53)

The standard account of the debate, presented by Bergson (1948) and Schumpeter (2003), is as follows: the initial impulse by Mises was countered by a group of English-speaking neoclassical economists such as Fred Taylor (1929), Henry Dickinson (1939), and Lange (1936), who were arguing that this problem had been solved even before Mises set up his challenge.[4] In particular, it was pointed out that an Italian economist, Enrico Barone, in 1908 had already considered the situation with technical knowledge, and he put forward the formulation of a system of equations describing a socialist economy. The solution of this system is guaranteed to achieve the optimum allocation of all kinds of goods to different uses. Therefore, it cannot be the case that socialism is theoretically impossible under these idealized conditions (Lange, 1936, p. 54).

As Hayek (1935, p. 212) and Robbins (1971, p. 151) quickly noticed, even if this was true, Barone and his teacher Vilfredo Pareto did not consider this approach a practical one. Clearly, the size of the algebraic problem grows quadratically with the number of goods so it was claimed to be impossible to be solved efficiently. Contrary to popular wisdom, Barone thought that only "technical coefficients" could be solved, whereas he believed it to be "inconceivable" for the "economic determination" of them to be solved *a priori* (Barone, 1908, pp. 287–288).

In addition, Hayek pointed to the existence of dispersed knowledge in the economic process: each agent has non-verbal knowledge about particular circumstances of time and place, which he cannot use outside of the action itself. Thus, any central planning board would not be able to collect the required information. Moreover, the time needed to gather data e.g. from questionnaires would make them obsolete, as the markets in the developed, interconnected economy are very dynamic and generate inherent knowledge assimilated during the process (Hayek, 1935, 1940, 1945).

In response, Lange (1936, pp. 56–57) triumphantly announced that Hayek and Robbins had abandoned the original argument by Mises and admitted socialism as a coherent theoretical possibility, only doubting its practical feasibility. Second, he argued that there exists a way to overcome the problem of dispersed knowledge. His solution, dubbed market socialism, is an economic system in which managers in each industry would try to imitate the market: they would set some (at the beginning possibly arbitrary) numbers as "socialist prices" and they would observe the physical surpluses or shortages. In each case, they would adjust prices in the proper direction. By engaging in this trial-and-error approach the prices would eventually converge and all the mismatches in the production structure would eventually disappear. Ultimately, this procedure as an algorithm for solving general equilibrium equations is supposed to be identical to the one in capitalist systems, where every agent acts in coordination without recourse to complex computations (Lange, 1936, pp. 66–71).[5]

It was not only the flourishing and overall acceptance of the neoclassical model (ironically despite the greatest economic crisis in modern history) that was an important factor against Austrian economists in the debate. An institutional analysis of the principal–agent problem came exactly at the same time to attack the idea of private property as a central feature of efficiently functioning markets. As Lange and other neoclassical economists wanted socialism to mimic most functions of capitalism (consumer markets, labor markets, management, etc.), there remained a most crucial function specifically highlighted later by Mises that could not be replicated under socialism: private property in the capital markets. Unfortunately, this was ignored by theoreticians, and it was explicitly invoked only later in the debate by Mises in his *Nationalökonomie* and *Human Action*, i.e. in the 1940s, when the debate was already over. On the institutional side, Adolf Berle and Gardiner Means were arguing for the existence of separation of ownership and control in the contemporary stock markets, thus downplaying the importance of capital ownership (Berle & Means, 1933). If most market functions can be replicated under socialism and the function of ultimate ownership is irrelevant, then why cry for capitalism?

MOVING FORWARD WITH THE ARGUMENT

The debate, labeled by economic historian Mark Blaug as "one of the most significant controversies in modern economics" (Blaug, 1997a, p. 557), ended after all these exchanges in the 1940s with a broad agreement that the Austrian camp was wrong, and their opponents proved decisively the possibility and even the practicality of the economic calculation under socialism (Vaughn, 1994, p. 481). However, it is crucial to note that all the responses came from economists such as Lange, who supported socialism politically, but who were at the same time avowed neoclassical economists and followers of the Walras general equilibrium tradition. This is not accidental, since even Schumpeter and Knight, hardly to be accused of socialist sympathies, acknowledged the correctness of Lange's position: there is no difference between the logic of capitalist and socialist economy and both systems diverge only in political and social matters (Knight, 1940, p. 269; Schumpeter, 2003, p. 172). As the concept of general equilibrium and the idea of capital as a homogeneous blob were getting very popular during the interwar years, it was not hard to establish the orthodox view on the debate, which Mises and his followers indisputably lost (Keizer, 1989, pp. 63–65; Lavoie, 1981, p. 42). This also coincides with Mises's view of the calculation debate as the break of the Austrian tradition from the neoclassical one within the broader marginalist-subjectivist heritage as the differences between these two approaches came to the forefront (Kirzner, 1988).

However, the triumph was short-lived. It turned out that the verdict relied on the particular milieu of the 1930s and 1940s, i.e. of the overconfidence of the static Walrasian general equilibrium framework – and on the misunderstanding of Mises and Hayek caused by forcing them within this paradigm. This concern was voiced for decades by Austrians, e.g. by Lavoie (1981, 1985) in his revision of the history of the socialist calculation debate. As years went by, the deficiencies of the neoclassical approach were becoming more and more visible: its blindness to the heterogeneity of capital goods, its inability to cope with the dynamics of the economy, and its neglect of entrepreneurship as a function peculiar to capitalism. Strikingly, the predictions made in neoclassical textbooks (e.g. Paul Samuelson's *Economics*) about the Soviet Union (USSR) overtaking the United States (USA) in terms of gross domestic product due to higher net investment were consistently failing not so much due to the socialist sympathies of the authors, but due to the weakness of the neoclassical apparatus (Levy & Peart, 2011, pp. 120–122). Finally, the point made by Austrians came to a broader acknowledgment with the fall of the USSR. To quote economic historian Robert Heilbroner, hardly sympathetic to Austrian economics: "It turns out, of course, that Mises was right. The Soviet system has long been dogged by a method of pricing that produced grotesque misallocations of effort" (Heilbroner, 1990, p. 92).

As mentioned, the main flaw of the neoclassical account of the issue of calculation was framing it as a static equilibrium problem. However, it is interesting to note that Mises already in 1922 was well aware that "the problem of economic calculation is of economic dynamics: it is no problem of statics

... the problem arises in an economy which is perpetually subject to change, an economy which every day is confronted with new problems which have to be solved" (Mises, 1951, p. 139). He even identified several particular factors influencing the constant economic changes: external nature, the quantity and quality of the population, the quantity and quality of capital goods, techniques of production, the organization of labor, and demand (Reynolds, 1998, p. 36).

In order to best understand the crux of the Misesian argument about the calculation and pricing process, and also to see why the Berle-Means doctrine does not violate it, let us turn to his *opus magnum, Human Action*, which contains important, but often overlooked elaborations on the topic. Mises admits there again that the problem does not concern all imaginary situations and that even under certain weaker assumptions in principle one could disregard monetary calculation as an allocation tool:

> the mere information conveyed by technology would suffice for the performance of calculation only if all means of production – both material and human – could be perfectly substituted for one another according to definite ratios, or if they all were absolutely specific. In the former case all means of production would be fit, although according to different ratios, for the attainment of all ends whatever; things would be as if only one kind of means – one kind of economic goods of a higher order existed. In the latter case each means could be employed for the attainment of one end only; one would attach to each group of complementary factors of production the value attached to the respective good of the first order. (Mises, 1998a, pp. 207–208)

That is, the requirement for the non-monetary calculation to work is twofold: we have to know the shapes of all production functions and, more importantly, all goods have to be either perfect substitutes for each other or they have to be perfectly specific, that is, without any substitutes.[6] Then, provided the knowledge of all possible needs with their order of importance and supplies of all factors of productions, we would be able to find an optimal allocation without resorting to any sort of price.

However, this is not the case in the real world, as Mises quickly notes. Therefore, we may say that calculation is all about determining trade-offs arising from the different allocations of partially specific capital goods. Since this is quite a compact description, we want to stress two implicit aspects of the economic calculation:

1. the existence of a common denominator for such comparisons – supposedly money as the common medium of exchange; and
2. the speculative character of the appraisement of potential alternatives – as opposed to merely mechanical evaluation based on past and present data.

Only when there are both prices expressed in the common denominator and people who use these prices to speculatively appraise different uses of controlled capital goods, there can exist a price-guided allocation of capital goods.

The lack of the first characteristic is obvious when we consider socialism with a central planning board. Of course, planners can envision some alternatives, but they can only arrive at the various amounts of heterogeneous goods needed for each production process – and they lack a way to decide on the proper trade-off between them other than simply making arbitrary decisions (setting the trade-offs internally).

It is worth noting that the lack of at least one of these traits (common denominator and speculative appraisement of alternatives) is not distinctive of socialism with central planning. We can apply it equally well to the market socialism schemes proposed by Taylor and Lange. Their trial-and-error approach, although possible in some accounting units, is purely past-oriented as it relies upon already existing shortages and surpluses under currently set prices. They did not care to state how often the prices should be updated, and there are practical limits to the frequency of changes (Vaughn, 1980, p. 546). But more importantly, past shortages and surpluses might be misleading as mechanistic indicators, no less than any pricing rule purely based on past prices would be. At any point present prices – or rather price offers – stem from the entrepreneurial future-oriented judgment as a factor crucial in understanding the whole of the market process (e.g. Foss & Klein, 2012).

The famous rule by Lerner (1937), who suggested that managers should equate prices with the respective marginal costs, is also dubious since it assumes the existence of costs as given, objective, and measurable independently of prices. Instead, as it was often repeated from the Austrian perspective, costs are subjective and framed in terms of foregone alternatives, thus dependent on a particular entrepreneurial judgment (e.g. Buchanan, 1973; Roberts, 1971, pp. 569–571; Rothbard, 1976, pp. 73–74; Thirlby, 1973). It is only via exchanges on the market that they give rise to objective quantities, i.e. prices.

This is especially important when we take into account innovations, for example, the introduction of a new method of production. In the market, to successfully implement innovations it is only needed to appraise the profitability as a difference between revenues and total costs in money terms. However, as a side effect, the higher the entrepreneurial profit, the greater the incentive for other entrepreneurs to compete with the innovation or to provide a way for outsourcing some tasks. This process allows maximizing the economic value of the innovation, possibly by creating some new markets for capital goods (Bylund, 2016, p. 130). However, it is easy to spot that in socialism, there exists no way to create a market for a new intermediary good other than the administrative one, and as such it has to be arbitrary, without any reference to its profitability. For one, every socialist manager can optimize only under the assumption that his set of possible inputs and outputs are fixed and known in advance:

> The management function is impotent with respect to reshaping an economy's capital structure and production apparatus, because it is limited to adjustments to, and within, already established supply functions ... Managers act within the boundaries of the supply functions created by entrepreneurs, and they therefore cannot produce an economy characterized by growth through value creation. (Bylund, 2018, p. 233)

Moreover, even the clear technical superiority of one production method over another does not preclude the economic inferiority given already existing capital structure, as noted by Mises back in 1931:

> Whether or not the plants equipped with the old, less efficient machines will discard them in spite of the fact that they are still utilizable and replace them by the new model depends on the degree of the new machine's superiority. Only if this superiority is great enough to compensate for the additional expenditure required is the scrapping of the old equipment economically sound. (Mises, 2003, p. 233)

In socialism, there is not only a problem with the pricing of innovations but also with the abolition of the capital market. As Mises once remarked to Murray Rothbard, "a stock market is crucial to the existence of capitalism and private property" (Rothbard, 2006, p. 426), and its existence delineates between capitalism and socialism as economic systems. To be more precise: capitalism needs a way to trade the titles of property to the original factors of production and capital goods. Of course, a stock market is an institution that allows and facilitates such trade, serving both as a primary and a secondary market for the masses.

All socialist schemes overlook that the abolition of the capital market has direct consequences: the abolition of the managerial market and market-based corporate governance. Ultimate ownership allows capitalists to appoint managers by judging their performance, e.g. measured in changes of the capital value of the firms managed. For stock companies, we have a direct way of getting public opinion about the current value of the assets of the company as shown by the value of the stocks. If people lose confidence, they sell their stocks, which pushes their price and thus the capital value of the company downwards. On the other hand, if more people have more confidence, they try to buy the stocks by outbidding the reservation price of their current owners. All of these features are absent without a proper stock market.

It becomes clear, then, that a socialist regime cannot use such rules to evaluate managerial skills. The whole process of governance can exist, but it has to be administrative, with top-down rules, thus promoting people who can adapt to them in the best – and most bureaucratic – way (Hayek, 1935, 1940). However, the lack of connection of such criteria to the efficiency of market allocation means that such ranking would be equally "arbitrary," or to be precise dependent on the monopolistic rule of the collective.[7]

Rothbard enriched the discussion by making a connection between the calculation argument and the monopoly theory. As he pointed out, monopoly is always a special privilege granted by the government that necessarily results in lower consumer satisfaction (Rothbard, 2004, p. 669). If there are suppliers forcefully excluded from making transactions, then apparently they were offering something beneficial, either in terms of lower prices or better (or different) quality. Henceforth, praxeologically every exclusion of the potential competitor worsens the position of the consumer, since she loses access to a product that under competitive conditions could offer something extra. The intervention can be local and applied to a minority of the market, but can also touch the whole sector, resulting in the majority of consumers being hampered by a monopolistic policy. In our thought experiment, step by step we can imagine the whole economy being monopolized by political regulations. Such would be full socialism, resulting in massive destruction of entrepreneurial allocations and pricing decisions. From this point of view, socialism is at the end of the spectrum of monopolization, amounting to the full exclusion of all competition between producers on the whole market.[8] Interestingly, this coincided with Hayekian insight about competition as a discovery procedure:

> Which goods are scarce, however, or which things are goods, or how scarce or valuable they are, is precisely one of the conditions that competition should discover: in each case it is the preliminary outcomes of the market process that inform individuals where it is worthwhile to search. Utilizing the widely diffused knowledge in a society with an advanced division of labor cannot be based on the condition that individuals know all the concrete uses that can be made of the objects in their environment. Their attention will be directed by the prices the market offers for various goods and services. (Hayek, 2002, p. 13)

As already noted, Mises in his *Socialism* provided a broader critique of socialism, not limited to the calculation argument, but taking under scrutiny its whole narrative about family, classes, profit motives, etc. This can be related to the point made by Deirdre McCloskey about bourgeois dignity as the pivotal element in the development of markets and capitalism (McCloskey, 2010). Briefly, her idea is that it was not until the time when being an entrepreneur was finally appreciated and stopped being regarded as an inferior way of living that the markets could really flourish and the finance and stock markets could be developed.

If we look at socialism from this perspective, we note its introduction amounts to the complete elimination of the bourgeoisie and all of the positive external effects associated with it. It may be physical (as in the USSR) and it may be reputational (as described by McCloskey). But under socialism it also becomes deeply institutionalized: any entrepreneur is deprived of some possibilities of executing his judgment by the very definition of this economic system.

MISES-HAYEK DEHOMOGENIZATION DEBATE

The renewed interest in the calculation debate within the Austrian School in the 1980s and 1990s gave rise to a fundamental question: is the argumentation presented by Hayek congenial to the one presented by Mises, or did he really retreat to another line of argumentation? It is well known that it was the influence of Mises which caused the young Hayek to turn his sympathies away from socialism (Hayek, 1976, pp. 189–190). Moreover, earlier Austrian writers on the subject ardently defended Hayek from Lange's accusation of a retreat to "the second line of defense" as from the Misesian-Hayekian perspective there was always an unbridgeable gulf between the consistency of the fictional model and its relevance to the real world (Lavoie, 1981, pp. 45–46; Rothbard, 1976, p. 68).

As Huerta de Soto (2013, p. 128) succinctly presented it, the dehomogenization question is about the difference between the two lines of argumentation:

1. Misesian algebraic or computational – the calculation scheme is not possible without prices as one cannot compute the profits and losses necessary to rationalize allocations.
2. Hayekian epistemological – it is simply impossible to properly centralize knowledge of a particular time and place related to not only concrete economic circumstances but also some aspects of entrepreneurial actions.

For authors such as Rothbard (1991, pp. 64–68), Salerno (1993, 1994, 1996), Herbener (1995), Hoppe (1996), and Hülsmann (1997), the Misesian argument was seen as a much stronger and fundamental one since it did not require the assumptions of incomplete knowledge on the side of the benevolent socialist planner. The crucial component from this perspective would be the lack of private property and free exchange of property titles as it directly makes exchange ratios non-existent under any additional assumptions. As a consequence, the Hayekian problem of knowledge would be limited only to the data that already exist, such as supply of consumer and producer goods or technology, but it could not include consumer taste. For the latter, we would need an intersubjective method of judging consumer satisfaction, independent of actual choices.

Salerno (1993, 2002) and Bostaph (2003) even go so far as to state that Hayek was a true disciple of Wieser, who was working within a verbal general equilibrium tradition, and thus he did not fully grasp the crux of the Misesian argument.[9] To support this, Salerno quotes from various economic works of Hayek from the 1930s and early 1940s, where he praised and used the static general equilibrium theory.[10] By the time Hayek published "The Use of Knowledge in Society," he had come to the conclusion that this model was wrong, but only due to the lack of information, and not because of any inherent problem with its internal pricing mechanism (Salerno, 1993, pp. 127–128).

The defenders of the opposite view (Boettke, 2001; Horwitz, 1998, 2004; Huerta de Soto, 2013; Kirzner, 1996; Yeager, 1994, 1995, 1997) claim that the difference between the two lines of argumentation and, in consequence, between Mises and Hayek is perhaps merely verbal. Huerta de Soto points out that for Mises both lines of argument are complementary:

> For it is impossible to make any economic calculation, nor the corresponding pre-liminary judgments, if the necessary information, in the form of market prices, is unavailable. Moreover, it is the free exercise of entrepreneurship which constantly results in the creation of such information. Entrepreneurs continually bear in mind the terms of trade or market prices which have applied in the past, and they try to estimate or discover the market prices which will apply in the future. They then act in accordance with their estimates, and in this way, actually bring about the establishment of future prices. (Huerta de Soto, 2013, p. 129)

Yeager in a similar vein admits "that there might be more to the calculation problem than the knowledge aspect" (Yeager, 1997, p. 135). And they all agree that Hayek was following and building on the original Misesian argument, just highlighting epistemic aspects already implicit therein (Boettke, 2001, p. 38; Horwitz, 1998, pp. 443–444; Kirzner, 1996, p. 153).

As in the case of many discussions, this one also has run its own course and sometimes involved ambiguous interpretations and misunderstandings.[11] Nevertheless, one can hardly deny that what flourished as a dehomogenization debate has certainly enriched our understanding of the nature of the economic calculation, especially what it really means to *know* something from the economic perspective, and perhaps even more importantly what it means to *calculate* something in economics. In particular, the three theoretical important points are worth mentioning: first, all sides accepted that it is simply not true that past prices can be automatically translated, but there is a necessary spec-ulative element in the economic calculation (Rothbard, 1991, p. 66; Yeager, 1997, p. 134). Thus, one cannot confuse economic calculations with mathe-matical operations – and both Mises and Hayek affirmed that the size of the computational problem was at best a secondary problem for socialism (Huerta de Soto, 2013, pp. 168, 171). Second, the debate clarified that there are no data about the "true" underlying relative scarcities out there in the world that prices merely reflect or summarize (Mahoney, 2012, pp. 63–67). Instead, every act of exchange creates information by changing price offers and quantities available for other participants, and without these exchanges the relevant data would not come into existence at all. And last, but not least, the private property and the market price system is what by necessity underlies any solution to both computational and informational problems in real-world circumstances (Machaj, 2018, pp. 155–169).

MEANING OF "IMPOSSIBILITY" AND CALCULATION VERSUS INCENTIVES

Bryan Caplan (2004, 2005) turned attention to some definitional and empirical issues related to the impossibility argument. From the outset he agreed with the Misesian argument that socialism destroys economic calculation while disagreeing that socialism has to be for that reason unsustainable chaos and as such it is impossible, contrary to what Mises (1998a, p. 680) and Rothbard (1991, p. 57, 2004, pp. 613–614) said.[12] Lower productivity of a socialist economy cannot be a decisive factor, since such a country still could sustain itself (e.g. by putting a large part of manpower in agriculture) while being viewed by its inhabitants as more egalitarian or moral compared to a capitalist one.

All these insights definitely have certain merits, as noted in the responses (Boettke & Leeson, 2005; Gonzalez & Stringham, 2005; Gordon, 2005). For example, Mises was already aware that his argument applies for dynamic advanced economies since for very simple processes of production no calculation is needed (Mises, 1998a, p. 210). And it would still be true that productivity would be reduced to the level of satisfaction of basic needs, and any more complex process of production would incur huge waste. In fact, the USSR, North Korea, and other communist countries are not examples of socialism but rather mixed economies due to their internal black markets. The impossibility of socialism, as opposed to the impossibility of rational allocation in socialism, would mean that such a system cannot be stable compared even to meager alternatives like black markets or open defiance against the state.

What also could be developed here is a notion of *structural compatibility* between a variety of sectors in the economy. It is certainly true that primitive economies can easily function without money and financial markets, and at the same time allow for many people not to die of hunger while integrating productively in alternative socio-economic arrangements. As such, an agricultural sector, with low yet sufficient productivity, which dominates 80 percent of employment can be envisioned without a production structure based on economic calculation. Instead it could have a very labor-intensive flat production structure fueled by a specific cultural system of barter, gifts, and early features of a sharing economy. Many early societies did precisely that without any chaos and collapse.

It becomes questionable, however, that such a system could be compatible with a highly industrialized country with aspirations to a higher and more significant part of the labor force not being employed in the agricultural sector. As agriculture employs a small part of the population and has to somehow match optimally variables of employment, capital equipment, logistics, and management, the calculation becomes absolutely indispensable. In agricultural societies most of the production is either used directly or for a direct local exchange, which can happen with minimal forms of calculation (and often a non-monetary one). That is not compatible, however, with developed industrial nations requiring most of the surplus of agricultural production to be distributed across all specialized economic sectors. Paradoxically such a *structural incompatibility* may result in food shortages that would not be present under more primitive societies. As such, that also explains why private land consisting of only 1 percent of the whole area supplied almost 30 percent of food in the Soviet system (Heller & Nekrich, 1986, p. 687).

Caplan (2004, pp. 41–44) also noticed that it is hard to judge the significance of the impossibility argument in practice since historical examples are mixtures of calculation and incentive problems. He argues that in fact the latter factors were more prominent in countries like the USSR. However, as Gonzalez and Stringham (2005, p. 191) point out, doing this properly would require at least a clarification of what could count in each category, and there can still be found plenty of cases supporting the case of the importance of calculation problems. Furthermore, the calculation problem is a root cause of many perverse incentives. Theoretically, a central owner has much more power to incentivize people negatively (punish) and in theory positively (enrich them by offering opportunities that are not available elsewhere). Yet under socialism people can only be incentivized to follow orders and specific plans defined by the monopolist owner. The crucial problem therefore remains: while incentives are derivates of plans and orders, how can those orders and plans embody economic rationalization without the pricing process?

A MARKET SOCIALIST STRIKES BACK

Another interesting approach to the calculation problem was offered by Denis (2015, 2017), who agreed that while exchange ratios are necessary to calculate, he believes that private property is not essential. As anarchocapitalist order is not a necessary prerequisite for economic calculation, Denis believes that to arrive at exchange ratios we need only "several" property, that is:

> divided property with a single legal owner, property which is no longer held in common or jointly, with plural owners, as tribal property was, but has been severed ... Several property is thus opposed to the common property of a community, but – and this is key – there is no particular requirement for it to be private, or non-governmental divided property, rather than public divided property. (Denis 2015, p. 614)

He also noted that Hayek cited approvingly the term "several property" over "private property" as more precisely indicating the decentralized control over resources. The prime example of several property can be the nationalized British Steel Corporation: it is neither private, nor common, i.e. available to use for everybody.

However, as Mises (1998a, pp. 301–302, 2008, pp. 36–37) emphasizes time and again, the crucial trait of the capitalists is bearing the burden of losses, unlike an appointed manager with a fixed salary. Capitalists are sovereign in decisions like where to invest or set up a firm, when to exit, and which manager to employ. And they perform these decisions based on economic calculation, guided by expected profitability of each investment. When the economy is within the hands of one owner, collective (democratic) or individual (auto-cratic), there is no way to assess the profitability of any production change. And managers always face the principal–agent problem, which causes them to force the riskier and less sustainable structure of production, disconnected from the customers' wishes but aligned with managers' incentives (Bylund & Manish, 2017, pp. 420–421).

It may be added that since public ownership is by definition a system with a single (possibly collective) owner, the only ultimate decision maker would not encounter any limitations from the other property owners, but only from the physical scarcity. This sets the stage for the managers to "compete," but they are not economic actors since they may overrule any opposition by their will. On the contrary, in a private ownership regime there is no supreme agent who establishes rules for others, but everyone is limited in their sovereignty to his or her property, confirmed by legal ownership titles and contracts, by which direct control is passed to other parties. Under socialism the ultimate owner adjusts *the* prices. Under capitalism the owner adjusts *to* prices (Machaj, 2018, pp. 163–169). Denis is certainly right that several property can produce some exchange ratios, but there remains a central question: what do they reflect and how do they interrelate? The central planner can also establish some ratios and perform arithmetical tasks in them – but what can those ratios tell us?

What are the consequences of the above-mentioned differences between private and public ownership? As we mentioned, as long as the ultimate will is never executed, but always delegated to some manager, it makes no difference. But an absolutely passive owner, not interfering with the disposal of his ownership or taking any advantage of its existence, whether public or private, would play no practical difference – it would be just the regime in which managers *are* owners in all but dead legal claim. Suppose for example that Congress passes an act that assigns all the property of US citizens to Joan Smith. However, suppose also that all the people in the world (including the people who passed this act) are certain that Smith is in no position whatsoever to enforce this regulation in any particular case. This would mean of course that the legal title belongs to Smith, but it is irrelevant since it would bear no economic consequences – and as such it does not provide any economic explanation or support.[13]

Within a system of private property there is no fixed "one will to rule them all," but the ultimate power of each will is proportional to the share of capital one owns. Moreover, as Mises notes, this is nowhere near steady, but keeps changing on a daily basis (Mises, 2008, p. 13). Every successful decision – direct or via delegation to a successful agent – is reflected in an increase of the value of capital under disposal. Every mistake is revealed as a loss. Every choice is made under conditions, which are to a large extent independent of an entrepreneur. The system of private property as we see today is, on the contrary, highly distributed between many individual wills. This entails the notion of *contestability* of the markets, as put in the notion introduced by Baumol (1982). It is a fact not only that at every moment the price of every good stems from an agreement between sides of the transaction, but also that it can be questioned by them as well as by third parties. The competition serves here as a way to economize on entrepreneurial abilities, as to pursue your plan you have to become the owner of the scarce means, which in turn requires you to outbid all other people with their plans concerning the usage of the same good (see more in Machaj, 2018, pp. 150–154).

Finally, we note that the existence of decentralized several property does not preclude the economic calculation. Mises (1951, pp. 270–275) described for example syndicalism as an example of such a property regime, and although he criticized it for hampering a division of labor and the rigidity of the production structure, he did not imply that it makes the economic calculation impossible.

ADDITIONAL CHALLENGES

The discussion ignited by Mises's essay has gone on for over 100 years and it has already touched many issues related to the calculation problem. However, there are still some vital areas of interest for future research.

The major challenge for any researcher in the Misesian vein is the question of delivering the basic goods, which are prerequisites to the sufficiently effective functioning of the exchange economy with the private property itself. A list of such goods includes national defense and the law, which Mises himself assumed to be the responsibility of the state (Mises, 2006, p. 37). Clearly, one has to consider how such goods are to be priced, even though especially in the case of the law there is no price system for it. It is said that many of these services offer positive externalities which cannot be easily internalized by the workings of the price system, which may cause a problem for the rational allocation of scarce goods for these goals: "where a considerable part of the costs incurred are external costs from the point of view of the acting individuals or firms, the economic calculation established by them is manifestly defective and their results deceptive" (Mises, 1998a, p. 653).

This issue is related to the observation put forward by Elinor Ostrom. She noticed that the effective order does not have to arise through price incentives, but there exist various communal solutions to the coordination problem. One can ask how this can be squared with the calculation argument, which unequivocally rates non-price mechanisms unfavorably. Is it the case that such solutions could be only second best? Can they be at least "good enough" in some sense? Which institutional setting leads to the most effective government or communal solution? Modern Austrian economists have offered their critique of the ineffectiveness of the government provision of such services also due to the problems with economic calculation (Coyne, 2015, p. 382; Coyne & Goodman, 2020, pp. 248–251). And they provided their own perspective on how market-based approaches could be applied to provide national defense (Hoppe, 2003).

Another problem arises with the widespread conviction that we live in the age of Big Data and sophisticated machine inference techniques, which could be useful in overcoming mathematical difficulties mentioned e.g. by Hayek and Robbins. However, as we have shown, the root of the calculation problem does not lie with a lack of computational power and the existence of computers by itself cannot solve the calculation problem; it even makes it even harder (e.g. Horwitz, 1996; Huerta de Soto, 2013, pp. 69–73). As a related problem, we can consider an example of an economy run fully with 3D printers. It may be asked whether this can simplify the problem to a level when it could be at least in principle solvable. After all, for 3D printers we could envision energy as a common unit at every stage of production – but would such accounting be sufficient to get rid of calculation in money terms without dire consequences in productivity?

Next, there remains not only theoretical but also historical and practical work to do. We have some descriptions of the workings of the system probably as close to socialism as one can get in practice, i.e. early USSR (Boettke, 1990; Brutzkus, 1935). However, we lack for example comprehensive historical works describing the privatization processes e.g. during the 1990s (with the sole exception of Boettke, 1993) together with some praxeological-thymologi-cal analyses of different privatization schemes and advice towards the best one possible.

Clearly, over 30 years after the fall of communism, the question of the fea-sibility of rational allocation of goods under socialism is not as prominent as it was earlier. The countries today with active and massive participation of the government in the economy definitely would not qualify in Mises's typology as a socialist. Rather, they should be classified as interventionist or, equiva-lently, as hampered market economies. One could wonder how far the argu-ment presented by Mises can be applied in such cases, where some markets are restricted but not fully absent (Ikeda, 1997). For example, one area, which is probably the most heavily regulated in modern economies, is the sphere of money production and distribution. The rule applies especially to the recent 15 years since the Great Recession of 2008, when an unprecedented amount of monetary interventions were not only applied but theoretically developed. The balance sheets of all the major central banks across the globe have risen to record levels not seen previously during any other crash (Bagus & Howden, 2016). It also changed significantly the quality of assets that were being accepted as collateral in the special tools of unconventional monetary policy. Naturally, such actions do not mean that capitalism in the financial market has been abolished, since first, the stock market still plays its crucial role, and second, the actions were just a part of market transactions. Nevertheless, despite relatively low volume, they still played a major role in short-term pricing decisions. The question whether this could be a potential option for the Schumpeterian path to the socialization of the financial markets remains to be solved (McCaffrey, 2009).

From a broader point of view, we point out that several later writers put forward other definitions of socialism as "an institutionalized policy of aggres-sion against property" (Hoppe, 2010, p. 18) or "any systematic or institutional coercion or aggression which restricts the free exercise of entrepreneurship" (Huerta de Soto, 2013, p. 59). Clearly, on such accounts interventionism is a kind of socialistic system, even though it is preserving the main feature of capitalism: the stock exchange, embodying the market for capital goods. However, the question arises: how do these definitional issues relate to the calculation argument? How irrational is allocation in hampered market economies?

This issue is directly related to the so-called Misesian Paradox (Ikeda, 2016): on the one hand, according to Mises, "the middle system of property that is hampered, guided, and regulated by government is in itself contradictory and illogical. Any attempt to introduce it in earnest must lead to a crisis from which either socialism or capitalism alone can emerge" (Mises, 1996, p. 38). On the other hand, it is clear that interventionist states thrive or at least do not seem to wane in the near future despite the well-known negative unintended consequences of particular interventions. It is an interesting question how this discrepancy could be resolved and to what extent we are able to apply the calculation argument to non-socialist systems (see discussion in Ikeda, 2016). Of course, the theoretical research on interventionism in the vein of Mises (1996, 1998b) may – and indeed should – be supplemented by extensive empirical research on the particular kinds of intervention.

Overall, it may be stated with confidence that the calculation argument is indeed *the* Austrian contribution to political economy (Boettke, 2001). And while it gives a solid theoretical foundation, at the same time it opens many further questions for comparative economic systems research.

NOTES

1. See Ebeling (1993, pp. 65–85) and Steele (1981, pp. 2–9) for an overview of critics of economic problems of socialism before Mises. However, as Mises (1998a, p. 697) himself notes, all but Nicolaas Pierson failed to get to the core of the problem and even Pierson did not integrate it within a broader theory.
2. Contrary to Boettke and Leeson (2005), the Misesian definition of socialism is solely property-oriented, without any reference to goals such as greater productivity. See also Gonzalez and Stringham (2005, pp. 180–182).
3. See also a similar exposition in Boettke (2001, p. 31) and Van Den Hauwe (2019, p. 192).
4. In fact, the first, largely forgotten round of the discussion occurred between Mises and German-speaking economists in the early 1920s. See Keizer (1987) and Chaloupek (1990) for details.
5. Interestingly, later in his life Lange (1972, pp. 401–402) came to believe in solving the equation using computers. However, as Engelhardt (2013) has shown, given the reasonable estimate of the number of goods on the market, the time needed to solve such a system of equations far exceeds the powers of today's computers.
6. Compare Hayek (1945, p. 525), who wrote that "a single mind could solve this kind of problem only by constructing and constantly using rates of equivalence (or "values," or "marginal rates of substitution"), i.e., by attaching to each kind of scarce resource a numerical index ... which reflects, or in which is condensed, its significance in view of the whole means–end structure."
7. There was a divergence of views on how this incentive would affect actions of managers: Mises argued that the lack of losses of personal wealth would make managers more prone to risk, and Hayek thought that they would be risk-averse due to the reputational consequences of eventual failures in pursuit of probable greater gains (Vaughn, 1994, p. 482).
8. Let us just mention in passing that the same connection was made by Rothbard (1976, pp. 75–76) between the calculation argument and the firm theory: there has to exist an upper limit on the size of a firm, since otherwise it would face the same problem as a socialist state.
9. Congenially, Blaug (1997b, p. 280) notes that Mises formulated his argument against the Wieserian framework presented in his 1889 book *Natural Value*.

And it was already Buchanan (1999, pp. 22–23) who observed that Hayek did not push his subjectivist conclusions far enough, as he was still clinging to the competitive equilibrium framework.

10. On the other hand, as early as 1935 Hayek warned against relying on the "hypothetical state of stationary equilibrium" by the Walrasians, as it misled them into objectifying the costs (Hayek, 1935, pp. 226–227).

11. See Vaughn (1980, p. 544), who noted well before the dehomogenization debate that Hayek did not present his case with sufficient clarity. Certainly, to Hayek's credit we note that he wrote in 1982 that if all the knowledge was centralized, then still the planning authority would not be able to rationally allocate the factors of production (Hayek, 1982, pp. 137–138; see also Machaj, 2015).

12. For example, Mises (1998a, p. 676) graphically compared a choice between capitalism and socialism to a choice between a glass of water and a glass of cyanide.

13. This is not a view that Denis had in mind when he described it as public ownership with a several property regime. He assigns to the state the tasks of protecting the environment, providing subsidies to the poor, and even manipulating the price system using Pigovian taxes (Denis 2015, pp. 620–621). Since they are all unrelated to the issue of several property they are criticized by the Austrians separately, e.g. using a framework provided by Rothbard (2004, pp. 875–1297).

REFERENCES

Bagus, P., & Howden, D. (2016). Central Bank Balance Sheet Analysis. *Betriebswirtschaftliche Forschung Und Praxis*, *2*(68), 109–125.

Barone, E. (1908). Il Ministro Della Produzione Nello Stato Collettivista. *Giornale Degli Economisti*, *37*, 267–283.

Baumol, W. J. (1982). Contestable Markets: An Uprising in the Theory of Industry Structure. *American Economic Review*, *72*(1), 1–15.

Bergson, A. (1948). Socialist Economics. In H. Ellis (Ed.), *A Survey of Contemporary Economics* (pp. 412–448). Philadelphia, PA: The Blakiston Company.

Berle, A., & Means, G. (1933). *The Modern Corporation and Private Property*. New York: Macmillan.

Blaug, M. (1997a). *Economic Theory in Retrospect*. Cambridge: Cambridge University Press.

Blaug, M. (1997b). *Great Economists before Keynes*. Cheltenham, UK and Northampton, MA, USA: Edward Elgar Publishing.

Boettke, P. J. (1990). *The Political Economy of Soviet Socialism: The Formative Years, 1918–1928*. Springer Science & Business Media.

Boettke, P. J. (1993). *Why Perestroika Failed*. London: Routledge.

Boettke, P. J. (2001). Economic Calculation: The Austrian Contribution to Political Economy. In *Calculation and Coordination: Essays on Socialism and Transitional Political Economy* (pp. 29–46). London: Routledge.

Boettke, P. J., & Leeson, P. T. (2005). Still Impossible after All These Years: Reply to Caplan. *Critical Review*, *17*(1–2), 155–170.

Bostaph, S. (2003). Wieser on Economic Calculation under Socialism. *Quarterly Journal of Austrian Economics*, *6*(2), 3–34.

Brutzkus, B. (1935). *Economic Planning in Soviet Russia*. London: Routledge & Sons.

Buchanan, J. M. (1973). Introduction: L. S. E. Cost Theory in Retrospect. In J. M. Buchanan & G. Thirlby (Eds), *L. S. E. Essays on Cost* (pp. 1–18). London: London School of Economics and Political Science.

Buchanan, J. M. (1999). Cost and Choice: An Inquiry in Economic Theory. In *The Collected Works of James M. Buchanan*, Volume 6. Indianapolis, IN: Liberty Fund.

Bylund, P. L. (2016). *The Problem of Production: A New Theory of the Firm*. London: Routledge.

Bylund, P. L. (2018). The Management Problem of Socialism: Cost at the Expense of Value. In M. McCaffrey (Ed.), *The Economic Theory of Costs Foundations and New Directions*. London: Routledge.

Bylund, P. L., & Manish, G. P. (2017). Private Property and Economic Calculation: A Reply to Andy Denis. *Review of Political Economy, 29*(3), 414–431.

Caplan, B. (2004). Is Socialism Really "Impossible"? *Critical Review, 16*(1), 33–52.

Caplan, B. (2005). Toward a New Consensus on the Economics of Socialism: Rejoinder to My Critics. *Critical Review, 17*(1–2), 203–220.

Chaloupek, G. (1990). The Austrian Debate on Economic Calculation in a Socialist Economy. *History of Political Economy, 22*(4), 659–675.

Coyne, C. J. (2015). Lobotomizing the Defense Brain. *Review of Austrian Economics, 28*(4), 371–396.

Coyne, C. J., & Goodman, N. (2020). Economic Pathologies of the State. In G. Chartier & C. Van Schoelandt (Eds), *The Routledge Handbook of Anarchy and Anarchist Thought* (pp. 247–261). London: Routledge.

Denis, A. (2015). Economic Calculation: Private Property or Several Control? *Review of Political Economy, 27*(4), 606–623.

Denis, A. (2017). Private Property or Several Control: A Rejoinder. *Review of Political Economy, 29*(3), 432–439.

Dickinson, H. (1939). *Economics of Socialism*. London: Oxford University Press.

Ebeling, R. M. (1993). Economic Calculation under Socialism: Ludwig von Mises and His Predecessors. In J. M. Herbener (Ed.), *The Meaning of Ludwig von Mises* (pp. 56–101). Norwell, MA: Kluwer Academic Press.

Engelhardt, L. (2013). Central Planning's Computation Problem. *Quarterly Journal of Austrian Economics, 16*(2), 227–246.

Foss, N. J., & Klein, P. G. (2012). *Organizing Entrepreneurial Judgment: A New Approach to the Firm*. Cambridge: Cambridge University Press.

Gonzalez, R. A., & Stringham, E. (2005). Incentives vs. Knowledge: Reply to Caplan. *Critical Review, 17*(1–2), 179–202.

Gordon, D. (2005). Calculation and Chaos: Reply to Caplan. *Critical Review, 17*(1–2), 171–178.

Hayek, F. A. von. (1935). The Present State of the Debate. In *Collectivist Economic Planning* (pp. 201–243). London: Routledge & Sons.

Hayek, F. A. von. (1940). Socialist Calculation: The Competitive "Solution." *Economica, 7*(26), 125–149.

Hayek, F. A. von. (1945). The Use of Knowledge in Society. *American Economic Review*. https://doi.org/10.2307/1809376

Hayek, F. A. von. (1976). Tribute to Mises by Hayek. In M. v. Mises (Ed.), *My years with Ludwig von Mises* (pp. 187–191). New Rochelle, NY: Arlington House.

Hayek, F. A. von. (1982). Two Pages of Fiction. *Economic Affairs, 2*(3), 135–142.

Hayek, F. A. von. (2002). Competition as a Discovery Procedure. *Quarterly Journal of Austrian Economics, 5*(3), 9–23.

Heilbroner, R. (1990). After Communism. *New Yorker*, 91–92.

Heller, M., & Nekrich, A. (1986). *Utopia in Power: The History of the Soviet Union from 1917 to the Present.* New York: Summit Books.

Herbener, J. M. (1995). Calculation and the Question of Arithmetic. *Review of Austrian Economics, 9*(1), 151–162.

Hoppe, H.-H. (1996). Socialism: A Property or Knowledge Problem? *Review of Austrian Economics, 9*(1), 143–147.

Hoppe, H.-H. (2003). The Myth of National Defense. In *Essays on the Theory and History of Security Production.* Auburn, AL: Ludwig von Mises Institute.

Hoppe, H.-H. (2010). *A Theory of Socialism and Capitalism.* Norwell, MA: Ludwig von Mises Institute.

Horwitz, S. G. (1996). Money, Money Prices, and the Socialist Calculation Debate. In P. J. Boettke (Ed.), *Advances in Austrian Economics*, Volume 3 (pp. 59–77). Bingley: Emerald Group Publishing.

Horwitz, S. G. (1998). Monetary Calculation and Mises's Critique of Planning. *History of Political Economy, 30*(3), 427–450.

Horwitz, S. G. (2004). Monetary Calculation and the Unintended Extended Order: The Misesian Microfoundations of the Hayekian Great Society. *Review of Austrian Economics, 17*(4), 307–321.

Huerta de Soto, J. (2013). *Socialism, Economic Calculation and Entrepreneurship.* London: Institute of Economic Affairs Monographs.

Hülsmann, J. G. (1997). Knowledge, Judgment, and the Use of Property. *Review of Austrian Economics, 10*(1), 23–48.

Hülsmann, J. G. (2007). *Mises: The Last Knight of Liberalism.* Auburn, AL: Ludwig von Mises Institute.

Ikeda, S. (1997). *Dynamics of a Mixed Economy: Towards a Theory of Interventionism.* London: Routledge.

Ikeda, S. (2016). The Misesian Paradox: Interventionism Is Not Sustainable. https://oll .libertyfund.org/page/liberty-matters-sanford-ikeda-mises-interventionism

Keizer, W. (1987). Two Forgotten Articles by Ludwig von Mises on the Rationality of Socialist Economic Calculation. *Review of Austrian Economics, 1*(1), 109–122.

Keizer, W. (1989). Recent Reinterpretations of the Socialist Calculation Debate. *Journal of Economic Studies, 16*(2), 63–83.

Kirzner, I. M. (1988). The Economic Calculation Debate: Lessons for Austrians. *Review of Austrian Economics, 2*(1), 1–18.

Kirzner, I. M. (1996). Reflections on the Misesian Legacy in Economics. *Review of Austrian Economics, 9*(2), 143–154.

Knight, F. H. (1940). Socialism: The Nature of the Problem. *Ethics, 50*(3), 253–289.

Lange, O. (1936). On the Economic Theory of Socialism: Part One. *Review of Economic Studies, 4*(1), 53–71.

Lange, O. (1972). The Computer and the Market. In A. Nove & D. M. Nuti (Eds), *Socialist Economics: Selected Readings* (pp. 401–402). London: Penguin Books.

Lavoie, D. (1981). A Critique of the Standard Account of the Socialist Calculation Debate. *Journal of Libertarian Studies, 5*(1), 41–87.

Lavoie, D. (1985). *Rivalry and Central Planning: The Socialist Calculation Debate Reconsidered.* Cambridge: Cambridge University Press.

Lerner, A. P. (1937). Statics and Dynamics in Socialist Economics. *The Economic Journal, 47*(186), 253.

Levy, D. M., & Peart, S. J. (2011). Soviet Growth and American Textbooks: An Endogenous Past. *Journal of Economic Behavior and Organization, 78*(1–2), 110–125.

Machaj, M. (2015). Hayek's Return to the Roots? *Argumenta Oeconomica, 2*(35), 49–65.

Machaj, M. (2018). *Capitalism, Socialism and Property Rights*. Newcastle upon Tyne: Agenda Publishing.

Mahoney, D. (2012). Mises' Calculation Argument: A Clarification. *Libertarian Papers, 4*, 53–76.

McCaffrey, M. (2009). Entrepreneurship, Economic Evolution, and the End of Capitalism: Reconsidering Schumpeter's Thesis. *Quarterly Journal of Austrian Economics, 12*(4), 3–21.

McCloskey, D. N. (2010). *Bourgeois Dignity: Why Economics Can't Explain the Modern World*. Chicago, IL: University of Chicago Press.

Mises, L. von. (1951). *Socialism: An Economic and Sociological Analysis*. New Haven, CT: Yale University Press.

Mises, L. von. (1990). *Economic Calculation in a Socialist Commonwealth*. Auburn, AL: Ludwig von Mises Institute.

Mises, L. von. (1996). *A Critique of Interventionism*. Irvington-on-Hudson, NY: Foundation for Economic Education.

Mises, L. von. (1998a). *Human Action: A Treatise on Economics*. Auburn, AL: Ludwig von Mises Institute.

Mises, L. von. (1998b). *Interventionism: An Economic Analysis* (B. B. Greaves, Ed.). New York: Foundation for Economic Education.

Mises, L. von. (2003). *Epistemological Problems of Economics* (Third Ed.). Auburn, AL: Ludwig von Mises Institute.

Mises, L. von. (2006). *Economic Policy: Thoughts for Today and Tomorrow*. Auburn, AL: Ludwig von Mises Institute

Mises, L. von. (2008). *Profit and Loss*. Auburn, AL: Ludwig von Mises Institute.

Neurath, O. von. (1973). Through War Economy to Economy in Kind. In M. Neurath & R. Cohen (Eds), *Empiricism and Sociology* (pp. 123–157). Dordrecht: Reidel Publishing.

Reynolds, M. O. (1998). The Impossibility of Socialist Economy, or, a Cat Cannot Swim the Atlantic Ocean. *Quarterly Journal of Austrian Economics, 1*(2), 29–44.

Robbins, L. (1971). *The Great Depression*. Freeport, NY: Books for Library Press.

Roberts, P. C. (1971). Oskar Lange's Theory of Socialist Planning. *Journal of Political Economy, 79*(3), 562–577.

Rothbard, M. N. (1976). Ludwig von Mises and Economic Calculation under Socialism. In L. Moss (Ed.), *The Economics of Ludwig von Mises: Toward a Critical Reappraisal* (pp. 67–77). New York: Sheed and Ward.

Rothbard, M. N. (1991). The End of Socialism and the Calculation Debate Revisited. *Review of Austrian Economics, 5*(2), 51–76.

Rothbard, M. N. (2004). *Man, Economy, and State A Treatise on Economic Principles with Power and Market Government and the Economy*. Auburn, AL: Ludwig von Mises Institute.

Rothbard, M. N. (2006). A Socialist Stock Market? In *Making Economic Sense* (pp. 425–428). Auburn, AL: Ludwig von Mises Institute.

Salerno, J. T. (1993). Mises and Hayek Dehomogenized. *Review of Austrian Economics, 6*(2), 113–146.

Salerno, J. T. (1994). Reply to Leland B. Yeager on "Mises and Hayek on Calculation and Knowledge." *Review of Austrian Economics, 7*(2), 111–125.

Salerno, J. T. (1996). A Final Word: Calculation, Knowledge, and Appraisement. *Review of Austrian Economics, 9*(1), 141–142.

Salerno, J. T. (2002). Friedrich von Wieser and Friedrich A. Hayek: The General Equilibrium Tradition in Austrian Economics. *Journal Des Economistes et Des Etudes Humaines*, *12*(2). https://doi.org/10.2202/1145-6396.1066

Schumpeter, J. A. (2003). *Capitalism, Socialism and Democracy*. London: Routledge.

Steele, D. R. (1981). Posing the Problem: The Impossibility of Economic Calculation under Socialism. *Journal of Libertarian Studies*, *5*(1), 7–22.

Taylor, F. M. (1929). The Guidance of Production in a Socialist State. *American Economic Review*, *19*(1), 1–8.

Thirlby, G. (1973). The Ruler. In J. M. Buchanan & G. Thirlby (Eds), *L.S.E. Essays on Cost* (pp. 163–200). London: London School of Economics and Political Science.

Van Den Hauwe, L. (2019). Ludwig von Mises' Argument against the Possibility of Socialism: Early Concepts and Contemporary Relevance. In J. Backhaus, G. Chaloupek, & H. Frambach (Eds), *The First Socialization Debate (1918) and Early Efforts towards Socialization* (pp. 191–222). Cham: Springer Nature.

Vaughn, K. I. (1980). Economic Calculation under Socialism: The Austrian Contribution. *Economic Inquiry*, *18*(4), 535–554.

Vaughn, K. I. (1994). The Socialist Calculation Debate. In P. J. Boettke (Ed.), *The Elgar Companion to Austrian Economics* (pp. 478–484). Cheltenham, UK and Northampton, MA, USA: Edward Elgar Publishing.

Yeager, L. B. (1994). Mises and Hayek on Calculation and Knowledge. *Review of Austrian Economics*, *7*(2), 93–109.

Yeager, L. B. (1995). Rejoinder: Salerno on Calculation, Knowledge, and Appraisement. *Review of Austrian Economics*, *9*(1), 137–139.

Yeager, L. B. (1997). Calculation and Knowledge: Let's Write *finis*. *Review of Austrian Economics*, *10*(1), 133–136.

9. Money

Joseph T. Salerno and Kristoffer J. M. Hansen

INTRODUCTION

One core feature of the Austrian school since its inception is the focus on monetary theory. Scarcely none of the great Austrians were not also monetary theorists (the possible exception is Böhm-Bawerk) and many great advances in monetary theory are due to Austrians. It is probably true to say that monetary theory is considered the core of economics by many Austrians, because as Mises (1998 [1949], p. 415) says: "Nothing can happen in the orbit of vendible goods without affecting the orbit of money, and all that happens in the orbit of money affects the orbit of commodities."

Be that as it may, in this chapter we will review contributions to and debates in monetary theory in the last generation or so. We will concentrate on the literature from the 1990s onward to show the current vitality of Austrian school monetary theory, but we will also mention some works from the 1980s that are still very much part of current discussion, as well as older, classic works that still inform modern Austrians.

The chapter is divided into three main parts: the supply of money; the demand for money; and monetary equilibrium. Although it is impossible to disentangle completely the fields of money and banking, here questions of banking theory are only cursorily treated. For a fuller discussion of banking, the reader is invited to consult Howden (this volume).

THE SUPPLY OF MONEY

Setting out from premises laid down by Menger (2009 [1892]) and Mises, the basic conception of money shared by all Austrians is that money is a market-produced good just like other goods. Government interference in the monetary system takes the form of price controls and, especially, control over the production of money. Legal tender laws and their consequences, known as Gresham's law, have been analyzed as a kind of price control (Mises, 2011, p. 25) and their importance for the development of the modern monetary system emphasized (Hülsmann, 2004).

Austrians depict the modern system of national paper moneys as the outcome of centuries of intervention (Hülsmann, 2008, pp. 193–236). The supply of money in this system is determined by monetary policy exogenous to the market. There is some debate over whether this is true of the supply of fractional-reserve bank money – fiduciary media – as well as central bank-controlled fiat money, as we briefly discuss in the section on free banking below. Be that as it may, the consequences of government interference with the supply of money have been a continued focus of Austrian research: Salerno (2012a) shows the relevance of the monetary theory of the business cycle for the recession of 2008 and White (2011) argues that the crisis was caused by the unconstrained monetary policy of the Federal Reserve.

More generally, the social and economic consequences of inflationary monetary policy have also received attention from Austrians in recent years: Hülsmann (2016) explains how fiat money leads to greater indebtedness, and how the inflation culture is marked by a pronounced increase in the present orientation of human planning and action and even the outright abandonment of the pursuit of long-term goals. Cantor (1994) and Salerno (2013) have considered the link between hyperinflation and changes to human personality. This focus on the more cultural and social aspects of inflation does not mean Austrians have abandoned more classic economic research: Sieroń (2017) examines how monetary inflation can have other effects than simply price increases, and he has also produced a thorough manual on the Cantillon effect, the unequal impact of inflation on different sectors of the economy and different people (Sieroń, 2019). One classical argument for the superiority of fiat money which can be traced back to Adam Smith is that it is more cost-efficient. This has been exploded by Israel (2021), who examines the real costs of modern central banking.

While of more theoretical concern, modern Austrians have also engaged in a deep analysis of deflation (Bagus, 2015a; Salerno, 2003; Thornton, 2003). Price deflation is a normal phenomenon in a growing economy and in fact beneficial, as the increase in output, ceteris paribus, causes a secular decline in prices. Government policy can also lead to deflation of the money supply. For instance, confiscatory or fiscal deflation – reducing the money supply either directly or through taxation – has been practiced as part of monetary reforms. Furthermore, in financial crises a credit crunch can lead to bank credit deflation, causing a severe restriction of the supply of fiduciary media. While painful, such a restriction in fact helps the recovery along, as it speeds up the adjustment of prices and the allocation of factors of production to profitable employments.

Commodity Money Production

While virtually all Austrian economists argue that a market-produced commodity money is superior, they do not simply restate a Misesian preference for gold. Rather, they have provided detailed analyses of how commodity money production responds to changes in the market data. The pioneer here was Hans Sennholz (1975, pp. 47–48), who in books and pamphlets arguing for a restored gold standard was the first to clearly indicate that commodity money production was subject to the law of costs in the same way as all other production in a market economy. Complementary factors of production will be allocated to money production – gold mining, minting and storage on a gold standard – until the marginal cost exceeds the expected marginal profit. That is, only if they have no other, more profitable uses, will factors of production be allocated to gold production.

Salerno (2010b [1982], pp. 357–361) expands on this key insight and, pairing it with the important article by Paish (1950 [1938]) describing the economics of gold mining, shows how the money supply under a gold standard responds to changes in the data of the market. The equilibrium in the money market occurs when demand and supply and hence the purchasing power of money (PPM) are constant. Gold-mining firms maximize profits by producing a quantity of gold per year just equal to the amount allocated to non-monetary uses plus the amount of monetary gold used up or destroyed during the year. From this equilibrium, we can now imagine an improvement in production technique that leads to greater output of gold. As a result, the prices of goods increase and the amounts of goods and service each gold ounce purchases declines. This also includes the prices of goods where gold is an input: their prices increase and a unit of gold now earns a net return in industrial uses greater than its own weight. Entrepreneurs reallocate gold to industrial uses, until eventually prices begin to fall and the discrepancy is eliminated. Salerno pursues a similar analysis in the case of rising costs of gold production and in the case of changes in demand for money. If demand rises, prices fall and gold production is stimulated, as each ounce can now purchase more, until a new equilibrium is reached. Conversely, if demand falls, gold is shifted to non-monetary use and its current production contracts.

Importantly, Salerno does not claim that there is one stable PPM to which the economy will tend to return after each disturbance. As in all other markets, the final price (or PPM) is constantly shifting as the data of the market change. However, we see in this analysis good economic reasons for the historical fact of long-term price stability in terms of gold that Rueff (1972, p. 45) remarked upon and which Jastram (2009 [1977]) explored at length.

White (1999, pp. 31–40) pursues a similar analysis of the economics of the gold standard showing the relations between the monetary and non-monetary demands for gold. However, unlike Salerno, White (1999, pp. 31–33) finds that in the long run, changes in the demand for monetary gold does not influence the PPM. A rise in the demand for monetary gold will in the long run only lead to a rise in cash balances and vice versa with a fall in demand. The tendency is rather for the money supply to respond to changes in demand or to demand "shocks" while keeping PPM stable in the long run. This difference speaks to a more fundamental disagreement to be described in the section on monetary adjustment.

Free Banking

White (1995 [1984]) and Selgin (1988) and a little later Horwitz (2000) argued that a free banking system can reliably supply the economy with the circulating medium it needs in the form of fractionally backed bank money or fiduciary media. Free banking has since then been a hotly debated topic. Here we will only consider some of the literature that pertains to the question of the supply of bank notes. Free banking argues that there are two principles constraining the issue of bank money: excess reserves and adverse clearings. Any bank will only keep reserves up to the point where the marginal cost (the foregone interest earned on additional loans) exceeds the marginal benefit (the expected value of avoiding a suspension of payment of notes and deposits due to insufficient reserves). Banks have to keep some reserves on hand for clearing with other banks, and this limits the possibilities of credit expansion. Within that limit, however, the supply of bank money is perfectly elastic and can expand to accommodate any demand for money (Dowd, 2015).

Critics of free banking dispute the argument that the supply of fiduciary media is stable. Following Rothbard, they see a fractional reserve banking system as inherently unstable and legal privileges and a central bank as necessary for its continued existence (Hülsmann, 2008, p. 93 and the following). Gertchev (2012), however, has argued that a central bank is not necessary for a fractional reserve banking system to keep expanding credit: such expansion can be coordinated through the interbank loan market. Herbener (2002) argues that only because the bank customers consider their claims fully secure can fractional reserve banking function, and Salerno (2012b) has interpreted Mises to show how free banking would really mean the strict limitation if not eradication of fiduciary media. In an exchange with White (2003), Hülsmann (2003a) argues that in a free market, fully backed money certificates would drive fiduciary media from circulation. Since these are only fractionally backed claims, there is necessarily a default risk. Building on this argument, Hansen (2021) tries to show that only widespread entrepreneurial error or legal privileges could lead to the circulation of bank liabilities as money.

Bitcoin and the Regression Theorem

While Austrian economists have great sympathy for market-produced money, the invention of bitcoin caused plenty of debate over basic monetary theory, both in the blogosphere and in the academic literature. Since bitcoin is a digital good designed to be a medium of exchange in peer-to-peer transactions from its very beginning (Nakamoto, 2009), does this not provide an empirical refutation of Mises's regression theorem? Mises argued that the PPM must be traced back to the moment when the monetary commodity was first used as money, i.e., that moment when a good which was not previously a medium of exchange was first demanded by an individual for that purpose. This is necessary if we want to understand the marginal utility of money today, but since it is not possible in the case of bitcoin – bitcoin was money from day 1 – Mises's theory is flawed.

This challenge has been met head on in the literature. Selgin (2015a) sees bitcoin as a synthetic commodity money, which shares some characteristics of both fiat money and commodity money: it is absolutely scarce, like a commodity, but like fiat money it has no non-monetary uses. Its value has been "bootstrapped" into existence: enough people speculate that it will have value for it to have it. Davidson and Block (2015), on the other hand, argue that the regression theorem is a non-issue, as it applies only when a new money comes into existence in a pure barter economy. Finally, Hansen (2019, pp. 41–42), in an article defending the regression theorem, shows how bitcoin and the theorem are perfectly compatible. When bitcoin was first in use, it was not demanded as a medium of exchange, but rather as a consumption good or by people speculating on its future value. Since bitcoin emerged in a monetary economy, all that was needed for its use as a medium of exchange was that its price be expressed in terms of dollars. The long process of adoption described by Menger is only necessary in barter; in a monetary economy, it's simply a question of bookkeeping, of using the dominant money for accounting purposes while using other media of exchange.

Monetary Reform Proposals

Gold, free banking and bitcoin sum up Austrian proposals for monetary reform: they all turn on the conditions of money production. There is thus a straight line from the older calls for a restoration of a classical or "pure" gold standard, as exemplified by Mises (1953 [1912], pt. 4) and Rothbard (2005 [1963]), to current Austrian reform proposals. A theme explicitly emphasizing the importance of a free market in money and choice in currencies emerged with Hayek's (1976, 1990 [1976]) books on the topic. Abolish legal tender laws and people will be free to choose the optimal money. Both Sennholz (1985) and

Ron Paul (Paul & Lehrman, 1982) emphasized this. Later proposals connected with free banking also emphasized the Hayekian heritage. White (2015) finds a return to gold coupled with free banking both attractive and feasible, and he elsewhere (White, 2012) suggests an intriguing "double-path" return to gold: path 1 is letting a parallel standard grow up alongside the current dollar system and path 2 is setting a date after which the dollar is again redeemed in gold. White thus merges the Misesian and Hayekian paths. George Selgin (1988, pp. 164–172), in his original free banking reform proposal, on the other hand, prefers a frozen stock of fiat money as the monetary base. More recently, he (Selgin, 2015b) has suggested a Hayekian argument for why a gold standard is not really a desirable free market reform: citing the work by Gallarotti (1995), Selgin argues that the classical gold standard was a spontaneous order, while a modern gold standard would simply be a case of uncredible public policy.

Among critics of free banking, the most detailed proposal is still Huerta de Soto's (2020 [1998], pp. 715–812) for a gold standard coupled with 100 percent banking. The main problem with these proposals is what to do with the uncovered fiduciary media. Some way of funding them or ensuring their orderly withdrawal from circulation is the goal. Huerta de Soto proposes turning bank deposits into shares in mutual funds. While this process is designed to protect private capital, it risks a sharp credit and monetary contraction, since mutual fund sharers do not provide the same monetary services that deposits do. The more recent proposal by Hansen (2020) for eliminating fiduciary media tries to avoid this danger, but instead risks involving the government in a costly process of converting all dollar claims to gold or silver coin.

Freedom in money is the goal, but there is probably truth in Hülsmann's (1995, pp. 51–52) claim that it is not enough. That is, it is not enough to proclaim monetary freedom and to abolish legal tender laws, the existing fiat currency must be replaced with some other kind of money.

THE DEMAND FOR MONEY

Austrian economists have a unique view on the demand for money. While other schools consider this demand somehow related to the flow or circulation of money and thus begin from an overall or macroeconomic viewpoint, Austrian economists insist on proceeding from the subjective demand of individuals. Furthermore, demand for money is always demand to hold. This latter position was, among modern economists, first explicitly stated by the English economist Edwin Cannan (1921, 1932, pp. 71–78). It is implicit in Mises's (1953 [1912], pp. 131–137) *Theory of Money and Credit*, and although Mises's monetary thinking did evolve in certain respects (Gertchev, 2004; Hülsmann, 2012), when it comes to the demand for money this wasn't the case.

By the time he wrote *Human Action*, Mises (1998 [1949], p. 399) was much more explicit that the demand for money is always demand to hold:

> There exists a demand for media of exchange because people want to keep a store of them. Every member of a market society wants to have a definite amount of money in his pocket or box, a cash holding or cash balance of a definite height ... Every piece of money is owned by one of the members of the market economy. The transfer of money from the control of one actor into that of another is temporally immediate and continuous. There is no fraction of time in between in which the money is not a part of an individual's or a firm's cash holding, but just in "circulation."

Rothbard (2008 [1983], pp. 29–35, 2009 [1962], p. 265) too emphasized that demand for money is demand to hold. However, Rothbard (2009 [1962], p. 756) also introduced a distinction, not found in Mises, between exchange demand and reservation demand for money, a distinction he took over from Wicksteed's (1910) total demand approach. This seems to offer us a contradiction, since it appears to contradict the emphasis on demand to hold. Exchange demand, after all, sounds like the exact contrary of demand to hold.

Exchange Demand and Reservation Demand

The Rothbardian analysis in terms of exchange and reservation demand has been expanded by Salerno (2010a [2006]). Reservation demand denotes the demand for money kept in cash balances, called post-income demand by Rothbard, while exchange demand is the demand for money in terms of other goods, what Rothbard also called the pre-income demand for money. Since the subjective value of money is based on the existence of objective prices, or rather on the individual's expectations of future prices, it is necessary that money is continuously exchanged against other goods in order for individuals to be able to value the monetary unit. It is through the exchange demand for money that the monetary adjustment process takes place, as changes in the data lead to a new array of money prices for goods and hence a new PPM.

The Rothbardian distinction allows us to highlight and better understand this process, without contradicting the insight that demand for money is always demand to hold. Exchange demand is prospective demand, or pre-income demand in Rothbard's terminology, exercised by those who wish, for the moment at least, to increase their cash balance. It is the inverse of the supply of all non-monetary goods: the supply schedule of every non-monetary good constitutes a partial exchange demand schedule for money (Davidson, 2012). All these partial demand schedules form part of the total demand for money no less than the reservation demand for money.

The possible contradiction is only too apparent, which is clearly seen when we recall that all supply and demand analysis is only a conceptual tool to understand price formation. Any demand curve is simply an abstraction, summing up and depicting the value scales of market actors at one point in time. It's a tool to either explain past prices or forecast future prices, but it is always a static analysis. In the case of money, the demand is dependent on the expected purchasing power, which is itself the inverse of money prices of goods. Separating out exchange demand for money in specific goods markets is therefore necessary to fully understand reservation demand and total demand. It is a way of showing more clearly how stocks of goods, reservation demand for goods, stock of money and reservation demand for money all are factors in determining the objective PPM, which in turn influence individuals' demand for money (Rothbard, 2009 [1962], p. 816). In other words, it's an attempt to explain the Misesian conception of money.

Monetary analysis along the lines of reservation and exchange demand highlights the interconnections between money on the one side and all the vendible goods, in Mises's phrase, on the other. Austrian economists have long excelled in drawing attention to and explaining the monetary adjustment process as drawn out over time and leading to price changes across the economy, a tradition continuing into the present (Huerta de Soto, 2020 [1998]; Sieroń, 2019). The conceptual tools developed by Rothbard and Salerno describing demand for money is a further advance in this tradition.

Demand for Money and Uncertainty

A core issue in monetary theory is the question of what motivates market actors to hold money at all. Austrians have been clear in explaining the role of population and the extent of the market in influencing the demand for money. As population grows, more people will be in existence and want to hold some money in their cash holding. As the division of labor intensifies, there are more exchange transactions and this too will increase the demand for money (Mises, 1953 [1912], p. 151; Rothbard, 2008 [1983], pp. 59–65). Conversely, if population declines or the market contracts as more individuals revert to autarky for whatever reason, the demand for money will tend to fall. Other factors also influence the height of demand. The establishment of clearing systems enabling the mutual cancellation of claims instead of transferring money back and forth allow market actors to economize on their cash holdings (Rothbard, 2009 [1962], pp. 771–772, 821–822). In all this, Austrians don't depart appreciably from the mainstream of economics, except for a greater clarity of exposition and a constant emphasis on the fact that these factors, important as they are, don't act directly on the demand for money. Only insofar as they enter into the plans and motivate the actions of individual market actors do they stand in any connection with the demand for money.

However, this does not explain what the fundamental cause of demand for money *is*, only how it might change. On this point, too, Austrian economists have broken new ground apart from the mainstream. When explaining the demand for money, mainstream economists will break it down into precautionary, transactions and speculative demand. Austrians, on the contrary, have developed a unitary explanation for the demand for money. The ultimate reason for holding any money at all is the fact of uncertainty. We live in an uncertain world, and holding money is a way of alleviating the felt uncertainty of the market actor.[1]

This argument was implicit already in *The Theory of Money and Credit* (Hülsmann, 2012), and Mises made the connection explicitly in *Human Action* (Mises, 1998 [1949], p. 249–250): in the absence of uncertainty in the imaginary construction of the evenly rotating economy, there would be no demand for money, since everyone would be able to structure their receipts and payments in such a way that their receipts would coincide perfectly with their expenditures. Rothbard (2009 [1962], p. 265) also emphasizes this point.

However, it is only more recently that the connection between uncertainty[2] and the demand for money has been made explicit. Hans-Hermann Hoppe (2012) has expanded on Hutt's (1956) notion of the yield from money as essentially derived from money's use as a hedge against uncertainty:

> [T]he investment in money balances must be conceived of as an investment in certainty or an investment in the reduction of subjectively felt uneasiness about uncertainty … [I]nsufficient attention has been drawn to the fact that, as the most easily and widely salable good, money is at the same time the most universally present – instantly serviceable – good (which is why the interest rate, i.e., the discount rate of future goods against present goods, is expressed in terms of money) and, as such, the good uniquely suited to alleviate presently felt uneasiness about uncertainty.

When a market actor's subjectively felt uncertainty increases, he will therefore increase his cash balance, either by exchanging some of his other assets for money or by refraining from purchases he would otherwise have made. Similarly, when a market actor feels less uncertain about the future, he will demand less money and spend more on consumption and investment.

The question of the role of uncertainty is one area of debate in the issue of free banking. While modern free bankers fully accept the role of uncertainty in the demand for money, they deny it has any role in the choice between money and money substitutes. For instance, George Selgin (1993, p. 362) denies that uncertainty would make bank notes issued by fractional reserve banks circulate at a discount – i.e., he denies that market actors think uncertainty enters into the evaluation of fiduciary media. Now, this is certainly true, since otherwise they could not form part of the money supply, but it still leaves the question open: are bank notes really as certain as money proper? If some uncertainty objectively attaches to only partially covered money substitutes – which seems intuitive, since they are mere promises to pay a sum of money and not that sum of money itself – then this has implications for the free banking debate. Hansen (2021) argues that since there is a fundamental difference between money proper and fiduciary media, as there is a default risk in the latter not present in the former, it is only due to widespread entrepreneurial error or intervention that fiduciary media circulates at par.

The Quality of Money

The quantity of money is usually what attracts the most attention among economists and the lay public alike. However, in recent years an Austrian literature has grown that focuses on the quality of money instead. Arguably, earlier economists also considered qualitative aspects of money. In Menger's (2009 [1892]) famous explanation of the origin of money, it is commodities with certain qualities that are used for media of exchange, until the commodity whose qualities best fulfill this function emerge as the dominant medium, that is, as money. However, this aspect of monetary theory has not been developed since then. Since it is always in respect of some quality that a thing possesses that it becomes serviceable as a means to an end and hence becomes an economic good, and since money is an economic good no less than consumer and producer goods, this is a real lacuna in economic science.

This hole has been filled in recent years, starting with Philipp Bagus (2009), who introduced the quality of money as a research topic in modern economics. In his initial article introducing the notion, Bagus defined the quality of money as its capacity to fulfill its main functions: those of medium of exchange, store of value and unit of account (2009, p. 22). This is consciously a departure from Mises's exclusive focus on the function of medium of exchange. Bagus makes the connection to the demand for money explicit, since the demand for money is determined by the marginal utility of the monetary unit, and the utility of money in turn is determined by its quality. If the quality of money changes, the ranking of units of money will change on people's value scales, leading to changes in the prices at which goods are offered in exchange for money. Thus, changes in quality can lead to changes in the PPM (2009, pp. 27–29).

Bagus lists widespread non-monetary demand for the money commodity as one important factor influencing its quality. In this he goes beyond the role of non-monetary demand in establishing a commodity as money, and follows Hülsmann (2003b) in stressing the continuing importance of this aspect. Bagus also considers the other traditional qualities of money: divisibility, transportability, durability and so on. When discussing the role of liquidity in determining the quality of money, Bagus (2009, p. 33) makes explicit the role of holding money in alleviating uncertainty.

Important, too, in the modern institutional setup, is the monetary philosophy of the central bank and the quality of the assets that fractional reserve banks hold (Bagus, 2009, pp. 35–39). Bagus (2015b) has extended the analysis of quality to include the quality of monetary regimes, naming White (1999) as a precursor. Bagus and Howden (2016) elaborate a schema for analyzing the quality of a given money by looking at the balance sheet of the central bank issuing it.

A hardcore Misesian might be annoyed by Bagus's rejection of the centrality of the medium of exchange function. Was Mises really wrong in his emphasis on this? If we focus on uncertainty as the fundamental cause of holding money, then the important qualities of money are those that allow it to fulfill this function. In a market economy, holding money brings acting man closest to the ultimate goal of action in the market: the acquisition of goods and services. If we keep this in mind the marketability of money is clearly its central and fundamental quality, and the function of money really is unitary. These remarks are not a critique of Bagus's work, but rather would suggest that a slight shift of emphasis is needed to align these two strands of Austrian thinking on the demand for money.

The focus on the quality of money has already proven fruitful, both in the work by Bagus and Howden and most recently by Žukauskas (2021). Žukauskas uses the theoretical tools pioneered by Bagus and Howden to construct an index to measure the quality of the euro. Perhaps unexpectedly, he concludes that the euro has deteriorated substantially over recent years to an extent not visible if we look only at the different monetary aggregates. Work along these lines could help us better understand the modern economy. For instance, the phenomenon of "financialization" (Krippner, 2012) might be connected to deteriorating quality of money, as market actors reduce their holdings of cash as its quality declines and instead invests in financial assets that serve as partial substitutes (cf. Žukauskas & Hülsmann, 2019). Reducing cash balances may also leave firms and individuals more vulnerable in times of crisis. Economic downturns will be more severe if most people have less cash on hand to tide them over, and panic sales of financial assets to realize much-needed purchasing power may lead to a crash of prices and the evaporation of liquidity. If these tentative hypotheses are correct, low-quality money is of great importance in understanding the instability and fragility of modern economies, as well as the drive for government interventions to protect fragile financial structures.

MONETARY EQUILIBRIUM

One key debate among Austrians is over the question of monetary equilibrium. As it is a part of the debates over free banking it often gets subsumed in these debates although it is really a question of the nature of money as such. We already alluded to it when we considered the differences between Salerno and White on the workings of the gold standard, and historical work suggests that it can be traced back to different conceptions of neutral money in the older Austrian school (Salerno, Dorobat, & Israel, 2020).

Free bankers accept monetary disequilibrium theory (Yeager, 1997) and argue that monetary equilibrium is necessary for the functioning of the real economy. Shocks originating from the "money side" can cause dislocations on the "real side" of the economy, both in the case of inflationary (business cycle) and deflationary shocks. The two "sides" can here be conceptualized with the equation of exchange: $MV = PY$. Crucially, instead of considering the stock of money, it is now the flow of spending, MV, that is the focus of attention. If MV is stable, then the real economy can grow according to productivity, even causing price deflation along the way.

The real debate is over the demand for money. An increase in demand (a fall of V in the equation) that is not compensated by an increased supply of money causes a fall in nominal income. Faced with menu costs and sticky prices, entrepreneurs have to cut production and this causes real economic dislocations and unemployment, as some factors of production can no longer be profitably employed due to the fall-off in demand (Horwitz, 2000, p. 141). In order to avoid this, the supply of money must increase and one of the advantages of free banking is that the banking system automatically increases the supply of money to meet higher demand. When this happens, there is no fall in nominal income and no disruptions to the real economy. When the demand for money falls again, the supply of bank money also shrinks.

Bagus and Howden (2011) in debate with Evans and Horwitz (2012) have disputed the importance of price stickiness. The argument is not that prices are perfectly flexible, responding to every slight variation in the data of the market. Rather, there is some degree of price stickiness in the free market because market actors prefer it this way. It can be costly to renegotiate long-term contracts, and more fundamentally, it is easier to calculate and plan one's actions if prices can be expected to be somewhat stable. However, prices are only sticky so long as this is desired by market actors: if they perceive that the data of the market change, then prices too can change and contracts be renegotiated. It is true that this is costly, but it is the business of the entrepreneurs to foresee changes in the market and adjust production and prices to them. A second point is that sticky prices in the real world are most often caused by some government intervention, be it price fixing, minimum wages or union power. Using inflation to overcome this problem is possible, but as Hayek (2009 [1972]) showed, only for a time. The interventionist government or wage-fixing union will get wise to the trick and simply make sure that prices or wages are index-linked to keep up with inflation.

Yet the fundamental disagreement appears to be over the notion of demand for money. Only reservation demand is considered demand for money by free bankers, as the exchange demand is met and "canceled out" by an equal exchange supply. Yet as Davidson (2012) argues, this is erroneous: we need to consider the total demand for money schedule when we analyze money, and this includes reservation demand and exchange demand for money. There is no essential difference between a change in the demand for money and a change in the demand for any other good. Both simply mean that the relative position on the acting person's value scale of the good in question has changed. In the case of money, this necessitates adjustment across several goods markets, since money uniquely enters into all other markets.

These critiques were already proposed by Huerta de Soto (1998) and they indicate that the core issue concerns the nature of money. Can money be kept neutral by the correct institutional setup, or does it always have, in Mises's (1998 [1949], p. 415) phrase, a driving force of its own? Hülsmann (2000) made the point in his review of White's (1999) *Theory of Monetary Institutions*: any change in the data of the market, be it in the supply of money or in the demand for money, leads to a change in the PPM. This, however, is the very quality for which money is demanded in the first place, and there is no need to adjust the supply of money to fit the changed conditions. Variations in PPM brought about by changing market data simply means that money itself constantly adjusts to the conditions of the market.

One example may help to show this: in a simple exchange between two persons, not only does money change hands, but the reason for why it is valued also changes. No person considers the whole objective array of prices when evaluating the addition or subtraction of a unit of money to or from his cash holding. Rather, each person only considers a subset of prices and forms his own estimate as to how these prices will change in the future. Therefore, not only does money change hands, but the estimate of prices on which demand for money depends also changes and the specific array of prices that informs the decision to hold money changes. Some people are vegetarian, others are not; some people enjoy alcoholic drinks, others do not; some go skiing for the holidays, others go to the beach. Rather than equilibrium, the value of money is in a state of constant flux.

CONCLUSION

This chapter has tried to review briefly some core contributions of modern Austrian economists to monetary theory. In general, Austrians tend to eschew any conception of money as neutral or merely a veil. Money can only be seen as constantly changing as well as being an agent of change, as Mises stressed.

The more specific areas where Austrians continue to focus with fruitful results are:

- Analyses of the processes of inflation and deflation, both when they pertain to business cycles and more generally. As a complement to these analyses, a thorough description of the principles governing money production in the free market has emerged.
- The importance of uncertainty and of the quality of money in explaining the demand for money.
- The role of the monetary system in shaping the economic order as a whole. This goes together with the Austrian rejection of the notion of neutral money or of money as a veil over economic reality.

NOTES

1. This does not mean that only Austrians consider the role of uncertainty – the Keynesian theory of liquidity preference also emphasizes this factor. Cf. Keynes (1930) and Hicks (1935, 1962).
2. Uncertainty is here to be understood as contrary to calculable risk, or as case probability *pace* Mises (1998 [1949], pp. 105–106, 110–113; cf. Hoppe, 1997).

REFERENCES

Bagus, P. (2009). The Quality of Money. *Quarterly Journal of Austrian Economics*, *12*(4), 22–45.

Bagus, P. (2015a). *In Defense of Deflation*. Cham: Springer International Publishing.

Bagus, P. (2015b). The Quality of Monetary Regimes. In P. L. Bylund & D. Howden (Eds), *The Next Generation of Austrian Economics: Essays in Honor of Joseph T. Salerno* (pp. 19–34). Auburn, AL: Ludwig von Mises Institute.

Bagus, P., & Howden, D. (2011). Monetary Equilibrium and Price Stickiness: Causes, Consequences and Remedies. *Review of Austrian Economics*, *24*(4), 383–402.

Bagus, P., & Howden, D. (2016). Central Bank Balance Sheet Analysis. *Betriebswirtschaftliche Forschung Und Praxis*, *2*(68), 109–125.

Cannan, E. (1921). The Application of the Theoretical Apparatus of Supply and Demand to Units of Currency. *The Economic Journal*, *31*(124), 453.

Cannan, E. (1932). *Money: Its Connexion with Rising and Falling Prices* (7th ed.). Westminster: P. S. King & Son.

Cantor, P. A. (1994). Hyperinflation and Hyperreality: Thomas Mann in Light of Austrian Economics. *Review of Austrian Economics*, *7*(1), 3–29.

Davidson, L. (2012). Against Monetary Disequilibrium Theory and Fractional Reserve Free Banking. *Quarterly Journal of Austrian Economics*, *15*(2), 195–220.

Davidson, L., & Block, W. E. (2015). Bitcoin, the Regression Theorem, and the Emergence of a New Medium of Exchange. *Quarterly Journal of Austrian Economics*, *18*(3), 311–338.

Dowd, K. (2015). Free Banking. In C. J. Coyne & P. Boettke (Eds), *The Oxford Handbook of Austrian Economics* (pp. 212–244). Oxford: Oxford University Press.

Evans, A. J., & Horwitz, S. (2012). On Not Doing Due Diligence: Bagus and Howden on Free Banking. *Review of Austrian Economics, 25*(2), 149–157.

Gallarotti, G. M. (1995). *The Anatomy of an International Monetary Regime: The Classical Gold Standard, 1880–1914.* New York; Oxford: Oxford University Press.

Gertchev, N. (2004). Dehomogenizing Mises's Monetary Theory. *Journal of Libertarian Studies, 18*(3), 57–90.

Gertchev, N. (2012). The Inter-Bank Market in the Perspective of Fractional Reserve Banking. In J. G. Hülsmann (Ed.), *Theory of Money and Fiduciary Media: Essays in Celebration of the Centennial* (pp. 209–228). Auburn, AL: Ludwig von Mises Institute.

Hansen, K. M. (2019). The Menger-Mises Theory of the Origin of Money: Conjecture or Economic Law? *Quarterly Journal of Austrian Economics, 22*(1), 26–48.

Hansen, K. M. (2020). The Populist Case for the Gold Standard. *Journal of Libertarian Studies, 24*(2), 323–361.

Hansen, K. M. (2021). Are Free Market Fiduciary Media Possible? On the Nature of Money, Banking, and Money Production in the Free Market Order. *Quarterly Journal of Austrian Economics, 24*(2), 286–316.

Hayek, F. A. von. (1976). *Choice in Currency: A Way to Stop Inflation.* London: Institute of Economic Affairs.

Hayek, F. A. von. (1990 [1976]). *Denationalisation of Money: The Argument Refined* (3rd ed.). London: Institute of Economic Affairs.

Hayek, F. A. von. (2009 [1972]). *A Tiger by the Tail: The Keynesian Legacy of Inflation* (S. R. Shenoy, Ed.) (3rd ed.). London: Institute of Economic Affairs and Ludwig von Mises Institute.

Herbener, J. M. (2002). Ludwig von Mises on the Gold Standard and Free Banking. *Quarterly Journal of Austrian Economics, 5*(2), 67–91.

Hicks, J. R. (1935). A Suggestion for Simplifying the Theory of Money. *Economica, 2*(5), 1–19.

Hicks, J. R. (1962). Liquidity. *The Economic Journal, 72*(288), 787–802.

Hoppe, H.-H. (1997). On Certainty and Uncertainty, or: How Rational Can Our Expectations Be? *Review of Austrian Economics, 10*(1), 49–78.

Hoppe, H.-H. (2012). The Yield from Money Held. In *The Great Fiction. Property, Economy, Society, and the Politics of Decline* (pp. 205–213). Baltimore, MD: Laissez Faire Books.

Horwitz, S. (2000). *Microfoundations and Macroeconomics.* London: Routledge.

Huerta de Soto, J. (1998). A Critical Note on Fractional-Reserve Free Banking. *Quarterly Journal of Austrian Economics, 1*(4), 25–49.

Huerta de Soto, J. (2020 [1998]). *Money, Bank Credit, and Economic Cycles* (M. Stroup, Ed. and Trans.) (4th ed.). Auburn, AL: Ludwig von Mises Institute.

Hülsmann, J. G. (1995). Free Banking and the Free Bankers. *Review of Austrian Economics, 9*(1), 3–53.

Hülsmann, J. G. (2000). Economic Principles and Monetary Institutions: Review Essay on The Theory of Monetary Institutions – Lawrence H. White. *Journal Des Economistes et Des Etudes Humaines, 10*(2). https://doi.org/10.2202/1145-6396 .1157

Hülsmann, J. G. (2003a). Has Fractional-Reserve Banking Really Passed the Market Test? *The Independent Review, 7*(3), 399–422.

Hülsmann, J. G. (2003b). Optimal Monetary Policy. *Quarterly Journal of Austrian Economics, 6*(3), 37–60.

Hülsmann, J. G. (2004). Legal Tender Laws and Fractional-Reserve Banking. *Journal of Libertarian Studies*, *18*(3), 33–55.

Hülsmann, J. G. (2008). *The Ethics of Money Production*. Auburn, AL: Ludwig von Mises Institute.

Hülsmann, J. G. (2012). The Early Evolution of Mises's Monetary Theory. In J. G. Hülsmann (Ed.), *Theory of Money and Fiduciary Media: Essays in Celebration of the Centennial* (pp. 1–36). Auburn, AL: Ludwig von Mises Institute.

Hülsmann, J. G. (2016). Cultural Consequences of Monetary Interventions. *Journal Des Économistes et Des Études Humaines*, *22*(1). https://doi.org/10.1515/jeeh-2016 -0010

Hutt, W. H. (1956). The Yield from Money Held. In M. Sennholz (Ed.), *On Freedom and Free Enterprise: Essays in Honor of Ludwig von Mises* (pp. 196–216). Irvington-on-Hudson, NY: Foundation for Economic Education.

Israel, K. (2021). The Fiat Money Illusion: On the Cost-Efficiency of Modern Central Banking. *The World Economy*, *44*(6), 1701–1719.

Jastram, R. W. (2009 [1977]). *The Golden Constant: The English and American Experience 1560–1976*. Cheltenham, UK and Northampton, MA, USA: Edward Elgar Publishing.

Keynes, J. M. (1930). *A Treatise on Money*, Vol. 1. New York: Harcourt, Brace and Company.

Krippner, G. R. (2012). *Capitalizing on Crisis: The Political Origins of the Rise of Finance*. Cambridge, MA: Harvard University Press.

Menger, C. (2009 [1892]). *On the Origins of Money* (C. A. Foley, Ed. and Trans.). Auburn, AL: Ludwig von Mises Institute.

Mises, L. von. (1953 [1912]). *The Theory of Money and Credit*. Auburn, AL: Yale University Press.

Mises, L. von. (1998 [1949]). *Human Action: A Treatise on Economics*. Auburn, AL: Ludwig von Mises Institute.

Mises, L. von. (2011). *Interventionism: An Economic Analysis* (B. B. Greaves, Ed.). Indianapolis, IN: Liberty Fund.

Nakamoto, S. (2009). *Bitcoin: A Peer-to-Peer Electronic Cash System*. www.bitcoin .org

Paish, F. W. (1950 [1938]). Causes of Changes in the Gold Supply. In *The Post-War Financial Problem and Other Essays* (pp. 149–186). London: Macmillan & Co.

Paul, R., & Lehrman, L. E. (1982). *The Case for Gold: A Minority Report of the U.S. Gold Commission*. Washington, D.C.

Rothbard, M. N. (2005 [1963]). *What Has Government Done to Our Money? And, the Case for a 100 Percent Gold Dollar*. Auburn, AL: Ludwig von Mises Institute.

Rothbard, M. N. (2008 [1983]). *The Mystery of Banking* (2nd ed.). Auburn, AL: Ludwig von Mises Institute.

Rothbard, M. N. (2009 [1962]). *Man, Economy, and State: A Treatise on Economic Principles with Power and Market Government and the Economy* (2nd ed.). Auburn AL: Ludwig von Mises Institute.

Rueff, J. (1972). *The Monetary Sin of the West* (Roger Glémet, Ed. and Trans.). New York: Macmillan Company.

Salerno, J. T. (2003). An Austrian Taxonomy of Deflation – with Applications to the U.S. *Quarterly Journal of Austrian Economics*, *6*(4), 81–109.

Salerno, J. T. (2010a [2006]). A Simple Model of the Theory of Money Prices. In *Money, Sound and Unsound* (pp. 131–151). Auburn, AL: Ludwig von Mises Institute.

Salerno, J. T. (2010b [1982]). Gold Standards: True and False. In *Money, Sound and Unsound* (pp. 355–373). Auburn, AL: Ludwig von Mises Institute.

Salerno, J. T. (2012a). A Reformulation of Austrian Business Cycle Theory in Light of the Financial Crisis. *Quarterly Journal of Austrian Economics, 15*(1), 3–44.

Salerno, J. T. (2012b). Ludwig von Mises as Currency School Free Banker. In J. G. Hülsmann (Ed.), *Theory of Money and Fiduciary Media: Essays in Celebration of the Centennial* (pp. 95–125). Auburn, AL: Ludwig von Mises Institute.

Salerno, J. T. (2013). Hyperinflation and the Destruction of Human Personality. *Studia Humana, 2*(1), 15–27.

Salerno, J. T., Dorobat, C. E., & Israel, K.-F. (2020). Two Views on Neutral Money: Wieser and Hayek Versus Menger and Mises. *European Journal of the History of Economic Thought, 27*(5), 682–711.

Selgin, G. A. (1988). *The Theory of Free Banking: Money Supply under Competitive Note Issue.* Totowa, NJ: Cato Institute; Rowman & Littlefield.

Selgin, G. A. (1993). In Defense of Bank Suspension. *Journal of Financial Services Research, 7*(4), 347–364.

Selgin, G. A. (2015a). Law, Legislation, and the Gold Standard. *Cato Journal, 35*(2), 92–99.

Selgin, G. A. (2015b). Synthetic Commodity Money. *Journal of Financial Stability, 17*, 92–99.

Sennholz, H. F. (1975). *Gold Is Money.* Westport, CT: Greenwood Press.

Sennholz, H. F. (1985). *Money and Freedom.* Spring Mills, PA: Libertarian Press.

Sieroń, A. (2017). The Non-Price Effects of Monetary Inflation. *Quarterly Journal of Austrian Economics, 20*(2), 146–163.

Sieroń, A. (2019). *Money, Inflation and Business Cycles: The Cantillon Effect and the Economy.* London: Routledge.

Thornton, M. (2003). Apoplithorismosphobia. *Quarterly Journal of Austrian Economics, 6*(4), 5–18.

White, L. H. (1995 [1984]). *Free Banking in Britain: Theory, Experience, and Debate, 1800–1845* (2nd ed.). London: Institute of Economic Affairs.

White, L. H. (1999). *The Theory of Monetary Institutions.* Malden, MA: Blackwell.

White, L. H. (2003). Accounting for Fractional-Reserve Banknotes and Deposits – or, What's Twenty Quid to the Bloody Midland Bank? *The Independent Review, 7*(3), 423–441.

White, L. H. (2011). A Gold Standard with Free Banking Would Have Restrained the Boom and Bust. *Cato Journal, 31*(3), 497–504.

White, L. H. (2012). Making the Transition to a New Gold Standard. *Cato Journal, 32*(2), 411–421.

White, L. H. (2015). The Merits and Feasibility of Returning to a Commodity Standard. *Journal of Financial Stability, 17*, 59–64.

Wicksteed, P. H. (1910). *The Common Sense of Political Economy.* London: Macmillan & Co.

Yeager, L. B. (1997). *The Fluttering Veil: Essays on Monetary Disequilibrium.* (G. A. Selgin, Ed.). Indianapolis, IN: Liberty Fund.

Žukauskas, V. (2021). Measuring the Quality of Money. *Quarterly Journal of Austrian Economics, 24*(1), 110–146.

Žukauskas, V., & Hülsmann, J. G. (2019). Financial Asset Valuations: The Total Demand Approach. *Quarterly Review of Economics and Finance, 72*, 123–131.

10. Banking

David Howden

INTRODUCTION

It is unfortunate that one word has come to describe two different activities. Central banking commonly refers to an extra-market body in control of the base money supply. Banking without a modifier refers most commonly to private banks with control over the money supply through their function as depositories. In their present forms, both types of banking have serious legal, economic, and ethical problems. A large body of research has documented these problems, but the Austrian school is unique among currents of economic thought in that it searches for the root problems of banking instead of addressing more superficial symptoms.

The student of economics is introduced to the topic of banking through a series of "Money and Banking" courses specifically dealing with the industry and its effect on the economy. The inquisitive student might consider why banking as an industry deserves special attention while others are neglected. This question is not addressed by the mainstream, and the starting point in analysis is the acceptance that banks—both commercial and central—function the way they do due to natural economic forces, but must be regulated to balance various malignant economic forces. It is this control through regulation that then makes up the bulk of the semester's work on banking and its relationship to money.[1]

The Austrian school of economics takes to heart Friedrich von Hayek's (1937, p. 34) adage that "before we can explain why people commit mistakes, we must first explain why they should ever be right." Stemming directly from its analysis of the bedrock of the banking system, money, the Austrian economist then looks at how the banking industry evolves naturally as a beneficial institution (i.e., how it can go "right"). When problems arise, e.g., an illiquidity-induced bank run, he can then compare the malfunctioning system under analysis with a pure type, and in this way understand the sources of instability. In contrast, the mainstream economist focuses on the "mistakes" of the banking system, which are really just symptomatic of deeper-rooted problems, and then devises a set of band-aid solutions to patch over these problems.

In this chapter I will focus on the private commercial banking sector, giving special attention to the legal, economic, and ethical aspects of fractional-reserve banking. I emphasize these aspects of commercial banking because they explain the extra-market origins of the central bank. In this way, we can sidestep the issue of central bank operations and results on the economy because the institution is an outgrowth of the fractional-reserve banking system. Understanding the latter, and why such a system is not necessary to a well-functioning economy, allows one to understand why central banks are also unnecessary.

The prevailing theory among mainstream economists on the origin of the central bank is that it is a natural response to safeguard fractional-reserve banks in times of unavoidable liquidity crises (Goodhart, 1988, chapter 7; Gorton, 1985). Within the Austrian camp, the central bank can be seen as a natural evolution of a fractional-reserve banking system that defends itself against external competition (Howden, 2014), to protect itself against liquidity shocks of its own making (Smith, 1990, chapters 169–170), or to aid the government in earning seigniorage revenue (Rothbard, 2010, chapter 3). In all cases, the absence of a fractional-reserve banking system precludes the formation of a central bank.

Private banks matter greatly for the economy under a fractional-reserve banking system. The way in which they influence events evolves partly in response to regulatory changes and partly as a natural outgrowth of the maturity of the system. I will first briefly overview the phenomenon of money to understand the foundation of the banking system. I then move on to describing how the legal and economic aspects of the bank's deposit-taking and lending facilities function within both an ideal-type banking system as well as the present system. With this legal-economic foundation, I give some examples of ways in which the fractional-reserve banking system influences the economy. I conclude with some short extensions of the analysis, confront some common criticisms, and point to thorny issues in theory that future economists must resolve.

MONEY, THE ROOT OF ALL BANKING

There are two theories of the role of banking prevalent today. On the one hand, banks serve as pure financial intermediaries offering a service—a deposit account—that converts an illiquid liability into a liquid asset for their customers (Freixas & Rochet, 2008, p. 4). Under this theory the primary role of the bank is to transform the maturity of its asset portfolio comprising mostly loans of various maturities into on-demand claims by way of demand deposits. These deposits then make up the majority of the bank's liabilities. Banks are successful to the extent that they (1) transform the greatest amount of deposits into loans, (2) earn the highest yield on their loan portfolio, and (3) incur the lowest cost for their deposit management services. I refer to this theory of banking as the maturity-transformation theory.

The prevailing alternative theory of banking views their *raison d'être* not as maturity transformation, but as storage providers. In this view the depositor entrusts his currency to the bank, which then converts the currency into a different form of money, a deposit. The depositor values this service to the extent that the bank specializes in safe-keeping activities (e.g., vaults, security systems, etc.) and increases the marketability of the money held so as to make it easier to use (as in Menger, 2007 [1871], p. 241). Checking services, debit cards, and more recently internet transfers have all increased the ease at which the customer can access his money. This increased ease of using money through a banking intermediary has increased the demand for banking services. Banks are profitable under this theory to the extent that they (1) offer the best storage services for money and (2) minimize their costs of providing this service. The bank competes on convenience, cost, and most importantly services that enhance the safety of the currency entrusted to it. I refer to this theory of banking as the warehousing theory.

Both theories of banking share in common a link between money and banking. They also share in common the initial condition of the bank's existence—a stock of money in the form of currency. This link is explicit in the warehousing theory of banking. Here the bank relies on an initial transfer of currency which it then converts to a deposit serving as a claim to the sum of currency. The initial link between money and banking is somewhat strained in the maturity-transformation theory of banking since banks here not only convert the form of money but also create money if they choose to offer loans in excess of their deposit base. Still, while the bank can create deposits by issuing loans once it is already in operation, it can only start this process by attracting an initial currency deposit.

Since the money–banking link is apparent in both theories of banking, any discussion of banking must start from first understanding what money is, and how the form of money most commonly associated with banks, the deposit, relates to it.

In the common story of the origin and evolution of money, one central aspect is the reduction of transaction costs (i.e., Menger, 1892, 2007 [1871], chapter 8). In a moneyless world there is a double coincidence of the wants problem, as elaborated by Jevons (1875, p. 3). As the scope of trades is limited and the costs associated with setting an agreeable price once trading partners do meet is high, there is an incentive for traders to use specific goods that are widely demanded to settle their transactions. As more individuals use these few specific goods to settle their exchanges, they gain a value for exchange purposes in addition to the value they possess for direct use. The process ends when one (or very few) goods begin to be traded solely for exchange purposes, and their acceptance is due to the knowledge that they can be easily traded with, and accepted by, another individual. Money is the outcome of this process, and it is also clear that whatever good functions as money will also be the generally accepted medium of exchange as a result.

Money's use during its evolutionary process is clearly for exchange purposes but there is also an additional factor of great importance. Mises (1949, pp. 244–251) sheds light on this by way of his equilibrium construct of the "evenly rotating economy" to demonstrate when money is *not* necessary. Only in a world of full certainty—one where all expenditures are known in advance, both in magnitude and timing—would money not be necessary.

Depart from the perfectly certain world and one runs into the intractable problem of how to best meet his future needs. As Mises (1949, pp. 14, 249) shows, money serves as a security hedge to guard against these uncertain situations. The key problem is that "[u]ncertain of what, when, where or the amount of future expenditures, individuals demand to hold an amount of money to safeguard against this uncertain future" (Bagus & Howden, 2013, p. 236).

Other highly liquid money substitutes can serve this role to some degree. Rothbard (1993 [1962], p. 713) refers to such goods as a type of "quasi money," but to the extent that they are not perfectly liquid assets or the final means of settlement, they cannot function as "money."

In this brief discussion of the evolution and use of money there are several roles taking place concurrently. The most obvious one is a medium of exchange—a unit to transfer in settlement of pecuniary obligations. There is also the role of money in mitigating our felt uncertainty. In order to function accordingly, we must identify what the relevant uncertainties are that the individual will face.

Having already commented on the unknowledge of what, how much, or when we will need purchasing power in the future, we can now comment on why money is held as a hedge against these expectations. After all, most individuals can and do hold a variety of liquid non-money financial assets to assist them with their future expenses, e.g., equities, short-term bonds, or certificates of deposit. All of these non-money financial assets have a risk inherent in them which the money holder must overcome.

In a superficial sense, money is demanded because it is highly liquid. Yet this cannot be the sole reason money is demanded, as other financial assets such as equities and heavily traded debt securities are also highly liquid. More to the point, money is demanded because of its uniqueness. Money is the only financial asset that is able to embed two features—par value and on-demand availability—into one good (Howden, 2015). It is this combination that makes money such an exceptional, and essential, part of a portfolio of financial assets. Money is demanded precisely because of these two features, which endow its holder with a guarantee that should an uncertainty arise, he will hold an asset of value to meet it.

Consequently, any good that serves as money can only do so to the extent that it offers par value and on-demand availability. This chapter focuses on the relationship between currency and deposits to the extent that they are widely acknowledged to serve as forms of money, and also since they have in common these two features.

DEPOSIT AND LOAN CONTRACTS

Within banking the link between the deposit base and the loan portfolio has legal as well as economic attributes and implications. This is because in converting his money from currency to a deposit the depositor has not altered the terms of how he views his money balance. In both instances, the currency and deposit function as an on-demand, par-value financial asset to be used in the exchange of goods and services. From the bank's point of view, however, a shift has been made at the moment it converts the currency to a deposit claim *and* when it uses the deposit to fund a loan. In this instance, the bank alters the deposit to a loan that it will repay in the future when demanded by the depositor. Thus, the bank views the deposit as a loan and the depositor views his deposit as a deposit. Given this conflict, a discussion about the distinctions and relationship between deposit and loan contracts is warranted.

Many aspects of both deposit and loan contracts are quite similar. Both can involve specific goods (e.g., art, cars, or homes) or fungible goods (e.g., money, wheat, or water). Both involve the physical transfer of a good from one person to another. An individual may deposit his art or wheat with a depository just as a lender can loan his car or money to a borrower.

Economic Differences between Deposit and Loan Contracts

There are three significant economic differences between deposit and loan contracts (Huerta de Soto, 2006, chapter 1). These economic differences create three corresponding legal distinctions.

The first economic difference is that the loan contract represents an exchange of a present good for a claim on a future good. A lender exchanges money units to a borrower and in return receives a claim to a set of future money units. This is quite distinct from the deposit contract in which there is no such intertemporal exchange (Mises, 1971, p. 269). The depositor, unlike the lender, does not renunciate the money in question, but rather retains a full claim to it. The depository does not gain the use of the money deposited in it. It must instead continually safeguard it for the depositor (as per the intent of the contract) as well as keep it continually and fully available for withdrawal.

A second economic difference is that in the loan contract the *availability* of the exchanged asset is transferred. By loaning money, the lender gives up both the availability and use of the sum over the duration of the contract. The borrower is at liberty to use the money as he pleases, until the contract's maturity when the predefined claim to a future good comes due. At this moment, the claim to a once-future good becomes the delivery of a present good to settle the debt. In contrast, in a deposit contract there is no such intertemporal exchange of the good's use. As the goal of the contract is the full and continual availability of the deposit, the depository is not in a position to make use of the deposit at *any* time during the contract's duration. As the deposit can be requested and must be provided by the depository at any time, there can be no transfer of availability during the interim. The depositor retains the full availability of the deposit (Mises, 1971, p. 268), and the depository must ensure that this is met by not using the deposit.

The third economic difference between the two contracts arises from the fact that a loan involves an intertemporal exchange of goods, while a deposit does not. Intertemporal exchanges involve an interest spread between the present and future prices of the exchanged good. In a loan contract the borrower will have to pay the lender for the use of the lent good over the contract's duration. As the deposit contract has no intertemporal element, there is no interest payment to compensate for the loss of the use of the deposited asset. These three fundamental economic differences raise three important legal distinctions.

Legal Differences between Deposit and Loan Contracts

These legal differences result in separate obligations for both deposits and loans, strictly limiting the activities that each contract allows for.

First, the legal *purposes* of the two contracts are radically distinct. The loan represents the transfer of property from the lender to the borrower. The lender will lose all availability and the use of the good for the duration of the loan contract, while the borrower gains these two features. Since the depositor's intent is the safekeeping of his deposited good, the depository does not gain the legal use or availability of the deposit. The legal *claim* to the contracted good remains distinct depending on which contract is exercised.

The second legal distinction is that the loan contract must necessarily establish a (at least implicit) contractual *duration* (Huerta de Soto, 2006, pp. 1–6). As the essential feature of a loan is the transfer of a good's availability, a maximum duration of this contract must arise.[2] A good "lent" with no term would be continually on demand, and hence be equivalent to a deposit. The borrower would never be at liberty to make use of the lent good as the lender could ask for its return at any moment. There could not be any transfer of the good's use in any meaningful sense of the word.[3]

The third legal distinction, and perhaps the most important, is the difference in contractual *obligations*. The legal obligations are defined by both the type of contract entered into (deposit or loan) as well as the type of good contracted for (specific or fungible) (Huerta de Soto, 2006, pp. 2–4).

A specific good lent results in a *commodatum* contract. Car leases, apartment rentals, or intermuseum loans for works of art exemplify these contracts. The borrower gains the use of the good in question for the contract's duration. The lender is reimbursed at the end of the contract with the return of the lent good—in either the same condition (qualitatively and quantitatively) or in a predetermined and contractually specified condition. A loan for a fungible good results in a *mutuum* contract. Money loans, a farmer borrowing wheat, or oil lent to a gas producer provide examples. As one unit of the good is indistinct from other units, the contract terminates with the return of the *tantundem*—a predefined quantity and quality of the lent good—at the contract's maturity. The homeowner repays the bank by returning a quantity of money to terminate his mortgage (but not necessarily with the same money as was originally lent), or a farmer may repay a mill by returning a quantity of wheat to terminate a *commodatum* loan.

Note that in these two types of loan contracts the obligation is only for the return of a good in the future. Nothing is said about the use or availability of the good borrowed in the present. The borrower is at full liberty to do what he may with the good over the contract's duration. The only requirement is that he returns the promised good upon maturity—the lent good for the *mutuum* contract, or the *tantundem* for the *commodatum* contract.

Deposits, both for specific and fungible goods, result in distinct legal requirements. As the depositor's intent is the safekeeping of a good, the depository's obligation is to keep the deposit safe and available at all times: he may not make use of the deposited good at *any* time during the contract's existence.[4] For specific goods, the depository must keep the original deposit on hand, to be available to return to the depositor upon request. For fungible goods, the bank must keep a *tantundem* available at all times. Note that the *tantundem* does not imply that the same deposited units be kept on hand, only that an equal quality and quantity be kept available. Thus a mill needs only to keep enough wheat on hand to honor the farmer's deposit, not his same deposited units. Likewise, the bank need only keep a similar quality and quantity of money units available to honor the depositor's withdrawal requests. These economic and legal differences are summarized in Table 10.1.

It is in this third legal distinction, the distinct obligations of the depository or borrower, where we note the largest contractual difference. The borrower in a loan contract (for both specific and fungible goods) need only return

Table 10.1   *Contractual differences of deposit and loan contracts*

	Loan contract	Deposit contract
Economic differences	Intertemporal exchange of present for future good. Lender transfers asset's availability to borrower. Borrower pays interest.	No intertemporal exchange of goods. Depositor retains availability of good at all times. Depositor pays for services.
Legal differences	Lender transfers legal claim of good to borrower. Lender establishes a maximum duration of loan. Borrower must return good (or *tantundem*) upon maturity.	Depositor retains legal claim to good. No explicit duration need apply to the deposit. Depository must keep good (or *tantundem*) on hand at all times.

a predefined good at the contract's maturity. Nothing is implied in this requirement concerning what he may or may not do with the borrowed good over the course of the loan's life. The depository in a deposit contract (again, for both specific and fungible goods) does not gain this same liberty. As the deposit must be fully available, and given that no right to use the deposit is transferred, the depository must keep the good (or its *tantundem*) safe until the depositor requests its return.

Table 10.2   *Typology of deposit and loan contracts*

		Purpose	
		Transfer of ownership	**Safekeeping**
Type of Good	**Specific**	*Commodatum*	Regular deposit
	Fungible	*Mutuum*	Irregular deposit

Thus the contracting parties have four different contracts that they may enter, as summarized in Table 10.2. Each contract for a specific good, whether *commodatum* or regular deposit, can be terminated by returning the same good as was originally subject to the contract. In cases of fungible goods, the mutuum or irregular deposit can be terminated by returning a *tantundem*. Note that while deposit contracts can also be for either fungible or specific goods, the distinction is moot for the analysis at hand. In each case the contractual obligation is to keep the deposited good, or its *tantundem*, available.[5]

These separate legal obligations imply that deposited money must be treated separately from lent money. This separation is tenuous in the modern banking system as banks partake in both activities. Deposit services are available (primarily through the use of checking accounts, but also through safety deposit boxes), while a sizable portion of banking activity (and the majority of profits) come from *mutuum* services—mortgages, consumer loans, or pension savings plans.

The Contradiction of the Fractional-Reserve Demand Deposit

The distinction between deposit and loan contracts is more evident if we assess the differences between the legal rights and duties of each party in a conventional deposit contract, as in Table 10.3.[6] These rights and duties follow specifically from the legal intent of the deposit contract, and also from the economic reality constraining its embodiment. It is notable that there is no apparent conflict with the contract. When we speak of a depositor's right to his deposit, there are several rights intermingled. The first is the right to withdraw his money as he wishes.[7]

Table 10.3   *Conventional deposit contract rights and duties*

	Depositor	Depository
Rights	Retains a claim to full deposit on demand	Gains a privilege to remuneration for services offered
Duties	Must remunerate depository for services provided	Must hold deposit continually for immediate redemption: • in kind for specific goods • the *tantundem* for fungible goods

Necessitating the right of the depositor to withdraw his funds on demand is the bank's duty to not make use of the deposited funds. The right to withdrawal on demand is what creates the corresponding duty on the part of the bank to safeguard the deposit. Both parties have clearly defined boundaries concerning their rights, and both have a clear understanding of their respective duties.

Loan contracts are also well defined in terms of rights and duties, as per Table 10.4. Note that none of these rights or duties for the lender or borrower conflicts with the rights or duties of the other.

As we observe, both contracts with their entailing rights and duties are mutually exclusive: combinations are not possible without creating conflict. No conflicts arise provided that the contracts that banks and individuals enter into concerning their deposits and loans follow these two pure examples. Recent evidence in the financial sphere has demonstrated that there is considerable dismay concerning the rights that depositors have to their deposits, as well as the duties that the bank must follow. A 2010 survey on attitudes towards banking commissioned by the Cobden Centre (2010) found that 74 percent of respondents thought the depositor retained ownership of his deposit, when in fact the bank is the legal owner. A third of respondents felt it was "wrong"

Table 10.4   Loan contract rights and duties

	Lender	Borrower
Rights	Claim to the future return of the lent good • The same good if it is specific • The *tantundem* if the good is fungible Receives an interest remuneration at termination of the contract	The full use of the good Availability of good over contract's duration
Duties	Must accept the return of the good upon termination of the contract Cannot request for the lent good to be returned before the contract's maturity	Must return the good upon termination of the contract • The same good if it is specific • The *tantundem* if good is fungible Must remunerate lender for use of good

that banks made use of their deposited funds, and almost 60 percent thought the legal system should address this discrepancy and subject banks to the same legal requirements as other depository institutions. In this legal-economic analysis, the issue arises because today's banking system uses a contract that does not follow either the traditional deposit or loan requirements. Although trying to safeguard and ensure the availability of a deposited sum, banks today do not abide by the same duties as laid out above.

Specifically, one of the duties of the depository is that it safeguards and keeps available at all times the deposited good (Bagus & Howden, 2016). Modern banks do not abide by this duty. A fractional-reserve banking system exists in a state of partial backing of its deposit base. There are superficial reasons to believe that this is a positive development. By using a portion of the deposit, the bank is able to pursue profit-enhancing activities. As a result, a depositor does not usually have to pay a fee to deposit his funds, but rather the bank earns this fee by making use of his deposit. It is also true that usually the depositor does not redeem his whole deposit at once. Since the deposit is made to guard against uncertainty, a sum will be on hand that is never, or at least only infrequently, redeemed. A fractional-reserve bank that prudently invests a portion of its deposit base will be able to earn a profit to reduce the costs of its operations. In most cases it will also be able to meet redemption requests by depositors.

The apparent problem arises in those circumstances when the bank cannot meet the redemption requests of its depositors. This problem arises when the bank's estimate of the depositor's liquidity demands does not accord with the depositor's actual demands. Since the bank holds only a fraction of the deposit on reserve it must appeal to its relatively illiquid investments to acquire money to honor the depositor's request. In these scenarios, the investments the bank

Table 10.5   *Fractional-reserve demand deposit contract rights and duties*

	Depositor	Borrower
Rights	A claim right to withdraw the full deposit on demand	Full use of the deposit Availability of the good over the contract's (undefined) duration
Duties	Remunerate depository for services provided May have to wait for the return of the deposited good May receive less than the full value of the deposit requested	Return of the *tantundem* on demand

made with the deposited funds either lose value or are of such a long duration that they leave the bank illiquid. Depositors have a claim to their money while the bank is unable to honor all these claims simultaneously. This apparent problem that arises only infrequently is merely symptomatic of a larger legal problem: the conflation of rights and duties.

Consider Table 10.5, which outlines the rights and duties stemming from the common fractional-reserve demand deposit contract.

These rights and duties define the modern deposit account. This contract amounts to a melding of a deposit and loan contract, with a resulting muddling of the legal rights and duties. Three important differences relative to a pure deposit or loan contract are apparent.

First, note that the legal relationship is no longer between depositor and depository, or lender and borrower. The deposit contract creates a union between depositors on the one hand and banks acting as borrowers on the other. This is an important shift, as it redefines the legal rights that the contract creates.

Second, note that while the depositor has the right to use the deposit on demand, the bank also has the right to make full use of the deposited funds.[8] The conflict that arises is that each party has a claim right to the same good, and there exists the impossibility that each claim can be exercised simultaneously (Hoppe, 1994, p. 67; Hoppe, Hülsmann, & Block, 1998, pp. 21–23). One solution to this problem is a waiver appended to some types of demand deposits, whereby the depositor will in certain circumstances be required to give a notice of withdrawal prior to making a redemption. In this way the bank gains time in being able to sell its investments to meet the redemption request. Note that this only superficially solves the problem of the conflicting claims, as it merely transfers the conflict from one party to another. The new conflict that arises is that the deposit was made originally with the intent that it could be redeemed on demand (to make the deposit a perfect money substitute). Including a waiver that alters this claim right puts the depositor in conflict with the original legal intent of his actions.[9]

Finally, if rights conflicts arise because the duties correlated with the rights are themselves in conflict, it is important to consider what specific duties the deposit contract entails. Returning to Table 10.5, we see that the rights of the depositor are misaligned with the duties of the bank. As the depositor has full claim to the deposit on demand, the bank must be able to return the deposit when notified. As the bank has the duty to return the good upon the contract's duration, an alignment of rights and duties seems to be in place. A salient issue arises as to when the right may be exercised and if a conflict arises with the duty undertaken. Since the depositor may request his funds on demand he may also terminate the contract at will.[10] Although in many circumstances the bank can fulfil its duty by returning the deposited sum (or its *tantundem*), this will not be possible in all cases.

Thus, the bank has a two-fold duty. First, it must return the *tantundem* on demand, and second, this entails that it must not use the deposited sum in its possession. That the fractional-reserve banking system does make use of deposited funds signals a conflict that exists between the duties required of banks and the claim rights of depositors.

IMPLICATIONS

The intermingling of features specific to the deposit and loan contracts has wide-reaching implications throughout the economy. One of the primary examples of a distortion caused by the creation of money through the fractional-reserve banking system is the instigation of an Austrian business cycle. Interest rates are normally set by the interaction between savers and borrowers. Savings are embodied by money, which represents unconsumed income and is borrowed to shift consumption from the future to the present. The fractional-reserve banking system's ability to create money augments the supply of money savings and gives the appearance that there is a greater amount of unconsumed income than consumption patterns allow for. As a consequence, the market interest rate that equilibrates the supply of savings with the demand for investment falls below what it would be absent this money-creation process (an interest rate Wicksell (1962) termed the "natural rate").

The market rate of interest falling below the natural rate sets in force several phenomena that distort the economy and ultimately culminate in a business cycle. On the one hand, producers are led to alter their production plans to favor longer-dated or more capital-intensive methods. This "malinvesment," as the shift in production is known, is one of the defining features of the Austrian business cycle (Hayek, 1967; Mises, 1949, chapter 20). Under this view, the fractional-reserve banking system motivates a change to investment patterns that are inconsistent with savers' preferences.

On the other hand, consumers are also misled by a reduction in the interest rate caused by the fractional-reserve banking system's creation of money. Overconsumption, as in Mises (1998, chapter 20) and Garrison (2004), results as a lower interest rate lures consumers to increase their present consumption in lieu of future consumption. While these new investment and consumption patterns give the appearance of an economic boom, their readjustment to a pattern more sustainable with the natural rate of interest is characterized by a recession. Thus, the fractional-reserve banking system is one of the primary instigators of the business cycle through its distortion of intertemporal production and consumption decisions.

No less important than the changes in the economic sphere are those the banking system invokes on the social or cultural sphere. The creation of money and its incipient reduction in the market rate of interest changes behavioral patterns, usually in ways that are consistent with activities that are short term-oriented and have an immediate payoff. Longer-oriented social activities (raising children, inculcating manners throughout society, etc.) are diminished as a lower market rate, caused by the fractional-reserve banking system, entices people to satisfy their wants sooner. Mises (1990, p. 105), Hülsmann (2008), Bagus and Howden (2011, pp. 70–71), and Howden and Kampe (2016) all explore negative changes to society that the fractional-reserve banking system creates.

Of a final note is that our understanding of the legal and economic perversion of the banking system allows us to understand its two most salient features. Fractional-reserve banks are often characterized as being "too big to fail" and as being highly interconnected with each other. The too-big-to-fail problem gains importance during economic crises when conditions of illiquidity call into question the solvency of large banks. While such crises are detrimental to many businesses, banks in particular are commonly seen as so large that the failure of one would have oversized effects on the economy (e.g., in terms of lost income, or unemployment). Given this large size, banks are in a politically advantageous position to be bailed out to stave off insolvency.

That banks are highly interconnected also bolsters the case for a bailout in times of distress. Unlike in other industries when the failure of a company is seen as good news for a competitor, in the banking sector the demise of one bank strains the liquidity of the others. In the money-creation process of the fractional-reserve banking system, the loans issued by one bank become deposits in another. Should one bank default on its loan and not repay it (or if it has a client default or not make a payment) then this loss of an asset compromises the ability of another bank to make good on its deposits. The failure of one bank contributes to the illiquidity of the others as the assets needed to honor the depositors' withdrawal requests disappear from the banking system.

It is commonly understood that banks are interconnected because of the nature of the deposit-creation process in the fractional-reserve banking system. Less well understood is why banks are so large (giving rise to the perception that they are too big to fail). A cursory look around the world reveals that banks count themselves among the largest companies in nearly all countries. This ubiquitous feature of the world's economic landscape can be understood by the fact that fractional-reserve banks are also the foundation of every financial system.

By using their clients' deposits, fractional-reserve banks are given access to low-cost funding not available to other businesses. When a manufacturer decides to invest, it raises funds on the capital markets and incurs the cost of prevailing interest or dividend rates. The fractional-reserve bank, in contrast, uses the deposits entrusted to it and which come at essentially no cost. The result of this low-cost funding source is that these banks can grow to sizes not possible for other firms, constrained as they are by higher borrowing costs.

It is important to note that there is nothing inherently wrong with banking as an activity. Indeed, as banks increase the marketability of money by converting currency into deposits, they greatly enhance trade and economic development. The legal aberration of fractional-reserve banking has, unfortunately, undermined consumer trust in this fiduciary industry. The conflation of loans and deposits has also wrought economic harm in the form of enhanced business cycles, and created a behemoth industry now viewed as too interconnected and large to allow market forces to curtail.

In light of these problems, a patchwork of regulations (e.g., deposit insurance, capital and liquidity requirements, etc.) has aimed to set the industry straight. Each new banking crisis brings forth new regulations that fail to set the industry on an even keel. By returning banks to their proper role as money depositories, economics, financial, and social stability will be promoted.

FUTURE DIRECTIONS

Despite the straightforward legal-economic analysis outlined here, there remain loose threads. After all, fractional-reserve banking is one of the most ingrained institutions in the economy. Banking reform has been slow. It usually proceeds in a piecemeal set of regulations aimed at correcting symptoms of the problems discussed in this chapter.

The most vocal critics of the analysis in this chapter belong to the fractional-reserve free banking school. This heterogeneous set of economists includes some members loosely affiliated with the Austrian school (Selgin, 1988; White, 1984, 1989). It also includes monetarists (Glasner, 1989; Timberlake, 1984, 1987, 1989; Yeager, 1997). Some differences in the economic analysis of banking is evident between the fractional-reserve free banking school and that contained in this chapter. These differences include (1) what comprises the demand for money, (2) the microfoundations of monetary equilibrium, (3) the relationship between saving and the demand for money, (4) the applicability of historical cases to the analysis at hand, and (5) the role that judicial arguments play in economic theorizing. Huerta de Soto (1998) and Bagus and Howden (2010) have addressed these differences in economic analysis thoroughly. To be successful in changing the theoretical and practical treatment of fractional-reserve banks, future research will focus on the final point of disagreement: the role of judicial arguments in economic theorizing.

One common rebuttal to the legal-economic analysis contained herein is that any voluntary relationship is permissible in a free society. (From personal experience, I can attest that almost every referee report I have received for a publication promoting these ideas contains some form of this reply.) The criticism has a grain of truth: freely consenting adults can contract with each other in a myriad of ways, including ways that are detrimental to their wellbeing. The link between judicial and economic analysis is that a legal consideration of property rights is necessary before analyzing how we can allocate goods economically. Understanding that not all mutually advantageous contracts are allowed has long been a staple of legal analysis. Any analysis of the banking system must include this legal constraint. Doing so is a consistent application of the role of costs in economic analysis, similar to the role of other constraints.

Some traditional analyses of fractional-reserve banking focused on the ethical aspect of the relationship between depositor and lender. Fraud and embezzlement are common themes in these analyses (e.g., Hoppe et al., 1998; Rothbard, 2001 [1974], 2007 [1994]). History is rife with cases of bankers misappropriating depositor funds. Yet even in those cases where fractional-reserve banking emerged under purely voluntary and uncoerced conditions there are reasons to doubt its legitimacy.

Under standard contract law, uncertainty of performance, incompatible objectives, and common mistakes of subject matter all prohibit otherwise voluntary transactions. All three of these reasons apply to one or both parties of the fractional-reserve demand deposit contract (Bagus & Howden, 2013). Before drafting banking policy and assessing its effects on the broader economy, one must start by understanding what legal constraints bind these financial arrangements. Judicial considerations form the bedrock of later analysis.

A legal foundation is implicit in other forms of economic analysis. The allocation of shirts in any principles of economics class presupposes a theory of property rights. Such rights allow for demanders and suppliers to transact with each other. This chapter is a more explicit application of this general reasoning to the case of banking. Future directions of research into the role of banking must consider these legal arguments. Consideration of legal arguments is not a complement to economic theory, but a prerequisite for its full development.

NOTES

1. There are other industry-specific courses, e.g., insurance, healthcare, etc. Such courses do not look at systemic implications of the industry on the economy and instead focus on the microeconomics of various policies targeted at specific areas of the economy. "Money and Banking" is unique as it jumps to analyzing systemic economy-wide effects of the industry without answering the questions of why banking is unique, and whether such uniqueness is optimal.

2. A good lent for an unlimited time period is a gift (Bagus & Howden, 2013). One such historical example of this financial product are British consols: "bonds" of perpetual maturity first issued by the British government in 1751. Though "perpetual" in name (and theory), the bonds were subject to frequent alterations in both their earned interest rate and their actual maturity (in practice being redeemed early at the option of the British Treasury).

3. While the bank may waive the interest payment for such loans out of reasons of attracting new business or friendliness, this will not negate the essential occurrence of the interest payment. It instead represents a loss for the bank that will be compensated (or expected to be so) through other avenues of business. Bagus and Howden (2009, p. 400, note 5) make a similar point.

4. Note that any use of a deposited good is a violation of the contract, even if the good can be returned when the depositor asks for it. If a painting is deposited with a depository that appropriates the painting for an exhibition, there is a misappropriation. It might be that the depositor asks for his painting only after the end of the exhibition and it can be returned on demand. Yet even in this case where the depositor is not aware of the act, a misappropriation occurs with a commensurate violation of the contract's safekeeping obligation.

5. Throughout this chapter we use the word deposit interchangeably for regular and irregular deposits. Deposits involving money are always irregular, though the safekeeping obligation of the depository is identical in each case.

6. This section borrows heavily from Bagus and Howden (forthcoming).

7. This does not imply that the depository cannot place constraints on these withdrawals out of practical convenience or necessity (e.g., business hours). It means that the depositor can access his funds within the limits as set out in the contract, and that the depository must also abide by this requirement. For example, if the deposit stipulates withdrawals are available during business hours only, the depository cannot deny the depositor's right to his funds during these hours. Furthermore, the full availability of the deposit has an economic definition that differs from the legal requirement, namely, that nothing can be done to impinge on the availability of the good, as discussed in Bagus and Howden (2016).

8. The dual claim nature of the fractional-reserve demand deposit contributes to a wealth effect whereby more than one party is made wealthier than would otherwise be the case as they (depositor and bank) each deem ownership of the deposit to reside with them. It is the duality of ownership claims to the deposit that Hoppe et al. (1998) find problematic, both economically and ethically, with the contract.

9. This is similar to the historical use of an "option clause" on deposits that gave a bank the ability to not redeem the depositor's funds on demand if constrained by liquidity. In a similar manner to the modern notice of withdrawal waiver, these clauses solved the apparent problem of an impossible-to-honor conflict of

rights while creating another conflict by altering the rights and forcibly converting the depositor into a lender.
10. The difficulty inherent in the bank returning the deposit on demand is complicated by the fact that not only does it not know when this deposit will be
requested, but also that the depositor himself lacks this knowledge. As money
and deposits are held to provide insurance against an unknown future event, it is
impossible to predict when this future event will occur, as well as in what amount
the required funds will be.

REFERENCES

Bagus, P., & Howden, D. (2009). The Legitimacy of Loan Maturity Mismatching:
A Risky, but Not Fraudulent, Undertaking. *Journal of Business Ethics*, *90*(3),
399–406.
Bagus, P., & Howden, D. (2010). Fractional Reserve Free Banking: Some Quibbles.
Quarterly Journal of Austrian Economics, *13*(4), 29–55.
Bagus, P., & Howden, D. (2011). *Deep Freeze: Iceland's Economic Collapse*. Auburn,
AL: Ludwig von Mises Institute.
Bagus, P., & Howden, D. (2013). Some Ethical Dilemmas of Modern Banking.
Business Ethics: A European Review, *22*(3), 235–245.
Bagus, P., & Howden, D. (2016). The Economic and Legal Significance of "Full"
Deposit Availability. *European Journal of Law and Economics*, *41*(1), 243–254.
Bagus, P., & Howden, D. (forthcoming). Consumer Rights and Banking Contracts.
Journal of Banking Regulation.
Cobden Centre. (2010). Public Attitudes toward Banking. www.cobdencentre.org/
?dl_id=67
Freixas, X., & Rochet, J.-C. (2008). *Microeconomics of Banking* (2nd ed.). Cambridge,
MA: MIT Press.
Garrison, R. W. (2004). Overconsumption and Forced Saving in the Mises-Hayek
Theory of the Business Cycle. *History of Political Economy*, *36*(2), 323–349.
Glasner, D. (1989). *Free Banking and Monetary Reform*. Cambridge: Cambridge
University Press.
Goodhart, C. (1988). *The Evolution of Central Banks*. Cambridge, MA: MIT Press.
Gorton, G. (1985). Clearinghouses and the Origin of Central Banking in the United
States. *Journal of Economic History*, *45*(2), 277–283.
Hayek, F. A. von. (1937). Economics and Knowledge. *Economica*, *4*(13), 33–54.
Hayek, F. A. von. (1967). *Prices and Production*. New York: Augustus M. Kelley.
Hoppe, H.-H. (1994). How Is Fiat Money Possible? Or, the Devolution of Money and
Credit. *Review of Austrian Economics*, *7*(2), 49–74.
Hoppe, H.-H., Hülsmann, J. G., & Block, W. (1998). Against Fiduciary Media.
Quarterly Journal of Austrian Economics, *1*(1), 19–50.
Howden, D. (2014). A Pre-History of the Federal Reserve. In D. Howden & J. T.
Salerno (Eds), *The Fed at One Hundred: A Critical Review of the Federal Reserve
System* (pp. 9–21). London: Springer.
Howden, D. (2015). Money in a World of Finance. *Money in a World of Finance*, *4*
(Papers and Proceedings of the 3rd Annual International Conference of Prices and
Markets, Toronto, November 6–7, 2014), 13–20.
Howden, D., & Kampe, J. (2016). Time Preference and the Process of Civilization.
International Journal of Social Economics, *43*(4), 382–399.

Huerta de Soto, J. (1998). A Critical Note on Fractional-Reserve Free Banking. *Quarterly Journal of Austrian Economics*, *1*(4), 25–49.

Huerta de Soto, J. (2006). *Money, Bank Credit and Economic Cycles*. Auburn, AL: Ludwig von Mises Institute.

Hülsmann, J. G. (2008). *The Ethics of Money Production*. Auburn, AL: Ludwig von Mises Institute.

Jevons, W. S. (1875). *Money and the Mechanism of Exchange*. London: C. Kegan Paul.

Menger, C. (1892). On the Origin of Money. *The Economic Journal*, *2*(6), 239.

Menger, C. (2007 [1871]). *Principles of Economics* (J. Dingwall, Trans. and B. F. Hoselitz, Ed.). Auburn, AL: Ludwig von Mises Institute.

Mises, L. von. (1949). *Human Action*. New Haven, CT: Fox & Wilkes and Foundation for Economic Education.

Mises, L. von. (1971). *The Theory of Money and Credit* (H. E. Batson, Trans.). Irvington-on-Hudson, NY: Foundation for Economic Education.

Mises, L. von. (1990). Inflation and You. In B. B. Greaves (Ed.), *Economic Freedom and Interventionism: An Anthology of Articles and Essay* (pp. 101–107). Indianapolis, IN: Liberty Fund.

Mises, L. von. (1998). *Human Action: The Scholar's Edition*. Auburn, AL: Mises Institute.

Rothbard, M. N. (1993 [1962]). *Man, Economy, and State: A Treatise on Economic Principles*. Auburn, AL: Ludwig von Mises Institute.

Rothbard, M. N. (2001 [1974]). *The Case for a 100 Percent Gold Dollar*. Auburn, AL: Ludwig von Mises Institute.

Rothbard, M. N. (2007 [1994]). *The Case against the Fed*. Auburn, AL: Ludwig von Mises Institute.

Rothbard, M. N. (2010). *What Has Government Done to Our Money?* Auburn, AL: Ludwig von Mises Institute.

Selgin, G. A. (1988). *The Theory of Free Banking: Money Supply under Competitive Note Issue*. Totowa, NJ: Rowman and Littlefield.

Smith, V. L. (1990). *The Rationale of Central Banking and the Free Banking Alternative*. Minneapolis, MN: Liberty Fund.

Timberlake, R. H. (1984). The Central Banking Role of Clearinghouse Associations. *Journal of Money, Credit and Banking*, *16*(1), 1.

Timberlake, R. H. (1987). Private Production of Scrip-Money in the Isolated Community. *Journal of Money, Credit and Banking*, *19*(4), 437.

Timberlake, R. H. (1989). The Government's License to Create Money. *Cato Journal*, *9*(2), 302–321.

White, L. H. (1984). *Free Banking in Britain: Theory, Experience, and Debate, 1800–1845*. Cambridge: Cambridge University Press.

White, L. H. (1989). *Competition and Currency: Essays on Free Banking and Money*. New York: New York University Press.

Wicksell, K. (1962). *Interest and Prices: A Study into the Causes Regulating the Value of Money*. (R. F. K., Ed. and Trans.). New York: Augustus M. Kelley.

Yeager, L. B. (1997). *The Fluttering Veil: Essays on Monetary Disequilibrium* (G. A. Selgin, Ed.). Indianapolis, IN: Liberty Fund.

11. On the origins of cryptocurrencies
William J. Luther and Nikhil Sridhar

INTRODUCTION

Bitcoin launched in early 2009 to little fanfare, but is now widely recognized as a revolutionary technology in money and payments. Its predetermined supply schedule precludes debasement. Its distributed ledger technology enables individuals to transact pseudonymously without relying on a trusted third party. And its open source code has inspired thousands of alternative cryptocurrencies, or alt-coins. It would not be surprising if, in a hundred years, bitcoin were cited alongside automatic teller machines, redeemable banknotes, and the reeded edge as a remarkable advance in payments technology.

There is considerable overlap between those interested in Austrian economics and those interested in cryptocurrencies today. Many Austrians see bitcoin as exemplifying their ideas. Austrians have been critical of discretionary monetary policy, and those working in the tradition of Murray Rothbard tend to view a fixed money supply as ideal.[1] Libertarian-leaning Austrians generally like the privacy-protecting features of bitcoin, which might serve as a bulwark against meddlesome or confiscatory state actors.[2] At the same time, Austrian economics provides a rich intellectual history that those interested in cryptocurrencies might draw on. Some cryptocurrency proponents cite arguments advanced by Ludwig von Mises and Friedrich Hayek in the socialist calculation debate when discussing the decentralization afforded by cryptocurrencies like bitcoin (e.g., Voorhees, 2021). Others at the intersection have noted similarities between the modern-day market for cryptocurrencies and the competition in currency envisioned by Hayek (e.g., Nakayama, 2018; White & Luther, 2018).

The relationship between Austrian economists and cryptocurrency proponents was not always so cozy, however. At the outset, many Austrians were skeptical of bitcoin's potential to function as a medium of exchange. Mises's regression theorem, they claimed at the time, implied that an item must first have some non-monetary use value in order to be acceptable in exchange without government support. Since bitcoin lacked a non-monetary use, it did not meet the necessary conditions of the regression theorem and, hence, could not emerge as money in the absence of state coercion. Indeed, some argued—erroneously—that bitcoin was not money *despite* functioning as a medium of exchange *because* it violated the regression theorem.[3] As bitcoin gained traction, and it became impossible to deny it was functioning as a medium of exchange, those who had previously denied bitcoin could become money changed their tune. Some working in the Austrian tradition have attempted to rehabilitate the regression theorem in light of bitcoin. Others have been more inclined to cast it aside.

In what follows, we consider the conflict that cryptocurrencies like bitcoin created for the traditional Austrian understanding of the emergence of money and the more recent steps those working in the field have taken to resolve it. We describe the traditional view in the first section. We offer a brief survey of bitcoin and other blockchain-based media of exchange, then we discuss efforts to reconsider the regression theorem in light of bitcoin.

MENGER, MISES, AND THE EMERGENCE OF MONEY

The traditional Austrian view on the emergence of money begins with Carl Menger, who published "On the Origin of Money" in 1892. Menger sought to explain how an item might become a commonly accepted medium of exchange through the actions of decentralized individuals acting in their own interest. He shows that, without intending to do so or explicitly coordinating their actions, individuals will naturally come to accept a small set of items in exchange that they do not consume but, instead, use to acquire other goods and services. It is, to borrow a phrase from Adam Ferguson (1782), "the result of human action, but not the execution of any human design."

Menger's spontaneous order theory is perhaps best understood by starting with a simple thought experiment. Suppose a trader, who produces chickens, goes to the market in the hopes of acquiring grain. With each interaction, the trader must decide whether to swap the good he has with the good of his trading partner. Obviously, if the trader meets another who has grain, he will offer to exchange his chickens for grain. But, importantly, Menger also considered what the trader would do when meeting someone who does not possess grain. Will he offer to trade in that situation as well? Menger reasoned that the trader would offer to exchange his chickens for the non-grain good of his trading partner if he believed the non-grain good would enable him to trade for grain more quickly than he would be able to do so by continuing to hold chickens. Suppose further, for example, that grain producers rarely want chickens, never want beef, and frequently want salt. The trader might refuse to trade his chickens for beef, since holding beef will likely make it more difficult to trade for grain. He might trade his chickens for salt, though, since holding salt will likely make it easier to trade for grain.

To generalize the thought experiment described above, one might note that each agent produces some good i and consumes some good $j \neq i$. When matched with a potential trading partner, a self-interested optimizing agent asks herself two questions:

1. Does this person have j?
2. Does this person have some good $k \neq j$ that would make it easier for me to trade for j than the good I am currently holding (initially, i)?

If she answers yes to either, she offers to trade. If she answers no to both, she moves on to the next potential trading partner. And she continues doing this until she successfully trades for the good she wants to consume, at which point she returns home. She will revisit the market to repeat this process once she produces again.

With this basic idea in mind, Menger considered how the economy would evolve over time.[4] Note that accepting an item one does not want to consume on the grounds that it is more saleable does not merely help one trade for her consumption good more quickly. It also makes that item more saleable to others, by increasing the number of traders who readily accept the item in exchange. Menger reasoned that a positive feedback loop would result: accepting a more saleable item makes it even more saleable, which encourages others to accept it, making it more saleable still, and so on. Over time, an unplanned order would naturally emerge, where individuals accept a small set of highly saleable (or liquid) assets in exchange. "The theory of money," Menger (1892, p. 243) wrote, "necessarily presupposes a theory of the saleableness of goods."

Nearly a century after Menger published "On the Origin of Money," George Selgin and Lawrence White extended his account to explain the emergence of other monetary institutions. Commodity monies, like gold, are eventually minted into coins to reduce the cost of assaying at each transaction. Money-transfer services are developed to economize on the cost of transporting physical coins. To attract customers, banks come to provide convenient payment instruments like checkable deposits and negotiable banknotes. And, to reduce the cost of holding reserves sufficient to meet redemptions associated with those payment instruments, they develop routine clearing arrangements with rival banks. "[E]ach successive step in the process of evolution originates in individuals' discovery of new ways to promote their self-interest," Selgin and White (1987, p. 440) write, "with the outcome an arrangement at which no individual consciously aims."

The spontaneous order theory pioneered by Menger and extended by Selgin and White can account for the emergence of commodity-based outside monies and redeemable inside monies. It cannot account for the non-commodity, irredeemable monies widely used today. No one consumes the United States (US) dollar or the Chinese yuan. These monies are *intrinsically worthless*—that is, they lack any use apart from serving as a medium of exchange. Nor are these monies redeemable for some underlying commodity. The US dollar was redeemable for gold by foreign governments prior to 1971 and US citizens prior to 1933. But it is not redeemable today. The new yuan (or renminbi) was first issued in 1948 and has never been redeemable; the convertibility of its predecessor, the old yuan, into silver ended in 1935. Today, these monies—along with most other outside monies used around the world—are intrinsically worthless.

How, then, do Austrians explain the existence of intrinsically worthless monies? Traditionally, they have pointed to the regression theorem of Ludwig von Mises.[5] In order to estimate the value of money, Mises (1934, p. 131) maintained, a preexisting market exchange ratio between the item functioning as money and other goods is required. Thus, "it follows that an object cannot be used as money unless, at the moment when its use as money begins, it already possesses an objective exchange value based on some other use." In other words, intrinsically worthless monies must have some historical link to commodities—a link that can be broken by the government. Mises (1934, p. 132) finds this link in redeemable banknotes, which were ultimately "deprived of their character as claims" to commodities by the government but continued to circulate at a positive value since "money that already functions as such may remain valuable even when the original source of its exchange value has ceased to exist." Whereas some commodity use was required to get these monies off the ground, it is no longer required after a successful launch; after a successful launch, Mises (1934, p. 132) noted, the value of money might be "based entirely on its function as a common medium of exchange."

In the time since Mises wrote *The Theory of Money and Credit*, many intrinsically worthless monies have been issued by governments without ever being redeemable for some commodity. As Selgin (1994) explains, however, these monies also owe their success to historical commodity monies. When the renminbi was introduced, for example, it was not redeemable for silver, as the old yuan had once been. But it was introduced at a fixed exchange rate with the old yuan, making it redeemable, in a sense, for a money already in circulation that had once been redeemable for a commodity, in this case silver. The fixed exchange rate could only be dropped after the new yuan was in circulation. Similarly, when the euro was introduced in 1999, its exchange rate was initially fixed to monies already circulating in what would become the euro area: Austrian schilling (ATS 13.7603), Belgian franc (BEF 40.3399), Dutch guilder (NLG 2.20371), Finnish markka (FIM 5.94573), French franc (FRF 6.55957), German mark (DEM 1.95583), Irish pound (IEP 0.787564), Italian lira (ITL 1,936.27), Luxembourg franc (LUF 40.3399), Portuguese escudo (PTE 200.482), and Spanish peseta (ESP 166.386). Each of these monies had either been redeemable for some commodity when launched or similarly introduced at a fixed exchange rate to a money that had been redeemable for some commodity at its launch. Modern fiat monies, in other words, can trace their lineage to commodity monies of the past.[6]

The traditional Austrian view, from Menger through Mises to Selgin and White, maintains that commodity monies can emerge without government support; that redeemable claims for commodity monies will follow; and that intrinsically worthless monies will only circulate if a government suspends redemption of claims already in circulation or introduces an irredeemable money at a fixed exchange with some money already in circulation. The traditional Austrian view rules out the prospect that an intrinsically worthless item might emerge as money without government support.

That is not to say Austrians have not considered privately issued irredeemable monies. F. A. Hayek (1976) envisioned such monies circulating in *The Denationalization of Money*. However, he did not clearly explain how such monies would come to be accepted. And many Austrians dismissed his proposal on the grounds that the monies circulating in the system he envisioned violated the regression theorem. "Hayek's plan for the denationalization of money is Utopian in the worst sense: not because it is radical," Murray Rothbard (1985, p. 4) wrote, "but because it would not and could not work."

BITCOIN AND OTHER CRYPTOCURRENCIES

The cryptocurrency bitcoin was outlined in a 2008 white paper by the pseudonymous Satoshi Nakamoto and launched a few months later. While others, including David Chaum and Nick Szabo, had proposed earlier cryptocurrencies, bitcoin was the first to really take hold.[7] Unlike its predecessors, Bitcoin employed a novel blockchain technology, which enabled transactions to be processed on a distributed network and thereby eliminated the need to rely on a trusted third party.[8] As the community of users grew, the purchasing power of bitcoin climbed. As of December 1, 2021, one bitcoin exchanged for $57,180.

The blockchain technology consists of a shared ledger and protocol for updating that ledger. To make a transaction, the sender indicates the public address of her recipient and then signs the transaction from her public address with her private key. In practice, the transaction is often initiated by scanning a QR code with a smartphone app. Indeed, as Antonopoulos (2014) notes, "digital keys are very rarely seen by the users of bitcoin. For the most part, they are stored inside the wallet file and managed by the bitcoin wallet software." The authorized transaction is then bundled together with other recent transactions. Those running the bitcoin protocol compete to process this block of transactions—that is, to create an appropriate hash of the block, thereby chaining the block to the preexisting blockchain and effectively updating the shared ledger.

The bitcoin protocol employs a proof-of-work mechanism and recognizes the longest blockchain as legitimate. The proof-of-work mechanism requires the hash to include a given number of leading zeros, which can only be achieved via brute force. As a result, the probability of producing an appropriate hash—and, hence, processing a batch of transactions—is roughly equivalent to one's share of the computing power on the system. Since users randomly add blocks to the blockchain, and only the longest blockchain is recognized as legitimate, the protocol protects against double spending. And this protection is sufficient so long as no user or group of cooperating users has access to a majority of the computing power on the system.

To encourage users to run the bitcoin protocol, the system rewards the entity successfully hashing a block of transactions with a new balance of bitcoin. The reward amount is predetermined and is cut in half roughly every four years. The system also adjusts the difficulty of producing an appropriate hash to ensure one block of transactions is added to the blockchain roughly every ten minutes. When blocks are added more frequently than designed, the number of leading zeros required increases. This makes it more difficult to produce an appropriate hash, reducing the speed at which blocks are added. When blocks are added less frequently than designed, the number of leading zeros required in a hash declines, allowing blocks to be created more frequently. Taken together, the predetermined rewards and automatically adjusting difficulty ensure that the supply of bitcoin grows at a predictable, declining rate until 21 million coins have been issued, which should occur in late 2140.

After the maximum bitcoin supply is reached, the system will depend entirely on transaction fees to encourage users to run the protocol and, hence, process transactions. In fact, since the block reward falls very close to zero well in advance of 2140, it seems likely that the system will rely heavily on transaction fees much earlier. Transaction fees will encourage users to economize on transactions, perhaps by employing second-layer solutions. It will also ensure that the resources used to secure the bitcoin ledger do not exceed the value users place on transacting with bitcoin.

Following the launch of bitcoin, many other cryptocurrencies—known as alt-coins—have been introduced. Many early alt-coins were simply clones of the bitcoin protocol. In other words, a developer copied the bitcoin code and then issued a new cryptocurrency that functions exactly like bitcoin. Others deviate from the bitcoin design in potentially important ways. Some offer enhanced privacy features. Some make it convenient to run self-executing (or, smart) contracts. Some replace the proof-of-work mechanism with a proof-of-stake mechanism, which reduces the energy required to process transactions. Today, there are a host of alt-coins—more than 4,000!—vying for market share, though bitcoin has remained dominant.

One relatively new type of alt-coin is called a stablecoin. As the name implies, these cryptocurrencies attempt to stabilize their value relative to some other asset—typically an existing currency and, most often, the dollar. In the case of tether, the most popular stablecoin to date, the supply is managed at the discretion of the issuer to ensure 1 tether always trades for $1. Other algorithmic stablecoins, like ampleforth, frax, and empty set dollar, have attempted to remove the issuer risk inherent with stablecoins like tether by coding the value-stabilizing supply mechanism into the protocol.

Governments are also moving into the cryptocurrency space, with so-called central bank digital currencies (CBDCs). China's e-yuan is perhaps the most widely known example. China began considering its CBDC in 2014 and launched a pilot project in May 2020 (Yeung & Mullen, 2021). Some 45 other central banks have considered or are in the process of launching CBDCs, as well (King, 2020). CBDCs have an advantage over privately issued cryptocurrencies in pegging to the domestic currency, but they are expected to deliver less financial privacy than the typical cryptocurrency.

Cryptocurrencies like bitcoin would seem to pose a problem for the traditional Austrian view on the emergence of money. They are not commodities; nor are they generally redeemable for some commodity. With the exception of CBDCs, they do not typically enjoy government support. And, with the exception of stablecoins, they are not typically introduced at a fixed exchange with some existing money. How, then, have cryptocurrencies like bitcoin gained a positive value in the market?

RECONSIDERING THE REGRESSION THEOREM

Those working in the Austrian tradition were quick to note the tension between the regression theorem and bitcoin. Some, including Nikolay Gertchev (2013), maintained that bitcoin was consistent with the regression theorem. But many rejected this view. "[W]e might as well say that alchemy works," Patrik Korda (2013) wrote in response. Others hedged their bets. "Bitcoin may yet fail, in which case Mises' theorem will remain as a powerful argument," Logan Albright (2014) concluded. "If it ends up succeeding, however, an alternate explanation will have to be found."

In fact, as Robert Murphy (2020) has explained, there was no need to wait around. "[T]he regression theorem actually doesn't refer to a good becoming *money*, but rather a good becoming a *medium of exchange* ... Bitcoin has clearly *already* become a medium of exchange (though it is not money under any reasonable standard). So it must already be the case one way or the other:

either the emergence of Bitcoin as a medium of exchange violated the regression theorem, or it didn't."[9]

As bitcoin use increased, it became impossible to deny it was functioning as a medium of exchange. Those who had previously denied bitcoin could become money on the grounds that it violated the regression theorem had little choice but to revise their view. The question then turned to whether bitcoin required rejecting the regression theorem—or whether the regression theorem might be rehabilitated in light of bitcoin.

Some of those working in the Austrian tradition have tried to preserve the validity of the regression theorem by claiming its scope is narrower than has been widely claimed. Laura Davidson and Walter Block (2015, p. 318), for example, maintain that the regression theorem "is not an explanation for the origin of all monies or all media of exchange" and does not apply "once a calculational framework in terms of money prices is established." Instead, they say, it merely "explicates how a barter economy—where all economic calculation is conducted ordinally—becomes a monetary economy in which calculation is performed cardinally." Bitcoin does not threaten the validity of the regression theorem in their view because it was launched in an economy where other monies were already widely used.

Regarding the possibility of launching an intrinsically worthless item in a monetary economy despite no such possibility existing in a barter economy, Davidson and Block might be correct. But Mises (1949, p. 407) is quite clear that the regression theorem applies more broadly:

> This always happens when the conditions appear; whenever a good which has not been demanded previously for the employment as a medium of exchange begins to be demanded for this employment, the same effects must appear again; no good can be employed for the function of a medium of exchange which at the very beginning of its use for this purpose did not have exchange value on account of other employments. And all these statements implied in the regression theorem are enounced apodictically as implied in the apriorism of praxeology. It must happen this way.

In claiming that it is possible for a private actor to launch an intrinsically worthless item in a monetary economy, Davidson and Block advance a view that is irreconcilable with the regression theorem laid out by Mises.

Others considering the regression theorem in light of bitcoin rightly recognize that the debate hinges on whether bitcoin is intrinsically worthless.[10] However, some arguing in this vein ignore the conventional definition of the term. Evan Faggart (2014), for example, redefines the term intrinsic to mean objective:

> Those who claim that money needs "intrinsic" value fail to realize that there is no intrinsic value, it is created in the minds of individuals. So by saying that Bitcoin

value is imaginary is merely to confirm subjective value theory. All value that exists
in objects of human interaction and exchange is "imaginary." There is no value that
exists independently of the minds of human beings.

In other words, he dismisses the view that an item must initially have some
intrinsic worth in order to function as a medium of exchange on the grounds
that all value is subjective.

Elsewhere, I have referred to this view as the "superficial subjective value
argument" (White & Luther, 2018). Although the claim that all value is
subjective is true and *appears* to address the view that an item must have
some intrinsic value in order to function as a medium of exchange, it is not
actually relevant to the underlying debate. Monetary economists do not deny
that value is subjective. When they refer to an item's "intrinsic" worth, they
mean its value apart from any role it might play as a medium of exchange. Its
intrinsic worth, in other words, is derived from the subjective valuation of its
non-monetary use. To say that an item is intrinsically worthless, therefore,
merely notes that no individual values it (subjectively) for any purpose other
than its potential use as a medium of exchange.

Peter Šurda (2014, p. 22) seems to make a similar error in arguing that
bitcoin is a commodity money. A commodity money, as conventionally
understood, is a money that also has some intrinsic use. Šurda maintains that
bitcoin is a commodity money because it possesses "utility … derived from
a reduction of transaction costs of exchange." Although there is no denying
that people use a given medium of exchange to reduce transaction costs relative to barter or use of some alternative medium of exchange, that utility (or
subjective value) does not allow one to conclude that the item is a commodity
money. If it did, all monies would meet the definition of a commodity money!
Again, the term intrinsically worthless means that the item in question has no
utility *apart from its role as a medium of exchange*. If reducing the transaction
costs of exchange is the *only* source of utility, then the item in question does
not qualify as a commodity money and should, instead, be regarded as intrinsically worthless.

Konrad Graf (2013a, 2013b) makes a more persuasive case that bitcoin is
a commodity and, hence, its use as a medium of exchange does not contradict
the regression theorem. He points to non-monetary uses that are "primarily
psychological or sociological in character" (Graf, 2013a). He notes that it was
useful for testing the network—which might be valued by those with a theoretical or scientific interest in monetary economics or computer science (Graf,

2013b, pp. 27–28). It might also be used as a digital collectible, perhaps to signal the degree of one's participation in the bitcoin social project.[11]

> Even now, well after their initial emergence, there appears to be a "mystique value" and a "curiosity value" attached to bitcoins among widening circles of newcomers who, compared with founders and earlier adopters, tend to understand the underlying mechanics of the system less and less, but have the impression that participation is a way to be proud and to send a message of being techno-savvy, up to date, in the know, etc. (Graf, 2013a)

It is clear that bitcoin had some non-monetary use, Graf (2013b, p. 23) maintains, because "bitcoins had some value to some people, but going out and buying something with bitcoins—facilitating trades with them—was not among the available uses."

Graf's view, that bitcoin had some non-monetary use prior to functioning as a medium of exchange, might be correct. It is impossible to observe another's utility function directly and difficult to determine it indirectly from observed actions. One cannot really know *why* one demanded bitcoin prior to its use as a medium of exchange—and, in particular, whether it was for some non-monetary use. Admitting his position might be correct, however, also implies that the regression theorem has far less practical relevance than was previously thought.[12]

Prior to the introduction of bitcoin, the regression theorem was thought to tell one what types of items might emerge as media of exchange in the absence of government support. In particular, it maintained that commodities and redeemable claims to valuable assets might come to be used as media of exchange, while intrinsically worthless fiat monies could not do so without some support from the government. If one accepts Graf's approach, however, then the regression theorem no longer rules out any would-be media of exchange in practice. Anything might function as a medium of exchange, so long as someone thinks it is neat.

Of course, recognizing the implication of Graf's view for the practical relevance of the regression theorem in no way discredits his view. He does not seem too bothered by the implication. Indeed, he suggests that many historical monies were characterized by such trivial non-monetary uses. Gold and silver, Graf (2013b, p. 17; emphasis in original) maintains, were also mere collectible at the outset: "The sometimes-touted industrial and electronic uses of gold and silver are all quite modern and therefore entirely irrelevant to the *first emergence* of these metals in a monetary trading role in various places many centuries earlier." And he goes further still:

> That is, in each such case we have considered, a few of mankind's "crazy ones" were playing around with and collecting things that were useless for anything that

would have been considered a generally "practical" purpose at the origin phases in question, such as shell beads, shiny metals, or bitcoins. Eventually though, an additional economic use for these mere trinkets—actually using them to facilitate trades—was gradually and in fits and starts put into practice, with some favorable results. This practice then spread by some blend of imitation and recurring independent rediscovery.

Such experiments were quite likely met in every case with furrowed brows and disbelief on the part of more sober observers still unwilling to trade "real" things for the likes of shells, shiny soft metals, or in the current case ... they do not have the faintest idea what. The difference is, today, the process of more and more people discovering how to make use of Bitcoin to facilitate trade is taking place worldwide and at the speed of the internet and word of mouth. (Graf, 2013b, p. 29)

If this means the regression theorem lacks practical relevance, in other words, so be it.

While Graf's approach to reconciling the experience of bitcoin with the regression theorem is plausible, he goes too far in claiming bitcoin *must* have had some non-monetary use. "Thus, even if every single interpreter, including myself writing now, were to end up failing to find any prior direct-use or direct-exchange values," Graf (2013a) writes, "we would still know that bitcoins had had one. All that we would establish by not finding one would be the failure of our own interpretive efforts." There is, in fact, an alternative explanation.

The standard search-theoretic approach to monetary economics pioneered by Kiyotaki and Wright (1989, 1991, 1993) maintains that an intrinsically worthless item might function as a medium of exchange if individuals are able to coordinate their beliefs. This explanation, which I call the "coordination view," might reasonably account for the successful launch of bitcoin (Luther, 2016a, 2019). Krawisz (2013) reaches the same conclusion:

When Bitcoin was first invented, bitcoins had no exchange value and were given away free just to generate interest. However, once the right entrepreneurs began to suspect that bitcoins might actually be used as money some day, they were willing to pay dollars to have larger amounts than were available for free.

Proponents of the coordination view maintain that bitcoin lacked some non-monetary use at the outset; that bitcoin community members coordinated to generate a set of shared beliefs about the future acceptability of bitcoin as a medium of exchange; and that they were then able to act on those shared beliefs in the present, bootstrapping bitcoin's value. Failing to identify some non-monetary use at the outset need not indicate "the failure of our own interpretive efforts," as Graf maintains. It might instead indicate that no such non-monetary use existed, and that bitcoin gained a positive value in a way not anticipated by Menger or Mises.

CONCLUSION

The rise of bitcoin is a remarkable event in the history of money and banking. And many of those interested in Austrian economics have taken a keen interest in bitcoin, as well. But the success of bitcoin as a medium of exchange poses a problem for the traditional Austrian view on the emergence of money. In particular, it casts doubt on the regression theorem of Ludwig von Mises, which implies that an item cannot gain acceptance as a medium of exchange without government support if it does not first possess some non-monetary use value.

There are two potential ways to think about the regression theorem in light of bitcoin. The use-value view maintains that bitcoin had some non-monetary use at the outset and, hence, is entirely consistent with the regression theorem. This view preserves the validity of the regression theorem, while sacrificing its practical relevance for identifying items that cannot function as a medium of exchange without government support. The coordination view, in contrast, denies bitcoin had any non-monetary use prior to its use as a medium of exchange. Instead, it maintains that bitcoin gained value because people thought it might be useful as a medium of exchange and coordinated their beliefs to realize its potential as such. This view rejects the validity of the regression theorem as the only explanation for how an item might come to be used as a medium of exchange in the absence of government support. It poses an alternative, where an item is valued at the outset solely on the basis of its usefulness as a medium of exchange.

It is impossible to know whether bitcoin possessed some non-monetary use value prior to its use as a medium of exchange. We do not observe utility functions. Hence, one cannot definitively conclude that the existence of bitcoin violates the regression theorem. On the other hand, we see no reason to rule out the coordination view *a priori*. Why should one assume people cannot coordinate on a potential medium of exchange?

Acknowledging the prospect that people might coordinate on a medium of exchange opens up several interesting research questions for those working in the Austrian tradition. How do individuals coordinate? What characteristics of the potential medium of exchange, participants, or environment make coordination more likely? How might governments encourage or undermine coordination? When is coordination likely to break down? Strict adherence to the regression theorem, as put forward by Mises, rules out such questions in the context of intrinsically worthless monies lacking government support. Nonetheless, we think these questions are interesting—and those working in the Austrian tradition are well suited to address these questions in future research.

NOTES

1. Horwitz and Luther (2011) divide macroeconomists working in the Austrian tradition into two groups: Rothbardians and monetary equilibrium theorists.
2. Hendrickson and Luther (2022) compare the privacy-promoting features of cash and cryptocurrencies. See also Hendrickson et al. (2016) and Hendrickson and Luther (2017).
3. As Hazlett and Luther (2020) make clear, money is defined as a commonly accepted medium of exchange. An item is money if and only if it meets that definition.
4. Modern economists typically use search-theoretic models to consider questions of currency acceptance. For a brief survey, which considers these models from an Austrian perspective, see Luther (2014, 2016b).
5. Ellis (1937), Patinkin (1965), Moss (1976), Edwards (1985), and Timberlake (1987) offer critiques of Mises's theorem. See also Rothbard (1976), Salerno (1994), and Selgin (1994).
6. King (2004), Luther (2013), and Luther and White (2016) consider cases where government support for an intrinsically worthless item is removed and, yet, it continues to function as money. In doing so, they demonstrate that, even if government support is required to launch an intrinsically worthless money, it is not required to sustain it.
7. Luther (2019) provides a brief survey of the early history. See also Popper (2015).
8. Luther and Stein Smith (2020) denote differences between centralized, decentralized, and distributed payment mechanisms.
9. Murphy's clarification serves as a useful correction to Walter Block (2013), who acknowledges that "bitcoins were never a valuable commodity" but maintains that, "if we more sympathetically interpret the regression theorem not in terms of a commodity, but in terms of SOMETHING of value, then when and if bitcoin becomes a money, it will not contradict the regression theorem for, surely, before it became a money (if it does) it was SOMETHING of value, albeit not a commodity, because it cannot be denied that some people valued it." The issue, as Murphy explains, is not whether bitcoin was valuable prior to becoming a money (i.e., a commonly accepted medium of exchange). Rather, it is whether bitcoin was valuable prior to being used as a medium of exchange.
10. In a recent article, George Pickering (2020, p. 608) claims that I misinterpret "the purpose and requirements of the regression theorem." He is wrong on both counts (Luther, 2021).
11. On bitcoin's appeal to anarchocapitalists and technologists, see Luther (2016a) and Yelowitz and Wilson (2015).
12. I have written much the same about Davidson and Block (2015), who "preserve the regression theorem by rendering it irrelevant" (Luther, 2018).

REFERENCES

Albright, L. (2014). "What Does Bitcoin Mean for Austrian Money Theory?" Mises Canada. Retrieved from http://mises.ca/posts/blog/what-does-bitcoin-mean-for -austrian-money-theory/

Antonopoulos, A. M. (2014). *Mastering Bitcoin: Unlocking Digital Cryptocurrencies*. O'Reilly Media.

Block, W. E. (2013). Regression theorem and Bitcoin. *Probane, 9*.

Davidson, L., & Block, W. E. (2015). Bitcoin, the Regression Theorem, and the Emergence of a New Medium of Exchange. *Quarterly Journal of Austrian Economics, 18*(3), 311–338.

Edwards, J. R. (1985). *The Economist of the Country: Ludwig von Mises in the History of Monetary Thought*. Carlton Press.

Ellis, H. S. (1937). *German Monetary Theory, 1905–33*. Harvard University Press.

Faggart, E. (2014). Bitcoin Value: The Nature and Origin of Money. Retrieved from https://99bitcoins.com/bitcoin-value-money/

Ferguson, A. (1782). *An Essay on the History of Civil Society* (Fifth ed.). T. Cadell, in the Strand.

Gertchev, N. (2013). The Money-ness of Bitcoins. Retrieved from https://mises.org/library/money-ness-bitcoins

Graf, K. S. (2013a). Bitcoins, the Regression Theorem, and That Curious but Unthreatening Empirical World. Retrieved from www.konradsgraf.com/blog1/2013/2/27/in-depth-bitcoins-the-regression-theorem-and-that-curious-bu.html

Graf, K. S. (2013b). *On the Origins of Bitcoin: Stages of Monetary Evolution*. Retrieved from https://nakamotoinstitute.org/static/docs/origins-of-bitcoin.pdf

Hayek, F. A. von. (1976). *Choice in Currency: A Way to Stop Inflation* (Vol. 48). Institute of Economic Affairs.

Hazlett, P. K., & Luther, W. J. (2020). Is Bitcoin Money? And What That Means. *Quarterly Review of Economics and Finance, 77*, 144–149.

Hendrickson, J. R., & Luther, W. J. (2017). Banning Bitcoin. *Journal of Economic Behavior and Organization, 141*, 188–195.

Hendrickson, J. R., & Luther, W. J. (2022). Cash, Crime, and Cryptocurrencies. *The Quarterly Review of Economics and Finance, 85*, 200–207.

Hendrickson, J. R., Hogan, T. L., & Luther, W. J. (2016). The Political Economy of Bitcoin. *Economic Inquiry, 54*(2), 925–939.

Horwitz, S. G., & Luther, W. J. (2011). *The Great Recession and Its Aftermath from a Monetary Equilibrium Theory Perspective in the Global Financial Crisis*. Edward Elgar Publishing.

King, M. (2004). The Institutions of Monetary Policy. *American Economic Review, 94*(2), 1–13.

King, R. (2020). *The Central Bank Digital Currency Survey 2020: Debunking Some Myths*. Retrieved from www.centralbanking.com/fintech/cbdc/7540951/the-central-bank-digital-currency-survey-2020-debunking-some-myths

Kiyotaki, N., & Wright, R. (1989). On Money as a Medium of Exchange. *Journal of Political Economy, 97*(4), 927–954.

Kiyotaki, N., & Wright, R. (1991). A Contribution to the Pure Theory of Money. *Journal of Economic Theory, 53*(2), 215–235.

Kiyotaki, N., & Wright, R. (1993). A Search-Theoretic Approach to Monetary Economics. *American Economic Review, 83*(1), 63077.

Korda, P. (2013). Bitcoin: Money of the Future or Old-Fashioned Bubble? Retrieved from https://mises.org/library/bitcoin-money-future-or-old-fashioned-bubble

Krawisz, D. (2013). *The Original Value of Bitcoins*. Retrieved from https://nakamotoinstitute.org/mempool/the-original-value-of-bitcoins/

Luther, W. J. (2013). Friedman versus Hayek on Private Outside Monies: New Evidence for the Debate. *Economic Affairs, 33*(1), 127–135.

Luther, W. J. (2014). Evenly Rotating Economy: A New Modeling Technique for an Old Equilibrium Construct. *Review of Austrian Economics, 27*, 403–417.

Luther, W. J. (2016a). Cryptocurrencies, Network Effects, and Switching Costs. *Contemporary Economic Policy, 34*(3), 553–571.

Luther, W. J. (2016b). Mises and the Moderns on the Inessentiality of Money in Equilibrium. *Review of Austrian Economics, 29*(1), 1–13.

Luther, W. J. (2018). *Is Bitcoin Intrinsically Worthless?* AIER Sound Money Project Working Paper No. 2018–07.

Luther, W. J. (2019). Getting off the Ground: The Case of Bitcoin. *Journal of Institutional Economics, 15*(2), 189–205.

Luther, W. J. (2021). *The Relevance of Bitcoin to the Regression Theorem: Reply to Pickering*. AIER Sound Money Project Working Paper No. 2022–03.

Luther, W. J., & Stein Smith, S. (2020). Is Bitcoin a Decentralized Payment Mechanism? *Journal of Institutional Economics, 16*(4), 433–444.

Luther, W. J., & White, L. H. (2016). Positively Valued Fiat Money after the Sovereign Disappears: The Case of Somalia. *Review of Behavioral Economics, 3*(3–4), 311–334.

Menger, C. (1892). On the Origin of Money. *The Economic Journal, 2*(6), 239–255.

Mises, L. von. (1934). *The Theory of Money and Credit* (2nd ed.). Jonathon Cape.

Mises, L. von. (1949). *Human Action*. Fox & Wilkes and Foundation for Economic Education.

Moss, L. S. (Ed.). (1976). *The Economics of Ludwig von Mises: Toward a Critical Reappraisal*. Sheed and Ward.

Murphy, R. P. (2020). Bitcoin and the Theory of Money. Retrieved from https://mises.org/wire/bitcoin-and-theory-money

Nakayama, C. (2018). The Reconsideration of Hayek's Idea on the De-nationalization of Money: Taking the Growing Tendency of Digital Currencies in Consideration. In A. Godart-van der Kroon & P. Vonlanthen (Eds), *Banking and Monetary Policy from the Perspective of Austrian Economics* (pp. 207–221). Springer.

Patinkin, D. (1965). *Money, Interest, and Prices: An Integration of Monetary and Value Theory*. Harper and Row.

Pickering, G. (2020). The Relevance of Bitcoin to the Regression Theorem: A Reply to Luther. *Quarterly Journal of Austrian Economics, 22*(4), 603–619.

Popper, N. (2015). *Digital Gold: The Untold Story of Bitcoin*. Penguin.

Rothbard, M. N. (1976). The Austrian Theory of Money. In E. G. Dolan (Ed.), *Foundations of Modern Austrian Economics* (pp. 160–184). New York: Columbia University Press.

Rothbard, M. N. (1985). The Case for a Genuine Gold Dollar. In L. Rockwell (Ed.), *The Gold Standard: An Austrian Perspective* (pp. 1–17). DC Heath and Company.

Salerno, J. T. (1994). Ludwig von Mises's Monetary Theory in Light of Modern Monetary Thought. *Review of Austrian Economics, 8*(1), 71–115.

Selgin, G. A. (1994). On Ensuring the Acceptability of a New Fiat Money. *Journal of Money, Credit and Banking, 26*(4), 808.

Selgin, G. A., & White, L. H. (1987). The Evolution of a Free Banking System. *Economic Inquiry, 25*(3), 439–457.

Šurda, P. (2014). The Origin, Classification and Utility of Bitcoin. *SSRN Electronic Journal*. Retrieved from https://doi.org/10.2139/ssrn.2436823

Timberlake, R. H. (1987). Private Production of Scrip-Money in the Isolated Community. *Journal of Money, Credit and Banking, 19*(4), 437.

Voorhees, E. (2021). Decentralized Cryptocurrency Systems and Hayek's Unplanned Economy. Retrieved from www.aier.org/article/decentralized-cryptocurrency -systems-and-hayeks-unplanned-economy/

White, L. H., & Luther, W. J. (2018). Cryptocurrencies and the Denationalization of Money. Retrieved from www.aier.org/article/cryptocurrencies-and-the -denationalization-of-money

Yelowitz, A., & Wilson, M. (2015). Characteristics of Bitcoin Users: An Analysis of Google Search Data. *Applied Economics Letters*, *22*(13), 1030–1036.

Yeung, K., & Mullen, A. (2021, June 6). China Digital Currency: When Will the e-Yuan Be Launched, and What Will It Be Used For? *South China Morning Post*. Retrieved from www.scmp.com/economy/china-economy/article/3135886/china -digital-currency-when-will-e-yuan-be-launched-and-what

12. The pure time preference theory of interest

Robert P. Murphy

INTRODUCTION

Capital and interest theory has always featured prominently in the Austrian School.[1] Economists of all schools recognize the tremendous influence of Eugen von Böhm-Bawerk, whose "agio theory" of interest was the forerunner of both the standard approach in the neoclassical mainstream as well as the Austrian approach, namely the pure time preference theory (PTPT) of interest.

This chapter traces the origin of the PTPT, explaining its emphasis on the subjective preference for present versus future goods, as opposed to the neoclassical focus on the "marginal product of capital." This chapter aims to equip up-and-coming researchers in the Austrian tradition, so wherever possible it "translates" verbal Austrian insights into formal modeling, which will be familiar to neoclassical colleagues.

Because the legacy of Böhm-Bawerk is so critical in understanding modern disputes in interest theory, this chapter spends relatively more time on older contributions than the other chapters do in this volume. However, the final sections feature summaries of recent criticisms and extensions of the PTPT, pointing researchers toward the future of a more robust, yet still distinctly Austrian, theory of interest.

BÖHM-BAWERK'S FORMULATION OF THE INTEREST PROBLEM AND HIS CRITIQUE OF THE "NAÏVE PRODUCTIVITY THEORY"

Before assessing the contributions of other writers or offering his own explanation, from the very first sentence of his grand work Böhm-Bawerk sets out exactly what phenomena we are trying to explain when it comes to interest:

> It is generally possible for any one who owns capital to obtain from it a permanent net income, called Interest.

This income is distinguished by certain notable characteristics. It owes its existence to no personal activity of the capitalist, and flows in to him even where he has not moved a finger in its making. Consequently, it seems in a peculiar sense to spring from capital, or, to use a very old metaphor, to be begotten of it. It may be obtained from any capital, no matter what the kind of goods of which the capital consists: from goods that are barren as well as from those that are naturally fruitful; from perishable as well as from durable goods; from goods that can be replaced and from goods that cannot be replaced; from money as well as from commodities. And, finally, it flows in to the capitalist without ever exhausting the capital from which it comes, and therefore without any necessary limit to its continuance. It is, if one may use such an expression about mundane things, capable of an everlasting life.

Thus it is that the phenomenon of interest, as a whole, presents the remarkable picture of a lifeless thing producing an everlasting and inexhaustible supply of goods. And this remarkable phenomenon appears in economic life with such perfect regularity that the very conception of capital has not infrequently been based on it.

Whence and why does the capitalist, without personally exerting himself, obtain this endless flow of wealth?

These words contain the theoretical problem of interest. When the actual facts of the relation between interest and capital, with all its essential characteristics, are described and fully explained, that problem will be solved. (Böhm-Bawerk, 1959 [1884], pp. 1–2, emphasis added)

With the interest problem so formulated, Böhm-Bawerk then proceeds in his first volume (1959 [1884]) to classify and critique the entire history of explanations offered to date. Of particular relevance in the Austrian tradition is Böhm-Bawerk's treatment of (what he termed) the naïve productivity theory of interest,[2] which he describes and then critiques in this manner:

Here the productive power ascribed to capital is, in the first instance, to be understood as physical productivity only, that is to say, a capacity on the part of capital to furnish assistance which results in the production of more goods or of better goods than could be obtained without its help. But it is assumed as self-evident that the increased product, besides replacing the costs of capital expended, must include a surplus of value. Just how convincing is this interpretation?

I grant without ado that capital actually possesses the physical productivity ascribed to it, that is to say, that more goods can actually be produced with its help than without. I will also grant ... that the greater amount of goods produced with the help of capital has higher value than the smaller amount of goods produced without it. But there is not one single feature in the whole set of circumstances to indicate that this greater amount of goods must be worth more *than the capital consumed in its production*. And that is the feature of the phenomenon of excess value which has to be explained.

To put it in terms of [Wilhelm] Roscher's familiar illustration, I readily admit and understand that with the assistance of a boat and net one catches 30 fish a day, while without this capital one would have caught only 3. I readily admit and understand, furthermore, that the 30 fish are of higher value than the 3 were. But that the 30 fish must be worth more *than the pro rata portion of boat and net which is worn out in catching them* is an assumption which the conditions of the problem do not prepare us for, or even cause to appear tenable, to say nothing of making it obvious. If we did not know from experience that the value of the return to capital is regularly greater than the value of the substance of capital consumed, the naïve productivity theory would not furnish a single reason for regarding such a result as necessary. It might very well be quite otherwise. Why should not capital goods that yield a great return be highly valued on that very account and indeed, so highly that their capital value would be equal to the value of the abundance of goods which they yield? Why, for instance, should not a boat and net which, during the time that they last, help to procure an extra return of 2,700 fish be considered exactly equal in value to those 2,700 fish? But in that event, in spite of the physical productivity, there would be no excess value. (Böhm-Bawerk, 1959 [1884], I, pp. 93–94, emphasis in original)

Although he does not use the terms, what Böhm-Bawerk isolates in his critique of the naïve productivity theory is the distinction between the *rental price* of a capital good (for its services during a unit of time) versus the *return on invested financial capital* accruing to a capitalist who purchases such a good. In principle, we can logically imagine an economy in which capital goods still earn their rental income (according to their marginal productivity) per unit time, even though the owners who invest in these goods do not earn a positive return on their financial capital.

For example, suppose there is a simple economy consisting of a consumption good, namely corn, and a capital good, namely a tractor. Further suppose that a brand-new tractor lasts for five years (after which it is discarded as worthless scrap), and that during each of its working years the tractor boosts a farmer's yield by 1,000 bushels of corn relative to what the farmer would have harvested *without* the tractor.

Even though our stipulated tractor is physically productive, and even if we naturally assume that the farmer subjectively prefers more corn to less, these facts alone do not guarantee that the farmer who invests in a tractor earns a positive return. Specifically, suppose that the initial purchase price of a brand-new tractor is (the money equivalent of) 5,000 bushels of corn. After the first year of operation, the tractor has boosted output by 1,000 bushels, but its market price has fallen to (the money equivalent of) 4,000 bushels. After the second year of operation, the tractor has again contributed 1,000 bushels to output, but this further depreciation has reduced its market value to 3,000 bushels. This process recurs every year, so that by the time the tractor has completely worn out, the farmer has merely recouped his initial 5,000 bushels of corn in additional output from its assistance in his operations. In real terms, our farmer has not increased his wealth over time, merely from investing in the tractor; he invested the money worth 5,000 bushels of corn into the acquisition of a brand-new tractor, and by the time it was discarded he was left holding enough money to buy 5,000 bushels of corn. In our example, having possession of an initial stock of 5,000 bushels of corn in hand does *not* enable the farmer to "put it to work" and generate a potentially endless flow of future corn consumption, which is what happens with capitalists in the real world. Hence, as Böhm-Bawerk demonstrated so long ago, the mere physical productivity of capital goods, along with a positive valuation placed on the extra output that they yield, are *not* sufficient to explain the existence of interest.

BÖHM-BAWERK'S AGIO THEORY OF INTEREST

After providing an exhaustive taxonomy and critique of all previous attempts, in his second volume (1959 [1889]) Böhm-Bawerk proceeds to offer his own positive theory to solve the interest problem. After devoting 200+ pages to an investigation of capital and subjective value theory, Böhm-Bawerk begins his treatment of interest with this bold declaration:

> *Present goods are as a general rule worth more than future goods of equal quality and quantity.* That sentence is the nub and kernel of the theory of interest which I have to present. All threads of the explanation of phenomena of interest lead through it, and it constitutes the focal point...of all the tasks we have to perform in the way of examination into economic theory. Half of the explanation is devoted to demonstrating the truth of that sentence. The other half will then consist in showing how the fact that present goods exceed future goods in value constitutes the source from which, naturally and necessarily, emanate all the variegated forms in which the phenomenon of interest manifests itself. (Böhm-Bawerk, 1959 [1889], p. 259, emphasis in original)

As Böhm-Bawerk's remarks make crystal clear, his fundamental explanation for interest is that present goods have a higher valuation than comparable future goods; this is why he classifies his own explanation as an "agio theory" of interest (where in common parlance "agio" refers to a premium in currency exchanges). We will here reverse the order of tasks, however, and first show how this statement—namely, that present goods are more valuable than future goods—solves the interest problem, and second we will summarize Böhm-Bawerk's arguments for *why* present goods should trade at such a premium against future goods.

Consider again our corn/tractor example from the previous section. Suppose that, for whatever reason, the people in that simple economy subjectively prefer present bushels of corn to (airtight) claims to future bushels of corn. Relying on the new subjective marginal utility approach that had been pioneered by Menger, Böhm-Bawerk would use such a stipulated difference in subjective valuations to explain why present bushels of corn would trade on the market at a premium to future bushels. For example, suppose that 1,000 bushels of corn to be delivered in one year only have a market value *right now* of 952 bushels, reflecting a 5 percent annual discount. Similarly, an airtight

Table 12.1   *Coconut consumption by period (each harvests 100 per period)*

	1	2	3	4	5	6
Alice	80	101	101	101	101	101
Bill	120	99	99	99	99	99
Total	200	200	200	200	200	200

claim to 1,000 bushels of corn to be delivered in two years has a market value *right now* of only 907 bushels of corn, and so on, finally with an airtight claim to 1,000 bushels to be delivered in five years only having a current market value of 784 bushels.[3] Because a tractor represents (technological) "claim tickets" on these five bursts of future deliveries of corn, by arbitrage it must have the same market value as these five claims, which works out to a total of about 4,330 bushels of corn in the present.

Consequently, *because of our assumed 5 percent annual subjective discount* on future corn relative to present corn, we have concluded that the spot price of a brand-new tractor must be about 4,330 bushels. If the farmer invests 4,330 bushels of corn today to buy a new tractor, and then stockpiles each year's extra output of 1,000 bushels made possible by the tractor, after all is said and done the farmer will end up with 5,000 bushels of corn, which is more than he started out with. We have thus seen how a stipulated premium on present versus future goods can explain why our hypothetical farmer earns a positive return on his investment in tractors, while in the previous section we saw that the tractor's physical productivity *by itself* was insufficient to explain the phenomenon.

To see just how robust Böhm-Bawerk's explanation is, we can apply it to a pure endowment economy, where there is no physical production (or even physical saving) at all. For example, suppose Alice and Bill each owns a coconut tree that yields 100 coconuts per period. Further suppose that the coconuts are perishable and must be eaten in the period they are harvested.

Even so, if Alice and Bill have different subjective preferences for the timing of coconut consumption, they might both increase their utility by engaging in intertemporal trades. Suppose in equilibrium there is a 5 percent premium on present versus future coconuts, so that Alice (assuming she is more patient) can trade 20 present coconuts to Bill in exchange for his promise to deliver her 21 coconuts in the next period. If Alice and Bill repeat this exchange every period, the consumption flows look as depicted in Table 12.1.

To reiterate, in this simple endowment economy there is no possibility of physically carrying coconuts into the future; in each period, the two trees shoot out a combined 200 coconuts, which must be eaten in some combination by Alice and Bill.

Even so, the Böhm-Bawerkian framework still applies. In the first period, out of her 100 coconuts of "real income," Alice saves 20 coconuts and lends them to Bill, at a 5 percent real interest rate. In period 2, Bill gives Alice her due 21 coconuts, out of which she consumes the net interest of one coconut, but she then rolls over the loan by lending the principal of 20 coconuts back to Bill. They repeat this trade indefinitely, with Alice enjoying a permanently higher level of consumption that is physically possible because of Bill's permanently lower level of consumption (which he interprets as the interest service on his carried debt). Thus the higher subjective valuation of present versus future coconuts allows Alice to parlay her initial capital stock of 20 saved coconuts into a perpetual flow of one coconut in real interest income per period. The higher valuation of present versus future goods is all that is necessary for this result; Alice's perpetual flow of interest income is certainly not due to the productivity of capital or even of "waiting."

As our simple tractor and coconut examples illustrate, the higher valuation of present goods versus future goods fully explains the interest problem as it was formulated by Böhm-Bawerk. We also note that Böhm-Bawerk offered a *real* theory of interest, explaining the phenomenon in terms of goods rather than sums of money. From a modern perspective, we would say that Böhm-Bawerk's framework ultimately explains the *real* rate of interest (and its associated flow of "real" consumption without impairing the capital stock) rather than the *nominal* interest rate, although Böhm-Bawerk himself did not stress this distinction[4]—presumably because there was no systematic and large purchasing power premium necessary in loan contracts during the classical gold standard.

Böhm-Bawerk's Three Grounds

Finally in this section, we summarize Böhm-Bawerk's three "grounds" or causes of the higher valuation of present versus future goods. In order to facilitate discussion with neoclassically trained economists, we present this summary in the context of an agent with a two-period utility function of the form $U(t)=ln(C_t)+\beta ln(C_{t+1})$, where $0<\beta\leq1$ is the subjective discount on future utility per se, and C_t is the amount of consumption (of coconuts, let us say) in period t.

Before proceeding, let us reiterate that the "nub and kernel" of Böhm-Bawerk's agio theory is that interest flows from the higher valuation of present versus future goods. In the context of our two-period model here, that means a positive (real) rate of interest occurs when a coconut at time t offers a higher marginal utility than the prospect of a future coconut at time $t+1$—when both are judged *from the perspective of the agent at time t*. For example, if the marginal utility of a unit of present coconuts is twice as high as the marginal utility of a unit of coconuts to be delivered at $t+1$, then present coconuts trade two for one against future coconuts, and the real rate of interest is 100 percent. But how to explain *why* the marginal utility of coconuts at time t should be twice as high as the prospect of a unit of coconuts to be delivered at $t+1$? To repeat, Böhm-Bawerk offered three main reasons.

First, there could be differences in the relative provisioning of coconuts across the time periods. In general, the quantities of goods available for consumption increase over time, thus lowering their marginal utility. With our specific function of the natural logarithm—which is a popular choice among mathematical economists because it exhibits diminishing marginal utility along with other convenient properties—the marginal utility of additional consumption in each of the time periods is given by $1/C_t$ and $1/C_{t+1}$. Absent any other considerations (and setting $\beta=1$), if consumption were one coconut in period t and two coconuts in period $t+1$, then the marginal utility of coconuts would be one in period t and one-half in period $t+1$, giving the desired result of one coconut in period t trading on the margin for two coconuts in period $t+1$.

Second, there could be a discount placed on future satisfactions *simply because they are in the future*. (Böhm-Bawerk argued that "lack of willpower" was one reason, though not the only one, that this might occur in an individual.) In terms of our example, we could have a constant level of consumption of one coconut each period, but $\beta=\frac{1}{2}$. Thus from the perspective of the agent at time t, the marginal utility of consumption at t is 1, but the marginal utility of a promised future unit of consumption is only $\frac{1}{2}$, even though the agent will subjectively gain a full utility of 1 at the moment of consumption as the future prospect ripens into a present reality (at time $t+1$). To explain the phenomenon of a 100 percent real rate of interest, we merely need to explain why—at the moment of trading present versus future goods at time t—the agent values a present unit of coconuts twice as much as a prospective future unit.

Third—and controversially—Böhm-Bawerk argued that present goods tend to be more valuable than future goods because of their superior net technical productivity. It just so happens to be the case that if a unit of a factor of production is invested in a suitably chosen, more "roundabout" process, then its physical yield can be increased.

To continue working with our specific example, suppose that a unit of labor can yield one coconut if deployed in a one-period production process, or two coconuts if deployed in a two-period process. In that case, regardless of any other facts about subjective preferences or levels of consumption in the different time periods, it is obvious that our agent would prefer to have a unit of labor available at time t rather than at time $t+1$. This is because the immediately available labor can yield an additional coconut in period t *or* it can yield two additional coconuts in period $t+1$. In contrast, the unit of labor not available until the start of $t+1$ yields zero units of coconuts at time t, *or* it yields one coconut at time *t+1*. Since the agent prefers more consumption in a given period to less, these technical facts about labor's physical productivity are enough to conclude that "present labor" trades at a premium for "future labor." This third category, Böhm-Bawerk argued, is independent of the first two grounds; it's not working through the first two "in disguise," as Irving Fisher claimed.

DEVELOPMENT OF THE PURE TIME PREFERENCE THEORY BY FETTER AND MISES

In the standard Austrian tradition, Böhm-Bawerk is credited with brilliantly paving the way to a correct theory of interest—and in particular, with unmasking the fallacies of the productivity approach—but alas, he inexplicably relapsed into these same errors with his own positive explanation.[5] As the American economist Frank Fetter lamented:

> Interest thus expressing the exchange ratio of present and future services or uses is not and cannot be confined to any class of goods: it exists wherever there is a future service. It is not dependent on the roundaboutness of the process; for it exists where there is no process whatever, if there be merely a postponement of the use for the briefest period. *A good interest theory must develop the fertile suggestion of Böhm-Bawerk that the interest problem is not one of product, but of the exchange of product—a suggestion he has not himself heeded.* It must give a simple and unified explanation of time value wherever it is manifest. It must set in their true relation the theory of rent as the income from the use of goods in any given period, and interest as the agio or discount on goods of whatever sort, when compared throughout successive periods. *For such a theory the critical work of Böhm-Bawerk was an indispensable condition; but, the more his positive theory is studied, the more evident it is that it has missed the goal.* (Fetter, 1977 [1902], p. 188, emphasis added)

In his introduction to a collection of Fetter's essays, Murray Rothbard agrees with Fetter's assessment:

> In his 1902 review of Böhm-Bawerk ... Fetter quite rightly pointed to *the major textual contradiction in Böhm-Bawerk's theory of interest*: Böhm-Bawerk's initial finding that interest stems from time preference for present over future goods is contradicted by his later claim that the greater productivity of roundabout production processes is what accounts for interest. (Rothbard, 1977, p. 7, emphasis added)

On this score, Rothbard is echoing what his mentor, Ludwig von Mises, had earlier written in *Human Action*: "Böhm-Bawerk in the elaboration of his theory did not entirely avoid the productivity approach which he himself had so brilliantly refuted in his critical history of the doctrines of capital and interest" (Mises, 1998 [1949], p. 486).

Rather than the eclectic approach of Böhm-Bawerk—which (allegedly[6]) explained interest in terms of both subjective preferences and objective productivities—Fetter advanced what he called a "capitalization theory" of interest. In Fetter's framework, productive factors—be they land (natural resources), labor, or capital goods—provide a flow of services at different points in time, and therefore generate rental income at those future points. But in order to engage in current transactions involving these future events, an individual must arrive at a present-value capitalization by *discounting* the future rents, according to their remoteness. In Fetter's approach, a capital good's productivity explains the height of its rental price during the period in which it provides those services, whereas the *gap* between the initial purchase price and the expected flow of future rental income is the source of interest. Thinking of it like this, it's clear that interest is fundamentally about the subjective preferences for income sooner rather than later; the "productivity of capital" is completely irrelevant. This is why later Austrian economists would refer to their view as the *pure time preference* theory of interest.

Mises fully embraced Fetter's approach (but renamed it explicitly as the PTPT), but with one major innovation: whereas Fetter had appealed to widespread positive time preference on empirical grounds (perhaps rooted in biological and psychological considerations), Mises recast positive time preference as an apodictic feature of human action per se. In his words:

> [A]cting man does not appraise time periods merely with regard to their dimension. His choices regarding the removal of future uneasiness are directed by the categories *sooner* and *later*. Time for man is not a homogeneous substance of which only length counts. It is not a *more* or a *less* in dimension. It is an irreversible flux the fractions of which appear in different perspective according to whether they are nearer to or remoter from the instant of valuation and decision. Satisfaction of a want in the nearer future is, other things being equal, preferred to that in the farther distant future. Present goods are more valuable than future goods.
>
> Time preference is a categorial requisite of human action. No mode of action can be thought of in which satisfaction within a nearer period of the future is not—other things being equal—preferred to that in a later period. The very act of gratifying a desire implies that gratification at the present instant is preferred to that at a later instant. He who consumes a nonperishable good instead of postponing consumption for an indefinite later moment thereby reveals a higher valuation of present satisfaction as compared with later satisfaction. If he were not to prefer satisfaction in a nearer period of the future to that in a remoter period, he would never consume and so satisfy wants. He would always accumulate, he would never consume and enjoy. He would not consume today, but he would not consume tomorrow either, as the morrow would confront him with the same alternative. (Mises, 1998 [1949], pp. 480-481, emphasis in original)

In the telling of modern Austrians, Böhm-Bawerk showed that interest was fundamentally about *value* and not about capital productivity, but for some reason he failed to carry this insight to its logical conclusion. It took Fetter and Mises to perfect the standard Austrian explanation of interest, namely the PTPT.

Before leaving this section, we make a claim that may surprise both Austrians and neoclassicals alike: when we distill exactly what post-Misesian Austrians mean by a *pure* time preference theory, it turns out that Böhm-Bawerk *and* the typical neoclassical are arguably PTPT adherents! Specifically, the PTPT doesn't deny that the higher productivity of more time-consuming processes might affect the equilibrium rate of interest. Their modest but emphatic point is that those technical facts must work *through* subjective intertemporal preferences; there is not an "interaction" between subjective impatience and objective productivity, the way a standard economist (in the tradition of Irving Fisher) might describe it.

But when we recall Böhm-Bawerk's own approach, we see that this is exactly how he proceeded. Interest was caused by the higher valuation of present versus future goods—the "nub and kernel" of his agio theory—and then *one of the three grounds* for this subjective premium involved productivity. And even in Irving Fisher's framework, the (real) rate of interest, whether positive or negative, corresponds directly with the marginal rate of substitution of present for future goods. To be sure, in the Fisherian framework exogenous subjective preferences interact with exogenous objective productivities to mutually determine the endogenous market premium on present goods, but even so Fisher would readily admit that *that premium* was the direct expression of the (real) rate of interest, in the sense that one was necessary and sufficient for the other.

Although just about everyone in the doctrinal disputes would disagree with the position taken here—namely, that *every* post-Böhm-Bawerkian economist is a PTPT theorist in the sense its adherents mean—we close this section with Mises' praise[7] for Irving Fisher's role in the development of the PTPT: "These observations do not detract at all from the imperishable merits of Böhm-Bawerk's contributions. It was on the foundation laid by him that later economists—foremost among them Knut Wicksell, Frank Albert Fetter and Irving Fisher—were successful in perfecting the time-preference theory" (Mises, 1998 [1949], p. 486).

INTEREST AND THE MARGINAL PRODUCT OF CAPITAL: DANGERS OF THE ONE-GOOD MODEL

Modern economics students trained in formal methods may dismiss Böhm-Bawerk's quaint verbal reasoning as somehow mistaken, because standard workhorse models seem to show quite clearly that in equilibrium, the real rate of interest equals the "marginal product of capital," just as the real wage rate equals the marginal product of labor. For example, when explaining the famous Solow model where K and L represent the levels of capital and labor, while A represents a technology parameter, David Romer writes:

> As described in Chapter 1, the marginal product of capital, $\partial F(K, AL)/\partial K$, is $f'(k)$, where $f(.)$ is the intensive form of the production function. Because markets are competitive, capital earns its marginal product. And because there is no depreciation, the real rate of return on capital equals its earnings per unit time. Thus the real interest rate at time t is $r(t)=f'(k(t))$. (Romer, 1996, p. 41)

In other words, Romer is arguing that when markets are competitive and absent depreciation, the real interest rate is equal to the increment in real output yielded by an increment in the physical capital stock. Although we are not quoting him here, Romer would analogously argue that because labor markets are competitive, the real wage rate is equal to the marginal product of labor, i.e. the derivative of the production function with respect to L.

At first blush, Romer's analysis—which is standard in neoclassical economics—seems to openly embrace the naïve productivity theory that Böhm-Bawerk presumably demolished in the 1880s. Indeed, generations of economists have been raised to believe that interest reflects the marginal product of capital, by which they have in mind, "You produce more output when you input more capital." A minority of older economists might vaguely be aware of an event called the Cambridge Capital Controversy, but authorities like Paul Krugman (2014, 2021) assure younger readers that they can safely ignore it.

What the typical neoclassical economist fails to appreciate is just how *special* the case of a one-good economy is, for it sweeps away all of the thorny problems of capital and interest theory. But once we allow for an economy with *two* goods, then the Böhm-Bawerkian perspective regains its relevance.

Imagine an economy with two goods, namely a consumption good ("coconuts") and a capital good ("machines") that augment labor in the production of consumption goods. At time t, an investor spends p_t units of the consumption good in order to acquire an additional unit of machinery M_t that will boost the amount of consumption good yielded by the production process at time $t+1$. In addition to having this increment in consumption good, the investor will retain the additional machinery at time $t+1$, but its market value (measured in units of the consumption good) may have changed in the interim, whether because of physical depreciation and/or changing market conditions. In this scenario, the real rate of return r_t on the investor's funds is given by the formula:

$$r_t = \left[\left(\Delta Y_{t+1} / \Delta M_t \right) + \left(p_{t+1} - p_t \right) \right] / p_t. \tag{12.1}$$

Equation 12.1 is quite intuitive. For example, suppose in period 1 that a unit of brand-new machinery (useful in harvesting coconuts) sells on the market for 100 coconuts. The investor trades 100 coconuts out of his saved stockpile to acquire the extra machine, which boosts his physical harvest of coconuts in period 2 by 20 coconuts (relative to how many coconuts he would have harvested if he *hadn't* acquired this additional unit of machinery). Thus, in period 1 we would say the "marginal product of capital" is 20 (future) coconuts; this is how much the owner of the new machine could rent it out for a single period use. However, to compute the total financial return to our investor, we also need to know how much the market value of the machine (measured in coconuts) changes in the interim. Suppose that in period 2, a one-period-old machine sells for 85 coconuts. Overall, then, our investor at the end of period 2 is left with 20 additional coconuts in physical output, less the drop in market value of his machine by 15 coconuts (from 100 down to 85), for a net yield of five coconuts. Divided by the original investment of 100 coconuts, the total net real rate of return to our investor is therefore 5 percent over the period; his initial property of 100 coconuts has been transformed one period later into property with a market value of 105 coconuts.

Now the interesting twist: suppose that instead of a distinct capital good ("machine"), we assume a one-good economy, such that capital and consumption goods *are the same physical thing*. In this very special case, the price of a capital good (measured in the consumption good) at any time *t* is necessarily 1, because a unit of a good necessarily trades one for one with a unit of itself. But if we set $p_t=1$ for all *t* and plug this into our above formula, it becomes:

$$r_t = \left[\left(\Delta Y_{t+1} / \Delta M_t\right)+\left(1-1\right)\right]/1,$$

which reduces to

$$r_t = \Delta Y_{t+1} / \Delta M_t. \tag{12.2}$$

In other words, *in a one-good economy*, the real rate of interest is always equal to the marginal physical product of capital, which also equals capital's rental price.[8] Yet this correspondence isn't due to a deep economic relationship, but instead is driven by the obvious fact that a unit of a good must trade one for one with itself. Far from simplifying the analysis to isolate the important issues, when it comes to capital and interest theory the standard one-good model is wildly inappropriate because its unrealistic assumptions drive the answers to the questions we are asking (see appendix in Murphy, 2003, 2007).

PRODUCTIVITY OR VALUE? KIRZNER VERSUS SAMUELSON

In the previous section, we argued that the Austrian tradition in interest theory remains relevant to this day, as modern neoclassical economists take (correct) results from one-good models and erroneously extrapolate those results to more general cases, and thereby falsely conclude that the (real) rate of interest is intimately tied to the marginal product of capital. Israel Kirzner (2011 [1993])[9] highlighted an example of Paul Samuelson (1982)[10] committing this very mistake. In this section we will first reproduce the relevant statements from Samuelson and Kirzner, and then illustrate Kirzner's verbal critique with a numerical counterexample to Samuelson's claim.

Relying on reasoning that is familiar in the Austrian tradition, Joseph Schumpeter argued that in a stationary economy, the rate of interest would have been pushed down to zero, such that a decomposition of the circular flow would show all income accruing to land and labor factors, with none being left for the capitalists as net interest income. (To avoid confusion, we should stress that the typical Austrian would *not* agree with Schumpeter's conclusion, even though he relied on "Austrian" reasoning to reach it.)

In a critical response, Samuelson (1982) posited a hypothetical case of a farmer in possession of 100 units of rice that will ripen—without any input from labor or (scarce) land—into 110 units of rice one year later. This farmer can then perpetually consume 10 units of rice per year, which Samuelson argued surely must be counted as real income when decomposing national output into its respective factors. Now since Schumpeter had discussed the mechanism by which, in a zero-interest world, the future value of a forest is fully imputed back to the value of the saplings, Samuelson knew that a Schumpeterian might argue the same thing regarding his rice counterexample. But Samuelson rejected such a rhetorical move as

> pure deception. Real rice *is* being produced net. Kuznets can measure it. You can eat 10 [units of] rice every year and still not impair your circular flow income ... No hocus-pocus of backward imputation—of forest to sapling, or rice grain to rice grain—evades the naive fact of productive interest. (Samuelson 1982, p. 23, quoted in Kirzner, 2011 [1993], p. 108, emphasis in original)

Kirzner (2011 [1993]) is sympathetic to Samuelson, and in fact may have been *too* kind. Kirzner seems to concede that Samuelson's analysis is correct insofar as it goes, but denies that it provides a challenge to Austrians who have embraced the PTPT and its associated framework for defining the interest problem. Kirzner explains:

> The interest problem [in the Böhm-Bawerkian tradition] asked how it is possible for an individual to invest capital funds in a way that yields a perpetual net income. Why does not the market bid up the price of all the "machines" ... so that no net annual yield remains. This question, it should be noted, did not challenge the physical possibility of a tree of infinite life producing an annual crop of fruit (or a tree of finite life producing an annual crop of fruit large enough to permit the planting, out of fruit output, of a replacement tree when the parent tree dies). The question merely asked why, in the absence of any other theory of interest, the market does not bid up the price of the tree to the point where in fact no net annual financial yield is possible from investing in trees ... Samuelson has proven that ownership of rice permits an indefinite stream of annual rice consumption; he has not disproved the contention that the anticipated perpetual flow of rice consumption is already fully recorded in the market valuation of the initial rice source. Samuelson does not, in fact, appear to wish to deny this contention; he appears merely to conclude that this contention constitutes a meaningless incantation which does not affect the undeniable realities of perpetual annual consumption flows—duly measured by Kuznets, or somebody.
> One hundred units of 1987 rice are expected to ripen into 110 units of 1988 rice. Suppose that the "value" of the 100 units of 1987 rice has indeed risen to anticipate this physical growth. Then in terms of the interest problem (formulated at the outset of this paper) the perpetual annual rice consumption income so made possible *does not present an example of interest.* (Kirzner, 2011 [1993], pp. 110–112, emphasis in original)

Kirzner's response is certainly correct and represents the PTPT position well, but it might give the appearance that Samuelson was right according to a different framework. Yet this is not the case. Even using the neoclassical approach, Samuelson's hypothetical rice example does *not* guarantee a positive interest rate. The fact that Samuelson (as well as Gordon, 1984 in a review in the *Journal of Political Economy*) thinks otherwise, shows how deeply mathematical economists have sunk into the bog of the one-good model.

A Two-Good Counter-Counterexample to Samuelson

Specifically, we stipulate Samuelson's rice crop and add an additional good, namely an initial stockpile of figs that deteriorates at one-twelfth (i.e. approximately 8.3 percent) per year, and cannot be increased with future production. Further suppose that in this two-good economy, we define a household commodity basket as consisting of one unit of rice and one unit of figs. With standard utility functions (even including an exogenous discount on future utils per se),[11] we can calibrate the initial stockpiles of rice and figs such that their market value is equal in the initial period. With these assumptions, in equilibrium it must be the case that a commodity basket today trades one for one with a commodity basket to be delivered with certainty next year. That is to say, even according to a neoclassical economist, the real net rate of interest in this economy is zero. The positive (10 percent) own rate of interest on the rice is exactly counterbalanced by the negative (approximately 8.3 percent) own rate of interest on the figs.

In this equilibrium, the market value of rice falls over time while that of figs rises. To see what's happening, we can pick specific numbers so that the hypothetical economy evolves like this: in year 1, a unit of rice sells for $1 while a unit of figs also sells for $1. (Notice that our household commodity basket thus has a price of $2.) But by year 2, these spot prices have moved; a unit of rice now sells for (a little less than) 91 cents while a unit of figs sells for (a little more than) $1.09. The household commodity basket still has a total price of $2, meaning that money's purchasing power has remained the same, and that we need not worry about real/nominal distinctions in this example. The crucial point is that investors in either of these physical goods will merely tread water: an investor who buys 100 units of rice for $100 in year 1 will see them physically transform into 110 units of rice by year 2. But the market value of 110 units of rice in year 2 is exactly $100, because the spot price (both nominal and real, by construction) of rice has fallen in the interim. Thus our investor in rice has earned a 0 percent real (and nominal) rate of return on his capital funds.

The same is also true for an investor in figs. Putting $100 into figs fetches 100 units in year 1. This stockpile deteriorates to approximately 91.7 figs by year 2, but in the meantime the price of figs has risen such that the market value of this smaller stockpile of figs is exactly $100. Despite the negative own rate of interest, the investor in figs has earned a 0 percent real (and nominal) rate of return on his capital funds.

As this simple two-good *counter*-counterexample demonstrates, Samuelson was simply wrong. A positive own rate of interest on a particular good does *not* establish that investors in such an economy can earn a positive real return on their financial capital. Embedded in our two-good rice/fig world, if Samuelson's hypothetical rice farmer were to continually eat 10 units of rice each year, it's true that he would maintain his physical inventory of 100 units of rice, but the *market value* of his assets would continue to fall over time (at the rate of about 8.3 percent annually). In *financial* terms, he would be consuming his capital.[12] It lies outside the scope of the present chapter to comment on whether Kuznets would look at our hypothetical economy and classify the perpetual flow of "real rice consumption" as net interest income, but if he *would*, then it poses a problem for conventional gross domestic product accounting,[13] not for the Austrian framework.

Before leaving this section, we should relate it to the previous one. Presumably the reason an economics giant like Samuelson made such an elementary mistake[14] was that he is so used to the workhorse one-good model that he forgot which of its features *only* apply to a one-good model. As we showed in the previous section, *in the special case of a one-good economy*, the "marginal product of capital" must be equal to the real rate of interest (in equilibrium); the own rate of interest on a particular good is the same thing as the real rate of interest on consumption in general, *because* there is only one good in the economy. So yes, if we imagine an economy consisting *only* of rice that physically grows at a rate of 10 percent annually, that is enough information to conclude that the real rate of interest must be 10 percent in that world.

Yet in the context of his response to Schumpeter, Samuelson seems to be arguing something much stronger, namely that *even in a multi-good economy*, a farmer in possession of the ever growing rice stockpile would necessarily earn interest income. As our simple counter-counterexample demonstrated, Samuelson's stronger claim is simply incorrect; his hypothetical rice farmer could in fact earn zero interest income, notwithstanding the stipulated physical facts of the situation. The episode underscores the dangers of the one-good model, and why it is particularly ill-suited for teaching lessons in capital and interest theory.

PROBLEMS WITH THE CANONICAL PTPT

Although the canonical PTPT has enjoyed relatively recent defenses (e.g. Garrison, 2002; Manish, 2018), there are problems with the standard exposition of the doctrine. Perhaps most serious is an ambiguity in the definition of "time preference" itself. At some points in the standard PTPT exposition, the term refers to the endogenously determined, *marginal* preference for present units of a good versus future units. Yet at other times, "time preference" refers to an exogenous preference for "the same" satisfaction in the present versus the future, holding "other things" equal. If we translate into neoclassical terminology, "time preference" in the PTPT literature sometimes means the marginal rate of substitution between present and future goods, while at other times it refers to the discount on future utility (often denoted by the letter beta) per se.

Of course, there is nothing wrong with either definition, but the typical PTPT defender is not consistent. For example, Hans-Hermann Hoppe argues that "if a negative event such as a flood is expected, the marginal utility of future goods rises. The time-preference rate will fall and savings will increase" (1999, p. 458). This usage construes time preference as a marginal concept, which *can* be affected by the relative supplies of goods in the present versus future. In principle, one might suppose that the expectation of a sufficiently catastrophic future flood might reduce time preference so much that it becomes negative, meaning an individual would prefer a marginal promise of additional future goods rather than having them in the present. But Hoppe earlier in the article denies that time preference can ever be negative (Hoppe, 1999, p. 456), which suggests that he is using the concept in an "other things equal" fashion.

This leads to another problem with the typical PTPT exposition, in that its insistence on the universality of positive time preference leads its defenders to use a definition of "the same good" in an intertemporal context that is inconsistent with the standard approach in an intratemporal context. To illustrate, we can consider the famous example of ice-in-the-winter versus ice-in-the-summer. Wouldn't an individual in December prefer a promise of a unit of ice to be delivered in six months, rather than an immediately available unit of ice? And if so, doesn't this prove that time preference can sometimes be negative? Below we quote Rothbard's answer to this concern:

> *Time preference* may be called the preference for *present satisfaction* over *future satisfaction* or *present good* over *future good*, provided it is remembered that it is the *same* satisfaction (or "good") that is being compared over the periods of time. Thus, a common type of objection to the assertion of universal time preference is that, in the wintertime, a man will prefer the delivery of ice the next summer (future) to delivery of ice in the present. This, however, confuses the concept "good" with the material properties of a thing, whereas it actually refers to subjective satisfactions. Since ice-in-the-summer provides different (and greater) satisfactions than ice-in-the-winter, they are *not* the same, but *different* goods. In this case, it is different satisfactions that are being compared, despite the fact that the *physical* property of the thing may be the same. (Rothbard, 2009 [1962], pp. 15–16, note 15, emphasis in original)

The problem here is that earlier in his treatise (pp. 22–23) Rothbard explained that multiple units of "the same" good are to be defined as inter-changeable from the point of view of the individual actor. For example, the first unit of water might be devoted to drinking, the second unit to bathing, and the third unit to watering the lawn. They are three units of the same good ("water") because each of the units is interchangeable from the individual's perspective, even though a chemist might point out that "the first" unit of water actually had a slightly higher volume, or a slightly lower acidity, than "the second" unit. These physical differences do not matter for subjective utility theory, however; what matters is that the individual would not distinguish between the physical items, and each would be equally useful in quenching thirst or filling the bathtub.

Notice, however, that the first unit of water *provides different and greater satisfactions* than the second unit. (This fact underscores the law of diminishing marginal utility.) So if we were to adopt Rothbard's defense of the PTPT, we would be forced to conclude that our individual does *not* have three units of "the same good" (namely, water), but sole units of three separate types of goods, namely one unit of water-for-drinking, one unit of water-for-bathing, and one unit of water-for-lawn-maintenance. (See Murphy, 2003, pp. 141–149 for a fuller discussion on how to apply standard subjective utility theory in an intertemporal context.)

RECENT ATTEMPTS TO REHABILITATE AUSTRIAN INTEREST THEORY

In this final section we will summarize three recent attempts to offer an Austrian theory of interest that improves upon (or entirely replaces) the PTPT.[15]

Murphy (2003) observes that the PTPT is a "real" theory of interest, when ironically the Austrian (and specifically Misesian) perspective characteristically emphasizes the driving force of money, and criticizes the neoclassical economists for analyzing price relations in a hypothetical barter economy. Murphy argues that interest is, first and foremost, an intertemporal exchange of *money*. Just as it would be nonsensical to explain the exchange rate between the yen and dollar by saying "American goods are preferred to Japanese goods," Murphy argues that it is equally at odds with other tenets in Austrian economics to explain the premium on present dollars by issuing blanket statements that "present goods are preferred to future goods." One drawback with Murphy (2003) is that by describing his own framework as a *monetary* (as opposed to a real) theory of interest, he may understandably have led some Austrians to worry that the approach imports fallacies associated with Keynes' theory of interest.

Hülsmann (2002) critiques the PTPT and then offers what he terms a "realist explanation of interest." Specifically, Hülsmann argues that in a means–end framework, although the means derives its (subjective) value from the end, it clearly cannot acquire *the same* value, for otherwise the actor would never exchange the means for the end. This simple yet powerful insight leads Hülsmann to offer a bold new definition: "Originary interest is the fundamental spread between the value of an end and the value of the means that serve to attain this end" (2002, p. 87). Although Hülsmann's logic is unassailable, it is unclear why the spread between the valuation of means and ends should correspond so closely to the passage of time. Furthermore, by grounding originary interest in the nature of action itself, Hülsmann's approach too ignores the special role of money.

Finally, Herbener (2011, pp. 11–58) gives hints of what may be called a *calculation* theory of interest. Herbener's approach retains the essence of the PTPT while restoring the primacy of monetary prices, as any quintessentially Austrian explanation must. Furthermore, Herbener argues that he is merely rekindling the explanation of interest that we find in Menger and Fetter: "Following Menger, pure time preference, for Fetter, is the preference people have for a given satisfaction sooner instead of the same satisfaction later. The rate of interest, reflecting pure time preference, emerges in the exchange of present money for future money" (Herbener, 2011, p. 38). Later in his essay Herbener quotes from Fetter directly:

> But two or more quite different things may be expressed in terms of another thing and so be made comparable. *Money becomes the value-unit through which different things may be reduced to the same terms for comparison.* With this mode of expressing the value-equivalence of various goods, the interest contract first becomes possible, money (the standard of deferred payments) being the thing exchanged (possibly only in name) at two periods of time. (Fetter quoted in Herbener, 2011, p. 47, emphasis added)

The italicized sentence in particular shows the sense in which Herbener offers a *calculation* theory of interest, in which the attributes of economic calculation—which Mises stressed in his debate with the market socialists—are applied across time and manifest themselves in the market rate of interest. If Austrians want to claim these virtues for the "time market," they cannot ignore the role of money, which the canonical PTPT does.

At the present time, Herbener's suggested calculation theory of interest seems the most promising as a refinement of the traditional PTPT. It retains the essential element of time valuation in the explanation of interest, but it includes the importance of money prices at the ground floor. As an added benefit, Herbener argues that this theory merely rehabilitates the approach of Menger and Fetter, and thus (we argue) it qualifies as an "Austrian" theory in both content and pedigree. The only major drawback is that the development of a calculation theory of interest is quite nascent in Herbener (2011) itself, with the bulk of his views remaining unpublished as of this writing.

NOTES

1. The author would like to thank Per Bylund, Jeff Herbener, Pavel Potužák, Matt Machaj, David Gordon, and William Denyer for their comments and discussion on these issues.
2. Strictly speaking, in the text we are quoting Böhm-Bawerk's critique of what he called the "second variant" of naïve productivity theories; see Murphy (2003, pp. 7–15) for a fuller discussion.
3. Note that the 1,000 bushels of corn to be delivered in five years has a current value of $(1000/(1.05)^5)=784$ bushels (with rounding).
4. See Potužák (2016, pp. 160–166) for further discussion on real versus nominal interest rates in the Böhm-Bawerkian framework.
5. The historical sketch presented here is necessarily constrained by space. For comprehensive summaries of the history and application of the PTPT see Herbener (2011, pp. 11–58) and Kirzner (2011 [1993]).
6. It lies outside the scope of the present chapter, but its author strongly denies that Böhm-Bawerk is guilty of contradiction (Murphy, 2003, chapter 1). For

one thing, Böhm-Bawerk criticized the *naïve* productivity theory; that adjective wasn't rhetorical, the way a critic might castigate the "silly Marxist theory of interest."

7. See also Hayek (1945, p. 22) who argues that "I. Fisher, F. A. Fetter, and particularly L. v. Mises" emphasized time preference in interest theory rather than the productivity of capital.

8. In his (excellent) book-length treatment of capital and interest in a neoclassical framework, Hirshleifer (1970) too notes that the traditional proposition falls apart when we move away from simplistic "Crusonia plant" models, explaining that "it is no longer true, when H is a distinct capital good, that the marginal future-product of (real) capital ... equals the rate of interest" (p. 183). Even so, throughout his chapter Hirschleifer repeats the claim that interest equals the marginal product of capital, though being careful to explain (at one spot, on p. 171, in a footnote!) the caveats involved.

9. We are citing Kirzner's essay on the pure time preference theory (2011 [1993]), because its original publication was apparently the Herbener (1993) collection (also cited in the references). However, in Kirzner's essay he refers to Paul Samuelson "quite recently" responding to a claim from Schumpeter, when Samuelson's essay appeared in 1982 (though Kirzner cites it as 1981). Moreover, Kirzner elaborates upon Samuelson's argument by positing 100 units of 1987 rice transforming into 110 units of 1988 rice. This leads the present writer to surmise that Kirzner may have originally written his essay (or at least portions of it) in 1987, not 1993.

10. We are dating Samuelson's remarks on Schumpeter to 1982, which is the publication date of the collection of ten papers delivered at a conference on Schumpeter held at the Austrian Academy of Sciences in 1980 (see Gordon, 1984). Also note that in Kirzner's (2011 [1993]) essay, he (apparently erroneously) dates the book collection as being published in 1981.

11. The preferences of the households affect the equilibrium, but by working through the amounts of rice and figs consumed in each period. Other things equal, if the households have a higher degree of exogenous impatience (i.e. discount on future utility per se), then consumption is concentrated more heavily in early periods, in order to make the *marginal* rate of substitution (of rice or figs) from period 1 to period 2 (etc.) the constant value it needs to be, as determined by the physical facts.

12. This is the precise point on which Kirzner arguably conceded too much to Samuelson. Kirzner referred to the perpetual flow of ten units of annual rice consumption as "income," and merely denied that it was *interest*. But in our example at best it would be *gross* (not net) income; the market value of the rice consumed each year would correspond exactly with the reduction in market value of the (constant) rice stockpile carried into the next period. If *income* is defined as the flow of consumption that is possible without impairing the value of the capital base, then the rice farmer in our two-good rice/fig economy has *no* income generated by his ownership of rice. This is simply another way of stating that the market rate of interest in this world is zero.

13. This is not a rhetorical statement. Modern students of Austrian interest theory would do well to critically assess the techniques used in national income accounting. For example, textbook discussions explain that the money spent by the baker on flour isn't included in gross domestic product so as to avoid "double counting" it with the final sale price of the bread, but the money the baker spends

on a new oven *is* counted as net investment. Yet over a longer timeframe in which the oven fully depreciates, wouldn't it be analogous to the flour? If there are indeed problems with the fixed/circulating capital distinction and other issues in conventional gross domestic product accounting, Austrians have an advantage in spotting them.

14.   To be clear, Samuelson was truly a genius in the field of mathematical economics, and moreover he published more on Böhm-Bawerkian capital and interest theory than most Austrians. As the discussion and list of references in Murphy (2007) make clear, Samuelson was aware of the nuances we are raising in the main text; he understood, for example, that a Schumpeterian could argue that the spot price of future rice would fall, in order to keep the rate of interest zero. Nonetheless, Samuelson did not take the lesson to heart, and insisted that his hypothetical rice farmer would necessarily earn interest income even though we have demonstrated that this is simply not true. As a closing observation we note that the real problem here might be the awkwardness in classifying physical flows of output correctly. After all, in a normal setting with a positive interest rate, if a patch of ground produces ten bushels of wheat per year, that clearly seems to be land rent (income) to the owner, but his accountant would also inform him that he earned the market rate of interest (adjusted for risk) on his financial investment in that very same patch of ground.

15.   The interested researcher should also consult Pellengahr (1996) and Lewin (1997), though they do not propose a new Austrian theory of interest per se, but rather seek to give an exposition of the PTPT free from unnecessary ambiguities or errors.

REFERENCES

Böhm-Bawerk, E. von. (1959 [1884, 1889, 1921]). *Capital and Interest*, 3 vols. South Holland, IL: Libertarian Press.

Fetter, F. A. (1977 [1902]). *Capital, Interest and Rent: Essays in the Theory of Distribution*. Kansas City, MO: Sheed, Andrews and McMeel.

Garrison, R. W. (2002). Capital, Interest, and Professor Kirzner. *Journal Des Economistes et Des Etudes Humaines, 12*(2). https://doi.org/10.2202/1145-6396 .1065

Gordon, S. (1984). Untitled Review of Schumpeterian Economics by Helmut Frisch. *Journal of Political Economy, 92*(1), 168–170.

Hayek, F. A. von. (1945). The Use of Knowledge in Society. *American Economic Review*. https://doi.org/10.2307/1809376

Herbener, J. M. (1993). *The Meaning of Ludwig von Mises: Contributions in Economics, Sociology, Epistemology, and Political Philosophy*. Auburn, AL: Ludwig von Mises Institute.

Herbener, J. M. (Ed.). (2011). *The Pure Time-Preference Theory of Interest*. Auburn, AL: Ludwig von Mises Institute.

Hirschleifer, J. (1970). *Investment, Interest, and Capital*. London: Prentice-Hall International.

Hoppe, H.-H. (1999). Time Preference, Government, and the Process of DeCivilization: From Monarchy to Democracy. In J. V. Denson (Ed.), *The Costs of War*. New Brunswick, NJ: Transaction Publishers.

Hülsmann, J. G. (2002). A Theory of Interest. *Quarterly Journal of Austrian Economics*, *5*(4), 77–110.

Kirzner, I. (2011 [1993]). The Pure Time Preference Theory of Interest: An Attempt at Clarification. In J. M. Herbener (Ed.), *The Pure Time-Preference Theory of Interest* (pp. 99–126). Auburn, AL: Ludwig von Mises Institute.

Krugman, P. (2014). On Gattopardo economics. *New York Times Blog*. http://krugman.blogs.nytimes.com/2014/04/24/on-gattopardo-economics/

Krugman, P. (2021). Twitter thread on Joan Robinson. Retrieved April 25, 2021, from https://twitter.com/paulkrugman/status/1386337811889065990

Lewin, P. (1997). Rothbard and Mises on Interest: An Exercise in Theoretical Purity. *Journal of the History of Economic Thought*, *19*(1), 141–159.

Manish, G. P. (2018). A Brief Defense of Mises' Conception of Time Preference and His Pure Time Preference Theory of Interest. *Quarterly Journal of Austrian Economics*, *21*(2), 95–109.

Mises, L. von. (1998 [1949]). *Human Action: The Scholar's Edition*. Auburn, AL: Ludwig von Mises Institute.

Murphy, R. P. (2003). *Unanticipated Intertemporal Change in Theories of Interest*. New York: New York University.

Murphy, R. P. (2007). Interest and the Marginal Product of Capital: A Critique of Samuelson. *Journal of the History of Economic Thought*, *29*(4), 453–464.

Pellengahr, I. (1996). *The Austrian Subjectivist Theory of Interest: An Investigation into the History of Thought*. New York: Peter Lang.

Potužák, P. (2016). *Capital and the Monetary Business Cycle Theory: Essays on the Austrian Theory of Capital, Interest, and Business Cycle*. Prague: Prague University of Economics and Business.

Romer, D. (1996). *Advanced Macroeconomics*. New York: McGraw-Hill.

Rothbard, M. N. (1977). Introduction. In *Capital, Interest and Rent: Essays in the Theory of Distribution by Frank A. Fetter*. Kansas City, MO: Sheed, Andrews and McMeel.

Rothbard, M. N. (2009 [1962]). *Anatomy of the State*. Auburn, AL: Ludwig von Mises Institute.

Samuelson, P. A. (1982). Schumpeter as an Economic Theorist. In H. Frisch (Ed.), *Schumpeterian Economics*. New York: Praeger.

13. Capital theory and the theory of the firm

Nicolás Cachanosky and Peter Lewin

INTRODUCTION

In this chapter, we focus on important implications for the theory of the firm derived from applying finance to capital theory. Admittedly, some of the issues we discuss below can be derived or deduced without finance. However, a financial approach to capital theory brings clarity and facilitates supporting a different view of the theory of the firm. Since firms are the economic agents that decide how to allocate resources, the relationship between capital theory and the theory of the firm should be clearly evident. Even though in this contribution we may talk in terms of capital theory in general, it should be clear that our emphasis is on the so-called "Austrian" capital theory, in particular on the contributions of Menger, Böhm-Bawerk, Mises, Hayek, and Lachmann.

We have previously explored the implications of applying finance to capital theory (for a comprehensive discussion, see Lewin & Cachanosky, 2020a). On this occasion, we extend our analysis to the theory of the firm, an area we have only marginally treated so far (Cachanosky, 2017; Lewin, 1982, 2017; Lewin & Cachanosky, 2020b). We do not offer a complete and finished financial take on the theory of the firm. We intend to explore the implications of our work but leave research questions open. In other words, we do not want to make another history of thought narrative. We want to offer a contemporary analysis where current research is still ongoing or needs further work.

We divide this chapter into two main sections. The first one offers a short account of the historical development of capital theory. We emphasize the roadblocks that capital theory has encountered in order to understand its theoretical and historical development. We offer a linear account to simplify the narrative. This form of exposition does not mean capital theory evolved in such a simple linear fashion. The reason for providing a historical discussion of capital theory is to provide historical context and a common-sense understanding of the issues at hand. The section that follows discusses implications for the theory of the firm. In particular, we offer an alternative to the static neoclassical view of the firm, one that is built on everyday financial concepts that provides a more satisfying picture of the what and why of business firms in a dynamic world. We conclude with the hope that what we have started here will be taken up and further developed by others working in the Austrian tradition.

AUSTRIAN CAPITAL THEORY: A BRIEF HISTORICAL ACCOUNT

Roadblock 1: Time and the Period of Production

The first episode in the story of the development of capital theory starts with a simple observation by Carl Menger (1871, p. 152): production takes time. Menger's disciple Eugen von Böhm-Bawerk greatly expanded on this simple undeniable observation. Perhaps the most important addition made by Böhm-Bawerk is the claim that the greater the time taken in production the greater will be the value of the product produced. In modern terms "production time" and production value are positively correlated because the longer time taken must be paid for. In Böhm-Bawerk's terminology, production value is positively related to the degree of "*roundaboutness*."[1] A modern translation of this term might be "complexity." Whatever we call it, trying to "operationalize" this intuitive and important idea has proven to be quite problematic.

Consider the following three questions that arise from acknowledging that production takes time:

1. In which sequence must the producer order inputs for production to occur? This question is the problem of the *structure of production*.
2. What is the value of the time consumed in the production process? Time preference is the subjective valuation of time (or waiting). Therefore, the interest rate is the price of time (rather than the price of money or capital as commonly stated in the economic literature).
3. Given that different production techniques can take the same amount of time, how is economic time (or value time) supposed to be measured?

Question 1 leads to the development of the concept of stages of production. We will deal with this in more detail in the next section. Question 2 will not be a centric topic in this chapter. Consider, however, that in the typical neoclassical theory of the firm, the interest rate is the price of capital. In contrast, in the Austrian literature, the interest rate is the price of time. Question 3 is the main topic of this section.

Going from the easy-to-understand statement that production takes time to how much time is involved in any given production process is far from easy.

Consider two production techniques. The first one requires us to invest \$2 for three periods of time, and the second one needs us to invest \$3 for two periods of time. Which one is longer, the first one or the second? Or do they consume the same amount of (economic) time? Böhm-Bawerk (1890, p. 87) famously offered an example of how to measure time consumed in a production process.[2] As much of a contribution as Böhm-Bawerk's work is, some issues remain questionable and subject to critical debate.[3]

There are two problems with Böhm-Bawerk's approach. The first problem is that, in a surprisingly un-Austrian turn, Böhm-Bawerk uses units of labor (labor hours) to weigh the different periods of time. If we rephrase our example above, Böhm-Bawerk's question becomes: which production technique takes longer, one that uses two units of labor for three periods of time or one that uses three units of labor for two periods of time? An issue with this representation is that labor must be assumed to be homogenous and objectively measurable. Clearly, in reality, labor is heterogeneous, yet, in his treatment, Böhm-Bawerk must assume it is homogeneous. There is no reason why an hour's work by a surgeon should be considered equivalent to an hour's work by an entry-level clerk. One might imagine that this problem could be avoided by adjusting for the different qualities of labor involved. However, doing so would involve losing the objectivity of any labor measure. No longer could we simply count up the number of labor hours; instead we would now have to count some labor hours differently from others according to some (subjectively?) estimated scaling. The second issue is that this approach to measuring production time ignores any influence of factors of production other than labor.[4] To be sure, Böhm-Bawerk realizes this and by offering an example that used only labor and land (original inputs) implicitly suggests that "capital-goods" (produced means of production) must be measured in terms of the labor hours necessary to produce them, reducing all inputs to their labor content. Apart from the fact that this still ignores the role of land (which Böhm-Bawerk pushes aside by suggesting that it is an insignificant complication), it can be seen that this approach, even if its logic could be salvaged, is hopelessly impractical. It is useless as a working tool for gauging the actual production time involved in any real production process, as the explanation in the following paragraph shows.

In his zeal to answer question 3 in a logically defensible way, Böhm-Bawerk actually inadvertently abandoned Menger's essential insight regarding the role of time in production as it influences the decision-maker. This is because Böhm-Bawerk takes a *backward-looking* approach to measuring the period of production. He asks the question of how long *it took* to produce a consumer good (how much (economic) time did it use?). By contrast, a forward-looking (Mengerian) approach would ask the question of how long *it will take* to make a consumer good (how much economic time will it use?). The backward-looking approach may seem the more natural. Once a consumer has a gadget in his hand, the natural question to ask is how long it took the producer to develop and produce this gadget. Yet, the backward-looking approach is problematic for a number of very important reasons.

One basic reason is that the starting point of the production process is undefined. Let us say a producer must use a hammer to forge some iron into a consumer good. Would the period of production depend on whether the producer bought the hammer or produced it himself? What if he contracted the hammer to create the first gadget and then used it again to create a second gadget? The starting point of the production process, and therefore the time consumed by the producer, depends on subjective and arbitrary decisions. The alternative, which is to go back in time all the way to the beginning of history, is trivially impractical. In that case, all production processes take the same time, or the production period is infinity for all final goods. Either way, the period of production is meaningless and useless.

We do not want to be unfair to Böhm-Bawerk. Even if his example of the period of production is problematic, his overall contribution and the intuitions concerning the relationship between time and production are valuable. We suspect that his critics gave too much attention to an illustration of a principle rather than to the principle itself.

Roadblock 2: The Stages of Production

When Hayek moved to the London School of Economics in 1931, he needed to present an accessible version of the Austrian theory of the business cycle. A first general representation of the theory is in Mises's *Theory of Money and Credit* (Mises, 1912). The basic construct of the theory is quite simple. Mises puts together Böhm-Bawerk's insight about the period of production with Wicksell's natural rate of interest. In straightforward terms, if interest rates fall below their natural (equilibrium) value, then the relative price of time decreases, and more time is consumed by producers. The increase in the consumption of time requires a reallocation of factors of production to allow for a lengthier production process. When the central bank reverses its low interest rate policy, then the relative price of time increases and an inverse reallocation of factors of production must occur. This policy reversal produces a bust because the reallocation of heterogeneous labor and capital goods across time is costly.

When Hayek delivers his lectures on *Prices and Production* (1967), he is not trying to move the Austrian business cycle theory into new theoretical territory. Rather he is trying to communicate his Austrian insights to his fellow British economists as easily and convincingly as possible. To achieve this, Hayek uses what later comes to be known as the Hayekian triangle. This simple graph shows how value grows linearly from the beginning of a production process until its final stage before emerging as a valuable consumption good. This straight line starts at zero value and grows with time at the rate (slope) equivalent to the market interest rate. Hayek's pedagogical approach was quite influential; seven decades later it became a crucial component of Garrison's trendy model (2001).

Hayek's triangular treatment has two advantages over Böhm-Bawerk's formulation. The first is that time is measured in value terms; that is, value time is how many dollars are assigned to a production process for how many periods of time. Using our above example, $2 invested for three periods of time is the same as £3 invested for two periods of time. As will be more apparent later, this change from time to value time is fundamental in a financial approach to this problem. The second advantage over Böhm-Bawerk is that Hayek is looking at market values of rather than the physical units of labor.

However, the most well-known addition in the Hayek-Garrison treatment is the presence of stages of production. The use of stages of production is a compelling pedagogical device. It clarifies that if production takes time, then the *order* in which production must take place is crucial. For instance, mining oil must come before refining.

It is clear now that manipulating the interest rate can lead to a misallocation of resources across stages of production (time). However, the use of stages of production is not free of problems itself, particularly when used to guide empirical work intended to assess the validity of the Austrian business cycle theory. The idea of stages of production is a mental construct, not an objective feature of reality. Besides problems such as looping, it is not apparent how exactly to slice the production process into its component stages. For instance, in some industries, the order of two stages of production may be inverted (Cachanosky & Lewin, 2018). Another issue is that Hayek's treatment, at least implicitly, is backward looking as well.

Hayek's theories were initially well received. But later, as the Keynesian approach took over the profession, they came under severe critical scrutiny. In the Keynesian view, time and capital heterogeneity take a back seat, and labor and inflation take center stage. Hayek's triangular treatment assumes that capital is homogeneous. For him, the triangle was a communication device to capture an idea; it was not the message itself. However, critics took the triangle as the message itself similar to what happened to Böhm-Bawerk's, whose critics took his example as *the* message rather than an illustration of the underlying principle. Therefore, a transition away from Hayek towards Keynes was an easy step to take. Hayek returned to the problem of the period of production in his *Pure Theory of Capital* (Hayek, 1941), only to finally give up the project.[5]

From Menger to Böhm-Bawerk to Hayek, the quest to provide a measure of the intuitive fact that production takes time proved to be a labyrinth that inevitably leads to a roadblock.

Roadblock 2: Capital Heterogeneity

With the period of production hitting a roadblock, attention shifted to the issue of capital heterogeneity. The work of Ludwig Lachmann (1947, 1956, 1977) is of particular relevance.[6] Capital heterogeneity stands on another basic intuition. Capital goods are different and can only be combined by producers in limited yet very different ways. Suppose 0 represents perfect homogeneity (all capital goods can be combined in one aggregate) and 100 means absolute heterogeneity (capital goods cannot be substituted for one another in any way). Then each capital good exhibits a different degree of heterogeneity. For instance, a microchip that only specific car manufacturers can use is less homogeneous than a desk, which can be used for several different jobs. Whether capital goods are complements or substitutes does not depend only on their physical qualities, it also depends on what similar valuable functions they perform; physical form in itself is irrelevant. Economic function is the key. Two capital goods that appear different, but perform exactly the same productive function are economically homogeneous.

Horwitz (2011) illustrates the idea of heterogeneous capital as pieces of a jigsaw puzzle that can be combined in different yet limited ways to produce several (but not infinite) shapes. To add clarity, the role of the producer is not to solve how to put the jigsaw pieces together to form a *given* shape but to figure out *what* shape the market demands in the first place. Mincing words, we can refer to the *entrepreneur* as the one who has the economic role of discovering the appropriate shapes of the pieces and how they must be combined, and the producer as the economic agent in charge of putting the pieces together.

If the period of production clashed with its own attempts at measurement, capital heterogeneity clashed with the mathematical turn in economics. The mathematics used in economic theory is not well suited to deal with the type of heterogeneity that exists in real-world economies. It is much simpler and mathematically more elegant to work with homogenous capital than to attempt to account for the complications of heterogeneity. For better or for worse, the mathematical way of doing economics biased the analysis against considering capital heterogeneity. It is also simpler to mathematically represent the role of the producer (solve a problem) than that of the entrepreneur (innovate and discover).[7] To be clear, the issue is not just about mathematical complexity; it is also about logical consistency. Taking capital heterogeneity seriously means that the neoclassical production function is unfeasible (Felipe & Fisher, 2003,

2006; Lewin & Cachanosky, 2020a). Yet, "big K" plays a central role in standard economic theory across all fields.

As intuitive and realistic as capital heterogeneity is, it hit its own roadblock owing to methodological limitations in formal economics. Capital heterogeneity is, of course, accepted in the narrative of formal models, but not in the substance. Various strategies are found for reducing the relevance of heterogeneity in formal modeling. For example, by assuming that a plan-coordination equilibrium exists the decision-maker is able to combine heterogenous capital items in a way that allows them to be aggregated in terms of money values (Lewin & Cachanosky, 2019a). Formal economic theory is an essential homogeneity at its base, and therefore heterogeneity plays a secondary or exceptional role. If capital heterogeneity played a central role, as it does for entrepreneurs in the real world, the use of the "big K" itself would be nonsensical.

Arguably, most of modern Austrian capital theory remained stagnant in these two blocks. The relevance of the period of production and the heterogeneous nature of capital goods are, of course, considered when needed. Yet, the difficulty of moving forward in capital theory led to a lack of interest in the subject. Revitalizing the subject with a renewed appreciation of its relevance tractability requires a fresh approach that started by returning to the fundamental question: What, then, is capital, really?

Going Back to the Beginning: What Is Capital?

It is already problematic that if you ask an economist, a financial analyst, and an accountant what capital is, you will get three different answers. It is even more disconcerting that you can get three different answers if you ask three economists what capital is. The fact that the same term, even the same mathematical symbol K, can have different meanings is far from helpful.

Consider a simple and familiar example. In the neoclassical production function, K represents the aggregation of physical stuff. In the profit statement of the firm, K represents the monetary amount invested in the firm.[8] If you now insert the production function into the profit function, you have the same big K with two different meanings. Yet, we proceed to teach students how to solve for profit maximization by considering changes in labor (L) and K. No explanation or warning about the *economic meaning* of what is being optimized is typically given.

The same K can mean at least three different things. Capital can be (1) the (macroeconomic or firm level) *aggregate of capital goods*, (2) (following Böhm-Bawerk's insights), *embodied time* in a production process, or (3) the *market value of all productive assets* of any type or form (incidentally, this is close to Mises's (1949) approach).

The third approach is the one that is consistent with the way that practitioners in the market traditionally understood the term. (Financial) capital is the monetary amount provided to a firm for its operations. This financial capital can originate in investors (owners) or creditors. The origin does not define the economic nature of the funds, even if it has legal, fiscal, or accounting implications. A hammer used to produce gadgets is a capital *good* regardless of whether it was bought by the owner or borrowed from his neighbor.

There are a few implications of understanding capital in *value* (rather than *physical*) terms. First, the value of productive assets other than material stuff should also be considered capital. Acquiring an intangible such as a reputable brand can be considered acquiring capital. Second, capital is contingent on the historical and institutional context (Mises, 1949). Suppose institutions do not allow for private property over the means of production. In that case, there can be no capital (though there can be productive resources that we usually call capital goods), and the economic calculation of profits and losses would be impossible. Capital as value is a connecting point with the field of institutional economics (Braun, Lewin, & Cachanosky, 2016). The third implication relates to how the value of capital is calculated. Answering this question requires a financial application in capital theory, which is a way out of the roadblocks discussed above.

Escaping the Roadblocks: Capital and Finance

The previous sections offer a summary of both empirical and theoretical roadblocks encountered in the development of capital theory. The situation looks grim. Economics cannot do without a capital theory, yet it is a struggle to find one that is consistent.[9] A financial application to capital theory goes a long way in solving many of the issues behind the roadblocks.

It is easier to start with the problem of the period of production. We mentioned before that this idea had been approached using a backward-looking point of view. Instead of approaching this question as an armchair theoretician, consider what the period of production looks like for a practitioner: an investor out there in the real world. The investor's question is not how long it took to produce the factors of production he needs to deliver the goods he is going to sell. The investor's question, in financial terms, is what is the net present value of this project: the investor is looking at the (net) *present value* of the expected *future* cash flows. The investor is forward looking, not backward looking. This simple change goes a long way. Any cash flow, expected or certain, has a well-defined average period of payment called the Macaulay duration. In addition, in continuous time, the Macaulay duration is equivalent to the modified duration, which measures the sensitivity of present values to changes in the discount rate. Furthermore, duration provides a well-known, tractable, and finite measure of time embedded in a cash flow *even if* its cash flow has an infinite horizon. APP, understood as the Macaulay duration, does not have to be either arbitrary or infinity. There is more: duration analysis shows that the estimated value of investment projects that take more time are more sensitive to changes in the discount rate. This supports the intuition behind Böhm-Bawerk's *roundaboutness* and the distinctive building block in the Austrian business cycle theory.

There is an interesting historical fact that went unnoticed for decades by scholars of capital theory. Hicks (1939, p. 186) offers a way out of the trap of APP being either arbitrary or infinite. Loyal to an economics approach, Hicks calculates the elasticity operator to the cash flow produced by a capital good. More precisely, he estimates the sensitivity of the price of a capital good, which is the present value of its cash flow, to movements in the discount rate. Hicks's approach is mathematically equivalent to the concept of financial duration mentioned in the previous paragraph. In an ironic turn of events, Böhm-Bawerk and Hayek's examples of APP can also be interpreted as simple or special cases of duration. One way or another, financial duration has been present in capital theory since the inception of APP by Böhm-Bawerk.

We can now move to a second implication of applying finance to capital theory. Such application relates to nothing less than the question of *what capital is*. Once again, allowing theory to take the practitioner's point of view, the conventional definition of capital is a value construct rather than a homogeneous aggregation of heterogeneous tools devoid of any market value (Hodgson, 2014). Thinking of capital as the value (as it appears to the decision-maker) of any productive good of any form or shape escapes the problem of aggregating heterogeneous tools. It moves the attention away from physical qualities of tools towards the subjective valuation of any type of productive input. It also clarifies that, because prices are involved, capital is not independent of the institutional framework in place or of specific regulations like price controls (Braun et al., 2017).

A financial framework can be broader than just capital theory. In Lewin and Cachanosky (2020a), we offer some general roadmaps of other paths that finance can lead to. We can now explore in more detail implications in one of these areas: the theory of the firm and entrepreneurship.

IMPLICATIONS FOR THE THEORY OF THE FIRM

What Is Capital to the Firm?

We start with a view of capital extensively developed in our recent work (for a summary see Lewin & Cachanosky, 2019a) and a definition of capital offered by Ludwig von Mises:

> Capital is the sum of the money-equivalent of all assets minus the sum of the money-equivalent of all liabilities as dedicated at a definite date to the conduct of the operations of a definite business unit. It does not matter in what these assets may consist, whether they are pieces of land, buildings, equipment, tools, goods of any kind and order, claims, receivables, cash, or whatever. (Mises, 1949, p. 262, emphasis added; see also Braun, 2017; Braun et al., 2016)

Mises is here seemingly departing from the preoccupation of Austrian capital theorists with the physical structure of production and its relation to time, and embracing a much more mundane everyday conception of capital that would appear to obscure or gloss over such fundamental concerns. At first sight it seems that in this passage Mises endorses an aggregate approach to capital. Our recent work on capital aims to explain that this impression is wrong, that Mises did not depart from the fundamental insights of his fellow Austrians, but, rather, provided a perspective that enhanced the relevance of those insights. As explained above, he did this in a way that had not been appreciated for decades. Seeing capital as finance provides the necessary connection between theory and practice that was until now missing, the absence of which made capital theory appear esoteric and irrelevant.

At one level Mises's definition appears to be about *accounting*; about the balance of assets and liabilities. Taken literally, Mises is talking about the equity in a balance sheet (assets minus liabilities). He seems to be describing a normal balance sheet as of a particular point of time with no reference to the production structure of the business and seems almost to downplay the heterogeneity of productive resources. But, understood in the context of Mises's work as a whole, and his preoccupation with money as a social institution that enables the calculation of profit and loss that guides decision-making (Lewin, 1998), one realizes that he is taking as given the insights of Böhm-Bawerk and Hayek regarding the complexities that characterize capital theory and is going beyond that to a discussion of how an Austrian view of capital informs the operations within an ongoing business concern. Capital is not seen to refer to inputs of a production function. Rather, Mises's capital (as finance) is a key component of the profit and loss calculation. Crucially, he distinguishes capital from capital goods, which *are* inputs in the production process. Rather than looking at just one input, or ignoring the differences between them, we think that a proper reading of Mises's take on capital theory emphasizes these differences (of which more below).

Above all, Mises is clarifying that capital is about *evaluation*. In order to make business decisions the entrepreneur/manager/investor needs to evaluate the attractiveness (profitability) of various alternatives. In a monetary economy this is facilitated using money values, the advantage of which cannot be overemphasized. Only in a (well-functioning, financially stable) monetary economy is it possible to estimate the value of the diverse heterogenous productive resources available to any business venture, and thus to the economy as a whole, in terms of a common metric. To be sure, there is nothing objectively fixed about the values thus estimated. They are based on the judgments of the decision-makers as to what can and will happen in various circumstances. Also, there is no implication that only money estimates are involved in any decision. Non-pecuniary elements (to which the decision-maker may well subjectively assign money values) might be important. But, without the ability to use money as a measuring rod, most modern-day business decisions could simply not be made at all. Money valuation is an essential aspect of the functioning of the capitalistic economy (see Cachanosky, 2017).

Thus, Mises talks about the *money-equivalent* of assets and liabilities. Capital is the value put upon a business concern, or business project, by whomever it is that gets to evaluate in money terms the existing assets and liabilities as of the moment of the decision/evaluation. For Mises, capital is always capital-*value*. Such value would not exist in the absence of the productive resources we colloquially call capital goods, though, as mentioned, Mises distinguishes capital sharply from capital goods, and suggests the latter would better be called productive resources. By implication this includes also labor resources (human capital services). He is effectively conceiving of capital as a subjective (frequently complicated) cost–benefit exercise. And this implies due notice be taken of the importance of time in production. The costs and benefits to be incurred over the time of the decision-making horizon are what (are used mentally to) determine the current values (the money-equivalents) of the assets and liabilities of the business. We are talking about cash flows over time that must be discounted to arrive at current values, a practice which reflects the time preference of the decision-maker(s). The link to the practice of managerial finance and accounting should be obvious.

This view of capital is closely bound up with the role of entrepreneurial decision-making in a disequilibrium world. By contrast, in standard neoclassical economics, the producers maximize profit with given (known) market values and cash flows. Compare this to an Austrian approach. First, while there are known production technologies, the entrepreneur must choose production combinations in the face of unknown future parameters and expectations of what prices he thinks his product will be sold for in the market in the future. With the same information, different entrepreneurs will arrive at different valuations. This is harder to see in a neoclassical profit maximization problem than it is in a typical discounted free cash flow (FCF) framework. Standard economics theory encourages us to think of profit as an objective function to be maximized with a unique solution. Using a financial (FCF) framework encourages us to recognize the subjective components involved. The discount rate is the subjective time preference of the investors and future FCFs depend on subjectively expected prices and quantities. Thinking of capital and the production process in terms of finance moves the focus away from objective maximization towards the subjective evaluation of productive assets. It also puts the economist in a framework closer to how business decisions are actually made in the real world.

Only in such a world does the economic way of thinking conform to the perspectives of the accountant, the financial manager, and the entrepreneur. A static neoclassical framework cannot tell the accountant anything that may help him understand what numbers may be useful to the real-world decision-maker. The very concept of "capital," and the closely related concept of "cost," as understood in that static model, depart crucially from what is relevant to the decision-maker.

(Capital) Value, Cost, and Choice

Consider Mises's definition of capital again. In evaluating the money-equivalent of the assets and liabilities of a business, the decision-maker must estimate the future outlays and inflows of funds over the relevant horizon. These will differ depending on the uses to which productive resources at hand, or yet to be acquired, are put. In other words, part of the process of evaluating the capital of a business consists of deciding the best use of the resources available, which involves comparing, as best one can, *different possible scenarios*.

The *cost* of any such decision, any such choice, is appropriately conceived of as the value of the best alternative use for the resources. This is the familiar "opportunity cost" idea embraced by almost all economists, but adhered to consistently by only very few. The outlays anticipated by the decision-maker attributing an estimated capital value to a chosen project, do not constitute the true economic cost borne in pursuit of that project. Rather, the appropriate economic cost is *the estimated capital value of the best alternative available but, in the event, not chosen*. This is a key distinguishing feature of the Austrian approach that differs from the neoclassical theory of the firm. In the latter we teach that "costs" are the outlays incurred by any chosen project (or the business as a whole). They are the objective *results* of a choice, not the *ongoing choice influencing* considerations of a real business.

The difference between the Austrian and the neoclassical conceptions is most apparent in the absence of system equilibrium. In static equilibrium, with complete shared information regarding all available alternatives, the marginal cost of producing one additional unit of output represents the minimum "cost" at which that unit will be produced because it is the value (money-equivalent) of the next best use of the resources necessary to produce that unit. For that choice the outlay involved corresponds to the opportunity cost. In a disequilibrium world this is no longer generally true. In disequilibrium perceptions of what is possible and what the sacrifices involved in any chosen course of action are will differ across decision-makers. Competition is a discovery procedure in which entrepreneurs are the explorers and profit (absent in static equilibrium) is the reward. At the start of the business its observed capital value is the money put up for its establishment, but, in the mind of the entrepreneur, this value understates its real value given the potential of the business to create value. There is economic value to be added over and above the alternative uses of the resources which is the real measure of profit that motivates the decision-maker. Whereas, as Buchanan (1999 [1969]) explains, the neoclassical approach can be understood as an exercise in empirical hypothesis derivation, the London School of Economics-Austrian approach must be understood as an exercise in explicating the necessary logic of choice that impels individual human action.

Thus, capital and choice belong together in the same way as do cost and choice. Capital as value requires a valuer. And valuing, evaluating, is associated with decision-making. Capital theory has sometimes failed to make this clear. Perhaps it would be better understood if the viewpoint of the would-be investor in any production project were always kept front and center.

Accounting data on cost and earnings do not deliver a complete understanding of the ingredients of the mental processes that inform the decisions that produced that data. In an important sense, accountants look back while economists look forward. Accountants report results (history), economists analyze decisions – using the economic way of thinking about decisions in general as a guide to ongoing decisions or in order to explain past decisions. An economic understanding of the history of a business is not told by the accounting data alone. This has to be augmented by an analysis of the subjective estimates that motivated the decisions taken. A productive, but difficult, research opportunity exists in exploring the interaction between accounting data generation and economic decision-making.

A Brief Formalization (to Contrast with the Typical Neoclassical Version)

Some of the essential points discussed in the foregoing paragraphs can be illustrated as follows. Consider the elements contained in any investment decision. The capital values are the subjective imaginings of the relevant decision-maker (the manager, the entrepreneur). Following Irving Fisher (1906), we consider all productive resources to be capital assets, divided between human capital (labor) and physical capital. The firm can either rent or own physical capital assets and use their services, but can only rent human capital and pay a wage to purchase its services. We designate $i=1, ..., n$ set of heterogeneous outputs (in contrast to the rigidly one-product neoclassical firm) and $j=1, ..., m$ heterogeneous inputs. Second, following Mises (and Menger), we insist that capital must refer to the *value* of the business venture (or production project) as a whole and not to the quantity of any class of physical inputs (see Braun et al., 2016; Lewin & Cachanosky, 2019a). Accordingly, the variable K is to be understood as the capital value of the firm – evaluated by whomever is the relevant decision-maker. Thus we have:

$$\pi = p_i o_i - p_j q_j \tag{13.1}$$

$$K = \sum_{t=1}^{T} f^t \cdot \pi_t . \tag{13.2}$$

In this formulation, K is the present value of the expected FCF.

$$FCF = K = \sum_{t=1}^{T} \frac{FCF}{(1+r)^t} . \tag{13.3}$$

Also, for any K the decision-maker can estimate the average period of production (APP) or the duration (D) of the project's cash flow, the average time for which one has to wait to earn a dollar from the investment. As explained, this is also the elasticity of K with respect to the discount factor ($f^t = (1+r)$). The "longer" any K, the more sensitive it will be to any change in the rate of discount. The relevance of this for monetary policy should be obvious.

$$D = \sum_{t=1}^{T} t \cdot \left(\frac{f^t \cdot \pi_t}{K} \right) = APP . \tag{13.4}$$

Note, the prices in Equation 13.1 are either (expected) market prices or the entrepreneur's estimate of the cost of using owned assets (the payment for their services to the firm, thus including "user cost" or depreciation). They are not equilibrium prices. And yet, *the marginal conditions still apply*, though in a very different way. To be sure, the theoretical constructs refer to financial accounting estimates and are subjective evaluations by the relevant decision-makers, not observable by outside analysts. They are no less real and are descriptive of what happens in the real world. Furthermore, these prices are not generally "costs" in the opportunity cost sense of the word discussed above. Rather they are the necessary outlays required to produce and sell outputs to earn the revenue that will result. They are a consequence of the production plan, the production budget. Later, ex post, they will become part of the account of the production history, the accounting record of what has taken place. As such they will be closer to or further from the values as envisaged by the investor ex ante to the extent to which the investor's appraisals are shared by the accountant.

In choosing a particular project the entrepreneur will compare all investments that she considers to be available alternatives and choose the one with the highest capital value (due account being taken of any non-pecuniary elements involved). If investment A is chosen, then K_A is considered to be the one with the highest estimated capital value. It is the project that maximizes economic profits over time. The (opportunity) cost of the investment is the value of K_B, which is the next highest value alternative. The decision elements involved in estimating K_B are the same as those involved in estimating K_A, though, of course, the estimated values are different. K_A and K_B are two alternative ways of deploying the "same resources" (Thirbly, 1952, pp. 209–214).

Financial Management: Whose Valuations Should Count?

We may conceive of the decision-maker following a *production plan*. When considering an individual or a single-person firm, there is no ambiguity associated with this. But, when, as is usually the case, the firm's activities are the result of decisions made by a (large or small) number of individuals working together, the components of the production plan will depend on who actually has the responsibility for implementing it, or implementing that part of it. Thirbly (1952, arguably a much undervalued article) offers the distinction between policy decisions and operating decisions. The latter take the form of rules designed to have the actors conform as much as possible to the production plan as conceived by the responsible planner. The planner makes the *policy decisions*, decisions which embody his idiosyncratic evaluations. To effectively manage the firm to conform to the policy-maker's vision requires a judicious selection of resource values to be provided to the rule followers.

Thirbly's insights may be seen as quite prophetically anticipating the evolution of the business firm from a hierarchical structure to a more "democratic" one in which, of necessity, because of the rapid complexification and specialization of knowledge within the firm, more of the "workers" need to have policy-making authority. Hayek's knowledge problem (the problem of coordinating the contributions of people with specialized knowledge dispersed throughout the organization – including tacit knowledge and creative knowledge) come to mind (analyzed by Jensen & Meckling, 1992, among many others).

Thus, understanding capital valuation has important implications for general principal–agent situations. Incentives interact with information (interpreted into knowledge) to materialize in decisions that need to be coordinated within the firm. These are details of any production plan that simply cannot be specified and articulated to any great degree and constitute an aspect of the pervasive uncertainty connected to any production plan. Coordinating management must be seen as a significant productive resource whose uncertain value is every bit as crucial as any other input. As events unfold the market serves as the ultimate adjudicator of the estimated capital values. The economics textbook view of capital, cost, and the firm is but a pale reflection of the richer perspective offered here.

CONCLUSION: WHAT SHOULD A GOOD AUSTRIAN ECONOMIST DO ABOUT THE THEORY OF THE FIRM?

For Austrians, the neoclassical theory of the firm presents an interesting challenge (Lewin, 2021). On the one hand, firms are clearly indispensable elements in all market economies. There is a vital symbiotic relationship between the firm and the market. Following Coase (1937), firms can be seen as islands of planning in a market sea, islands in which specified production relationships are fixed by contract (like implicit and explicit employment contracts) that reduce the uncertainty associated with the production plan. The firm serves as the institutional device for facilitating the calculations necessary for production decision-making. And, as such, it depends crucially on being able to refer to market prices. The firm as we know it could not exist in a non-market economy (Lewin, 1998). It is equally true that the market process depends on the existence of firms, the islands of calculation and organized planning competing with one another. Any good theory of the market economy would seem to need a good theory of the market firm. Yet, as we have seen, the firm, as depicted in static neoclassical economics, does not satisfy this need.

There are a few ways in which the theory of the firm and capital theory can move forward. First, extend the financial framework we discuss above and in our work to decision-making in terms of deciding on the period of production and also in deciding how to allocate different capital goods. Second, develop an empirical research program looking at the different implications of looking at capital from a financial lens (see Cachanosky & Lewin, 2016). There seems to be a natural blend with the field of management in this area. A third example would be to frame an Austrian approach to entrepreneurship theory in financial terms (as explained above). This third line of research would have the advantage of offering a more realistic connection of the Austrian theory of the firm.

NOTES

1. To be sure, Menger did indicate briefly that he too saw this implication, but it was Böhm-Bawerk who tried, sometimes unsuccessfully, to make it more concrete.
2. See the discussion and the example in Lewin and Cachanosky (2020a).
3. J. B. Clark offered a critical reaction to Böhm-Bawerk's work. For an account of this episode see Cohen (2008).
4. This is a reason why, by leaving capital out of the equation, one encounters problems like "reswitching." Besides our work cited above, on this issue see Lewin and Cachanosky (2019a), Garrison (2006), Osborne and Davidson (2016), Yeager (1976), and the exchange between Fratini (2019) and Lewin and Cachanosky (2019b).
5. Hayek (1941): "I rather hoped that what I'd done in capital theory would be continued by others … [Completing it myself] would have meant working for a result which I already knew, but I had to prove."
6. For a summary treatment see Lewin (2013) and Powell (2010).
7. Two key references regarding this issue are Kirzner (1973) and Lachmann (1986). For more recent work see Bylund (2015, 2016).
8. Incidentally, the profit of the firm is very similar to the EVA representation of the value of the firm (Cachanosky, 2017; Lewin & Cachanosky, 2020a).
9. This resembles the outcome of the Cambridge-Cambridge controversy. Serious issues in capital theory went unresolved as formal theory continued ignoring the deep implications of said shortcomings.

REFERENCES

Böhm-Bawerk, E. von. (1890). *Capital and Interest*. London: Macmillan and Co.

Braun, E. (2017). The Theory of Capital as a Theory of Capitalism. *Journal of Institutional Economics, 13*(2), 305–325.

Braun, E., Lewin, P., & Cachanosky, N. (2016). Ludwig von Mises's Approach to Capital as a Bridge between Austrian and Institutional Economics. *Journal of Institutional Economics, 12*(4), 847–866.

Buchanan, J. M. (1999 [1969]). *The Collected Works of James M. Buchanan, Volume 6: Cost and Choice*. Carmel, IN: Liberty Fund.

Bylund, P. L. (2015). The Realm of Entrepreneurship in the Market: Capital Theory, Production, and Change. In P. L. Bylund & D. Howden (Eds), *The Next Generation of Austrian Economics: Essays in Honor of Joseph T. Salerno*. Auburn, AL: Mises Institute.

Bylund, P. L. (2016). *The Problem of Production: A New Theory of the Firm*. London: Routledge.

Cachanosky, N. (2017). Austrian Economics, Market Process, and the EVA® Framework. *Journal of Business Valuation and Economic Loss Analysis, 12*(s1). https://doi.org/10.1515/jbvela-2016-0014

Cachanosky, N., & Lewin, P. (2016). An Empirical Application of the EVA® Framework to Business Cycles. *Review of Financial Economics, 30*(September), 60–67.

Cachanosky, N., & Lewin, P. (2018). The Role of Capital Structure in Austrian Business Cycle Theory. *Journal of Private Enterprise, 33*(2), 21–32.

Coase, R. H. (1937). The Nature of the Firm. *Economica, 4*(16), 386–405.

Cohen, A. J. (2008). The Mythology of Capital or of Static Equilibrium? The Böhm-Bawerk/Clark Controversy. *Journal of the History of Economic Thought, 30*(2), 151–171.

Felipe, J., & Fisher, F. M. (2003). Aggregation in Production Functions: What Applied Economists Should Know. *Metroeconomica, 54*(2–3), 208–262.

Felipe, J., & Fisher, F. M. (2006). Aggregate Production Functions, Neoclassical Growth Models and the Aggregation Problem. *Estudios de Economía Aplicada, 24*(1), 127–163.

Fisher, I. (1906). *The Nature of Capital and Income.* New York: Macmillan.

Fratini, S. M. (2019). A Note on Re-Switching, the Average Period of Production and the Austrian Business-Cycle Theory. *Review of Austrian Economics, 32*(4), 363–374.

Garrison, R. W. (2001). *Time and Money. The Macroeconomics of Capital Structure.* London: Routledge.

Garrison, R. W. (2006). Reflections on Reswitching and Roundaboutness. In R. G. Koppl (Ed.), *Money and Markets, Essays in Honor of Leland B. Yeager* (pp. 186–206). New York: Routledge.

Hayek, F. A. von. (1941). *The Pure Theory of Capital.* Chicago, IL: Chicago University Press.

Hayek, F. A. von. (1967). *Prices and Production.* New York: Augustus M. Kelley.

Hicks, J. R. (1939). *Value and Capital.* Oxford: Oxford University Press.

Hodgson, G. M. (2014). What Is Capital? Economists and Sociologists have Changed Its Meaning: Should It Be Changed Back? *Cambridge Journal of Economics, 38*(5), 1063–1086.

Horwitz, S. G. (2011). Contrasting Concepts of Capital: Yet Another Look at the Hayek-Keynes Debate. *Journal of Private Enterprise, 27*(1), 9–27.

Jenson, M. C., & Meckling, W. H. (1992). Specific and General Knowledge and Organizational Structure. In L. Werin & H. Wijkander (Eds), *Contract Economics* (pp. 252–274). Oxford: Blackwell.

Kirzner, I. M. (1973). *Competition and Entrepreneurship.* Chicago, IL: University of Chicago Press.

Lachmann, L. M. (1947). Complementarity and Substitution in the Theory of Capital. *Economica, 14*(54), 108.

Lachmann, L. M. (1956). *Capital and Its Structure.* Kansas City, MO: Sheed Andrews and McMeel.

Lachmann, L. M. (1977). *Capital, Expectations, and the Market Process: Essays on the Theory of the Market Economy.* Kansas City, MO: Sheed Andrews and McMeel.

Lachmann, L. M. (1986). *The Market as an Economic Process.* New York: Basil Blackwell.

Lewin, P. (1982). Pollution Externalities: Social Cost and Strict Liability. *Cato Journal, 2*(1), 205–229.

Lewin, P. (1998). The Firm, Money, and Economic Calculation: Considering the Institutional Nexus of Market Production. *American Journal of Economics and Sociology*, *57*(4), 499–512.

Lewin, P. (2013). Hayek and Lachmann and the Complexity of Capital. In R. W. Garrison (Ed.), *Elgar Companion to Hayekian Economics* (pp. 165–194). Cheltenham, UK and Northampton, MA, USA: Edward Elgar Publishing.

Lewin, P. (2017). Capital Valuation, What Is It and Why Does It Matter? Insights from Austrian Capital Theory. *Journal of Business Valuation and Economic Loss Analysis*, *12*(s1). https://doi.org/10.1515/jbvela-2016-0018

Lewin, P. (2021). How Should an Austrian Economist Teach the Theory of the Firm? Do the Equi-marginal Conditions Still Apply? *Review of Austrian Economics*. https://doi.org/10.1007/s11138-020-00540-7

Lewin, P., & Cachanosky, N. (2019a). *Austrian Capital Theory: A Modern Survey of the Essentials*. Cambridge: Cambridge University Press.

Lewin, P., & Cachanosky, N. (2019b). Re-Switching, the Average Period of Production and the Austrian Business-Cycle Theory: A Comment on Fratini. *Review of Austrian Economics*, *32*(4), 375–382.

Lewin, P., & Cachanosky, N. (2020a). *Capital and Finance: Theory and History*. London: Routledge.

Lewin, P., & Cachanosky, N. (2020b). Entrepreneurship in a Theory of Capital and Finance: Illustrating the use of Subjective Quantification. *Managerial and Decision Economics*, *41*(5), 735–743.

Menger, C. (1871). *Principles of Economics*. New York: New York University Press.

Mises, L. von. (1912). *The Theory of Money and Credit*. New York: Liberty Fund.

Mises, L. von. (1949). *Human Action*. New Haven, CT: Fox & Wilkes and Foundation for Economic Education.

Osborne, M., & Davidson, I. (2016). The Cambridge Capital Controversies: Contributions from the Complex Plane. *Review of Political Economy*, *28*(2), 251–269.

Powell, B. (2010). Some Implications of Capital Heterogeneity. In P. J. Boettke (Ed.), *Handbook on Contemporary Austrian Economics* (pp. 124–135). Cheltenham, UK and Northampton, MA, USA: Edward Elgar Publishing.

Thirbly, G. F. (1952). The Economist's Description of Business Behavior. *Economica*, *19*(74), 148–167.

Yeager, L. B. (1976). Toward Understanding Some Paradoxes in Capital-Theory. *Economic Inquiry*, *14*(3), 313–346.

14. Austrian business cycle theory

Jonathan R. Newman and Arkadiusz Sieroń

INTRODUCTION

Austrian business cycle theory (ABCT) is one of the most important contributions and distinctions of the Austrian school of economics, along with capital theory, the economic calculation critique of socialism, and the praxeological modus operandi. Ludwig von Mises first developed ABCT while discussing the effects of fiduciary media in *The Theory of Money and Credit* (1953 [1912]). Mises relied on theories from Wicksell on interest, the British Currency school on business cycles, and Böhm-Bawerk on capital and production, but offered a wholly new explanation for the business cycle based on fractional reserve bank credit expansion and its effects on the structure of production. The theory was developed, refined, and reformulated by Mises (e.g. 1998, chapter 10, pp. 535–583, 2006 [1928], chapter 2), Hayek (e.g. 2008c [1935]), Rothbard (2000 [1963], 2009 [1962], pp. 989–1023), Garrison (e.g. 2000), Huerta de Soto (e.g. 2006), Salerno (e.g. 1993, 2012),[1] and other Austrian economists over the course of the twentieth and early twenty-first centuries. The housing bubble (2002–2006), financial crisis (2007–2008), and the ensuing Great Recession exhibited markedly "Austrian" features, which "sparked a remarkable renewal of interest in Austrian Business Cycle Theory" (Salerno, 2012, p. 4). This included interest among the general public (see Figure 14.1), students, mainstream economists (e.g. Borio, 2011, 2014), and popular financial news media,[2] but also among Austrian scholars.

We seek to examine the trends that have emerged in academic literature on ABCT since this episode. First, we outline ABCT step by step, with emphasis on particular points of interest in recent literature. Then, we collect and review the current trends in ABCT research, noting gaps and other areas ripe for development. In particular, future research on ABCT should take the following into account:

- the consequences of the shift from the gold standard to a purely fiat standard, including the emergence of new banking practices, and other financial sector developments;

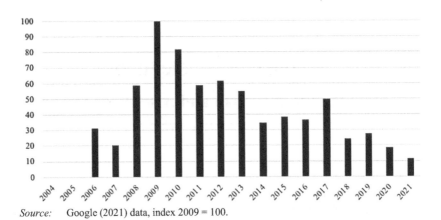

Source: Google (2021) data, index 2009 = 100.

Figure 14.1   Search interest for "Austrian business cycle theory"

- the rational expectations critique;
- the real aspects of the business cycle, including Cantillon effects, the insufficiency of the subsistence fund, and the nature of the malinvestment, overconsumption, and capital consumption during the boom; and
- international spillover and synchronization of the business cycle.

Of course, much work has already been done along these lines. We acknowledge this great work and recognize these areas as having the most potential to further our understanding of ABCT and its relevance to modern economies.

AUSTRIAN BUSINESS CYCLE THEORY: A REVIEW

ABCT refers to the explanation of general economic booms and busts set in motion by artificial credit expansion. The boom period, marked by malinvestment and overconsumption, is followed by an inevitable period of correction. This is contrasted with the theory of sustainable growth, in which real saving frees up resources for entrepreneurs to embark upon more roundabout and productive lines of production.[3] Longer production projects are only feasible if the resources necessary to complete them have been set aside first. This is true for Crusoe, who can only create a new fishing net by first stockpiling enough berries to last him through the stages of fishing net production. But it is also true in an advanced, industrial, and money-using division of labor, in which entrepreneurs respond to changes in the supply of credit (and therefore economy-wide saving) and interest rates to decide which lines of production to pursue. None of the added layers of complexity between these two economies voids the fundamental logic that saving must precede any sustainable lengthening of production. This logic is just more plainly seen in Crusoe's primitive situation, which is why it serves as an excellent pedagogical tool.

Identifying Business Cycles and Their Cause

Rothbard (2000 [1963]) emphasized the *general* character of the boom and bust. Changes that only occur at the firm or industry level are not business cycles. They are mundane business fluctuations that entrepreneurs seek to anticipate by combining scarce factors of production to make goods that consumers value. Profits are realized when the discounted revenues exceed the costs of production. Thus, economic calculation, i.e. comparing costs of production to anticipated revenues, is an essential process for the profit-seeking entrepreneur. Realized profits or losses inform entrepreneurs of the accuracy of their prior forecasts about consumer demand and the length and costs of production. This is the process by which production is economized in the unhampered market economy. The normal workings of the profit and loss mechanism incentivize profitable, economizing production and provide reliable information about consumer valuations and the availability of factors of production. If this is true, then what disrupts this process in a business cycle such that entrepreneurs in general seem to make the same kind of errors at the same time? A good business cycle theory needs to explain what would cause this "general cluster of business errors" (Rothbard, 2000 [1963], p. 8).

We can narrow our search for the cause of business cycles by considering factors that permeate the entire economy (due to the general, economy-wide character of the cycle) and factors that would cause entrepreneurs to make mistakes in their production plans. Money and credit markets are suspect areas for a few reasons:

1. Money is exchanged for goods and services in virtually all transactions, i.e. the prices of all factors of production and consumer goods are denominated in the money unit.
2. Entrepreneurs use the interest rate (revealed in time markets) to discount anticipated cash flows.
3. Entrepreneurs demand present money in credit markets to start or expand production projects.
4. The supply of credit represents forgone present consumption and therefore the present availability of resources for production and preferences for delayed consumption.
5. The production of fiat money and fiduciary media are not regulated by profit and loss.

Considering the first suspect area, money, we realize that changes in the money relation per se cannot explain the cluster of entrepreneurial errors. The malinvestments made by entrepreneurs in the boom involve an intertemporal reshuffling of factors in the stages of production, and the errors are only realized at a later point in time. This means that a mere change in money demand or money supply, for example, could not explain such a rearrangement of production.[4] It is important to note that changes in money supply and money demand are not necessarily related to changes in time preferences and intertemporal resource allocation. The interplay of *present* money supply and *present* money demand results in money's *present* purchasing power. Consumption and investment proportions could stay the same or tip either way with a change in money demand—there is no causal relationship that dictates that an increase in money demand must be associated with either an increase or decrease in time preference.[5] Said another way, "Even with constant proportions of consumption and investment expenditures the demand for money can increase. Actors may simply abstain from consumption and investment in the same proportions in order to increase their real cash balances" (Bagus & Howden, 2011, p. 386, note 6). If, however, new money enters through credit markets, there are real effects for economic calculation, production and consumption decisions, and the integrity of the structure of production. Thus, ABCT points to artificial credit expansion, not monetary disequilibrium, as the cause of an unsustainable boom.

The Unsustainable Boom: Malinvestment and Overconsumption

The boom period features both malinvestment and overconsumption, which describe the misallocations of capital into longer-term projects and the overall capital consumption that occurs due to consumers' overly optimistic view of their own income and wealth. When new credit is created that does not originate with savers' intentions to save and this credit is made available to entrepreneurs, entrepreneurs embark upon new lines of production that only appear to be profitable due to the inflated supply of credit and artificially low interest rates. The increased supply of funds allows entrepreneurs to increase their demands for factors of production and the artificially low interest rate causes entrepreneurs to decrease the discount applied to anticipated future revenues. However, the new funds are not backed by real savings and the artificially low interest rate does not reflect a real change in the social rate of time preference.

Salerno (2012) reemphasized the nature and importance of overconsumption in the boom. In so doing, he quoted Mises (1998) at length:

> It would be a serious blunder to neglect the fact that inflation also generates forces which tend toward capital consumption. One of its consequences is that it falsifies

economic calculation and accounting. It produces the phenomenon of imaginary or apparent profits … If the rise in the prices of stocks and real estate is considered as a gain, the illusion is no less manifest. What makes people believe that inflation results in general prosperity are precisely such illusory gains. They feel lucky and become openhanded in spending and enjoying life. They embellish their homes, they build new mansions and patronize the entertainment business. In spending apparent gains, the fanciful result of false reckoning, they are consuming capital. It does not matter who these spenders are. They may be businessmen or stock jobbers. They may be wage earners. (Mises, 1998, quoted in Salerno, 2012, p. 16)

Therefore, the malinvestment and overconsumption mean the new projects cannot be completed due to the lack of resources needed to complete them— the investments and project selections of entrepreneurs diverged from the preferences and consumption patterns of consumers.

The Inevitable Bust

Eventually, this disconnect is realized and anticipated profits turn into losses. The boom turns to bust when the central bank (perhaps with a dual mandate to keep prices stable and maintain full employment) sees that prices are increasing at an unacceptable rate, and so allows interest rates to increase with contractionary policy (or less expansionary policy).[6] The producers of capital goods face an unexpected decrease in demand for their output because the easy credit that enabled it was finally restricted. Before we review the correction phase of the cycle, it is worth noting that another way that the unsustainable boom could progress is with a "crack-up boom." In this case, the monetary authority doubles down on the inflation with even more inflation, temporarily preventing the necessary corrections from taking place. The destination of this chaotic scenario is hyperinflation, a complete breakdown of the structure of production, and eventual monetary replacement.

The inevitability of the bust is due to the malinvestment and overconsumption that occurs during the boom. The new, longer-term projects involve the production of new specific capital goods, and this includes the complementary employment of labor. The liquidation of these projects involves selling the malinvested capital at a discount and terminating the employment of the laborers. Factor owners must find profitable employment based on real-time preferences and availability of resources, which is one of those "easier said than done" processes. The economy-wide correction involves laid-off workers finding new jobs, capitalists reluctantly accepting low prices to minimize losses, stock prices collapsing as expected firm profitability turns into real-ized losses, and, often, general entrepreneurial malaise "that occurs when the recession reveals their cluster of miscalculations and errors and saps their confidence in their ability to identify and calculate profitable investments"

(Salerno, 2012, p. 6). Governments, with an action bias, incentives to capitalize on a perceived economic emergency, and/or sincerely held but incorrect
economic views, often get in the way of the necessary adjustments with myriad
interventions that usually take the form of propping up the malinvestments
and exacerbating the overconsumption with monetary and fiscal "stimulus."
It is clear, however, that the smoothest recession-adjustment process would
involve the government getting out of the way—halting monetary expansion,
decreasing taxes and spending, and removing regulatory burdens.[7]

Summary

The core elements of ABCT may be summarized briefly:

- An artificial credit expansion creates a mismatch between nominal and real
  funds available for investment.
- The increased supply of funds causes the loan rate of interest to fall below
  the interest rate that would be determined on an unhampered market.
- Entrepreneurs embark upon new lines of production that only appear to be
  profitable due to the inflated supply of credit and artificially low interest
  rates.
- This unsustainable boom period is marked by malinvestment and overconsumption. Malinvestment is when "entrepreneurs rush to invest and to
  widen and lengthen the real productive structure, even though economic
  agents have not decided to augment their saving by the volume necessary to finance the new investments" (Huerta de Soto, 2006, p. 351).
  Overconsumption describes people being misled "into a falsely optimistic
  appraisal of their real income and net worth that stimulates consumption
  and depresses saving" (Salerno, 2012, p. 15).
- A readjustment ("bust") is triggered when a significant restriction of the
  flow of artificial credit, perhaps due to a central bank responding to an
  undesirable increase in prices or when entrepreneurs (or their lenders)
  otherwise realize the unsoundness of current production plans.

NEW INSTITUTIONS AND BANKING PRACTICES

The first step in the preceding outline of ABCT claims that an artificial credit
expansion sets the business cycle in motion. The way this is commonly
explained is that commercial banks in a fractional reserve banking system
(with the support and facilitation of the central bank) are the primary channel
by which credit is expanded artificially. However, this standard line needs
updating due to new banking practices (including the credit creation process

and the emergence of shadow banking), monetary policy tools, and other financial-sector developments.

The Credit Creation Process and New Monetary Policy Tools

According to standard money and banking textbooks and many Austrian economists, commercial banks create loans based on the monetary base created by the central bank and the reserve requirement rate it sets. This approach assumes that a commercial bank must first receive a deposit to generate a loan. From this initial deposit the bank sets aside the reserve and the rest is allocated for loans. Borrowers spend the funds on various goods and services, making payments by card or wire transfer. Hence, the initial sum of money granted as a loan is credited to the seller's account, held most likely at another bank. This bank treats the sum like any other new deposit and extends its own credit. That process "will be continued as long as the amounts are merely transferred from bank to bank and are not taken out in cash," and it will "only stop when the last part of this cash is required for the [minimum] reserve of the deposits" (Hayek, 2008b [1933], pp. 83–87). The total amount of loans that commercial banks can extend is determined by a money multiplier.

However, the standard money multiplier approach has been called into question and debated especially since the Bank of England published "Money Creation in the Modern Economy" (McLeay et al., 2014). The opposing view is that the causation is the other way around: commercial banks extend loans based on expected profitability, these loans become deposits in the banking system, and finally the level of deposits determines the banks' demand for reserves which are supplied by the central bank ("in normal times, supplied on demand") (p. 15). The two sides are ultimately debating whether money is exogenous (the central bank has ultimate control over the money supply) or endogenous (the central bank passively responds to banks' demand for reserves). It is not within the scope of the present chapter to come to a conclusion on this ongoing debate,[8] but we may consider the implications for ABCT if money is purely endogenous.

If the endogenous money view is true, one potential implication for ABCT is that the central bank cannot be blamed (at least not directly) for artificial credit expansion and that monetary policy in general has a more uncertain effect on credit expansion and starting business cycles.[9] However, even in Mises's (2009 [1912]) original exposition of ABCT, he identifies "credit-issuing banks" (p. 357) and their issuance of fiduciary media as the cause of a new discrepancy between the Wicksellian natural rate of interest and loan rates such that production is unsustainably lengthened beyond what the subsistence fund would allow. This mechanism of credit expansion (new issues fiduciary media) operates in both the exogenous and endogenous money scenarios.

Murphy (2019) also shows that Mises and Hayek pointed to fractional reserve banking per se as the primary cause of cycles. While Rothbard (2009 [1962]) claims that inflations "may be effected either by the government or by private individuals and firms in their role as 'banks' or money-warehouses" (p. 990), in his main discussion of business cycles, unsustainable booms begin with commercial banks expanding credit (p. 995). Only later does Rothbard explain how a central bank can willfully expand reserves upon which commercial banks may extend new credit. In *America's Great Depression*, Rothbard (2000 [1963]) also begins his theoretical overview of ABCT with "what happens when banks print new money (whether as bank notes or bank deposits) and lend it to business" (p. 10), not with the actions of a central bank.[10] Therefore, it cannot be said that Austrian economists have built and developed their business cycle theory upon a particular view of the money creation process and that ABCT only applies to environments in which money is exogenous. Whether money is endogenous, exogenous, or both has no bearing on ABCT per se, only in the historical analysis of cycles and how they were started.

The Austrian school should, however, pay more attention to bank capital (Jabłecki, 2010). Although Austrian economists often write about the fractional reserve system, the use of reserve requirements for prudential reasons and monetary control is largely outdated (Gray, 2011). In the modern monetary system, changes in the required reserve ratio may not significantly affect banks' ability to lend if central banks supply base money on demand at prevailing interest rates. Indeed, "central banks typically accommodate the extra demand for reserves fully to maintain interest rate stability. Thus, reserve requirements do not act as a direct constraint on the bank lending" (Disyatat, 2008, p. 16). Instead, minimum *capital* requirements are nowadays the main exogenous constraint on the expansion of credit (Borio & Disyatat, 2010). After the financial crisis of 2007–2008, the capital requirements were tightened, which is another reason why the increase in bank reserves did not translate into a similar rise in the broad money supply.

One can argue that the money-multiplier model is still valid, that other factors, which can be explained within the model, outweighed the increase in the monetary base, curbing its inflationary effect. For example, Selgin (2018) emphasizes the payment of interest on excess reserves (IOER), which increased the reserve-to-deposit ratio. However, focus on IOER as an explanation of weak credit expansion and the low inflation rate misses the point. It assumes that if not incentivized by the Federal Reserve System (Fed) to hold excess reserves, commercial banks would loan these reserves into the real economy. Figure 14.2 supports this by showing that IOER does not determine to a great degree the extent of bank lending—other considerations must be driving commercial banks' decisions to hold excess reserves.

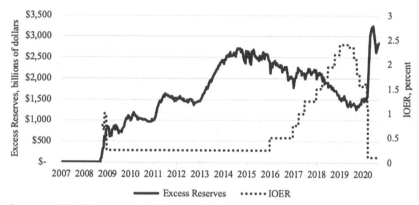

Source: Federal Reserve Bank of St. Louis (2022a).

Figure 14.2   *Excess reserves of depository institutions (left axis, solid line) and IOER (right axis, dotted line) January 2007 to September 2020*

Figure 14.2 shows that the excess reserves of United States depository institutions decreased from around $2.7 trillion in August 2014 to around $1.5 trillion in January 2019, despite the fact that IOER had increased from 0.25 to 2.40 percent, making reserves kept at the Fed even more attractive. Moreover, when IOER decreased sharply from 2.4 percent in mid-2019 to 0.10 percent in early 2020, excess reserves climbed from about $1.5 trillion to over $3.2 trillion. Of course, there are confounding factors that prevent a clear interpretation of the relationship between IOER and bank lending. At the very least, however, IOER is not an overriding concern for banks in their decisions to extend credit or accumulate reserves.

Shadow Banking and Other Financial Sector Developments

Sieroń (2016, p. 309) argues that "the Austrian business cycle theory should be extended to take into account the way in which shadow banking activity changed the conduct of credit expansion." Indeed, securitization, a key activity of shadow banking,[11] changed banks' business model from "originate and hold" to "originate and distribute." This means the "contemporary banking system is largely market-based, in which origination of loans is done mostly to convert them into securities (instead of holding them in banks' balance sheets)" (Sieroń, 2016, p. 313).[12] Indeed, Jordà et al. (2016) find that from 2001 to 2007, the broad excess credit measure, which includes shadow banking loans, rose by five percentage points of gross domestic product per year, significantly above the 1.75 percentage points for just traditional bank loans.

Thus, securitization increases the capacity of the banking system to supply new credit. This is because converting loans into securities and selling them on the market removes the loans' credit risk from the banks' balance sheets (although the credit risk remains within the broad banking sector). Meanwhile, the quality of the securitized loans is often lower as the process can reduce banks' incentives to carefully monitor and screen borrowers.[13] Hence, securitization may increase the vulnerability of the financial system and make the busts more severe.[14]

Shadow banking also weakens the relationship between the monetary base and the supply of credit, as securitization insulates banks' lending activity from the funds obtained from the central bank or retail depositors (Gertchev, 2009). Therefore, shadow banking affects the transmission mechanism of monetary policy while increasing the role of capital markets.

Another important development in the financial sector that also affects the transmission mechanism of monetary policy is that commercial banks are no longer practically the only institutions that can create new money and credit. There are strong arguments that collateral intermediation allows shadow banks to expand credit by themselves (Sieroń, 2016). ABCT should take into account the diminished role of banks' loans in credit expansion in modern finance, as "the process of lending and the uninterrupted flow of credit to the real economy no longer rely only on banks, but on a process that spans a network of banks, broker-dealers, asset managers, and shadow banks funded through wholesale funding and capital markets globally" (Pozsar et al., 2013, p. 10). For example, Shin (2014) argues that since 2010 the importance of the bond market in the international transmission of changes in the money supply has increased at the expense of bank loans.

RATIONAL EXPECTATIONS CRITIQUE

It is often remarked that entrepreneurs are "tricked" into thinking that there are enough resources to complete all the new, more roundabout production projects. While this statement is mostly harmless,[15] it does grant entrepreneurs more of a bird's eye view of the economy than they necessarily have, and it leads to the question of whether business cycles would occur if entrepreneurs would learn from the mistakes of the past and not take the new loans. This question is the essence of the "rational expectations critique" of ABCT.[16] There are quite a few ways to respond to this critique. One is that even entrepreneurs who are well versed in Austrian economics and its business cycle theory, who are skeptical of fiat money and bank credit creation, and who are "on the lookout" for impending financial crises would still find it profitable to participate in the unsustainable boom with the hope of exiting at the top.[17] Secondly, economic calculation is distorted for everyone, which means that even the most cautious investor will make mistakes.[18] Thirdly, the set of people who would need to learn these lessons is continually changing as entrepreneurs enter and exit the market,[19] and credit expansion itself induces marginal individuals to decide to join the entrepreneurial class.[20] Finally, even knowledge of ABCT does not impart detailed information about how a particular cycle will play out. This includes the particular realizations of Cantillon effects, the complex rearrangements of production, how to differentiate between credit backed by real saving versus credit created "out of thin air," the moment-by-moment changes in factor prices and consumption good prices, and the precise timing of the cycle.

Engelhardt (2012) provides a summary of the rational expectations critique and defends ABCT. Carilli and Dempster (2001) responded to the rational expectations critique by positing that the situation for entrepreneurs in the artificial boom is game theoretical in nature, and that the dominant strategy for investors with rational expectations is to invest and participate in the boom due to the opportunity for profits in the short run. Engelhardt (2012) acknowledges that while this response to the rational expectations critique has some merit, it does make some "problematic assumptions" about entrepreneurs' true payoffs, what their options are during the boom, and the length of their time horizons (pp. 179–182). The main point of Engelhardt's paper, however, is to extend the analysis of Evans and Baxendale (2008), who claimed that marginal, low-quality entrepreneurs find it easier to obtain funds and invest when credit is made easy by artificial credit expansion. Engelhardt explains that not only do fools become entrepreneurs, but that the incumbent entrepreneurs who are more likely to be wise to the effects of easy credit will sell off their investments, which further increases the share of resources in fools' hands. Engelhardt (2012) also provides econometric analysis of how housing prices respond to short- and long-term interest rates to showcase the foolishness of entrepreneurs (or the entrepreneurship of fools) during the housing booms of the early 1990s and 2000s. If entrepreneurs had rational expectations, it would not be the case that housing prices are influenced more by short-term, adjustable rates than long-term, fixed rates.

Another way to respond to the question of why business cycles keep occurring in a way that assumes rational expectations on the part of market participants, especially in historical analysis, is to consider the effect of expectations of bailouts, stimulus checks, and other government interventions that would mitigate losses in a downturn. This is essentially the opposite of Mises's proviso: "if, for example, an excess profit tax were imposed at the same time as the credit expansion occurred, then 'entrepreneurs will abstain from expanding their ventures with the aid of the cheap credits offered by the banks because they cannot expect to increase their gains'" (2012, p. 117, quoting Mises, 1998,

p. 552). Instead of an excess profit tax, it seems likely that many financial institutions, entrepreneurs, and households expect (perhaps not with certainty, but at least that there is a non-negligible chance of) bailouts in one manner or another. These may take the form of stimulus checks, last-resort loans, unemployment checks, monetary stimulus to revive stock markets, etc., which have all become predictable features of government responses to economic crises.[21] The expectation of being on the winning end of these transfers (or one of the early receivers of a fresh round of monetary expansion) would encourage riskier behavior (in the form of both malinvestment and overconsumption) even for actors who understand the consequences of artificial credit expansion. These expectations may be considered "rational," too, given the actors' recent observations of their government's actions. Also, as mentioned earlier, those in government have an action bias, incentives to capitalize on a perceived economic emergency, and/or sincerely held but incorrect economic views. Individuals may update these expectations given their perceptions of politicians' and bureaucrats' vanity, greed, and ignorance.

REAL ASPECTS OF BUSINESS CYCLES

One of the more important themes in recent literature on ABCT has been a reemphasis on the real aspects of business cycles. A few notable contributions along these lines are Salerno (2012), Braun and Howden (2017), and Sieroń (2019b). Salerno (2012) discusses the nature and pattern of real overconsumption and malinvestment in the business cycle. Braun and Howden (2017) rediscover the importance of the real resource constraint (subsistence fund) in explaining ABCT. And Sieroń (2019b) shows how ABCT is a special application of the Cantillon effect, which describes the real effects of money entering the economy at a particular point and "rippling out" from there. These contributions are not directly connected, but together they showcase the fruitfulness of recognizing and clarifying the real effects of business cycles.

Salerno (2012) reformulated ABCT while defending it against those who misconstrued it as a hydraulic, sectoral shift theory of overinvestment. Amid the renewed interest in ABCT after the financial crisis of 2007–2008 and ensuing recession, many mainstream economists claimed that "ABCT cannot explain the positive correlation of consumption and investment that occurs over the course of the business cycle. In particular they allege that the theory predicts a slump in investment and capital goods' industries and a corresponding boom in consumer spending and retail sales during the recession" (Salerno, 2012, p. 5).

In the hydraulic, sectoral shift theory, "the cycle is driven exclusively by the relative swelling and contracting of current spending streams directed toward different sectors of the economy" (Salerno, 2012, p. 10). Salerno shows that this is a misconception of ABCT—the Mises-Hayek-Rothbard theory of the business cycle accounts for malinvestment *and* overconsumption (but a decrease in real investment overall due to capital consumption) during the boom phase and curtailments of both consumption and investment during the recession as households and entrepreneurs reestablish the monetary calculations of net worth, factor productivity, and business profitability that had been falsified in the boom. Entrepreneurship, economic calculation, and expectations are critical elements of ABCT, not only because they explain the "stylized facts" of observed cycles, but also because the theory itself explains cycles as distinguished from mundane, reversible (to an extent) business fluctuations. A mere change in the profitability of producing capital goods versus consumer goods due to a lower interest rate may explain a shifting of resources toward higher stages, but this by itself is nothing but a description of a business fluctuation akin to any change in apparent profitability.

Braun and Howden (2017) trace the history of the subsistence fund concept and its attempted use by Mises (2009 [1912]), Strigl (2000 [1934]), and Hayek (2008a [1937]) to explain the necessity of the bust in ABCT. Braun and Howden (2017) conclude that the subsistence fund concept has not been used to explain in a precise way why entrepreneurs' investments in the boom are destined to fail—it has mainly been used as a metaphorical device[22] and attempts to go beyond that have been unsuccessful.[23] There is an opportunity to explain the resource constraint in more detail. Braun and Howden (2017) have diagnosed the problem—future research should aim to solve it.

Sieroń (2019b) discusses the role of Cantillon effects in the economy, pointing out that "the way in which new money is introduced into the economy is of fundamental importance" (p. 112). He claims that the Cantillon effect is the core of ABCT, as it analyzes a particular variant of monetary inflation, i.e. a case in which new money enters the economy unevenly, through the credit channel. This method of injecting money lowers the market interest rate below the level normally established by social time preference and redistributes purchasing power towards the recipients of credit, which sets in motion the boom–bust cycle. Sieroń (2019b) makes two more important points. First, "the existence of the Cantillon effect justifies why business cycles, which obviously have some common traits, do not progress the same way. Their course depends on how the new money 'dissipates' through the economy, which is influenced by institutional conditions and actions of the government, banks, and entrepreneurs" (Sieroń, 2019b, p. 25). Second, there are distinct channels of credit expansion, as commercial banks can grant different types of loans or purchase various assets, and their decisions in this respect affect the course of the business cycle. To be clear, these distinct channels do not affect the basic mechanism of the business cycle, but they are responsible for differences in their so-called secondary effects.

In particular, the process of credit creation has evolved over time, and the presumption that "basically the loans are granted for the production processes" (Huerta de Soto, 2006, p. 348) is not true any longer. It was the case in the time of Mises's and Hayek's early writings, but over the second half of the twentieth century, the share of household mortgages has increased considerably, which later contributed to the 2000s housing bubble. Figure 14.3 clearly shows that although commercial and industrial loans remain important elements of commercial banks' asset structure, their share has declined while the share of real estate loans has risen since the 1970s.

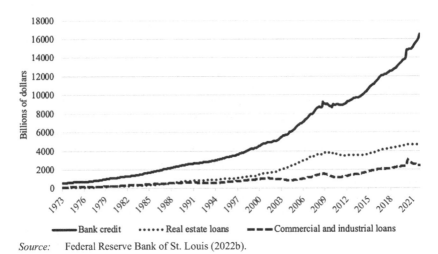

Source: Federal Reserve Bank of St. Louis (2022b).

Figure 14.3   Total credit, real estate loans, and commercial and industrial loans of all commercial banks, 1973–2021

According to Jordà et al. (2016), who analyze 17 advanced economies, "Household borrowing accounts for about 2/3 of the total increase in bank credit since 1960, predominantly driven by real estate lending" (pp. 14–15). Hence, commercial banks now primarily provide mortgages to households. This change in modern banking raises important questions about the relevance of the canonical model of ABCT. For example, does credit expansion that occurs mainly in the form of mortgage loans encourage entrepreneurs to pursue more roundabout production methods (Young, 2012)? And does it lead to the redistribution of income from consumers to entrepreneurs in the form of forced savings, as Hayek (2008c [1935]) argued?

A more recent example of the relevance of Cantillon effects is the economic crisis of 2020. The United States, and world economy in general, recovered from the recession (as officially measured) with much higher inflation than after the Great Recession. One reason for that is that the money created entered the economy primarily through the so-called real sector, as the Fed implemented more programs oriented towards "Main Street," while the fiscal stimulus was bigger and included checks sent to virtually all Americans.

Hence, a more disaggregated study of credit expansion, in the spirit of Cantillon's (1959 [1755]) dynamic analysis, examining how exactly the new money enters and is spent unevenly, should enable us to better understand the subtleties of the business cycle. As Hayek (2008c [1935]) argued, "progress in the field of monetary theory will depend on rejecting the concept of a general price level and turning to study the causes of changes in the structure of relative prices, i.e. the effect of money on different ratios of exchange" (Sieroń, 2019b, p. 25).

INTERNATIONAL SPILLOVERS AND SYNCHRONIZATION

ABCT was originally developed in the context of a closed economy and the classical gold standard (Cachanosky, 2014),[24] though Hayek (2008a [1937]), in *Monetary Nationalism and International Stability*, considered

> the interconnectedness of the economies in various countries under three different monetary regimes: a homogeneous commodity standard; a national reserve system (e.g., the classical gold standard); and independent national currencies (e.g., fiat monies during the decade before the Bretton Woods system). (Block et al., 2019, pp. 347–348)

A promising trend in Austrian literature is to situate ABCT in a modern, open economy international fiat standard: Engelhardt (2004), Hoffmann (2010), Cachanosky (2014), Hoffmann and Schnabl (2013), Dorobăţ (2015), Bilo (2018), and Block et al. (2019).[25] Indeed, Dorobăţ (2015) notes: "Austrian monetary and business cycle theory is best suited for this task [explaining the international transmission of inflation] because the theory is built on an integrated view of the market process, in which monetary changes and real changes are analyzed as an indivisible phenomenon" (p. 148). In what follows, we will review just a few points made in this recent literature with the intention of stimulating future research.

Cachanosky (2014) applies ABCT to open economies with fiat money. In particular, he focuses on the international effects of a credit expansion in a large economy whose money is used as a reserve currency by other countries, much like the United States and the dollar today. One issue for the monetary policy authority is selecting indicators to use to inform policy decisions—in a closed economy with a gold standard, adverse clearing of reserves serves as an indicator of too expansionary a monetary policy, but in an open economy with fiat money, there are a variety of indicators, domestic and foreign, to choose from, and none are as direct as adverse clearing (Cachanosky, 2014, pp. 284–285). The implication for ABCT is that booms could last longer in today's global economy and international fiat standard. A longer boom means more malinvestment and overconsumption before these mistakes are realized and liquidated.

Credit expansion in the modern monetary system leads not only to excessive lengthening of the structure of production, but also to horizontal disturbances—more specifically, distortions in exchange rates and capital allocation between tradable- and nontradable-goods industries (as the credit expansion leads to currency depreciation and increased profitability of exports). Cachanosky (2014) discusses the distortions in capital allocation between tradable and non-tradable goods industries. Depending on the exchange rate regime (e.g. fixed or floating), there are different effects of a large economy's credit expansion on the relative prices of tradable and nontradable goods in both the large and periphery countries.[26] This, combined with the lack of direct monetary policy indicators for the large economy's central bank and the fact that periphery countries may accumulate reserves and export more tradable consumption and production goods means that the unsustainable boom can be prolonged in an international, fiat money context. Therefore, the conclusion of Cowen (1997) that open economies can dilute the effects of credit expansion (i.e. the same credit expansion over a larger geographic area) may be true, but it should be qualified with the potential for booms to be prolonged in an international context. Cachanosky (2014) concludes "which effect dominates is an empirical question" (p. 296).

Dorobăţ (2015) skillfully outlines the international Cantillon effects (with open economies, fiat monies, and integrated time markets) of one country's credit expansion (pp. 149–159). In so doing, she observes a parallel to the well-known ABCT component of intertemporal misallocations of capital: international (i.e. spatial or geographic) misallocations of capital. Capital flows in response to a credit expansion do not correspond to real changes in demand for money between countries or the expectation of profitable, productive investment in a particular country. Dorobăţ (2015) explains:

> First, during periods of monetary expansion, the increase in the capital available for trade finance and foreign investments is not due to the higher savings of the population. By the same token, the movements of capital across borders are not the result of an increase in the foreign demand for money, or a real increase in opportunities for production in foreign countries (so-called pull factors). The outgoing flows of capital from expansionary countries, and the transmission of inflationary booms

among open economies are rather the by-product of artificially low interest rates. (p. 158)

Hence, in today's global economy, a country, especially if it is a small and open economy, can experience inflationary booms, even when it conducts relatively restrictive monetary policy, because of international spillovers, especially if the central banks of the leading economies ignore international factors and thus conduct too expansionary a monetary policy.[27] It also works the other way around. Because of the international spillovers (the newly created money may flee and be invested abroad), credit expansion in a given country does not necessarily lead to a (relatively fast-developing) economic boom and (relatively high) price inflation, contrary to what would follow from the canonical model of the ABCT in a closed economy.

Therefore, capital flows prolong the artificial boom in the exporting country and cause or intensify it in the importing country. Rothbard (2000 [1963]) provides an example to follow in *America's Great Depression*, in which he follows the inflations of the 1920s to foreign lending it generated. One prominent effect of the 1921–1922 inflations was to "stimulate foreign lending" and "increase or sustain foreign demand for American farm exports" (p. 138). When new United States tariffs indirectly harmed agricultural exports, the government's response was not to remove the tariffs but to double down on the inflation that stimulated foreign demand, which lasted from 1924 to 1928 (p. 139). Thus, the Austrian school should not look solely at changes in the credit supply at the national level; it should adopt a more international perspective and pay more attention to international capital flows, which in the current monetary system with freely floating fiat currencies seem to exacerbate the global business cycle.[28]

There are a few directions for future research on international business cycle spillovers, transmission, and synchronization. First, there is not a consensus about the severity of business cycles with open economies. Are they merely diluted, or do some of the transmission mechanisms prolong or exacerbate the cycle? Block et al. (2019) recommend historical analysis of this question, too.

Secondly, Cachanosky (2014) notes that one country "can be in the periphery of two centers at the same time" (p. 289). While Dorobăț (2015) considers a case with three large and three small countries, it would be interesting to consider the effects of "dueling" large countries. Instead of starting the analysis with one country's credit expansion, what of the scenario in which multiple large economies and their central banks pursue similar policies simultaneously?

Thirdly, what is the optimal or likely response of one central bank to another? Is there a game theoretical analysis of this scenario? Cachanosky (2014) and Dorobăț (2015) expect that the monetary authorities of smaller countries will follow the policies of their larger counterparts, most likely due to the small country's desire to peg their currency to the large economy's. Block et al. (2019), however, note that one country can be insulated from the distortionary effects of another's credit expansion by adopting a market-based commodity money regime. This suggests that a similar sort of insulation may be provided by allowing one's currency to appreciate against the inflationary economy's.

Fourthly, Dorobăţ (2015) raises the theoretical possibility of a different kind of malinvestment based on international misallocations of capital, as opposed to the more well-known intertemporal misallocations in the structure of production. What are the implications of this kind of malinvestment, if different from intertemporal misallocations?

Finally, the risk channel is particularly neglected in international ABCT literature. In the contemporary monetary system, credit expansion affects other countries through five channels: trade channel, exchange rate channel, interest rate channel, risk channel, and credit channel (Sieroń, 2019b). In short, credit expansion lowers the interest rates in the country of origin, which triggers capital outflows to other economies because of interest rate arbitrage. The fall in interest rates in the credit-expanding economy may also be accompanied by a search for higher yields through accepting investments in countries considered as riskier.

CONCLUSION

This obviously does not exhaust the current research and potential for ABCT research. We have not discussed: the microeconomics of firms' investment decisions in the context of an economy undergoing a business cycle (Wood, 1984); the debate over fractional reserve free banking; all of the changes to monetary policy since the 2007–2008 financial crisis; the structure of interest rates (Austrians write usually as if there was only one interest rate);[29] the many attempts to validate (or invalidate) ABCT using empirical methods, including models with heterogeneous agents; the debate over the link between interest rates and the structure of production;[30] and the role of the risk premium[31] and factors other than interest rates affecting investment decisions and the demand for loans.

ABCT is intellectually invigorating, and it is a constantly evolving research area. It is a powerful tool for understanding the business cycle, but it could be even more powerful after making some refinements, as it was developed several decades ago within different monetary and financial systems. We addressed a few current trends in ABCT research that appear to be promising for future research as well. These trends are:

- bringing ABCT in line with new banking practices and financial sector developments;
- dealing with the rational expectations critique;
- emphasizing the real aspects of the business cycle, including Cantillon effects, the real resource constraint, and the nature of the malinvestment, overconsumption, and capital consumption during the boom; and
- explaining international spillover and synchronization of the business cycle.

Even though it was originally developed in 1912, ABCT truly represents a vast area of fertile ground in economics today.

NOTES

1. This is where Salerno disentangles the contributions made by Mises and Hayek, including their business cycle theories. In the latter essay, Salerno clarifies Mises's views on fractional reserve free banking, which involved dehomogenizing Mises and Adam Smith as well.
2. Tempelman (2010) recounts some instances of mainstream economists and publications having to reckon with ABCT due to the way it so clearly corresponded to the macroeconomic events of 2002–2008.
3. "We must first understand how things could go right before considering how they might go wrong" (Garrison, 2000, p. 144).
4. Of course, this is stated with the exception of an increase in the money supply that is channeled through credit markets, as in the case of new issues of fiduciary media, which do have a particular effect on the structure of production. There are certainly real consequences to changes in the money relation—as Mises repeatedly emphasized, money is non-neutral. But ABCT includes claims about *particular* real changes (i.e. malinvestment, overconsumption, capital consumption, etc.) that happen as a result of credit expansion via new fiduciary issues, not just that there are real effects in a nonprecisive way.
5. We realize some economists consider money demand and saving to be the same, but this conflates valuations for money and intertemporal valuations. According to Rothbard (2009 [1962]): "If the demand for money increases, there is no reason why a change in the demand for money should affect the interest rate one iota. There is no necessity at all for an increase in the demand for money to raise the interest rate, or a decline to lower it—no more than the opposite. In fact, there is no causal connection between the two; one is determined by the valuations for money, and the other by valuations for time preference" (p. 774).
6. There may be other mechanisms by which interest rates rise, including commercial banks tightening their own standards, or consumers "overriding" the disproportionate spending on higher-order goods with their increase in demand for lower-order goods (Rothbard, 2000 [1963], pp. 11–14). Of course, all of these— central bank tightening, commercial bank tightening, and a reestablishment of

demands for goods in various stages according to real-time preferences—may be coordinated.

7.   According to Rothbard (2000 [1963]), "The most important canon of sound government policy in a depression, then, is to keep itself from interfering in the adjustment process ... There is one thing the government can do positively, however: it can drastically lower its relative role in the economy, slashing its own expenditures and taxes, particularly taxes that interfere with saving and investment" (pp. 21–22). For those interested in historical analysis of this claim, Woods (2009), Grant (2014), and Newman (2016) examine the United States government's generally laissez-faire response to the "forgotten" 1920–1921 depression and compare it to the interventionist response to the famously pro-tracted Great Depression. Biggs and Mayer (2014) compare the late 2000s debt crises in Latvia and Greece and conclude that immediate decreases in credit growth and aggressive deleveraging in Latvia explain its fast recovery, especially compared to Greece's slower deleveraging and resultant prolonged economic contraction.

8.   "There is no simple answer to the question of whether money is endogenous or exogenous. Money can be either endogenous or exogenous, depending on several factors" (Sieroń, 2019a, p. 335).

9.   This would mean that there are other factors influencing credit expansion and thus the money supply, such as the demand for loans, creditworthiness of borrowers, value of collaterals, expected bank profitability, and the risk-taking channel of the monetary transmission mechanism.

10.   Rothbard (2000 [1963], p. 10, note 6) notes that savings and loan institutions and life insurance companies may also expand credit artificially, which opens the door to consider other institutions, like shadow banks, discussed below, that may trigger a business cycle.

11.   According to the most common definition, shadow banking is "credit interme-diation involving entities and activities outside the regular banking system" (Financial Stability Board, 2013, p. 1), while securitization is "a process that, through tranching, repackages cash flows from underlying loans and creates assets that are perceived by market participants as fully safe" (Claessens et al., 2012, p. 7). See Sieroń (2016) for more details about shadow banking.

12.   The decades preceding the Great Recession were characterized by a build-up in debt in most advanced economies that has been coined "the Great Leveraging" (Taylor, 2013) and by a securitized fractional reserve banking system (Becke & Sornette, 2017).

13.   See Dell'Ariccia et al. (2008), who find that during the sub-prime mortgage crisis, "lending standards declined more in areas with higher mortgage securiti-zation rates" (p. 1).

14.   See Jabłecki and Machaj (2009) for a detailed description of the regulated melt-down of 2008 and the role of shadow banking in this process.

15.   However, it may be safe to say that entrepreneurs are "tricked" into thinking that their new projects will be profitable. This does not assume as much about what is going on in entrepreneurs' minds. We doubt that entrepreneurs, once acquiring a new business loan that is backed by real savings, say to themselves, "I am grateful to society for setting aside the resources I need to pursue a longer production process!" In terms of what must be going on inside their minds, entre-preneurs need only compare anticipated revenues to costs and act in a way that would bring about those anticipated profits. Economic calculation and the profit

and loss mechanism ensure their actions tend to be economizing even if they have no specific intention to align their own production decisions with the rest of the economy. Said another way, "It is not from the benevolence [or economic knowledge] of the butcher, the brewer, or the baker, that we expect our dinner, but from their regard to their own interest [and ability to calculate]" (Smith, 2010 [1776]).

16. Engelhardt (2012) notes that Caplan (n.d.), Tullock (1988), Cowen (1997), and Wagner (1999) make this critique.

17. Engelhardt (2012) makes this point: "Consider the case of an individual, rational, Austrian-informed, entrepreneur. Clearly, this entrepreneur would not want to be caught with investments on the eve of the crisis. So, such an entrepreneur will seek to sell the investments they have before the crisis occurs. As long as there are a substantial number of poor-quality entrepreneurs that do not foresee the crisis, a rational, Austrian-informed entrepreneur can reasonably expect to be able to invest in the early stages of the boom and exit the market shortly before the crisis" (p. 181).

18. According to Rothbard (2000 [1963]), "entrepreneurs are trained to estimate changes and avoid error. They can handle irregular fluctuations, and certainly they should be able to cope with the results of an inflow of gold, results which are roughly predictable. They could not forecast the results of a credit expansion, because the credit expansion tampered with all their moorings, distorted interest rates and calculations of capital" (p. 35). Hülsmann (1998) questions this claim and considers the possibility that entrepreneurs anticipate the effects of inflation and a business cycle would be avoided. He suggests that the errors made in the boom period of a cycle are more appropriately attributable to the errors and illusions inherent in government and its interventions, including the imposition of a fractional reserve banking system and fiat money. For those interested, Macovei (2015) analyzes Hülsmann's (1998) critique and concludes that malinvestments are unavoidable after an artificial credit expansion.

19. Likewise, credit booms are not repeated games (in the game theoretical sense), so both the players and the games are not the same each time.

20. "[D]uring the boom either entrepreneurs become foolish—or, as suggested by Evans and Baxendale (2008), fools become entrepreneurs" (Engelhardt, 2012).

21. Note that this argument does not rely on these measures having their intended result, or even generally beneficial results. It only relies on individuals' expectations that they will get at least some benefit in the post-crisis government transfers.

22. "There is no precise and comprehensive discussion of the resources that are supposed to constrain monetary policy and the consequent economic expansion in ABCT" (Braun & Howden, 2017).

23. One issue, noted by Braun and Howden (2017), involves the time period for which the subsistence fund is supposed to sustain the population. The current availability of consumer goods may not suffice for the planned period of production, but as current production yields new consumer goods, the plans may be completed with the help of consumer goods that are produced in the process. Newman (2016) compares and combines two models of the wages (subsistence) fund—a long-run model and a short-run model—to show that neither model on its own can produce all the main outcomes of the wages fund doctrine as described by classical economists.

24. As Hummel (1979, p. 50) puts it: "Rather than being a specific problem, this is an area where Austrian theory needs to be more fully worked out. Austrian economists have for the most part developed their business cycle theory within the context of a closed economy and have rarely applied it to an international setting."

25. Meanwhile, mainstream economists have also noted the synchronization of the business cycles and the international spillovers of monetary policy (Bordo & Helbing, 2011; Canova et al., 2007). Some even argue that inflation is a global phenomenon and that international factors are largely responsible for the observed inflation rates in national economies (Borio & Filardo, 2007; Ciccarelli & Mojon, 2005).

26. In so doing, he comments on the relevance of the rational expectations critique of ABCT: if the entrepreneurs expect the change in relative prices to be temporary, then the increase in demand for each sector would be met by an increase in prices rather than in real resource allocation. Just as a loose monetary policy should not fool the entrepreneur's rational expectations on interest rates, it should not do so in the behavior of the relative prices of nontradable and tradable goods either (Cachanosky, 2014, p. 288).

27. Again, Hayek (2008a [1937], p. 422) was aware of that, writing that "there is no means, short of complete autarchy, of protecting a country against the folly or perversity of the monetary policy of other countries."

28. As Garrison (2000, 121) says: "To understand the bubble economies of the emerging nations, we have to refocus attention on the international aspects of the market process and augment the role of circulation credit to account for modern developments in international finance."

29. The notable exceptions are Cwik (2004), Murphy (2011), and Bagus and Howden (2010).

30. For example, there is an ongoing debate about the link between interest rates and the structure of production. See Fillieule (2007), Howden (2016), Hülsmann (2011), Machaj (2015), and Newman (2016).

31. Young (2012) argues that the ABCT should incorporate the risk structure and the time structure of consumption.

REFERENCES

Bagus, P., & Howden, D. (2010). The Term Structure of Savings, the Yield Curve, and Maturity Mismatching. *Quarterly Journal of Austrian Economics*, *13*(3), 64–85.

Bagus, P., & Howden, D. (2011). Monetary Equilibrium and Price Stickiness: Causes, Consequences and Remedies. *Review of Austrian Economics*, *24*(4), 383–402.

Becke, S. von der, & Sornette, D. (2017). Should Banks Be Banned from Creating Money? An Analysis from the Perspective of Hierarchical Money. *Journal of Economic Issues*, *51*(4), 1019–1032.

Biggs, M., & Mayer, T. (2014). *Latvia and Greece: Less is More. CEPS High-Level Brief*. Brussels. www.ceps.eu/ceps-publications/latvia-and-greece-less-more/

Bilo, S. (2018). The International Business Cycle as Intertemporal Coordination Failure. *Review of Austrian Economics*, *31*(1), 27–49.

Block, W. E., Engelhardt, L., & Herbener, J. M. (2019). Is the Virus of International Macroeconomic Interventionism Infectious? An ABCT analysis. *Quarterly Journal of Austrian Economics*, *21*(4), 339–374.

Bordo, M. D., & Helbing, T. F. (2011). International Business Cycle Synchronization in Historical Perspective. *The Manchester School, 79*(2), 208–238.

Borio, C. (2011). Rediscovering the Macroeconomic Roots of Financial Stability Policy: Journey, Challenges, and a Way Forward. *Annual Review of Financial Economics, 3*(1), 87–117.

Borio, C. (2014). The Financial Cycle and Macroeconomics: What Have We Learnt? *Journal of Banking and Finance, 45*, 182–198.

Borio, C., & Disyatat, P. (2010). Unconventional Monetary Policies: An Appraisal. *The Manchester School, 78*, 53–89.

Borio, C., & Filardo, A. J. (2007). *Globalisation and Inflation: New Cross-Country Evidence on the Global Determinants of Domestic Inflation* (BIS Working Paper No. 227). Basel.

Braun, E., & Howden, D. (2017). The Rise and Fall of the Subsistence Fund as a Resource Constraint in Austrian Business Cycle Theory. *Review of Austrian Economics, 30*(2), 235–249.

Cachanosky, N. (2014). The Mises-Hayek Business Cycle Theory, Fiat Currencies and Open Economies. *Review of Austrian Economics, 27*(3), 281–299.

Canova, F., Ciccarelli, M., & Ortega, E. (2007). Similarities and Convergence in G-7 Cycles. *Journal of Monetary Economics, 54*(3), 850–878.

Cantillon, R. (1959 [1755]). *Essay on the Nature of Trade in General.* London: Frank Cass and Co.

Caplan, B. (n.d.). Why I'm Not an Austrian Economist. https://econfaculty.gmu.edu/bcaplan/whyaust.htm

Carilli, A. M., & Dempster, G. M. (2001). Expectations in Austrian Business Cycle Theory: An Application of the Prisoner's Dilemma. *Review of Austrian Economics, 14*(4), 319–330.

Ciccarelli, M., & Mojon, B. (2005). *Global Inflation* (ECB working paper No. 537).

Claessens, S., Ratnovski, L., & Singh, M. (2012). *Shadow Banking: Economics and Policy.* International Monetary Fund.

Cowen, T. (1997). *Risk and Business Cycles: New and Old Austrian Perspectives.* Routledge.

Cwik, P. F. (2004). *An Investigation of Inverted Yield Curves and Economic Downturns.* Auburn University. www.proquest.com/docview/305218492/fulltextPDF/ECF89C46D4964597PQ/1?accountid=4117

Dell'Ariccia, G., Igan, D., & Laeven, L. (2008). *Credit Booms and Lending Standards: Evidence from the Subprime Mortgage Market* (IMF Working Paper No. WP/08/106, April).

Disyatat, P. (2008). *Monetary Policy Implementation: Misconceptions and Their Consequences* (BIS Working Paper No. 269). Basel. www.bis.org/publ/work269.htm

Dorobăț, C. E. (2015). *Cantillon Effects in International Trade: The Consequences of Fiat Money for Trade, Finance, and the International Distribution of Wealth.* Université d'Angers.

Engelhardt, L. (2004). *Business Cycles in an International Context.* Ludwig von Mises Institute.

Engelhardt, L. (2012). Expansionary Monetary Policy and Decreasing Entrepreneurial Quality. *Quarterly Journal of Austrian Economics, 15*(2), 172–194.

Evans, A. J., & Baxendale, T. (2008). Austrian Business Cycle Theory in Light of Rational Expectations: The Role of Heterogeneity, the Monetary Footprint, and Adverse Selection in Monetary Expansion. *Quarterly Journal of Austrian Economics*, *11*(2), 81–93.

Federal Reserve Bank of St. Louis. (2022a). Excess Reserves of Depository Institutions. www.fred.stlouisfed.org

Federal Reserve Bank of St. Louis. (2022b). Total Credit (Solid Line), Real Estate Loans (Dotted Line), and Commercial and Industrial Loans (Dashed Line) of All Commercial Banks, 1973 to 2021. www.fred.stlouisfed.org

Fillieule, R. (2007). A Formal Model in Hayekian Macroeconomics: The Proportional Goods-in-Process Structure of Production. *Quarterly Journal of Austrian Economics*, *10*(3), 193–208.

Financial Stability Board. (2013). *Global Shadow Banking Monitoring Report 2013*. Basel. www.financialstabilityboard.org/publications/r_131114.pdf

Garrison, R. W. (2000). *Time and Money*. Routledge.

Gertchev, N. (2009). Securitization and Fractional Reserve Banking. In J. G. Hülsmann & S. Kinzella (Eds), *Property, Freedom, and Society: Essays in Honor of Hans-Hermann Hoppe* (pp. 283–300). Ludwig von Mises Institute.

Google. (2021). Austrian Business Cycle Theory. www.google.com/trends

Grant, J. (2014). *The Forgotten Depression: 1921: The Crash That Cured Itself*. Simon and Schuster.

Gray, M. S. (2011). *Central Bank Balances and Reserve Requirements*. IMF Working Paper, WP/11/36.

Hayek, F. A. von. (2008a [1937]). Monetary Nationalism and International Stability. In J. T. Salerno (Ed.), *Prices and Production and Other Works* (pp. 331–422). Ludwig von Mises Institute.

Hayek, F. A. von. (2008b [1933]), Monetary Theory and the Trade Cycle. In J. T. Salerno (Ed.), *Prices and Production and Other Works* (pp. 1–130). Auburn, AL: Ludwig von Mises Institute.

Hayek, F. A. von. (2008c [1935]). Prices and Production. In J. T. Salerno (Ed.), *Prices and Production and Other Works* (pp. 189–329). Ludwig von Mises Institute.

Hoffmann, A. (2010). An Overinvestment Cycle in Central and Eastern Europe? *Metroeconomica*, *61*(4), 711–734.

Hoffmann, A., & Schnabl, G. (2013). Monetary Nationalism and International Economic Instability. *Quarterly Journal of Austrian Economics*, *16*(2), 135–163.

Howden, D. (2016). The Interest Rate and the Length of Production: A Comment. *Quarterly Journal of Austrian Economics*, *19*(4), 345–358.

Huerta de Soto, J. (2006). *Money, Bank Credit and Economic Cycles*. Ludwig von Mises Institute.

Hülsmann, J. G. (1998). Toward a General Theory of Error Cycles. *Quarterly Journal of Austrian Economics*, *1*(4), 1–23.

Hülsmann, J. G. (2011). *The Structure of Production Reconsidered* (No. 2011–09, 34). Angers.

Hummel, J. R. (1979). Problems with Austrian Business Cycle Theory. *Reason Papers*, *5*, 41–53.

Jabłecki, J. (2010). "Show me the Money"—or How the Institutional Aspects of Monetary Policy Implementation Render Money Supply Endogenous. *Bank i Kredyt*, *41*(3), 35–82.

Jabłecki, J., & Machaj, M. (2009). The Regulated Meltdown of 2008. *Critical Review*, *21*(2–3), 301–328.

Jordà, Ò., Schularick, M., & Taylor, A. M. (2016). The Great Mortgaging: Housing Finance, Crises and Business Cycles. *Economic Policy*, *31*(85), 107–152.

Machaj, M. (2015). The Interest Rate and the Length of Production: An Aattempt at Reformulation. *Quarterly Journal of Austrian Economics, 18*(5), 272–293.

Macovei, M. (2015). The Austrian Business Cycle Theory: A Defense of Its General Validity. *Quarterly Journal of Austrian Economics, 18*(4), 409.

McLeay, M., Radia, A., & Thomas, R. (2014). Money Creation in the Modern Economy: Bank of England Quarterly Bulletin (p. Q1). London.

Mises, L. von. (1953 [1912]). *The Theory of Money and Credit*. Yale University Press.

Mises, L. von. (1998). *Human Action: The Scholar's Edition*. Ludwig von Mises Institute.

Mises, L. von. (2006 [1928]). *The Causes of the Economic Crisis: And Other Essays before and after the Great Depression* (P. L. Greaves, Jr., Ed.). Ludwig von Mises Institute.

Mises, L. von. (2009 [1912]). *The Theory of Money and Credit*. Ludwig von Mises Institute.

Murphy, R. P. (2011). Multiple Interest Rates and Austrian Business Cycle Theory. http://consultingbyrpm.com/uploads/Multiple Interest Rates and ABCT.pdf

Murphy, R. P. (2019). More Than Quibbles: Problems with the Theory and History of Fractional Reserve Free Banking. *Quarterly Journal of Austrian Economics, 22*(1), 3–25.

Newman, J. R. (2016). *Three Essays in Labor Economics*. Auburn University. https://etd.auburn.edu/bitstream/handle/10415/5122/jonathan newman three essays labor economics.pdf?sequence=2

Newman, P. (2016). The Depression of 1920–1921: A Credit Induced Boom and a Market Based Recovery? *Review of Austrian Economics, 29*(4), 387–414.

Pozsar, Z., Adrian, T., Ashcraft, A., & Boesky, H. (2013). *Shadow Banking: Federal Reserve Bank of New York Policy Review*. New York. www.newyorkfed.org/research/epr/2013/0713adri.pdf

Rothbard, M. N. (2000 [1963]). *America's Great Depression* (5th Edition). Ludwig von Mises Institute.

Rothbard, M. N. (2009 [1962]). *Man, Economy, and State: A Treatise on Economic Principles with Power and Market Government and the Economy* (2nd Edition). Ludwig von Mises Institute.

Salerno, J. T. (1993). Mises and Hayek Dehomogenized. *Review of Austrian Economics, 6*(2), 113–146.

Salerno, J. T. (2012). A Reformulation of Austrian Business Cycle Theory in Light of the Financial Crisis. *Quarterly Journal of Austrian Economics, 15*(1), 3–44.

Selgin, G. A. (2018). *Floored! How a Misguided Fed Experiment Deepened and Prolonged the Great Recession*. Cato Institute.

Shin, H. S. (2014). The Second Phase of Global Liquidity and Its Impact on Emerging Economies. In K. Chung, S. Kim, H. Park, C. Choi, & H. S. Shin (Eds), *Volatile Capital Flows in Korea* (pp. 247–257). Palgrave Macmillan.

Sieroń, A. (2016). The Role of Shadow Banking in the Business Cycle. *Quarterly Journal of Austrian Economics, 19*(4), 309–329.

Sieroń, A. (2019a). Endogenous Versus Exogenous Money: Does the Debate Really Matter? *Research in Economics, 73*(4), 329–338.

Sieroń, A. (2019b). *Money, Inflation and Business Cycles: The Cantillon Effect and the Economy*. Routledge.

Smith, A. W. (2010 [1776]). *An Inquiry into the Nature and Causes of the Wealth of Nations*. Harriman House.

Strigl, V. R. (2000 [1934]). *Capital and Production*. Ludwig von Mises Institute.

Taylor, A. M. (2013). The Great Leveraging. In *The Social Value of the Financial Sector: Too Big to Fail or Just Too Big?* (pp. 33–65). https://doi.org/10.1142/9789814520294_0004

Tempelman, J. H. (2010). Austrian Business Cycle Theory and the Global Financial Crisis: Confessions of a Mainstream Economist. *Quarterly Journal of Austrian Economics*, *13*(1), 3–15.

Tullock, C. (1988). Why the Austrians Are Wrong about Depressions. *Review of Austrian Economics*, *2*(1), 73–78.

Wagner, R. E. (1999). Austrian Cycle Theory: Saving the Wheat while Discarding the Chaff. *Review of Austrian Economics*, *12*(65–80), 65–80.

Wood, J. S. (1984). Some Refinements in Austrian Trade-Cycle Theory. *Managerial and Decision Economics*, *5*(3), 141–149.

Woods, T. E. (2009). Warren Harding and the Forgotten Depression of 1920. *Intercollegiate Review*, *44*(2), 22–29.

Young, A. (2012). Austrian Business Cycle Theory. In C. J. Coyne & P. Boettke (Eds), *The Oxford Handbook of Austrian Economics* (pp. 185–212). Oxford University Press.

15. Austrian sociology

Richard G. Ellefritz

INTRODUCTION

"Less Marx, more Mises," reads a slogan appearing on several placards at protests in Brazil (McMaken, 2015). Championing such slogans among the more than 200,000 Brazilians who took to the streets to protest socialist policies, Students for Liberty (Laer, 2019) helps citizens and students oppose socialist policymakers and Marxist professors wishing to bring about "real utopias" (Wright, 2010). The presumption of the slogan is that Ludwig von Mises (1881–1973), a founding father of the Austrian school of economics, is relatively unknown in popular culture when compared to Karl Marx (1818–1883), considered the father of communism. Along these lines, the presumption of the protestors is that Mises' philosophy and theory is the opposite of Marx's, and secondly, that Marx is generally read more than Mises, which is especially true when it comes to those who write educational and research material for the academic discipline of sociology. Two approaches to economic thought could not be further apart in their assumptions and conclusions (Steele, 1992), yet Marx is widely known throughout the world and ubiquitous in contemporary sociological works. Those with even a cursory familiarity with Austrian economics will no doubt be familiar with both names, yet evidence shows that *if* researchers, instructors, and students of sociology have encountered Mises' name it is through the lens of Marxian perspectives, tinting it with a reddish hue.

When it comes to an Austrian approach to sociology, associated with Mises is a name in the hall of fame of the social sciences and a founder of sociology, Max Weber (1864–1920). That there are Marxian and Weberian veins of sociology could not be questioned, for both originators' namesakes are considered the earliest practitioners of two paramount sociological paradigms, the conflict perspective and interpretivist perspective, respectively. Though their publications contain explicit sociological analyses and material otherwise useful to sociological studies, Mises' name, and those of other founders of the Austrian school of economics, seldom appear as credible citations in the writings of sociologists. Even though their works contain much explicit and implicit sociological analyses, sociologists tend to marginalize Mises and label Austrian economics in general with the pejorative "neoliberalism." At worst, this amounts to the use of obvious rhetorical fallacies designed to demonize this school of thought through guilt by association and strawman fallacies, and in the end the *ad hominem* of "neoliberals" is used to refer to Austrian proponents of free market capitalism as dangerous to the world order. Observations of the free market-oriented populist uprisings in Brazil, for example, are dismissed as the effects of "right-wing" demagoguery (Oliveira, 2019) resulting in "neofascism" (Caldeira Neto, 2020).

This chapter discusses Austrian sociology, a term conscripted here from its current use to refer to sociology developed and practiced in Austria. This discussion is carried out with reference to the reigning school of thought in sociology, namely the conflict tradition rooted in Marxian theories, as well as to the positivistic approach found in Durkheimian sociology. Attention is also directed to the interpretivist tradition found in Weberian sociology as it has the strongest link to the Austrian school of economics (Yu, 2020). Though few sociologists have rigorously entangled with Austrian economic theory, sociologists use the pejorative label of "neoliberalism" to associate Austrian axioms with what they believe to be the evil of the world, free market capitalism. In the end, Austrian sociology is oriented toward Weber's sociological works (Weber, 2019 [1922]) on meaning-making processes and social action, as well as to bureaucracy and the role of culture in economic transformations in society. Further, Austrian sociological analysis is rooted in methodological individualism traced to Mises' (1949) method of praxeology that deduces from human action how the economic order arises. This chapter highlights the existing works of Austrian sociology, limited in number as they are, but the style is inspired by broader approaches to the history of economic thought (see also Boettke, 2002; Rothbard, 1995a, 1995b). Also, in the style of a sociology of sociology (Curtis & Petras, 1972) and metatheory (Ritzer, 1990), the discussion proceeds with a contextualization of the dominant approaches to sociology to better understand the future of this nascent subfield. Lastly, the audiences considered are those with a familiarity with the history of either the Austrian school of economics or of sociology, not both simultaneously.

AUSTRIAN SOCIOLOGY DISAMBIGUATED

To begin, it is useful to distinguish *geographic* Austrian sociology as the type of sociology developed and practiced in the country of Austria from the matter of our concern. Readers of this book interested in further studying *theoretical* Austrian sociology on their own will likely encounter many search results pertaining to the former while seeking the latter. Up to the date of this writing, "Austrian sociology" has typically been used to refer to its geographic sense akin to American as compared to European sociology (e.g., see Münch, 1991). One instructive result produced by a search for "Austrian sociology" shows that, like sociology generally, the sociology developed and practiced in Austria has been heavily influenced by Marxian thought, and current discussions and debates have become only more entrenched in sociological Marxism (Kranebitter & Reinprecht, 2018). While I pick up on these issues below, the aim of this section (and chapter) is to reorient "Austrian sociology" from its current geographic reference. Compared to its popular usage up to this date, Austrian sociology in this chapter refers to: (1) existing sociological analyses by Austrian economists; and (2) the inclusion in sociological studies of principles, concepts, theories, methodologies, and findings in line with those of the Austrian school of economics. These points are discussed further below, but our immediate concern is with how the legacy of Marx has shaped sociology up to date and how this has and will likely continue to make problematic the establishing of an Austrian sociology as a formal subdiscipline.

For these purposes, John Torrance's (1976) history of geographic Austrian sociology is useful to explore at some length. Referring to the late 1800s and early 1900s, Torrance (1976) outlines how "Austro-Marxism as a new sociological departure arising from class struggle [in Austria]" (p. 186) eventually took over the prior predominant approach: positivism. Highlighting the positivism of a central figure in the early sociology of Austria, Torrance reviews the work of Ludwig Gumplowicz (1838–1909). In the following passage, we can see the fissure that has and will continue to exist between positivistic sociology and an Austrian sociology, a cleavage parallel to that of an Austrian sociology and sociological Marxism (e.g., see York & Clark, 2006):

> Gumplowicz proclaimed the autonomy of the social no less trenchantly than [Emile] Dürkheim, defining sociology as "an inductive experimental method, which, to explain social phenomena, relies on social facts." He argued the irrelevance of methodological individualism for the study of "social units," for "it is not possible to ascertain their mutual relations from the properties of their constituent parts." Psychological and cultural phenomena must be secondary for sociology, for which "the social phenomenon is always primary. The thought of the individual, and socio-ethical products such as religion, rights, morals, etc., are derivative." He claimed both that "the psychological method" – the pride of the contemporary Austrian school of economics – was "not at all useful for explaining social phenomena" and that "economic phenomena are also basically social." (p. 187)

In a section below I pick up on a discussion of the sharp contrast between the positivistic sociology established by Émile Durkheim (1858–1917) and the Austrian school of economics that we see spelled out in the above passage. The main contrast is between the methodological individualism and interpretations of subjective states of mind as compared to considering "society" to be *sui generis*, i.e., as an objective thing in itself to be studied as if it were similar in nature to a solar system or biological ecosystem open to naturalistic and inductive scientific observations.

In terms of important names and references for an Austrian sociology, Torrance (1976) notes that one of the few "academic Austrians to have made an enduring contribution to sociology, Joseph Schumpeter (1883–1950), having been the *'enfant gâté et terrible'* of the Vienna faculty" (p. 191), acknowledged his influences by founders of classical sociology, Georg Simmel (1858–1918) and Emile Durkheim. Schumpeter was an Austrian-born economist, and while studying at the University of Vienna, he "came under the intellectual influence of two of the leading members of the Austrian School of Economics, Eugen von Böhm-Bawerk (1851–1914) and Friedrich von Wieser (1851–1926)" (Ebeling, 2020, n.p.). It would be questionable to label Schumpeter an Austrian economist due to his flirtations with socialism and positivistic stance toward objectifying economics. This contrasts sharply with the Austrian economics approach of deducing from individual human action the principles of economics that result in the conclusion that private ownership and market transactions are the only viable mechanics of economic prosperity and human flourishing (Mises, 1949, 1951; Vanberg, 2015).

It is worth noting that Schumpeter's (1942) most famous work, *Capitalism, Socialism and Democracy*, "goes far beyond economics into political science and sociology" (Skousen, 2016, p. 429), and is considered foundational for economic sociology. To that end, Richard Swedberg (1991) notes at the outset of his book, *Joseph Schumpeter: The Economics and Sociology of Capitalism*, a useful point for purposes here:

> Schumpeter tried throughout his life to find a way to connect "theoretical economics," "economic sociology," "history," and "statistics" to each other in one broad concept of economics that he called "social economics" or *Sozialokonomik*. This effort, which is also connected to the work of Max Weber, has been forgotten – but perhaps needs to be resurrected since mainstream economics has tended to isolate itself from the other social sciences during the twentieth century. (p. vii)

Considering his impact on economic sociology, Schumpeter's part in an Austrian sociology should be treated as a point of comparison (Gloria-Palermo, 2002; Simpson, 1983), whereas, as we shall see, the works of Max Weber are foundational and unifying (Callahan, 2007; Kolev, 2020; Yu, 2020).

To demonstrate the disunity between mainstream sociology and Austrian economics, it is useful once again to return to Torrance's (1976) history of geographic Austrian sociology. "As the socialist threat mounted in Vienna," says Torrance,

Böhm-Bawerk shifted the polemical target to Marx, and in later years, von Mises and Hayek have kept the rear guard action going in exile. From Menger to Hayek, these economists remained consistent champions of the dogmatic laissez-faire outlook of Austrian liberalism in its heyday of the 1870's, blaming most of the evils of modernity on its demise. (p. 202)

Here, dismissed as dogmatic cranks for their adherence to classical liberalism, are key founders of the Austrian school of economics, including Carl Menger (1840–1921) and his student, Eugen von Böhm-Bawerk, who in turn was Joseph Schumpeter's teacher. For comparison, a search on July 31, 2021 of all sociology journals in *JSTOR* returns the following results for significant founders' names in the Austrian school of economics and sociology: Böhm-Bawerk (N = 202), Menger (N = 1,487), Mises (N = 12,707), Durkheim (N = 24,400), Weber (N = 38,975), and Marx (N = 39,967). An imprecise method to be sure, these results suggest by an order of magnitude a marked unfamiliarity or, perhaps, an unwillingness to contend with founders of Austrian economics by sociologists as compared to founders of sociology. This should not be surprising considering how and why Marx, Durkheim, and Weber came to be known as the founders of sociology (e.g., see Cuff, Dennis, Francis, & Sharrock, 2016; Royce, 2015). What this suggests is that, for example, educators and researchers in the field of sociology will be far less likely to know of, let alone promote, Böhm-Bawerk's (1949) devastating critiques of Marx's theories of exploitation and labor theory of value (see also Britton, 2020; Ebeling, 2004). In part, this is likely due to how contemporary sociologists conceive the works of these founders of Austrian economics, i.e., as "neoliberalism."

In the above passage, Torrance (1976) also marginalized two other founders of Austrian economics, Ludwig von Mises (1881–1973) and Friedrich August von Hayek (1899–1992), for their defense of laissez-faire economic liberalism. Currently, Mises and Hayek are implicated as the originators of the so-called "neo-liberal agenda" (Ritzer, 2011, p. 77) that has allegedly "threatened to destroy society" through "the evils of the free market" (p. 44). To counteract neoliberalism, contemporary sociologists encourage their colleagues to look to how Mises and Hayek engaged in epistemological critiques of founding works in sociology (Gane, 2014) and how the ideas of Austrian economists and other "neoliberals" cause contemporary global social problems, including the 2008 global financial crises (Birch, 2015; Centeno & Cohen, 2012; Davies, 2014; Dean, 2014). Specifically, neo-Marxists have gone so far as to argue that Hayek's (2007) seminal book, *The Road to Serfdom*, is a threat to democracy itself. First, this is allegedly because its critique of collectivism and government interventionism "fails to recognize that corporations are giant bureaucracies that, themselves, can take away the power of people central to democracy" (Derber & Magrass, 2016, p. 133), and second, allegations abound that neoliberalism is part of "a trend in the institutional organization of inter-locking state and corporate power" (Maher & Aquanno, 2018, p. 33; see also Ritzer, 2011), i.e., corporatism.

Even with its strong Marxist program, sociology practiced in Austria, like elsewhere in the world, was eclectic in its origins and practices (Fleck & Nowotny, 1993). For his analysis, Torrance (1976) looked at sociology in Austria through the lens of Austro-Marxism, which remains a staple of sociol-ogy practiced in Austria (Kranebitter & Reinprecht, 2018), similar to the soci-ological Marxism practiced there and elsewhere throughout the world (e.g., see Burawoy & Wright, 2002). Mises and Hayek were familiar with a variety of works foundational for the sociology of the late 1800s and early 1900s, but their critiques are cast as part of a neoliberal program that contemporary sociologists blame for many of the world's problems. In its geographic sense, Austrian sociology failed to produce a coherent school of thought, and so it is appropriate to define Austrian sociology as it is used in this chapter, which will likely be labeled as neoliberal sociology by mainstream sociologists.

AUSTRIAN SOCIOLOGY DEFINED

In addition to producing the founding fathers of the Austrian school of economics, Austria also produced two of sociology's most influential social theorists, Alfred Schutz (1899–1959) and Peter Berger (1929–2017). Along with their mutual coauthor, Thomas Luckmann (1927–2016), Schutz's (Schutz & Luckmann, 1973) and Berger's (Berger & Luckmann, 1966) major contri-butions to modern sociological theory, *The Structures of the Life-World* and *The Social Construction of Reality*, respectively, advanced a vein of classical sociological theory established by Max Weber. There exist strong connections between Austrian economics and the works of Weber, Schutz, and Berger (Boettke, 2012; Ebeling, 1999; Kolev, 2020; Prendergast, 1986; Yu, 2020), namely in the analytic realms of economic subjectivism and sociological interpretivism (Yu, 2015). Weberian sociology has been and continues to be a mainstay of the field of sociology broadly (Collins, 1986; Mommsen, 2021; Swedberg, 1998, 2003), and Weber's central concepts have been widely incor-porated into Austrian economics already, including the following: *Verstehen* (Koppl & Mongiovi, 1998; Lachmann, 1971); *social action* (Lachmann, 1982; Zafirovski, 2010); *rationality* (Oakley, 1997; Parsons, 2003); and *ideal types* (Crespo, 1997; Csontos, 1998). Peter Boettke and Virgil Storr (2002), who have produced much of what can said to be the current work on Austrian sociology, argue that it is Weber's concept of *Verstehen* that provides the clearest connection to Mises' Austrian approach to economics vis-à-vis methodological individualism.

Schumpeter (1909) is credited with creating the term methodological individualism, which was only decades later taken on by such scholars as Hayek (1942) and Mises (1949) to pronounce their own positions, and so its use to describe Weber's (2019 [1922]) sociological approach was posthumously ascribed (Hodgson, 2007). Though he did not coin the phrase, Carl Menger's (1985 [1883], 2007 [1871]) pioneering books, *Principles of Economics* and *Problems of Economics and Sociology*, paved the path forward for Austrian economists to analyze complex economic phenomena in terms of their most fundamental constituent parts, individual humans and our purposive actions (Arrow, 1994; Oakley, 1999). This necessarily entails considering individuals' subjective orientation toward the world, and it was the inclusion of this subjectivist outlook, while wildly contested (Eabrasu, 2011), that served as the unique analytic positions of Austrian economics (Zanotti, 2007) and Weberian sociology (Rehbein, 2020). Menger's revolutionary reorientation of economic thought from the treatment of economic value as objective to subjective contributed to Weber's (2019 [1922]) treatment of sociology as a matter of methodically interpreting individuals' subjective reasons for their social actions (Parsons, 2007; Tribe, 2012; Udehn, 2001). In turn, Weber influenced Mises' (1949) magnus opus, *Human Action*, wherein Mengerian subjectivism took a leap forward from a focus on individuals' wants and desires (consumption) to evaluating the means individuals choose for reaching their goals (Lachmann, 1982). For Austrian economics, methodological individualism is foundational and a given starting place (Boettke & Coyne, 2005), but for sociology it demarcates one side of the battlegrounds over which the war for the epistemological, ontological, and methodological grounds are fought for adequately or accurately studying society (Udehn, 2002).

"Other than the quite trivial claim that sociology is the study of society," says Christian Robitaille (2019) in his article, "Ludwig von Mises, Sociology, and Metatheory," "there is no epistemological consensus on what sociology is and on how it should be studied" (p. 245). This creates an opportunity for Austrian sociology. Robitaille (2019) notes that aside from calling for the theoretical incorporation of praxeology into the field of study, Mises (1949, 2003) conceptualized sociology as a historical discipline divided between the holism of its founders, Auguste Comte and Emile Durkheim, and the interpretative sociology of Max Weber, yet he could not at the time of his writing see just how fragmented sociology would become. Contemporary sociology is well known to be a highly specialized and fragmented field (Hand & Judkins, 1999; Scott, 2005; Steinmetz & Chae, 2002; Zhao, 1993) with periodic moments of crisis (Gouldner, 1970; Vaughan, 1993). Witnessing signs of fragmentation in his own time, Weber (2019 [1922]) concluded that science generally had "entered a phase of specialization previously unknown and that this will forever remain the case" (p. 134), yet somewhat contradictorily Weber's conceptual contributions to the cultural and social sciences helped resolve epistemological and methodological problems among them, thus leading toward unification (Ringer, 1997). Following Weberian and Misesian lines of inquiry, Austrian sociology is uniquely positioned to fit into the fissures of the field of sociology to help redress, for example, widespread assumptions by sociologists that markets and "neoliberalism" are to blame for the 2008 global financial meltdown (Allison, 2013; Centeno & Cohen, 2010, 2012; Lounsbury & Hirsch, 2010; Woods, 2009). For example, rather than viewing the business cycle as an inherent feature of capitalism, sociologists could consider the roles that state intervention and central banking play in market processes, which are themselves the summation of individual choices in economic transactions of all types.

Max Weber and Ludwig von Mises serve as the unifying sources for Austrian sociology (Kolev, 2020; Zafirovski, 2002). Mises' (2003) critique of Weber's theory of action, which typologized it between rational and non-rational, is that all action is rational, albeit with differences between calculable and non-calculable actions (Mises, 1949; Zafirovski, 2010). In essence, whereas the analysis of human action is concerned with the praxeology of how individuals satisfy their consumption needs (Mises, 1949), social action is about the sociology of actions oriented toward others within specific socio-cultural and historical contexts (Weber, 2019 [1922]). Weber's (1946, 1947, 2019 [1922]) breadth of work, like Mises', expands to politico-economic and socio-cultural analyses as well, with special attention to one of Mises' central topics covered in his book of the same name, *Bureaucracy* (Mises, 1944; see also Anderson, 2004). Their shared concern is that bureaucratic structures that monopolize and legitimize the use of force will inevitably bound humans to a life of perpetual servitude. As Boettke and Storr (2002) conclude, "the Weber-Austrian connection promises to avoid many of the pitfalls that plague their economic brethren and the 'new sociology of economic life' and may represent what has appeared so elusive in the twentieth century: a social theory that is at once logically coherent, empirically useful, humanistic in its method and humanitarian in its concerns" (p. 182). In the sections below, the discussion proceeds from the Austrian critique of sociological holism and then to a discussion of how an Austrian sociology can play counterpoint to sociological Marxism. In essence, Austrian sociology brings humans and the human condition back into the analysis of the social – namely in terms of the prisons of our subjectivity and salvation in intersubjective, voluntary associations.

BETWEEN HOLISM AND INDIVIDUALISM

In the 1830s, Auguste Comte (1798–1857) famously established a branch of science rooted in positivism that he called social physics. Coining this discipline as sociology, Comte (1855) proposed that empirical methods of the natural sciences could be similarly applied to society in order to identify its fundamental structures and governing laws. This new social physics was aimed at becoming the queen of the sciences by encompassing all other branches with the purpose of establishing a scientifically governed social order. In *The Counter-Revolution of Science*, Hayek (1952) discredited the scientism behind this type of thinking by demonstrating that the subjective orientations of humans make us distinctly different than the objects of study in the natural sciences. Moreover, though their treatment of political economy contrasted (Swingewood, 1970), both Comtean and Marxian notions about the inevitable path(s) of history toward scientifically manageable societies inexorably require a state to coerce or force individuals into action rather than allowing spontaneous order to arise from voluntary or consensual action (Hayek, 1960; Nisbet, 1994; Thomas, 2008). Of this way of thinking, Mises (1949) notes that his method, praxeology, does not, "like the works of Hegel, Comte, Marx, and a host of other writers, claim to reveal information about the true, objective, and absolute meaning of life and history" (Shantz & Williams, 2013, p. 28). Austrian sociology assumes human reasoning is simultaneously the reason we need specific methods for the subject of study as well as the ethics behind denying the legitimacy of statism.

To clarify the difference in approaches beyond ambiguity, Mises (1949) stakes the following claim:

> The terms society and state as they are used by the contemporary advocates of socialism, planning, and social control of all the activities of individuals signify a deity. The priests of this new creed ascribe to their idol all those attributes which the theologians ascribe to God – omnipotence, omniscience, infinite goodness, and so on.
>
> If one assumes that there exists above and beyond the individual's actions an imperishable entity aiming at its own ends, different from those of mortal men, one has already constructed the concept of a superhuman being. Then one cannot evade the question whose ends take precedence whenever an antagonism arises, those of the state or society or those of the individual. The answer to this question is already implied in the very concept of state or society as conceived by collectivism and universalism. (p. 151)

Those who rebuke Hayek and Mises on the grounds that they are making political rather than epistemological claims seem to be using a double standard by not interrogating the inherent political nature of assuming that society or the state take precedence over individuals (e.g., see Gane, 2014). Sociologists and other social scientists, like most members of society, operate within the social paradigm of statism, which assumes the primacy and naturalness of the state. Under this ideology, the state rightfully and pragmatically should serve as *the* regulating force in society, if not itself then through proxies like the educational system, military, media, medicine, and other social institutions, namely governments (Shantz & Williams, 2013).

Heavily influenced by Comte's positivist creed, Emile Durkheim (1858–1917) established the first department of sociology, became the first professor of the discipline, and published what are considered the first major sociological studies, *The Division of Labor in Society* (1984 [1893]), *The Rules of the Sociological Method* (1982 [1895]), *Suicide* (1951 [1897]), and *The Elementary Forms of Religious Life* (1965 [1912]). From Durkheim's collective works, sociologists have continued to elaborate and do empirical research on many of his central concepts, including collective effervescence (Shilling & Mellor, 1998), collective representations (Pickering, 2000), collective memory (Misztal, 2003), and collective consciousness (Smith, 2014). Similar to Comte's positivistic purposes for sociology, Durkheim eventually proposed that a moral society could and should be manufactured by means of its central institutions, specifically education (Durkheim, 1956). If sociologists subscribe to either the type of collectivism espoused by Durkheim or Marx, then it is no wonder that they lament, or warn that "neo-liberalism is radically individualistic" (Ritzer, 2011, p. 41).

Austrian economists argue from evidence-based approaches that market-based societies foster morality through the sociability of exchanges and the discipline necessary for economizing behavior (Storr & Choi, 2019). Durkheim's diagnosis was that industrialization and other processes of modernity were transforming social integration and cohesion to the point that society was becoming ever more atomized, and his social engineering prognosis was given in order to counteract rising individualism and the "cult of the individual" (Marske, 1987). Durkheimian logic goes like this: sociology should be practiced as a unique discipline with its own explanandum and explanatory reasoning; individuals' ideations and behaviors are created by society's social structures, which exist *sui generis* as social facts; social facts exist independently of individuals and are coercive to them, and are only explainable by other social facts, not the psychology or actions of individuals; social order and cohesion are desirable ends that should and can only be established by manipulating the social structures of society, particularly its organizations and institutions.

Mises (1949, 1951, 2007) sharply disagrees with this line of thought not only because it positions society and the state as sovereign over individuals, but because it passes over the unit of analysis in the praxeological study of human action, the individual. Here is Mises' (2007) take on the issue:

> Emile Durkheim and his school deal with the group mind as if it were a real phenomenon, a distinct agency, thinking and acting. As they see it, not individuals but the group is the subject of history.
>
> As a corrective of these fancies the truism must be stressed that only individuals think and act. (p. 190)

Methodological individualism (Hodgson, 2007) flies in the face of both Durkheimian positivism and Marxian assumptions and methodologies (Romm, 1991). Both are said to be part of the same paradigm – the social facts paradigm – since both systems of analysis privilege society as an objective social fact acting as a social force coercive to individuals (Ritzer, 1975). Although there is a proposed middle ground (Ritzer & Gindoff, 1992) between the methodological individualism of Weberian and Austrian styles of analysis (Prychitko, 1990), on the one hand, and the methodological holism of structural analyses said to be the true hallmark of sociology on the other (Mayhew, 1980; Warriner, 1956), a key point is that neither Weberian nor Austrian analyses resolve into psychological reductionism sometimes confused with methodological individualism (Webster, 1973). Rather, interpretations of the subjective states and rational choices of human agents are used for theory construction of how the economic order arises from human decision making and exchanges (Boettke, 1998; Boettke, Lavoie, & Storr, 2004).

Durkheimian sociology comes at odds with the thinking of Austrian economists in several ways, but consider just one discrepancy in *Socialism: An Economic and Sociological Analysis* that Mises takes with Durkheim's theory of the division of labor. In a footnote, Mises (1951, p. 293) remarks that Durkheim had reversed the logical order of economic productivity leading to population growth. Concerned that these types of critiques laid the foundations of neoliberalism, Gane (2014) disagrees, pointing out that Durkheim's interest in the social integration of members of society was at the heart of his analysis of the division of labor, not the economy or economic activity. Comte and Durkheim are not the only founding sociologists Mises took to task, though. In *Epistemological Problems of Economics*, Mises (2003) dedicates an entire chapter to dissecting the early program of sociology and spends much time critiquing Max Weber's methodology of using ideal types to distinguish different types of social action. For Mises (1949, 2007), all human action is rational, but Gane (2014) again criticizes this for missing the point that Weberian and other types of sociological analysis differ from praxeology in that sociology broadens the scope beyond economic activity (e.g., see Zafirovski, 2010). Gane (2014), though, perhaps misses Mises' (1949, 2003) vision for praxeology as *the method of the social sciences* rather than as one of many competing methodological programs within the discipline of economics.

As a brief aside, it is useful to highlight the unique features of praxeology as compared to other academic disciplines concerned with human action. Murray Rothbard's (1926–1995) essay, "Praxeology: The Methodology of Austrian Economics" (1997), serves as a general overview of praxeology, answering many questions about its distinctive methodological contributions to the social sciences.

> In brief, *praxeology* consists of the logical implications of the universal formal fact that people act, that they employ means to try to attain chosen ends. *Technology* deals with the contentual problem of *how* to achieve ends by adoption of means. *Psychology* deals with the question of *why* people adopt various ends and *how* they go about adopting them. *Ethics* deals with the question of what ends, or values, people *should* adopt. And *history* deals with ends adopted in the past, what means were used to try to achieve them – and what the consequences of these actions were.
>
> Praxeology, or economic theory in particular, is thus a unique discipline within the social sciences; for, in contrast to the others, it deals not with the *content* of men's values, goals, and actions – not with what they have done or how they have acted or how they should act – but purely with the fact that they *do* have goals and act to attain them. The laws of utility, demand, supply, and price apply regardless of the type of goods and services desired or produced. (p. 70; italics in original)

Weberian sociology, on the other hand, *does* deal with the content of the reasons people act, particularly when action is in reference to other people, hence it is called social action. From even Rothbard's (1997) phrasing, though, it can easily be mistaken that praxeology is only concerned with economics and that economics should be considered the main driver, which can seem to say that it assumes an economically deterministic model of the social world.

Considering this very issue of an econocentric analytic framework, Boettke and Storr (2002) reconcile the differences between Durkheimian and Misesian concepts through a Weberian approach. Boettke and Storr (2002) view social actors as embedded within a Venn diagram of overlapping spheres of the social, political, and economic orders, not as a concentric set of spheres with the economy at the center surrounded by the polity and then the social sphere. Another ring to be included in the Venn diagram might be culture, which includes cultural variations and sources of values, beliefs, and norms that impact and contextualize decision making (Storr & John, 2020). Within each ring should be considered the more micro-level situations involving individuals' social embeddedness and social capital that produce norms like the trust and reciprocity necessary for mutually beneficial exchanges (Lewis & Chamlee-Wright, 2008). In this way, Austrian sociology retains a focus on rational actions of humans, but in a way that shows how embeddedness within different contexts shifts what type of rational action is used. It is unlikely that an Austrian sociology, following Mises and Weber, will have much in common with the positivist programs of Comte or Durkheim, but there might be, surprisingly enough, room for Marx.

FROM FUNCTIONALISM TO CONFLICT THEORY TO AUSTRIAN SOCIOLOGY

Though their theories and perspectives differ considerably, sociological text-books often associate Comte and Durkheim with other "conservative" social theorists, such as Herbert Spencer (1873, 1892, 1897), Bronislaw Malinowski (1936, 1939), Talcott Parsons (1937, 1977), and Robert Merton (1936, 1968; see also Coser, 1975). Together, their works constitute the theoretical perspective or framework known as (structural-)functionalism (Turner & Maryanski, 1977). Currently, "structural-functionalism" exists primarily within university textbooks rather than as a viable research program in research journals (Manza, Sauder, & Wright, 2010). The pedagogical use of functionalism is as a strawman against the predominant perspective that places group conflict at the beginning and/or end of all analyses. Here is an illustrative statement to that end from the beginning of a popular textbook for introductory sociology, now in its thirteenth edition: "The conflict perspective addresses the deficiencies of structural functionalism by viewing the structure of society as a source of inequality that benefits some groups at the expense of other groups" (Newman, 2020, p. 39). From there, these types of textbooks typically set up a discussion of any given topic with the structural-functionalist perspective but then students are led to the preferred analysis vis-à-vis the conflict perspective.

"Karl Marx, perhaps the most famous scholar associated with the conflict perspective," instructs David Newman (2020, p. 39) in his well-sold textbook, "focused exclusively on economic arrangements." Though he never wrote an explicitly sociological treatise nor held a professorship of any kind, Marx, like Durkheim, is considered a founding figure by contemporary sociologists (Cuff et al., 2016). As such, instructors and scholars of sociology promote Marx's and Marxian ideas as legitimate ways to explain social problems, inequalities, and stratification ostensibly arising from capitalism and class relations to the means of production. Few other economic frameworks are offered, save for Keynes and Krugman. Beginning in the 1960s, Marx's and (neo-)Marxian theories have become staples of sociology textbooks, journal articles, and monographs, comprising a deeply entrenched tradition practiced by a glut of contemporary sociologists (Bottomore, 1966; Deflem, 2013; Manza & McCarthy, 2011). The American Sociological Association (ASA) even has an entire section dedicated to Marxist sociology (ASA, 2021) – no other specific theoretical or ideological tradition has its own ASA section. Proponents of sociological Marxism envision it as both an ideological and scientific program aimed at propagating "real utopias" in the public imagination and building alternatives to capitalism within existing institutions (Burawoy & Wright, 2002). Those engaging with theoretical Austrian sociology should consciously contend with this tradition in sociology, and they already have.

In *The Economics and Ethics of Property Rights*, Hans-Hermann Hoppe (1949–present) supplants a Marxist class analysis with an Austrian class analysis all the while accepting the premises of "the hard-core of the Marxist belief system" (2006, p. 117). In brief, Marx's premise is that class exploitation manifests in arrangements of property rights monopolized by a unified, oligarchical ruling class that wields ideological power that produces a false consciousness among the exploited class. The important distinction between the two approaches is that, in typical fashion of the political theory of Austrian economists (Gordon, 2021; Higgs, 2004; Rothbard, 2004, 2009), Hoppe identifies the state, not capitalism, as the source of these exploitative abilities. Jeffrey Tucker (1963–present; 2009) expresses shock at Hoppe's acceptance of Marx's premises considering that Ludwig von Mises (1949, 1951, 2003) had problematized polylogism – structural, rather than mental sources of different forms of logical thinking – at the outset of his magnus opus, *Human Action*, and had surgically dismantled Marx's theories otherwise. Marx's polylogistic theory operates like this: ideology in the form of ruling ideas are produced by the ruling class, i.e., capitalist owners of the means of production. In turn, the ideologies of the ruling class generate a false consciousness within and among the exploited class, workers "forced" to sell their labor. This, ostensibly, explains the lack of class consciousness in the working class that, if and when achieved, would (inevitably, in Marx's surmising) result in a dictatorship of the working class. Class consciousness would, eventually, bring about global communism and, somehow or for some reason, the state would just whither away like dried petals of a dying dandelion – at least, that's the gist of the theory (Eyerman, 1981; Lukes, 2011; Pines, 1993; Rosen, 1996).

Max Weber also dismissed this type of thinking in a biting remark distinguishing the aggregated construct of "classes" from actual communities of living human beings:

> To treat "class" conceptually as having the same value as "community" leads to distortion. That men in the same class situation regularly react in mass actions to such tangible situations as economic ones in the direction of those interests that are most adequate to their average number is an important and after all simple fact for the understanding of historical events. Above all, this fact must not lead to that kind of pseudo-scientific operation with the concepts of "class" and "class interests" so frequently found these days, and which has found its most classic expression in the statement of a talented author, that the individual may be in error concerning his interests but that the "class" is "infallible" about its interests. Yet, if classes as such

are not communities, nevertheless class situations emerge only on basis of communalization. (Weber, 1946, pp. 184–185)

The "talented author" Weber refers to is, no doubt, Karl Marx (Collins, 1980; Mommsen, 1977), and Austrian theorists likely agree that Marx's conclusions are pseudoscientific. The rejection of these holistic constructions on the grounds of methodological individualism extend as well to Durkheim's concepts of collective representations and collective consciousness (Zafirovski, 2002). Weber's classic distinction between class, status, and party, as well as his attention to the dominant forces of capitalism, bureaucracy, and the state, positions him among the early conflict sociologists (Alexander, 1983; Chan & Goldthorpe, 2007; Collins, 1975; Gane, 2005; Giddens, 1972; Sayer, 2002). This Weberian combination of interpretivist methodologies with attention to sources of social inequality paves the way for considering how an Austrian sociology fits in with the conflict perspective.

Randall Collins (1975) created conflict sociology by systematically reviewing and synthesizing the existing sociological research on conflict up to the time of his writing (see Collins & Sanderson, 2015 for an updated edition). Though "structural-functionalists" are said to represent the consensus perspective, which is often contrasted with the conflict perspective (Cuff et al., 2016; Lipset, 1985), Collins (1975) utilized structural-functionalist theories to explain conflict via the formations and operations of society's communities, organizations, and institutions and how they differentially affect individuals' life chances in terms of social classes and status groups. If the structural-functionalist framework that is tracked back to Durkheim is eschewed for being too "conservative," then the fact that Austrian economics is considered "neoliberalism" in mainstream textbooks (e.g., see Derber & Magrass, 2016; Ritzer, 2011) means that it is less likely to be taken seriously when students are learning how to do sociology. Consider, for example, how Marxian sociologists mythologized Talcott Parsons, a main figure in the school of structural-functionalism, as a defender of the status quo despite the fact that he paid much attention to social inequality and social change (Staubmann, 2021). Inequality is of central concern for conflict theorists, and so consider the fact that Mises authored "On Equality and Inequality" (Ebeling, 1990), which would fit with Collins' (1975) theme of exploring all roots of social conflict. More specifically, conflict theorists focus on inequalities based on social class and power, and there are several Austrian contributions in these matters as well (Hart, Chartier, Kenyon, & Long, 2018; Higgs, 2004; Lemke, 2015; Rothbard, 2004).

In terms of the various versions of conflict sociology, Collins' (1975) approach would likely be closest to Hoppe's (2006) position due to its not accepting Marx's premise that capitalism is at the root of producing systems of social stratification. Ralf Dahrendorf (1958, 1959, 2008) initiated a less theoretically eclectic vein of conflict sociology in that he directly argued with "Marx's ghost." Yet, Hoppe (2006) might also accept this type of conflict sociology due to Dahrendorf's theory that relations to positions of authority rather than to production are the sources of social inequality. Conflict sociologists who do play the game of blaming capitalism for producing society's problems are numerous, but major players reading from Marx's playbook include Erik Olin Wright (1997, 2010, 2019), Michael Burawoy (1979, 1990, 2003), John Bellamy Foster (1999, 2000, 2002), Simon Clarke (1991, 1994), and many others – notably, George Ritzer (2011) uses the works of Karl Polanyi (1944) and Zygmunt Bauman (2000) to side with Marx and malign Mises and Hayek as "neoliberals," thereby eschewing Austrian economics with the wave of a hand and blaming many of the world's problems on its "neoliberal agenda." The heavy presence of sociological Marxism in the discipline, along with the fact that Durkheimian sociology is viewed as too conservative, suggests that Austrian sociology will be, much like Austrian economics in the discipline of economics, not a welcome stranger in the discipline of sociology.

CONCLUSION

Readers interested in the geographic version of Austrian sociology are welcome, as are other sociologists, to thoroughly and honestly engage with the literature cited here on Austrian economics and its connections to sociology. My suggestion would be to replace any red-tinted sociological lenses that would prejudice one's reading from a Marxian perspective with *any* other lens. If that challenge cannot be accepted, Marxian readers can address any of the following issues raised by Austrian economics: the subjective versus labor theory of value, the price calculation problem in socialist systems, the business cycle theory with respect to government-granted monopolies to central banks, and the history of communism with respect to the democides and famines caused by communist regimes as compared to the fact that billions have been lifted from poverty under the system of capitalistic entrepreneurship. Due to the prevalence of sociological Marxism, I suspect there will be few sociologists who will, at all, take up this challenge, and even fewer who would do so earnestly. For readers hailing from the Austrian school, consider Boettke and Storr's (2002) decentering of the economy from your analytic lens: society is a multifaceted, multidimensional, multilevel, multilayered construct with mutually supporting and contradictory components and processes. Economic activity, important as it is in whatever respect, is not the only activity individuals engage in. Like a neglected child, sociological readers should consider directly nurturing methodological individualism back to life so that it might once again live well among those who have long since forgotten that, after all, individual humans are the heart, soul, and mind of society.

REFERENCES

Alexander, J. C. (1983). *Classical Attempt at Theoretical Synthesis: Max Weber*. London: Routledge.

Allison, J. A. (2013). *The Financial Crisis and the Free Market Cure: Why Pure Capitalism Is the World's Only Hope*. New York: McGraw-Hill.

Anderson, W. P. (2004). Mises versus Weber on Bureaucracy and Sociological Method. *Journal of Libertarian Studies, 18*(1), 1–21.

Arrow, K. J. (1994). Methodological Individualism and Social Knowledge. *American Economic Review, 84*(2), 1–9.

ASA. (2021). Marxist sociology. Retrieved July 14, 2021, from www.asanet.org/asa -communities/sections/marxist-sociology

Bauman, Z. (2000). *Liquid Modernity*. Malden, MA: Polity Press.

Berger, P. L., & Luckmann, T. (1966). *The Social Construction of Reality: A Treatise in the Sociology of Knowledge*. New York: Penguin Books.

Birch, K. (2015). Neoliberalism: The Whys and Wherefores ... and Future Directions. *Sociology Compass, 9*(7), 571–584.

Boettke, P. J. (1998). Rational Choice and Human Agency in Economics and Sociology: Exploring the Weber–Austrian Connection. In H. Giersch (Ed.), *Merits and Limits of Markets* (pp. 53–81). Berlin: Springer.

Boettke, P. J. (2002). The Use and Abuse of the History of Economic Thought within the Austrian School of Economics. *History of Political Economy, 34*(5), 337–360.

Boettke, P. J. (2012). *Living Economics: Yesterday, Today, and Tomorrow*. Oakland, CA: Independent Institute.

Boettke, P. J., & Coyne, C. J. (2005). Methodological Individualism, Spontaneous Order and the Research Program of the Workshop in Political Theory and Policy Analysis. *Journal of Economic Behavior and Organization, 57*(2), 145–158.

Boettke, P. J., Lavoie, D., & Storr, V. H. (2004). The Subjectivist Methodology of Austrian Economics, and Dewey's Theory of Inquiry. In E. L. Khalil (Ed.), *Dewey, Pragmatism and Economic Methodology* (pp. 327–356). New York: Routledge.

Boettke, P. J., & Storr, V. H. (2002). Post-Classical Political Economy: Polity, Society and Economy in Weber, Mises and Hayek. *American Journal of Economics and Sociology, 61*(1), 161–191.

Böhm-Bawerk, E. von. (1949). *Karl Marx and the Close of his System* (P. M. Sweezy, Ed.). New York: Augustus M. Kelley.

Bottomore, T. B. (1966). Karl Marx: Sociologist or Marxist? *Science and Society, 30*(1), 11–24.

Britton, J. E. (2020). Böhm-Bawerk Explains why "Marxist" Exploitation Is Nonsense. Retrieved July 31, 2021, from https://mises.org/wire/bohm-bawerk-explains-why -marxist-exploitation-nonsense

Burawoy, M. (1979). *Manufacturing Consent: Changes in the Labor Process under Monopoly Capitalism*. Chicago, IL: University of Chicago Press.

Burawoy, M. (1990). Marxism as Science: Historical Challenges and Theoretical Growth. *American Sociological Review, 55*(6), 775.

Burawoy, M. (2003). For a Sociological Marxism: The Complementary Convergence of Antonio Gramsci and Karl Polanyi. *Politics and Society, 31*(2), 193–261.

Burawoy, M., & Wright, E. (2002). Sociological Marxism. In Jonathan H. Turner (Ed.), *Handbook of Sociological Theory* (pp. 459–486). New York: Plenum Publishers.

Caldeira Neto, O. (2020). Neofascismo, "nova república" e a ascensão das Direitas no Brasil. *Conhecer: Debate Entre o Público e o Privado, 10*(24), 120–140.

Callahan, G. (2007). Reconciling Weber and Mises on Understanding Human Action. *American Journal of Economics and Sociology, 66*(5), 889–899.

Centeno, M. A., & Cohen, J. N. (2010). *Global Capitalism: A Sociological Perspective*. Malden, MA: Polity Press.

Centeno, M. A., & Cohen, J. N. (2012). The Arc of Neoliberalism. *Annual Review of Sociology, 38*(1), 317–340.

Chan, T. W., & Goldthorpe, J. H. (2007). Class and Status: The Conceptual Distinction and Its Empirical Relevance. *American Sociological Review, 72*(4), 512–532.

Clarke, S. (1991). *Marx, Marginalism and Modern Sociology: From Adam Smith to Max Weber*. Basingstoke: Macmillan.

Clarke, S. (1994). *Marx's Theory of Crisis*. Basingstoke: Macmillan.

Collins, R. (1975). *Conflict Sociology*. New York: Academic Press.

Collins, R. (1980). Weber's Last Theory of Capitalism: A Systematization. *American Sociological Review, 45*(6), 925.

Collins, R. (1986). *Weberian Sociological Theory*. Cambridge, MA: Cambridge University Press.

Collins, R., & Sanderson, S. K. (2015). *Conflict Sociology: A Sociological Classic Updated*. New York: Routledge.

Comte, A. (1855). *The Positive Philosophy of Auguste Comte*. New York: Calvin Blanchard.

Coser, L. A. (1975). *The Idea of Social Structure* (L. A. Coser, Ed.). New York: Routledge.

Crespo, R. F. (1997). Max Weber and Ludwig von Mises, and the Methodology of the Social Sciences. In *Methodology of the Social Sciences, Ethics, and Economics in the Newer Historical School* (pp. 32–55). Berlin: Springer.

Csontos, L. (1998). Subjectivism and Ideal Types: Lachmann and the Methodological Legacy of Max Weber. In R. Koppl & G. Mongiovi (Eds), *Subjectivism and Economic Analysis: Essays in Memory of Ludwig M. Lachmann* (pp. 80–130). New York: Routledge.

Cuff, E. C., Dennis, A. J., Francis, D. W., & Sharrock, W. W. (2016). *Perspectives in Sociology* (6th ed.). New York: Routledge.

Curtis, J. E., & Petras, J. W. (1972). The Sociology of Sociology: Some Lines of Inquiry in the Study of the Discipline. *The Sociological Quarterly, 13*(2), 197–209.

Dahrendorf, R. (1958). Toward a Theory of Social Conflict. *Journal of Conflict Resolution, 2*(2), 170–183.

Dahrendorf, R. (1959). *Class and Class Conflict in Industrial Society*. Stanford, CA: Stanford University Press.

Dahrendorf, R. (2008). *The Modern Social Conflict: The Politics of Liberty* (2nd ed.). New Brunswick, NJ: Transaction Publishers.

Davies, W. (2014). Neoliberalism: A Bibliographic Review. *Theory, Culture and Society, 31*(7–8), 309–317.

Dean, M. (2014). Rethinking Neoliberalism. *Journal of Sociology, 50*(2), 150–163.

Deflem, M. (2013). The Structural Transformation of Sociology. *Society, 50*(2), 156–166.

Derber, C., & Magrass, Y. R. (2016). *Capitalism, Should You Buy it? An Invitation to Political Economy*. New York: Routledge.

Durkheim, E. (1951 [1897]). *Suicide*. New York: The Free Press.
Durkheim, E. (1956). *Education and Society*. Glencoe, IL: The Free Press.
Durkheim, E. (1965 [1912]). *The Elementary Forms of Religious Life*. New York: The Free Press.
Durkheim, E. (1982 [1895]). *The Rules of the Sociological Method*. New York: The Free Press.
Durkheim, E. (1984 [1893]). *The Division of Labor in Society*. London: Macmillan Press.
Eabrasu, M. (2011). A Praxeological Assessment of Subjective Value. *Quarterly Journal of Austrian Economics*, *14*(2), 216–241.
Ebeling, R. M. (1990). *Money, Method, and the Market Process: Essays by Ludwig von Mises*. Norwell, MA: Kluwer Academic Press.
Ebeling, R. M. (1999). Human Action, Ideal Types, and the Market Process: Alfred Schutz and the Austrian Economists. In L. Embree (Ed.), *Schutzian Social Science. Contributions to Phenomenology*, Vol 37. Dordrecht: Springer.
Ebeling, R. M. (2004). Eugene Böhm-Bawerk Critique of Karl Marx. Retrieved July 31, 2021, from https://mises.org/library/eugen-von-boehm-bawerks-critique-karl-marx
Ebeling, R. M. (2020). Joseph A. Schumpeter, Outsider Looking In. Retrieved July 21, 2021, from www.aier.org/article/joseph-a-schumpeter-outside-looking-in/
Eyerman, R. (1981). False Consciousness and Ideology in Marxist Theory. *Acta Sociologica*, *24*(1–2), 43–56.
Fleck, C., & Nowotny, H. (1993). Marginal Discipline in the Making: Austrian Sociology in a European Context. In B. Nedelmann & P. Sztompka (Eds), *Sociology in Europe: In Search of Identity* (pp. 99–118). New York: De Gruyter.
Foster, J. B. (1999). Marx's Theory of Metabolic Rift: Classical Foundations for Environmental Sociology. *American Journal of Sociology*, *105*(2), 366–405.
Foster, J. B. (2000). *Marxism Ecology: Materialism and Nature*. New York: New York University Press.
Foster, J. B. (2002). *Ecology against Capitalism*. New York: New York University Press.
Gane, N. (2005). Max Weber as Social Theorist. *European Journal of Social Theory*, *8*(2), 211–226.
Gane, N. (2014). Sociology and Neoliberalism: A Missing History. *Sociology*, *48*(6), 1092–1106.
Giddens, A. (1972). *Politics and Sociology in the Thought of Max Weber*. New York: Macmillan Education.
Gloria-Palermo, S. (2002). Schumpeter and the old Austrian School: Interpretations and Influences. In R. Arena & C. Dangel-Hagnauer (Eds), *The Contribution of Joseph Schumpeter to Economics: Economic Development and Institutional Change* (pp. 21–39). New York: Routledge.
Gordon, D. (2021). Community and Civil Society over State: Review. *The Austrian*, 16–19.
Gouldner, A. W. (1970). *The Coming Crisis of Western Sociology*. New York: Basic Books.
Hand, C. M., & Judkins, B. (1999). Disciplinary Schisms: Subspecialty "Drift" and the Fragmentation of Sociology. *The American Sociologist*, *30*(1), 18–36.
Hart, D. M., Chartier, G., Kenyon, R. M., & Long, R. T. (Eds). (2018). *Social Class and State Power: Exploring an Alternative Radical Tradition*. Cham: Palgrave Macmillan.
Hayek, F. A. von. (1942). Scientism and the Study of Society. *Economica*, *9*(35), 267.

Hayek, F. A. von. (1952). *The Counter-Revolution of Science*. Glencoe, IL: The Free Press.

Hayek, F. A. von. (1960). *The Constitution of Liberty*. Chicago, IL: University of Chicago Press.

Hayek, F. A. von. (2007). *The Road to Serfdom: Text and Documents – Definitive Edition* (B. Caldwell, Ed.). Chicago, IL: University of Chicago Press.

Higgs, R. (2004). *Against Leviathan: Government Power and a Free Society*. Oakland, CA: Independent Institute.

Hodgson, G. M. (2007). Meanings of Methodological Individualism. *Journal of Economic Methodology*, *14*(2), 211–226.

Hoppe, H.-H. (2006). *The Economics and Ethics of Property Rights* (2nd ed.). Auburn, AL: Ludwig von Mises Institute.

Kolev, S. (2020). The Legacy of Max Weber and the Early Austrians. *Review of Austrian Economics*, *33*(1–2), 33–54.

Koppl, R., & Mongiovi, G. (1998). Introduction. In Roger Koppl & G. Mongiovi (Eds), *Subjectivism and Economic Analysis: Essays in Memory of Ludwig M. Lachmann* (pp. 1–11). New York: Routledge.

Kranebitter, A., & Reinprecht, C. (2018). Marxism Underground: Latent Marxism in Austrian Empirical Sociology. *Österreichische Zeitschrift Für Soziologie*, *43*(3), 219–229.

Lachmann, L. M. (1971). *The Legacy of Max Weber*. Berkeley, CA: Glendessary.

Lachmann, L. M. (1982). Ludwig von Mises and the Extension of Subjectivism. In I. M. Kirzner (Ed.), *Method, Process and Austrian Economics* (pp. 31–40). Lexington, MA: Lexington Books.

Laer, W. von. (2019). "Less Marx, More Mises" Shows Development: Students for Liberty Provides Professional Development Training for Students. Retrieved July 14, 2021, from www.wsj.com/articles/less-marx-more-mises-shows-development -11553031180

Lemke, J. S. (2015). An Austrian Approach to Class Structure. In C. J. Coyne & V. H. Storr (Eds), *New Thinking in Austrian Political Economy* (pp. 167–192). Bingley: Emerald Group Publishing.

Lewis, P., & Chamlee-Wright, E. (2008). Social Embeddedness, Social Capital and the Market Process: An Introduction to the Special Issue on Austrian Economics, Economic Sociology and Social Capital. *Review of Austrian Economics*, *21*(2–3), 107–118.

Lipset, S. M. (1985). *Consensus and Conflict: Essays in Political Sociology*. London: New Brunswick Publishers.

Lounsbury, M., & Hirsch, P. M. (Eds). (2010). *Markets on Trial: The Economic Sociology of the US Financial Crisis, Part B*. London: Emerald Group Publishing.

Lukes, S. (2011). In Defense of "False Consciousness." *University of Chicago Legal Forum*, *1*, 19–28.

Maher, S., & Aquanno, S. M. (2018). Conceptualizing Neoliberalism: Foundations for an Institutional Marxist Theory of Capitalism. *New Political Science*, *40*(1), 33–50.

Malinowski, B. (1936). Culture as a Determinant of Behavior. *The Scientific Monthly*, *43*(5), 440–449.

Malinowski, B. (1939). The Group and the Individual in Functional Analysis. *American Journal of Sociology*, *44*(6), 938–964.

Manza, J., & McCarthy, M. A. (2011). The Neo-Marxist Legacy in American Sociology. *Annual Review of Sociology*, *37*(1), 155–183.

Manza, J., Sauder, M., & Wright, N. (2010). Producing Textbook Sociology. *European Journal of Sociology*, *51*(2), 271–304.

Marske, C. E. (1987). Durkheim's "Cult of the Individual" and the Moral Reconstitution of Society. *Sociological Theory*, *5*(1), 1.

Mayhew, B. H. (1980). Structuralism versus Individualism, Part 1: Shadowboxing in the Dark. *Social Forces*, *59*(2), 335–375.

McMaken, R. (2015). Brazil Protestors: Less Marx, More Mises. Retrieved June 28, 2021, from https://mises.org/wire/brazil-protestors-less-marx-more-mises

Menger, C. (1985 [1883]). *Investigations into the Method of the Social Sciences with Special Reference to Economics* (L. Schneider, Ed.; F. J. Nock, Trans.). New York: New York University Press.

Menger, C. (2007 [1871]). *Principles of Economics* (J. Dingwall & B. F. Hoselitz, Ed. and Trans.). Auburn, AL: Ludwig von Mises Institute.

Merton, R. K. (1936). The Unanticipated Consequences of Purposive Social Action. *American Sociological Review*, *1*(6), 894.

Merton, R. K. (1968). *Social Theory and Social Structure*. New York: The Free Press.

Mises, L. von. (1944). *Bureaucracy*. New Haven, CT: Yale University Press.

Mises, L. von. (1949). *Human Action*. New Haven, CT: Fox & Wilkes and Foundation for Economic Education.

Mises, L. von. (1951). *Socialism: An Economic and Sociological Analysis*. New Haven, CT: Yale University Press.

Mises, L. von. (2003). *Epistemological Problems of Economics* (3rd ed.). Auburn, AL: Ludwig von Mises Institute.

Mises, L. von. (2007). *Theory and History: An Interpretation of Social and Economic Evolution*. Auburn, AL: Ludwig von Mises Institute.

Misztal, B. A. (2003). Durkheim on Collective Memory. *Journal of Classical Sociology*, *3*(2), 123–143.

Mommsen, W. J. (1977). Max Weber as a Critic of Marxism. *Canadian Journal of Sociology/Cahiers Canadiens de Sociologie*, *2*(4), 373.

Mommsen, W. J. (2021). *The Age of Capitalism and Bureaucracy: Perspectives on the Political Sociology of Max Weber*. New York: Berghahn Books.

Münch, R. (1991). American and European Social Theory: Cultural Identities and Social Forms of Theory Production. *Sociological Perspectives*, *34*(3), 313–335.

Newman, D. (2020). *Sociology: Exploring the Architecture of Everyday Life* (13th ed.). Los Angeles, CA: SAGE.

Nisbet, R. (1994). *History of the Idea of Progress*. Boca Raton, LA: Routledge.

Oakley, A. (1997). Human Agents and Rationality in Max Weber's Social Economics. *International Journal of Social Economics*, *24*(7/8/9), 812–830.

Oakley, A. (1999). *The Revival of Modern Austrian Economics: A Critical Assessment of Its Subjectivist Origins*. Cheltenham, UK and Northampton, MA, USA: Edward Elgar Publishing.

Oliveira, C. R. de. (2019). *"Menos Marx, mais Mises": uma gênese da nova direita brasileira (2006–2018)*. Universidade de São Paulo, São Paulo. https://doi.org/10.11606/T.8.2019.tde-19092019-174426

Parsons, S. D. (2003). *Money, Time, and Rationality in Max Weber: Austrian Connections*. New York: Routledge.

Parsons, S. D. (2007). Marginalizing Weber: A Critical Note. *Max Weber Studies*, *7*(4), 231–242.

Parsons, T. (1937). *The Structure of Social Action*, Vol. I. New York: Free Press.

Parsons, T. (1977). *Social Systems and the Evolution of Action Theory*. New York: Free Press.

Pickering, W. S. F. (Ed.). (2000). *Durkheim and Representations*. New York: Routledge.

Pines, C. L. (1993). *Ideology and False Consciousness: Marx and His Historical Progenitors*. Albany, NY: State University of New York Press.

Polanyi, K. (1944). *The Great Transformation*. Boston, MA: Beacon Hill Press.

Prendergast, C. (1986). Alfred Schutz and the Austrian School of Economics. *American Journal of Sociology*, *92*(1), 1–26.

Prychitko, D. L. (1990). Methodological Individualism and the Austrian School: A Note on Its Critics. *Journal Des Économistes et Des Études Humaines*, *1*(1). https://doi.org/10.1515/jeeh-1990-0107

Rehbein, B. (2020). Max Weber, Understanding and the Charge of Subjectivism. *Forum for Inter-American Research*, *13*(3), 33–45.

Ringer, F. (1997). *Max Weber's Methodology: The Unification of the Cultural and Social Sciences*. Cambridge, MA: Harvard University Press.

Ritzer, G. (1975). Sociology: A Multiple Paradigm Science. *The American Sociologist*, *10*(3), 156–167.

Ritzer, G. (1990). Metatheorizing in Sociology. *Sociological Forum*, *5*(1), 3–15.

Ritzer, G. (2011). *Globalization: The Essentials*. Malden, MA: Wiley-Blackwell.

Ritzer, G., & Gindoff, P. (1992). Methodological Relationism: Lessons for and from Social Psychology. *Social Psychology Quarterly*, *55*(2), 128.

Robitaille, C. (2019). Ludwig von Mises, Sociology, and Metatheory. *Quarterly Journal of Austrian Economics*, *22*(2), 242–270.

Romm, N. R. A. (1991). *The Methodologies of Positivism and Marxism: A Sociological Debate*. London: Macmillan.

Rosen, M. (1996). *On Voluntary Servitude: False Consciousness and the Theory of Ideology*. Malden, MA: Polity Press.

Rothbard, M. N. (1995a). *Classical Economics: An Austrian Perspective on the History of Economic Thought*, Vol. 2. Auburn, AL: Ludwig von Mises Institute.

Rothbard, M. N. (1995b). *Economic Thought before Adam Smith: An Austrian Perspective on the History of Economic Thought*, Vol. 1. Auburn, AL: Ludwig von Mises Institute.

Rothbard, M. N. (1997). Praxeology: The Methodology of Austrian Economics. In M. N. Rothbard (Ed.), *The Logic of Action One: Method, Money, and the Austrian School*. Cheltenham, UK and Northampton, MA, USA: Edward Elgar Publishing.

Rothbard, M. N. (2004). *Man, Economy, and State: A Treatise on Economic Principles with Power and Market Government and the Economy*. Auburn, AL: Ludwig von Mises Institute.

Rothbard, M. N. (2009). *Anatomy of the State*. Auburn, AL: Ludwig von Mises Institute.

Royce, E. (2015). *Classical Social Theory and Modern Society: Marx, Durkheim, Weber*. New York: Rowman and Littlefield.

Sayer, D. (2002). *Capitalism and Modernity: An Excursus on Marx and Weber*. New York: Taylor & Francis.

Schumpeter, J. A. (1909). On the Concept of Social Value. *Quarterly Journal of Economics*, *23*(2), 213.

Schumpeter, J. A. (1942). *Capitalism, Socialism and Democracy*. New York: Harper and Row.

Schutz, A., & Luckmann, T. (1973). *The Structures of the Life-World*. Evanston, IL: Northwestern University Press.

Scott, J. (2005). Sociology and Its Others: Reflections on Disciplinary Specialisation and Fragmentation. *Sociological Research Online, 10*(1), 71–78.

Shantz, J., & Williams, D. M. (2013). *Anarchy and Society: Reflections on Anarchist Sociology*. Boston, MA: Brill.

Shilling, C., & Mellor, P. A. (1998). Durkheim, Morality and Modernity: Collective Effervescence, Homo Duplex and the Sources of Moral Action. *British Journal of Sociology, 49*(2), 193.

Simpson, D. (1983). Joseph Schumpeter and the Austrian School of Economics. *Journal of Economic Studies, 10*(4), 18–28.

Skousen, M. (2016). *The Making of Modern Economics: The Lives and Ideas of the Great Thinkers* (3rd ed.). New York: Taylor & Francis.

Smith, K. (2014). *Émile Durkheim and the Collective Consciousness of Society: A Study in Criminology*. New York: Anthem Press.

Spencer, H. (1873). *The Study of Sociology*. London: Henry S. King & Co.

Spencer, H. (1892). *Social Statics Together with the Man versus the State*. New York: Appleton.

Spencer, H. (1897). *Principles of Sociology* (3 vols). New York: Appleton.

Staubmann, H. (2021). C. Wright Mills' *The Sociological Imagination* and the Construction of Talcott Parsons as a Conservative Grand Theorist. *The American Sociologist, 52*(1), 178–193.

Steele, D. R. (1992). *From Marx to Mises: Post-Capitalist Society and the Challenge of Economic Calculation*. La Salle, IL: Open Court Publishing.

Steinmetz, G., & Chae, O.-B. (2002). Sociology in an Era of Fragmentation: From the Sociology of Knowledge to the Philosophy of Science, and Back Again. *The Sociological Quarterly, 43*(1), 111–137.

Storr, V. H., & Choi, G. S. (2019). *Do Markets Corrupt Our Morals?* London: Palgrave Macmillan.

Storr, V. H., & John, A. (2020). *Cultural Considerations within Austrian Economics*. Cambridge: Cambridge University Press.

Swedberg, R. (Ed.). (1991). *Joseph Schumpeter: The Economics and Sociology of Capitalism*. Princeton, NJ: Princeton University Press.

Swedberg, R. (1998). *Max Weber and the Idea of Economic Sociology*. Princeton, NJ: Princeton University Press.

Swedberg, R. (2003). The Changing Picture of Max Weber's Sociology. *Annual Review of Sociology, 29*(1), 283–306.

Swingewood, A. (1970). Comte, Marx and Political Economy. *The Sociological Review, 18*(3), 335–349.

Thomas, P. (2008). *Marxism and Scientific Socialism: From Engels to Althusser*. London: Routledge.

Torrance, J. (1976). The Emergence of Sociology in Austria 1885–1935. *European Journal of Sociology, 17*(2), 185–219.

Tribe, K. (2012). Max Weber: the Works. *Economy and Society, 41*(2), 282–298.

Tucker, J. H. (2009). Marxism without Polylogism. In J. G. Hülsmann & S. Kinsela (Eds), *Property, Freedom, and Society: Essays in Honor of Hans-Hermann Hoppe* (pp. 37–44). Auburn, AL: Ludwig von Mises Institute.

Turner, J. H., & Maryanski, A. (1977). *Functionalism*. Menlo Park, CA: Benjamin/Cummings Publishing Company.

Udehn, L. (2001). *Methodological Individualism: Background, History and Meaning.* New York: Routledge.

Udehn, L. (2002). The Changing Face of Methodological Individualism. *Annual Review of Sociology, 28*(1), 479–507.

Vanberg, V. J. (2015). Schumpeter and Mises as "Austrian Economists." *Journal of Evolutionary Economics, 25*(1), 91–105.

Vaughan, T. R. (1993). The Crisis in Contemporary American Sociology: A Critique of the Discipline's Dominant Paradigm. In T. R. Vaughan, G. Sjoberg, & L. T. Reynolds (Eds), *A Critique of Contemporary American Sociology* (pp. 10–53). New York: General Hall.

Warriner, C. K. (1956). Groups Are Real: A Reaffirmation. *American Sociological Review, 21*(5), 549.

Weber, M. (1946). *From Max Weber: Essays in sociology* (H. H. Gerth & C. W. Mills, Eds). New York: Oxford University Press.

Weber, M. (1947). *Theory of Social and Economic Organization* (A. M. Henderson & T. Parsons, Eds). Glencoe, IL: The Free Press.

Weber, M. (2019 [1922]). *Economy and Society: A New Translation.* (K. Tribe, Ed.). Cambridge, MA: Harvard University Press.

Webster, M. (1973). Psychological Reductionism, Methodological Individualism, and Large-Scale Problems. *American Sociological Review, 38*(2), 258.

Woods, T. E. (2009). *Meltdown: A Free-Market Look at Why the Stock Market Collapsed, the Economy Tanked, and Government Bailouts Will Make Things Worse.* Washington, DC: Regency Publishing.

Wright, E. O. (1997). *Class Counts: Comparative Studies in Class Analysis.* Cambridge, MA: Cambridge University Press.

Wright, E. O. (2010). *Envisioning Real Utopias.* New York: Verso.

Wright, E. O. (2019). *How to Be an Anti-Capitalist in the 21st Century.* New York: Verso.

York, R., & Clark, B. (2006). Marxism, Positivism, and Scientific Sociology: Social Gravity and Historicity. *The Sociological Quarterly, 47*(3), 425–450.

Yu, F. L. T. (2015). Methodological Subjectivism and the Interpretive Approach in Political Economy. *International Journal of Pluralism and Economics Education, 6*(1), 51.

Yu, F. L. T. (2020). *Subjectivism and Interpretative Methodology in Theory and Practice.* New York: Anthem Press.

Zafirovski, M. (2002). Paths of the Weberian–Austrian Interconnection. *Review of Austrian Economics, 15*(1), 35–59.

Zafirovski, M. (2010). Weber's Sociological Elements in Mises' Economics of Human Action. *Social Epistemology, 24*(2), 75–98.

Zanotti, G. J. (2007). Intersubjectivity, Subjectivism, Social Sciences, and the Austrian School of Economics. *Journal of Markets and Morality, 10*(1), 115–141.

Zhao, S. (1993). Realms, Subfields, and Perspectives: On the Differentiation and Fragmentation of Sociology. *The American Sociologist, 24*(3–4), 5–14.

Index